CASS LIBRARY OF AFRICAN STUDIES

GENERAL STUDIES

No. 155

Editorial Adviser: JOHN RALPH WILLIS
Department of History, University of California, Berkeley

African Kingships
in Perspective

African Kingships
in Perspective
Political Change and Modernization
in Monarchical Settings

Edited by

RENE LEMARCHAND

Professor of Political Science
University of Florida

FRANK CASS & CO. LTD.

First published 1977 in Great Britain by
FRANK CASS AND COMPANY LIMITED
11 Gainsborough Road, London E11 1RS, England
and in United States of America by
FRANK CASS AND COMPANY LIMITED
c/o International Scholarly Book Services, Inc.
Box 555, Forest Grove, Oregon 97116

Copyright © 1977 René Lemarchand

ISBN 0 7146 3027 6

Library of Congress Catalog Card No. 73–84017

Printed in Great Britain by
Clarke, Doble & Brendon Ltd.
Plymouth

To Abu Rakaba

to remind him of other kingdoms . . .

CONTENTS

PREFACE

Can African monarchical systems regulate and institutionalize social change and at the same time adapt themselves to the exigencies of their environments? A decade or so ago this problem involved the destinies of some 30 million Africans living in independent (Libya, Morocco, Ethiopia) or soon to be independent (Rwanda, Burundi, Swaziland, Lesotho, Botswana) monarchies, and perhaps another 20 million distributed among several "incorporated kingships". Today the rulers of Morocco, Ethiopia and Swaziland are still plagued by this dilemma.

In suggesting possible answers to this question, the present volume seeks to fill a major gap in the current political science literature on Africa. While anthropologists and historians have devoted increasing attention in recent times to the comparative study of historic African kingdoms, political scientists have shown relatively little interest in the search for comparative generality about problems of social change in monarchical settings. Despite such pioneering monographic studies as Apter's classic work on *The Political Kingdom in Uganda*, and, more recently, Waterbury's *Commander of the Faithful: The Moroccan Political Elite*, the best general discussions of such problems have come from the pen of social anthropologists. Aside from one or two exceptions—the most notable being Huntington's seminal article on "The Political Modernization of Traditional Monarchies", first published in *Daedalus* (1966)—rarely have political scientists tried to deal systematically with the relationship of social change to the stability or instability of monarchical institutions.

There are several reasons for this neglect, the most obvious being that monarchical systems have seldom coincided with the boundaries of newly-emergent African states and hence have tended to be viewed as transient or secondary phenomena—in short, as epiphenomena. Where such coincidence did exist, or could be anticipated, as in Rwanda, Burundi, Lesotho, Swaziland, the presumption was that these polities were either too small or too atypical to deserve systematic attention. Moreover, for most political scientists of an earlier generation, the advent of independence meant the emergence of "new" political systems, destined to perform "new" functions, in particular to accelerate incipient trends toward development. And since political development was generally equated with Western political institutions and processes, it was only natural, though not always defensible, to de-emphasize traditional political structures, including monarchical ones, for the sake of "new" institutions and forms of leadership.

By focusing upon monarchical structures as independent variables, this

book offers a corrective to the biases of uncritical functionalism that have
come to characterize much of the social science literature on contemporary
Africa. The conspectus presented here is not meant to deny the utility of
systematic theory, but, rather, to suggest a shift of intellectual perspective
in the analysis of social change. The aim is to partially rehabilitate the
institutional approach in Africanist scholarship—by suggesting possible
correlations between the character of monarchical institutions and their
vulnerability to social change—while at the same time giving due
consideration to the impact of individual choices on institutional variables.

This book is the product of an intellectual gestation (some might say
"regression") that began in 1964, when I was first given the opportunity to
engage in a comparative analysis of African monarchical systems.
Although the scope of my analysis was initially limited to Rwanda and
Burundi, the subsequent emergence of three newly independent monarchies
(Lesotho, Swaziland and Botswana), almost immediately followed by the
overthrow of several monarchies elsewhere in Africa, prompted me to
attack this problem on a wider front and to solicit the collaboration of
scholars who shared my interest in African kingship.

Our choice of the eight kingships treated in this book has been dictated
by several considerations. One is that they provide a fairly broad geographical coverage of contemporary monarchical systems, broad enough
at least to illustrate the differential impact of various colonial legacies,
and in one instance (Ethiopia) how the absence of a sustained exposure to
colonial rule has affected monarchical structures. More importantly, they
offer enough diversity in terms of their political structures, operative norms
and social systems to make comparative analysis meaningful. Yet a third
consideration is that collectively and individually they shed a new light
on the different patterns of adjustment—and decay—experienced by
traditional African systems in their attempt to resist or regulate social,
economic and political change. Although some might question the advis-
ability of extending our treatment of African monarchies to monarchical
polities which are now (or used to be) incorporated into a wider territorial
framework, we believe that significant insights can be gained into problems
of political integration by including the case of "incorporated monarchies"
in our discussion of the generic monarchical type. In short, the sample of
polities presented here appears sufficiently diversified to warrant tentative
generalizations about the dynamics of change in monarchical settings.

As editor and co-author my responsibility is limited to my own essays,
including the Introduction and the Conclusion, and to soliciting the
remaining articles which make up the symposium. Each author is solely
responsible for his contribution. Except for one anthropologist (P. C.
Lloyd), the contributors are all political scientists. All were given a relatively free hand in the handling of their materials, and the conceptualiza-
tion of their respective kingships. This latitude may help to explain whatever differences of interpretation, or emphasis, can be discerned in this
book. Such a diversity of interpretation seems preferable to the kind of
artificial uniformity which might have been fostered through the
imposition of too rigid a conceptual framework.

To those authors who submitted their manuscripts before the others had even commenced theirs, I wish to express my apologies for the delay thereby enforced upon them. To each and every one of them however, I would like to express my sincere gratitude for their kind cooperation and exemplary patience while I tried to give final shape to the manuscript. Since this collection of articles was compiled, many of the authors' conclusions have been overtaken by events in Africa. This is particularly so in the case of Ethiopia.

NOTES ON THE CONTRIBUTORS

CHRISTOPHER CLAPHAM is Lecturer in Politics at the University of Lancaster. He previously taught at Haile Sellassie I University, Addis Ababa, and at the University of Manchester. He wrote his doctoral thesis for Oxford University on Ethiopian politics, and is the author of *Haile-Selassie's Government* (1969), and of several articles on Ethiopian and African politics.

MARTIN R. DOORNBOS is senior lecturer in political science at the Institute of Social Studies, The Hague. After graduating from Amsterdam University in 1960 he attended the University of California as a Harkness Fellow from 1962 to 1965. At one time research fellow of the East African Institute of Social Research and part time lecturer in the Department of Political Science at Makerere University College, Kampala, he has done extensive field research in East Africa. His professional interests centre upon problems of political change at the local and regional levels. He is editor of *Development and Change.*

RENÉ LEMARCHAND is Associate Professor of Political Science at the University of Florida. He received his education in France and at the University of California at Los Angeles. He received his Ph.D. from that institution in 1963. He taught at Lovanium University, Kinshasa, in 1960, and was subsequently on the research staff of the Institut de Sociologie Solvay in Brussels. He is the author of *Political Awakening in the Congo: The Politics of Fragmentation* (1964), and *Rwanda and Burundi* (1970), which was awarded the Herskovitz prize in 1971, and has contributed articles to American, British, French and Belgian journals.

PETER C. LLOYD is Reader in Social Anthropology at the University of Sussex. He taught at the University of Ibadan from 1959 to 1964, and previously served as Land Research Officer in the Ministry of Lands at Ibadan. He is the author of *Yoruba Land Law* (1962), *Africa in Social Change* (1967), *The Political Development of Yoruba Kingdoms* (1971), *Classes, Crises and Coups* (1971), the editor of *The New Elites of Tropical Africa* (1966) and co-editor of *The City of Ibadan* (1971).

CHRISTIAN P. POTHOLM is currently Associate Professor of Government and Legal Studies at Bowdoin College, and he previously taught at Vassar College and Dartmouth College. He is the author of *Four African Political Systems* (1970), *Swaziland: The Dynamics of Political Modernization* (1972) and co-author and co-editor of *Southern Africa in Perspective: Essays in Regional Politics* (1972). In addition, he has published numerous articles in such journals as *Africa Report*, the *Journal of Modern African Studies*, *International Journal*, *Africa Today*, the *Journal of Developing*

Areas, the *Journal of Asian and African Studies* and *World Politics*. His current research interests include Southern Africa, the international refugee situation and the politics of growth and decay.

RICHARD F. WEISFELDER is an instructor in the Department of Government at Ohio University. He was educated at Amherst (B.A. *magna cum laude*, 1960), and Harvard (M.A. 1965, Ph.D. candidate). His publications include *Defining National Purpose*, Papers in International Studies, Africa Series No. 3, (Ohio University, 1969), and "Lesotho", in Richard Dale and Christian Potholm eds., *Southern Africa in Perspective* (1972). His main research interest is in Africa south of the Zambesi.

M. CRAWFORD YOUNG has been associated with the University of Wisconsin since 1963. He has served as Chairman of the African Studies Program (1964–1968), Associate Dean of the Graduate School (1968–1971), and Chairman of the Department of Political Science (1969–1972). Part of the research for this chapter was accomplished while serving as Visiting Professor at Makerere University College in 1965–1966. He was educated at the University of Michigan (B.A., 1953) and Harvard University (Ph.D., 1964). He is the author of *Politics in The Congo* (1965), and, with Charles Anderson and Fred von der Mehden, *Issues of Political Development* (1967).

INTRODUCTION

IN SEARCH OF THE POLITICAL KINGDOM

In Africa, as elsewhere, history is fast catching up with historic polities. Between 1960 and 1970 two independent African monarchies (Burundi and Libya) met their doom at the hands of a new generation of republican elites; a third (Rwanda) was abolished on the very threshold of independence, in a pool of blood; a fourth (Buganda) managed to maintain itself for a while as a separate entity within the broader national framework of Uganda until it, too, suffered decapitation; less than a year later, in 1967, the three surviving kingships (Ankole, Bunyoro and Toro) still enclosed within the national boundaries of Uganda were, likewise, done away with—this time through constitutional surgery. To this rapidly extending list of monarchical casualties was added in 1970 the name of King Moshoeshoe II of Lesotho. As 1970 drew to a close, King Farouk's quip to Lord Boyd Orr had taken on a prophetic ring: "There will soon be only five kings left: The kings of England, Diamonds, Hearts, Spades and Clubs!"[1]

However novel its long-range implications, the phenomenon is by no means unprecedented. Kingdoms, after all, have been obliterated from the political map of Africa long before Europeans even heard their names. What sets the destinies of most contemporary African monarchs apart from their predecessors' is not that their legitimacy was challenged, but the grounds on which it was challenged—not that they were overthrown, but that they were overthrown in the name of "progress and democracy". For the sacredness of their dynastic claims has been substituted the sanctity of a secular religion, rooted in the exaltation of republican values; and the sanctity of the new order spells the desacralization of the old. Once the epicentres of their kingdom's political life, their palaces are now deserted; the thatched graves of their ancestors are neglected; and the august ceremonies that once commemorated the glory of their dynasties have all but passed into oblivion. As for the deposed monarchs who, only a few years ago, seemed the object of such public adulation, some are currently experiencing the frustrations of life in exile; others have been placed under house arrest; others still have been moved to cheap hotels.

For the historian in search of grand syntheses the phenomenon might conceivably be dismissed as part of an ineluctable trend in the direction of a secular political order, associated with the exercise of popular participation. For the student of contemporary African politics, however, the passing of African kingships is more than a matter of transient interest, as

1

it raises empirical and theoretical questions of some consequence. Why did some monarchical systems manage to survive in one form or another right up to the present time while others did not? Is the decline of African monarchies symptomatic of a source of instability inherent in their social systems, or were the monarchs themselves or their policies the cause of such instability? How can one reconcile patterns of "political decay" in monarchical settings with current theories of modernization, nation-building and political development? In the light of these and other theoretical questions the shedding of African kingships carries somewhat anomalous implications.

PARADOXES AND POSTULATES

That the blows struck against African monarchies simultaneously destroyed many of the concepts and typologies currently used by political scientists is not the least of these anomalies. Though much of the recent political science literature on Africa conveniently relegates monarchical systems to a residual category of deviant or *sui generis* cases,[2] the range of deviations is really too broad not to invite a questioning of current assumptions.

If the argument that "the prime condition for the building of nations is that they have an opportunity to age in the wood"[3] sounds reasonably convincing in the case of societies that were denied this opportunity, its relevance is far more dubious when applied to societies like Lesotho, Rwanda or Burundi, to cite only the most obvious examples. In none of these countries has "ageing in the wood" been of particular service in recent times in promoting internal cohesion and legitimacy; if anything, the result of this senescence has been a growing sclerosis of social and political structures, in time leading to violent confrontations. Nor is the correlation between centralization, on the one hand, and a system's capacity to innovate, on the other, any more convincing:[4] neither pre-coup Libya nor contemporary Ethiopia can be regarded as outstanding examples of innovating polities. And if the innovating properties once ascribed to "hierarchical-instrumental" systems such as Buganda or Rwanda cannot easily be detected from the facts of their recent history, the display of popular enthusiasm surrounding the investiture of Ashanti's 14th Ashantehene in July 1970, seems equally incongruous in the light of the system's presumed inability to cope with modernity.[5] Even when possessing those very features which some have singled out as the most crucial determinants of modernization (i.e. relatively stable territorial boundaries, a fairly homogeneous national culture, and a traditional ruler identified with the state as a whole),[6] African monarchies have performed rather unevenly in the realization of the fundamental and manifold transformations implicit in the notion of political modernization. On this score the gap between, say, Morocco and Ethiopia, or pre-1966 Buganda and pre-1966 Burundi, is as wide as might be conceived between any two other African states.

No less perplexing is the seemingly inexplicable frailty of what had commonly been regarded as the most "sacred" of African institutions. What, exactly, constitutes a derogation of sacredness is of course difficult to establish; nonetheless, if, as has been suggested, "the sacred characteristic becomes essential to maintaining solidarity in the community",[7] one is impelled to wonder why so many African kingships apparently failed to retain their sacred characteristics, or, assuming they did, why they proved so ineffectual in "maintaining solidarity in the community". Not only were African kingships traditionally regarded as sacred; in recent times this element of sacredness has tended to fuse with, and reinforce, the incipient sense of nationalism displayed by African "subjects". One only needs to recall in this connection the crucial stimulus given to Buganda "nationalism" by the exile of the Kabaka in 1953, the similarly important part played by Prince Rwagasore's struggles with Belgian authorities in giving temporary shape and cohesion to Burundi nationalism, and the significance of Haile Selassie's flight from Ethiopia, after the Italian invasion, for the rise of nationalist sentiment among black people both within and outside Africa. Since then, however, Buganda has been dismantled and carved into four administrative districts; Burundi has become a Republic; and there are some indications that Ethiopia might yet follow a similar path.

Recent attempts by political scientists to read into the style of non-monarchical African political systems evidences of "monarchical tendencies" make the decline of African kingships even more of a riddle.[8] For if the style of secular African leaders reflects a conscious attempt on their part to recapture the essence of monarchical rule, why should they expose themselves to the all too obvious risks in this type of behaviour? How, in other words, does one reconcile the monarchical tendencies of African republics with the republican leanings of African monarchies? If the former express, in Mazrui's words, "a quest for a royal historical identity", what is one to make of the latter tendencies? Could it be that the recent demise of African monarchies amounts to nothing more than an up-dated version of a traditional scenario in which the ritual killing of the sacrificial king establishes the continuity of the realm while at the same time ensuring its purification?

These, then, are the questions and paradoxes which this book seeks to elucidate; our conceptual search for the Political Kingdom can scarcely begin, however, without first indicating the postulates on which it rests.

1. Central to this discussion is the assumption that political institutions in general, and monarchical institutions in particular, not only have the capacity to cope with environmental strains, but to act upon and mould their social, economic and political environment. That this capacity is likely to vary significantly from one system (or subsystem) to another is made abundantly clear in this study; equally plain is that the capacity of African monarchies to come to grips with problems of social change and adaptation is inevitably affected by the nature of the social and political forces at work at any given time within and outside their traditional environments. Nonetheless, there is no justification for reducing political change in monarchical settings exclusively to the operation of social and

B

ecological variables.[9] None of the indicators of political development
available for the countries discussed in this book provides the slightest
clue to an understanding of their recent political fortunes (or misfortunes).
Whether one wishes to concentrate on such indices as literacy, urbanization, rate of agricultural employment, per capita income, or newspaper
circulation, no clear-cut correlation suggests itself between the levels of
political development attained by each of these countries and the stability
or instability of their respective monarchical institutions.

2. A more accurate index of the viability of African kingships lies in
their rulers' ability to generate and control new political resources from
their environment. Of special relevance in this connection is Eisenstadt's
interpretation of the development of bureaucratic empires as involving
continuous control on the part of the ruler and the bureaucracy over
"free-floating resources of various kinds": "They attempted to prevent
any one group or stratum within the society from controlling the use of
free-floating resources—whether wealth, prestige, communication or
political power and support itself—sufficiently to be able to challenge the
ruler's control of them".[10] To prevent scarce resources from passing into
the hands of potential opponents has been part of the "ruler's imperative"
since time immemorial: behind most of the historical and contemporary
struggles that have arisen between African monarchs and their opponents
lay fundamental disagreements over the use and allocation of political
resources.[11] Which is not to say that political norms and structures ought
to be relegated to the status of epiphenomena. The point, rather, is that
such norms and structures derive their main significance from the part
they play in expanding or restricting the flow of political resources available
at any given time to any given regime.

3. Although most of the case studies in this book focus upon changes
that have taken place over the last decade, they also demonstrate the
importance of historical depth for an understanding of contemporary
political phenomena. Vansina's statement that "trends in theoretical
anthropology require more and more diachronic evidence to test or refine
existing structural or functional theories"[12] would seem to apply equally
well to current theories of change formulated by political scientists:
historical depth is essential if one is to grasp the threads of continuity
between traditional and modern forms of intergroup conflict, how one has
interacted with the other, and with what consequences for the newly
emergent—or re-emergent—political system. Although there is no denying
the novelty of the conditions created in the wake of European colonization,
in many cases these have not so much eliminated traditional sources of
conflict as they have exacerbated them (as in Rwanda); alternatively, the
result may have been to make available new types of resources for the
resolution of age-old conflicts (as in Burundi and Morocco). Even where an
entirely new set of demands was made upon monarchical institutions as a
result of their incorporation into a wider territorial framework (as in the
case of the Lozi monarchy), traditional sources of conflict have not always
been dysfunctional from the standpoint of national integration. As these
and other examples might suggest, contemporary patterns of interaction

reflect varying mixtures of change and continuity. Only through a broad diachronic perspective can variations over time in the proportion of these components be properly identified.

But if history can help us disclose the subjective qualities of African responses to change, what of the subjectivity of the historian's response to the African experience of change? And if there are reasons to suspect that the historian's vision of the African past carries "metaphysical" implications, is it not equally plausible to expect similar distortions in the image which the anthropologist or political scientist seeks to convey of African institutions?

THE PHENOMENOLOGICAL DIMENSIONS OF KINGSHIP

All political objects have a phenomenological dimension that needs to be grasped before their forms and functions can be properly delineated. But in the case of African kingships, the problem is further complicated by the multiplicity of perspectives from which vision may depart from reality.

Like most kingships elsewhere in the world, African kingships incorporate a variety of analytical dimensions. Any of the monarchical systems discussed in this book may be seen as (1) the carrier of a cultural tradition, (2) the embodiment of symbolic or religious beliefs, (3) a legal institution defined in constitutional terms, (4) a method of transferring power, (5) the capstone of a particular administrative or political structure, (6) the apex of a particular system of stratification, or (7) the ultimate link in a chain of patron-client relations. This very richness of analytical referents generates confusion. Not only is the relevance of any of these referents likely to vary substantially from one context to another, but the way in which they "hang together" is, likewise, susceptible to wide variations. The problem is essentially one of selecting those analytical dimensions that are most appropriate for an understanding of political change in any given context.

Although the correctness of this choice can in part be controlled through empirical investigation, a major difficulty in Kluckhon's terms is that we need "to know as much about the eye that sees as the object seen".[13] We need to know as much about the way in which monarchical institutions are perceived by different sectors of society as about monarchical institutions themselves. Perceptions of monarchical legitimacy among Shoa and non-Shoa, Hima and Iru, Tutsi and Hutu, tell us at least as much—and perhaps more—about what monarchical rule in Ethiopia, Ankole and Rwanda implied as might be gathered from recorded traditions. The same applies to perceptions of legitimacy among the transitional sectors of society, including those whom Binder refers to, in another context, as the "dissatisfied moderns".[14] What some might describe as an anachronism may be seen by others as the embodiment of permanent values; what some might regard as a source of rewards others may denounce as an instrument of coercion. The horizons of meaning attached to African kingships are as varied as the social or ethnic landscape in which they are embedded.

Much the same type of epistemological difficulty arises from the image of monarchical systems projected by outside observers. Simply because people use the term "kingship" to describe a particular form of government is no guarantee that they mean the same thing. Although historians, political scientists and anthropologists all claim the mantle of science, their interpretations of kingship will necessarily reflect the teleological biases of their respective disciplines. At times the divergences are so wide as to impel one to wonder whether they are really talking about the same thing. Turning from the picture of the Ashanti bureaucracy drawn by a historian like I. Wilks to the description offered by a political scientist such as David Apter is like moving from one political universe to another.[15] Yet both are presumably dealing with the same society at roughly the same point in history. Even within the same discipline different theoretical twists may result in totally different versions of the same phenomena: at the hands of some anthropologists Frazer's Golden Bough has become little more than a "gilded twig";[16] and what some have tended to elevate to the status of a "sacred cow" others would regard as a cow *tout court*.[17]

Further distortions are liable to arise when the origins of African kingships are refracted through the prism of prior and often gratuitous assumptions about "African culture". An extreme example is Seligman's famous Hamitic hypothesis. Divine kingship, according to this view, was the hallmark of a more advanced civilization diffused from Egypt into black Africa through the vectors of Hamitic influences; Hamitic pastoralists were not only "better armed as well as quicker witted than the dark agricultural negroes",[18] but because of these superior endowments were also more capable of developing a centralized form of government. Scarcely more sophisticated is the explanation advanced by the proponents of the Sudanic civilizations thesis, as they draw attention to the diffusion of cultural and political influences on an east-west axis, some emphasizing the part played by Yemeni influences (Oliver and Fage), and others by Meriotic influences (Arkell).[19] There is little to be gained from a view of history which tends to lump together all African kingships under the rubric of "divine kingship". " 'Kingship' itself is much too vague," as Goody points out, "and to add the epithet 'divine' does little help".[20]

For the political scientist interested in the comparative study of African kingships these biases and preconceptions seriously complicate the task of definition and classification. In the absence of commonly accepted criteria for distinguishing between "kingdom" and "chiefdom" how is one to define a monarchical polity? "Kingship," according to J. H. M. Beattie, "applies not only to those states that, like most modern or recent European monarchies, are considerable in size and population, but also to the smaller traditional polities that centre upon a sovereign ruler or head."[21] But then how can one differentiate such large-scale entities as Morocco or Ethiopia from any of the small-scale chiefdoms scattered over any given African territory? The notion of "divine kingship" gives us little help in answering the question. However fashionable it may have been among earlier generations of anthropologists, today the Frazerian notion of "divine kingship" is subject to so many reservations and qualifications as

to make it virtually worthless for our purpose. In last resort one might turn
to customary usage, as we have done in this book. Yet neither European
nor African usage is always consistent. The rulers of Lesotho and Ashanti,
for example, have been alternatively referred to by Western observers
as "paramount chiefs" and "kings"; and in West Africa "one usually
speaks of 'kings' (*oba*) and chiefs in Yoruba kingdoms but of 'chiefs'
(*ohene*) and 'elders' for persons respectively of similar status in southern
Ghana".[22]

Nor is the definition of monarchical institutions made any easier by the
tendency of some historians (and sociologists) to project back into the past
structures which did not come into existence until much later, or, conversely, to exclude from their analyses structures which not only were in
existence but performed vital functions for the political system as a whole.[23]
Yet another source of confusion stems from attempts to generalize about
African kingships on the basis of limited empirical data, or in the light of
criteria which emphasize their cultural similarities and underplay their
differences. Some major counter-trends are already discernible among
historians and anthropologists, pointing to the complexity of African
monarchical systems;[24] these, however, have yet to be emulated by political
scientists.[25]

Whether arising from personal-cultural differences among social scientists or from the division of academic labour, such biases and prejudices
as we have tried to identify are not always avoidable. Nor is it entirely
certain that they should be avoided. "In the human sciences," writes
Bramson, "it is very often precisely the prejudices and biases of the observer which lead him to certain problems, which cause him to structure
his analysis in a certain way, and which allow him to see what he does see
and what he tries to report."[26] The critical question, for our purpose, is
whether "what he does see and tries to report" can in any way aid our
understanding of political realities. It is with this question in mind that we
now turn to a general analysis of processess of change in monarchical
settings.

THE RESOURCE–BASE OF TRADITIONAL KINGSHIPS

A tradition told of Emperor Sundiata of Mali reports that, having moved
his capital to a new site, he solicited the advice of a sage on how he could
best strengthen his rule. "Cut the trees." the elder replied, "transform the
forests into fields, for then only will you become a true king."[27] The
implications of this counsel of wisdom were grasped by historians and
anthropologists long before political scientists.[28] Only recently have
political scientists begun to raise critical questions about the use (and
misuse) of political resources, about the mechanism through which
resources are allocated, and how these in turn may affect the growth and
development of political systems. Although these questions are at times
raised at a level of generality that clearly transcends the scope of this discussion, that they are being raised at all suggests new ways in which to
further exploit the insights of historians and anthropologists.

Our assumptions, briefly stated, are as follows:

1. Monarchical *power*, like power in general, is not a given attribute handed from the Gods but, in Parson's words, "a generalized facility or resource in the society".[29] Kings, after all, derived their powers in many ways. They might use tribute received from their subjects in order to give gifts to their kinsmen and followers. They might impress their people through the splendour of ritual. Or they could wield the sword to secure compliance with their orders. Monarchical power, in short, involves the ability to secure compliance through the accumulation and redistribution of political resources, including economic wealth, whether in the form of tribute, taxation or booty, as well as status, coercion and authority.

2. Monarchical *legitimacy* stems from the nature of exchange relationships between the monarch on the one hand, and his "publics" or "sectors"[30] on the other. Mutually beneficial transactions between them enhances the regime's legitimacy. Whether such transactions are deemed mutually beneficial depends in part on their conformity to the scale of preference of the recipients (and hence on the monarch's ability to perceive and meet their preferences), and in part on their conformity to the order of priority established through legitimizing formulae or myths.

3. Although the operation of these allocative mechanisms invites the persistence of fairly stable power structures, certain basic transformations are likely to occur when wealth, status, coercion and authority are mediated through new "currencies".[31] When new economic, educational, ideological or informational "currencies" are injected into the system, significant changes are likely to take place in pre-existing patterns of allocation. In this case the problem of aggregating resources and securing compliance depends increasingly on the monarch's perception of the costs and advantages involved in particular types of transactions.

Our main concern in this section is to delineate the variant types of political systems described in this book in the light of traditional patterns of political resource allocation operative in the decade preceding the European conquest. Except for Ethiopia, only briefly subjected to Italian rule (1936–41), this time period coincides roughly with the last or penultimate decade of the nineteenth century.

Let us emphasize at the outset the somewhat arbitrary character of this effort, as it assumes a far greater degree of fixity in the format of monarchic institutions than seems to have been the case. Weisfelder's characterization of the structural fluidity of the Basotho monarchy applies equally well to Burundi on the eve of the German conquest or to Barotseland before it came under the control of the British South Africa Company: "The rapidity and regularity of significant changes in the functioning model of the monarchy meant that no definitive format was fully institutionalized or generally accepted as a normal standard." One might further add that any such attempt at systematization must necessarily de-emphasize regional

or local variations in standard patterns of resource allocation. To systema-
tize is to distort, and in suggesting possible ways of ordering the political
realities of African kingships our aim is more to minimize these distortions
than to eliminate them altogether.

(a) Traditional Patterns of Resource Allocation

Depending on the degree of control exercized by the Crown over the
distribution of political resources, two major types of monarchical systems
can be distinguished: (1) the "monopolistic" type, in which political
resources were in large part the monopoly of the Crown, and (2) the
"oligopolistic" type, in which monarchical control over resources was
shared with other sectors. The first type is best illustrated by Buganda and
Rwanda: control over political resources was overwhelmingly concentrated
in the hands of the king, whose omnipotence has often been seen as
synonymous with despotism. Examples of the second type include Burundi,
and Ijebu Ode: In Burundi control over political resources was widely
shared between the king and members of the royal lineage, and in Ijebu
Ode between the king and the titled chiefs. In none of these cases were the
chiefs wholly dependent upon the Crown for their authority, economic
standing or social status.

These, obviously, must be viewed as "ideal" types. For one thing royal
monopoly of a particular resource (i.e. authority) did not inevitably imply
a similar extension of monarchical control over other types of resources;
then a number of cases might be cited where the scope of monarchical
control tended to diminish as the distance from the centre to the periphery
increased. This "shading off of territorial sovereignty", to use Southall's
felicitous expression,[32] has tended to produce significant variations in
patterns of resource allocation.

Except for Burundi and Ijebu Ode—and where enclaves of residual
autonomy were still awaiting incorporation—most of the kingships
described in this book can be subsumed under the monopolistic type.
Yet the mere fact of a royal monopoly of political resources gives us no
clue as to who the beneficiaries were. In some kingdoms chieftaincies were
as a rule granted to members of the ruling caste (as in Rwanda), or to the
nobility (as at times happened in Ethiopia); in others the recipients were
drawn from all strata of society (as in Buganda); or else they were predominantly recruited from members of the royal clan (as in Ankole, where
the chiefs were for the most part members of the Bahinda clan). Hence the
need for further distinctions within each type, as between kingdoms in
which political resources tended to circulate rather freely through society,
and those in which their circulation was governed by fairly narrow,
ascriptive criteria. The nature of the distinction emerges most clearly from
a comparison between Ijebu Ode and Rwanda: unlike Rwanda, where
political resources were allocated on the basis of very rigid criteria, a major
characteristic of the traditional system of Ijebu Ode, in P. C. Lloyd's
terms, was that "some of the highest titled offices [were] open to all
citizens [and not restricted to men of a specific descent group]; hence very
wealthy men—who so often seem to come from humble homes—[could]

aspire to that political power which matches their economic status". Following the terminology adopted by Lloyd,[33] these sub-types may be described, respectively, as "open" and "closed"; where criteria of achievement and ascription tended to coalesce within the same political framework the resultant polity may be characterized as "mixed".

How these two sets of differentiating factors (oligopolistic-monopolistic; open-closed) might be used for purposes of classification is indicated in Table I.

TABLE I

DOMINANT PATTERNS OF RESOURCE ALLOCATION

I. Monopolistic	II. Oligopolistic

1. Open
    Buganda
    Lesotho
	1. Open
	    Ijebu Ode

2. Closed
    Rwanda
    Ankole
	2. Closed
	    (none)

3. Mixed
    Swaziland
    Ethiopia
	3. Mixed
	    Burundi

Buganda and Ankole, for example, were both "monopolistic" in the sense that in each kingdom the Crown was the principal supplier of political resources; Buganda, however, was evidently more "open" than Ankole, being not only one of the most politically centralized societies in the whole of Africa but one of the most upwardly mobile and opportunistic. In the allocation of political resources little attention was paid to ascriptive ties. In Ankole, by contrast, the Hima aristocracy clearly stood at the receiving end of the line, and left relatively little in the way of authority, wealth or status to Iru elements. Similarly, although Ijebu Ode and Burundi could both be described as "oligopolistic", the former was charactically more "open" in that wealth, status, authority and coercion circulated rather freely among heterogeneous descent groups. In Burundi, by contrast, ascriptive ties came into play with far greater force, though never quite as explicitly as in either Ankole or Rwanda. Burundi was both "oligopolistic" and "mixed".

However useful for purposes of classification, this typology tells us virtually nothing about the dynamics of change in monarchical settings. How were these allocative patterns established in the first place? Through what structures and mechanisms did they acquire a measure of persistence and stability over time?

As has been suggested by Goody and others, the key to the first question lies in the expansion and diversification of mobilizable resources available to African monarchs, or would-be monarchs.[34] Different types of economic and technological resources implied different types of opportunities for centralizing political power. Thus, if there is any truth to Gluckman's contention that the failure of the south-east Bantu to develop more ex-

tensive and centralized political units before the beginning of the nineteenth century "may have been due to the limited technology and the
availability of land, so that there was possibly little point in building up
power", one must also agree with Wrigley that the emergence of "an
ordered despotism" in nineteenth century Buganda was due in no small
way to the "exceptional potentialities of the Ganda economy"—to a
"concentration of wealth [made] possible and tolerable because the
aggregate income of Buganda was far above the general East African level
of bare subsistence".[35] Nonetheless, commercial, economic and technological resources were not in and by themselves generative of political
power. Only through deliberate and purposive manipulation could they
become productive of new political resources.

Such patterns of allocation of resources as we have sketched are thus
traceable to the varying skills displayed by individual monarchs in their
attempt to shift the supply of scarce resources away from autonomous
kinship and lineage groupings to the throne. Mutesa I (1856–84) of
Buganda, Moshoeshoe I (1823–1870) of Lesotho, Mswati (1839–1868)
of Swaziland, Menelik (1889–1913) of Ethiopia were all notably successful
in accumulating political resources. Under Mutesa I Buganda acquired for
the first time a permanent standing army, placed under the command of a
General (Mujasi) appointed by the king: "This was of particular importance to the nineteenth century," as Young points out, "as warfare was a
critical generator of resources to lubricate the monarchy ... The creation of
permanent royal regiments gave the Kabaka an alternative to relying on
the territorial chiefs (Bakungu)." Much the same conclusion suggests itself
when one considers Mswati's military innovations (centring around the
creation of regimental age-sets reminiscent of the Zulu system); or the
defensive use which Moshoeshoe made of the hill-top fortress of Thaba
Bosiu; or the efforts made by Menelik to improve the size and strength of
his military establishment. Varying mixtures of coercion and inducements
were employed, depending on the circumstances and the personalities
involved: against the rather low quotient of coercion which entered into
Moshoeshoe's tactics, one might point to the heavy reliance on military
strength displayed by Mutesa, or to the grim image evoked by a southern
Ethiopian proverb—"The King of Abyssinia wades in blood to his
Throne".[36] But along with the use of coercion came a considerable
accumulation of goods, whose conservation and redistribution were
essential to the building up of a centralized state.

In each of these cases a conscious effort was made to maximize the
production of new political goods—of prestige and obligation, tribute and
taxation, manpower and cattle—for purposes of territorial expansion and
political centralization. Economic, fiscal and manpower resources provided
the material base for the strengthening of monarchical power over the
chiefs, and of chiefly power over the masses. Just as in Tudor England the
patronage offered to and sought by the great Court favourites enabled
the Crown to exercize increasing control over political resources, in time
leading to the decline of the great territorial landlords, much of the
political centralization which occurred in African kingdoms must be

viewed in the light of the enhanced capacity of the Crown to aggregate support through the distribution of "prebends" and "benefices".

In coping with this problem African rulers could either resort to coercion, bargaining or manipulation, or they could reduce, though seldom eliminate, the area of choice involved in these strategies through appeal to immemorial prescriptive norms.

Whether control over scarce resources was predominantly in the hands of the chiefs or concentrated around the throne, the dice were never so loaded as to eliminate the possibility of bargaining between them. Even where the oligopolistic structure of the regime seemed to favour a weakening of monarchical power, the Crown could nevertheless enhance its resource base through a temporary alliance with one faction or another. Alternativively, even where the monopolistic features of the regime were most conspicuous, the monopoly of the Crown was never unlimited. Royal power was potentially limited by the factions and cliques swirling around the throne, by the residual strength and resilience of local kinship groups, and more generally by the sheer fluidity of political alignments. The pre-eminence of the throne was contingent upon the ability of the incumbent to maintain a measure of competitiveness among aspirants by a judicious balancing of the claims they made upon the regime. In summing up the problem faced by the Kabakas of Buganda, Rowe captured the essence of the dilemma faced by monopolistic kingships: "Each Kabaka faced anew the problem of preserving himself in power. His success would depend on his skill in maintaining an individually competitive atmosphere and constant mobility among office-holders and on utilizing to the full the natural allegiance of the people."[37] To "preserve themselves in their power", however, African monarchs were equally conscious of the need to formalize their prerogatives. They saw the need to maintain or develop "political myths" with which to stabilize and legitimize the incipient distributive patterns set through their entrepreneurial skills.

(b) Mythology as a Political Resource

In as much as they express certain fundamental assumptions about the ordering of political relationships, myths tend to impose a measure of continuity on existing patterns of resource allocation. In Malinowski's words, they are used "to account for extraordinary privileges or duties, for great social inequalities, for severe burdens of rank, whether this be very high or very low".[38] As most of the case studies in this book suggest, monarchical myths certainly played a major role in "accounting for the "extraordinary privileges and duties" of African kings; what these studies also demonstrate is that they incorporated much more—and in another sense much less—than the all-too-familiar myth of the "divine king". Although traditional African kings can be thought of as divine in the sense of being sacred, some were evidently more sacred than others.

In spite of these differences all of the monarchies discussed in this volume possessed a sacral element of some sort of another. "Sacredness" served as a major source of monarchical legitimacy, and because "the possession of legitimacy produces other resources at less cost to the regime"[39] it also served as a major resource in the hands of African rulers. Sacredness in this sense might be viewed as a political capital with which new resources could be generated at less cost.

If so, a convincing case can be made for the view that belief in the sacredness of royal office significantly increases the area of discretion open to the incumbent. His claim to "holiness", however dubious, imparts legitimacy to his demands. Material resources can be extracted with relative ease, at the same time that decisions regarding their allocation tend to acquire a final, sacrosanct character. As the incumbent's control over resources increases, so does his ability to attract and retain a body of loyal retainers. He thus emerges as the supreme "patron": His control of economic resources invites the formation of increasingly centralized clientage networks, more or less dependent upon Crown support.[40] The incumbent is also cast in the role of a "patron" in the sense in which Gellner refers to the Moroccan monarch as the "Great Patron"—as the "charismatic trimmer" who uses his holiness to arbitrate among competing clientage networks; "the use of his holiness is that it makes submission to the compromise palatable: the parties can submit without loss of face".[41] "Horse-dealing and faith," Gellner concludes, "are not incompatible." One might even add that faith in the divine origins of kings has often served to legitimize horse-dealing.

But the significance of myths is by no means limited to the symbolic role of kings. They incorporate normative judgments about the wider socio-political reality in which these roles are embedded; they are ideological statements about the way in which political resources ought to be mobilized and distributed. Not only do they lend moral sanction (or legitimacy) to the priorities set from above; they also give some predictability to the character of the transactions which take place in society.

Just as the structure, force and scope of monarchical myths varied from one state to another, so did the amount of leeway available to African kings for securing and distributing resources. The more rigid the *structure* of a myth, i.e. the more explicit its stipulations and the broader its "coverage", the lesser the area of choice open to political actors, including the monarch himself.

Moreover, the greater the *force* of mythical representations, i.e. the greater the "thoroughness with which [mythical] patterns are internalized in the personalities of the individuals who adopt them",[42] the higher the predictability of the choices open to the monarch—or perhaps more accurately, the higher the probability that certain choices will not be made. As an example of what is involved here one might point to the strong emphasis placed on status distinctions in the official mythologies of Rwanda, and to a lesser extent Ankole—distinctions that were not only thoroughly internalized by their respective aristocracies but carried forward into the definition of their social and political relationships with commoners. In each case innovation left off where the "premise of inequality" began, and the area of latitude open to the Crown tended to reflect this line of demarcation.

Variations in the *scope* of mythical beliefs constitute yet another variable.

Myths that are operative in "nuclear" areas may become increasingly tenuous as the distance increases between the core and the periphery. In these peripheral zones the choices made by the Crown are scarcely more predictable than the popular reactions which they may elicit. Clapham's statement that "the present Ethiopian empire contains many peoples incorporated only in the last hundred years, for whom the historic myths of the core highland areas can scarcely have much relevance" applies equally well to Rwanda.

The "functional" properties of monarchical myths may also be overstated for reasons other than those we just described. No matter how rigidly structured, myths are no more free of ambiguity than the value-significance they confer upon historical events. Lévi-Strauss's flat statement that "with myth everything becomes possible", and that "any characteristic can be attributed to any subject; every conceivable relation can be found",[43] scarcely exaggerates the point. As the case of Rwanda makes plain, the ideological resources associated with a given myth can be manipulated in very different ways. Mythical resources can be mobilized by potential aspirants against the ruling dynasty, or indeed against the very monarchical order they were intended to sustain.

Finally, changes may take place in the distribution of political resources which are simply not "covered" by the stipulations of "mythical charters" as when new legitimizing formulae and political currencies are introduced which no longer fit traditional patterns of expectations. Nowhere is this phenomenon more clearly evidenced than in the manifold transformations generated through the imposition of imperial controls. The changes wrought under the aegis of colonial rule were in many ways unprecedented, as were the types of "currencies" made available through the acculturative impact of the West.

THE REDEFINITION OF KINGSHIP UNDER COLONIAL RULE

To generalize about the transformations undergone by African kingships under colonial rule is a risky business: one only needs to look at the dramatic shifts which have punctuated the evolution of imperial policies; the varying goals and practices associated with the several agencies through which the European presence was mediated; the differences of attitude detectable among colonial civil servants; and the different responses which each and all of these factors have elicited from African kings and their subjects.

Little help, therefore, can be gained from the application of the classical dichotomy between "direct" and "indirect" methods of administration, useful though these may be in other contexts.[44] If Morocco can scarcely be cited as an ideal setting for observing French predilections for the first of these methods, neither is Lesotho a particularly apt illustration of British commitment to the second. Although it came to be acknowledged as the official policy of the colonizing power in virtually all of the states discusses in this book, indirect rule embraced very different kinds of policy.

But in spite of these differences indirect rule, once stabilized, everywhere led to the establishment of an enforced *quid pro quo* between colonial and "native" authorities: it brought in its wake new types of exchange processes, new types of resources, and new patterns of distribution and redistribution.

Major changes occurred in the *structure of processes of exchange* between monarchical regimes and sectors—between king and chief, chief and subchief, nobility and commoner. Both king and chief became increasingly dependent upon the colonial regime for the accumulation and retention of political resources. This new dependency relationship, backed by coercive sanctions, along with the new demands enforced through this relationship, seriously undermined the legitimacy of African kings. Devaluation of royal authority expressed itself in other ways: since kings and chiefs were now cast in the position of subordinates vis-à-vis the colonial authorities, the latter could choose to deal directly with the chiefs over the head of the monarch—as happened in Buganda when Sir Harry Johnston chose to negotiate the terms of the 1900 agreement exclusively with the Bakungu chiefs, and in Burundi in 1903 when Von Beringe formally recognized the independence of dissident chiefs from the Crown. But as P. C. Lloyd's discussion shows, the legitimacy of the Crown could also be affected by the reverse process: in Ijebu Ode the loss of legitimacy incurred by the Awujale came from an accumulation of authority at the expense of the titled chiefs, that is from a type of exchange which ran counter to the traditionally oligopolistic structure of the kingdom.

In specific instances the decline of monarchical legitimacy was further accelerated by the widening of its territorial base. By 1900 Buganda had approximately doubled its territory; by 1901 Ankole comprised an area several times the size of the nineteenth century kingdom of Nkore; similarly, by 1912 Rwanda had substantially expanded the scope of its northern boundaries. These territorial accretions, by opening up new sources of economic wealth and manpower, evidently enhanced the resource *potential* of the Crown. But they also entailed serious liabilities. The amalgamation of new sectors was not achieved through mutually beneficial transactions but through bureaucratic fiat. Though formally incorporated into the "political market" of monarchical systems the populations concerned had at first little or no sense of identification with their presumptive monarch. The demands enforced upon them were all the more costly for the kingship as these were seldom viewed as legitimate. Coercion, in short, tended to displace legitimacy. The significance of this phenomenon is nowhere more clearly illustrated than in the opposition to monarchical rule displayed by the populations of northern Rwanda during the terminal stages of the Belgian trusteeship. A rather different type of situation developed in Ankole, following the incorporation of a major portion of the Mpororo kingdom into its territorial base. Here amalgamation not only led to the elimination from the political scene of Ankole of its traditional royal clan (Bahinda) to the advantage of an exogenous clan (Bashombo), but, as Doornbos demonstrates, to a major restructuring of power relationships at the centre, that is between the king (Omugabe) and his chief councillor (Enganzi)—himself of Bashombo origins: "Divorced from his Bahinda kinsmen, the reigning Omugabe, Kahaya, thus came to stand rather isolated, and whenever possible (the Enganzi) did not fail to circumvent his bases of authority."

But if Ankole provides the clearest example of a restructuring of monarchical authority through a widening of its territorial base, it also exemplifies the nature of the costs and benefits involved in another phenomenon—the encapsulation of kingship into wider territorial organization. Even though the relevance of this situation is limited to only three of the kingships discussed in this book (Uganda, Ankole and Ijebu Ode), its implications are worth noting. Where opportunities for upward social mobility were initially circumscribed to members of a specific caste (as in Ankole), encapsulation offered alternative avenues for social and economic achievement, hence mitigating the asperites of intergroup conflict. Where several kingdoms happened to be juxtaposed to each other (as in Uganda and Nigeria), there has been a strong tendency on the part of colonial administrators to look upon some of these kingdoms as the "models" which others should try to emulate, major structural differences between them notwithstanding. Thus the heavily centralized authority systems exemplified by the Hausa emirates of northern Nigeria were often seen by British administrators as the ideal formula for administering Yoruba kingdoms; Rwanda provided the model polity which several German and Belgian Residents tried to replicate in Burundi; and Buganda, likewise, served as a model for administering Ankole. This quest for uniformity, one might add, did not stem solely from a lack of imagination on the part of European administrators, but from a realization that monopolistic structures were, on the whole, easier to deal with as well as more efficient for purposes of local government than oligopolistic ones. Whatever the motives, the result has been a restructuring of authority which tended to deviate substantially from pre-existing patterns of authority—a phenomenon nowhere better illustrated than in Lloyd's discussion of the growing tendency towards authoritarianism displayed by the Awujale of Ijebu Ode between 1933 and 1949.

Another consequence of encapsulation is that it has, at least in specific instances, created opportunities for the establishment of an internal "balance of power" situation among units which, in different circumstances might not have been administered with the same ease. The point is pertinently emphasized by Doornbos in his discussion of colonial rule in Ankole; but he also shows how the implications of this policy towards "balance of power" were carried over into the period after independence. After the forceful overthrow of the Buganda monarchy, in 1966, the kingdom of Ankole (along with the kingdoms of Toro and Bunyoro) had in a sense lost its *raison d'être* from the standpoint of the central Uganda authorities. Having served for a while, though not very successfully, to balance the power of the Buganda monarchy, the suppression of Ankole in turn served to balance the vacuum left by Buganda's own elimination from the political map of Uganda. Finally, encapsulation has evidently complicated the achievement of national integration once independence became a reality. The nature of the dilemma is aptly summarized by

Young: "Where they do not territorially coincide, nation and kingdom appear incompatible in the era of independence. The Buganda case suggests that either nation triumphs through dismantlement of kingdom, or kingdom mates nation through conquest of its central institutions, or through secession to render territory and kingdom congruent."

As the foregoing suggests, changes in the overall structure of exchange processes often involved major *shifts in the internal distribution of available resources*. Three basic patterns may be distinguished, involving either (1) a shift of resources away from the Crown to the traditional sectors of society, (2) or from the traditional sectors to the Crown, (3) or from one sector to another. The first pattern is exemplified by the massive distribution of land to the Bakungu chiefs, following the 1900 Buganda agreement—and by the formal recognition of the claims to "independence" made by members of the Batare segment of the Burundi royal family, after Von Goetzen's defeat of Mwami Mwezi Kisabo, in 1903. One might also point to the drastic curtailment of authority suffered by the Moroccan Crown after the passage of the famous *dahir berbère* of 1930, which in effect shifted authority away from the Maghzen to the dissident segments that gave its reputation of the Bled es-Siba ("lands of dissidence"). As P. C. Lloyd's discussion shows, it was precisely the reverse process that was inaugurated in Ijebu Ode after the issuing by Sir Donald Cameron of his 1933 policy statement. By recognizing the Awujale as "Sole Native Authority", and devolving upon his office far greater authority than had previously been the case, Cameron's statement in effect formalized a major transfer of authority from the titled chiefs to the Crown. The third pattern, involving a lateral transfer of resources from one sector to another, is again exemplified by Buganda and Burundi. In Buganda this process led, after 1900, to the absorption by the Bakungu chiefs of much of the resources previously held by the Bataka (clan chiefs). In Burundi a major portion of the resources held by the Batare segment of the royal family, eventually passed into the hands of their traditional rivals, the Bezi. A similar transfer took place in Ankole once the Bashombo had effectively supplanted the Bahinda as the prime depositors of wealth, status and chiefly authority.

The short-run implications of these transactions are relatively easy to pin down. Just as in Burundi the recognition of the Batare claims by the Residency had the effect of further restricting the authority of the incumbent Mwami, in Buganda the ascendancy of the Bakungu temporarily eclipsed the Kabakaship in the years following the 1900 agreement; similarly, the displacement of Bahinda chiefs by Bashombo elements undoubtedly weakened the authority and legitimacy of the Ankole kingship. How these transactions have ultimately affected the staying-power of monarchical systems is far more difficult to ascertain. For one thing, many of the patterns we have just described were extremely short-lived. Trends in one direction were often followed by countertrends in the opposite direction: For example, in Ijebu Ode and Burundi, the initial years of royal emasculation were followed by a period of gradual consolidation. Moreover, the conflicts of interest engendered by these transactions were handled differently by different monarchs. While some were able successfully to capitalize on the discontent of particular sectors, others were neither willing nor able to do so. Finally, rarely were these exchange processes reducible to a zero-sum game: what might be regarded as a loss of status and authority in terms of traditional political currencies, might be viewed as a net gain from the standpoint of the new criteria of status and authority introduced by the European colonizer.

Which brings us to yet another and even more fundamental dimension of change: shifts in the distribution of authority also tended to reflect *qualitative changes in the types of resources or currencies mediated through the European presence.* New forms of wealth, status and authority were injected in the political systems of African kingships which in many ways weakened the traditional resource-base of African monarchs. Major threats to monarchical legitimacy arose from the ideological resources made available through Christianity. The Christian God, in a way, emerged as a rival to the God-King. Meanwhile, those forms of coercion which the Church deemed unacceptable were eliminated from the arsenal of kingship, and what authority was left in the hands of the monarch was further devalued by the emergence of the Church as an alternative supplier of political resources—of status and wealth, and sometimes of coercion.[45] The lower the capacity of African kings to meet the expectations of Christianized elements, the greater the chances that the Church might act as a surrogate for the Crown.[46]

Similar consequences resulted from the inculcation of new attitudes and dispositions among Africans via new educational agencies and forms of commercialization. "The assumption, by members of the educated class, that they have a 'natural right' to rule",[47] gradually undermined the assumption held by African kings and chiefs that their rule was a natural birthright. Status, wealth and authority were no longer seen as originating from the Crown but from agencies and "currencies" external to it. Tensions arose between traditional holders of office and the newer generations of educated elites which came to reflect not only the different types of resources available to each, but basic disagreements over the way in which new resources ought to be allocated.

Extension of the suffrage to the masses implied a radically new way of distributing authority. Rather than being allocated by the Crown to the chiefs—or by the chiefs to the Crown—and on the basis of mutual loyalty or self-interested exchanges, authority was now allocated by the masses to their elected representatives on the basis of universal suffrage. No longer were authoritative decisions made by the Crown, or by a conclave of trusted and obedient servants, but by popularly elected officials. Just as "citizenship" shifted the bases of status away from royals and nobles to the masses, so the introduction of the suffrage displaced the political centre of gravity of monarchical systems away from the Court to the newly established, popularly elected conciliar organs. Inasmuch as these organs could serve as instruments for gaining control over new financial and economic resources (for example, through the awarding of contracts, and the setting of salary scales as well as through promotions and appointments), there occurred a drastic weakening of the resource-base of African kingships.

These general trends and phenomena are made abundantly clear by the various case studies contained in this book. It is equally plain that the "absorptive" capacity of the recipient systems varied widely, as did the ability of their respective monarchs to manage constructively the political resources made available through constitutional advance. Neither variable can be properly assessed independently of the other. The point is not only that a system's capacity to adapt itself to a changing environment is, in a fundamental sense, contingent upon the quality of its leadership, but that leadership is itself conditioned by the characteristics of the system. Two separate questions are involved in this proposition: (1) In what ways have the structural or normative characteristics of African kingdoms affected the *quality* of their monarch's leadership? (2) In what ways have these characteristics affected the *impact* of monarchical leadership on the course of recent events?

To the first of these questions Ferguson and Wilks provide one possible answer: inasmuch as monopolistic kingships invite the "politicization of high office", bringing the kingship "into the tumult of the political arena", they tend to place leadership at a premium.[48] Not only are the stakes involved in the capture of power higher than in the oligopolistic type, but the very concentration of resources around the throne implies the politicization of succession to royal office: "The politicization of the processes for determining the succession . . . obligates candidates to marshall and maximize their support, and has the clear effect of placing leadership at a premium."[49] This factor would presumably help to explain why a kingdom like Buganda, for example, was able to generate a more effective type of leadership than, say, Burundi or Ijebu Ode.

The conclusion reached by Wilks and Ferguson might gain further cogency from an examination of the socialization processes associated with the incumbency of monopolistic roles. Although the empirical evidence is as yet rather limited, one may, nevertheless, hypothesize that the emergence of a strong and effective monarchical leadership is as much a reflection of the politicization of succession to high office as of the require-ments of monarchical role performance in monopolistic settings.[50] Even so, the argument unduly minimizes the influence of age and personality on monarchical leadership, or else tends to exaggerate the influence of the political environment on the monarch's personality. Without going into the question of how best to assess personality characteristics, the least that can be said is that there is no self-evident relationship between the structural characteristics of any particular kingdom and the "modal personality" which might be attributed to its rulers. Very different types of personality may emerge from the same political environment.[51] Moreover, just as personality affects leadership, both are evidently affected by age. As Young's discussion makes clear, the age of the incumbent tends to impart "a clear rhythm to the exercise (of monarchical leadership)". In Buganda, as he goes on to note, "the early years [of a Kabaka's reign] were ones of cautious consolidation of power, of uncertainty . . . Old age was another perilous time; perspectives of imminent change were also likely to activate conspiracy". No attempt to assess the innovative or adaptive capacities of African kingships can overlook these cyclical variations in the exercise of monarchical leadership. On this score the evidence available from Lesotho, Rwanda and Burundi is fairly conclusive: although this is by no means the only relevant factor, in all three cases the crises of legitimacy faced by monarchical institutions were in part a reflection of the extreme youth and political inexperience of their respective rulers.

Finally, one is impelled to wonder whether the strength of a monarch's political leadership is the only relevant criterion for assessing his chances of political survival in a modernizing environment. If the recent history of Burundi is any index, a convincing case could be made for the view that the longevity of monarchical institutions is in part conditioned by the monarch's ability to keep clear of "the tumult of the political arena". This, of course, does not exclude other forms of leadership, whether they be moral, hortatory or symbolic. But in this case leadership becomes associated with qualities of a rather different nature from those alluded to by Ferguson and Wilks.

Which brings us to the next question: in what ways have the structural or normative characteristics of African kingdoms affected the impact of monarchical leadership on recent events? Taking as our premise the contention that "the likelihood of personal impact varies with the degree to which the actions take place in an environment which admits of restructuring",[52] the question can best be answered by taking into account the normative "propensities" of monarchical regimes, and the types of conflicts which these propensities have engendered. The more "open" the distributive patterns operative in the traditional society, the greater the likelihood of personal impact; conversely, the more restrictive the distributive patterns, and the more rigid the normative sanctions, the smaller the chances that monarchical leadership will have an impact on the environment in which it is exercised. In this connection one might point to the relative "openness" of the distributive formulae operative in Lesotho and Swaziland, and contrast the opportunities for political innovation afforded by their respective systems with the much more restrictive situation exemplified by Rwanda. For all its monopolistic tendencies the Rwanda monarchy was unable to innovate beyond the limits set through the "premise of inequality", and the leadership skills at the command of the incumbent Mwami were of little help to mitigate the asperities of ethnic conflict. As this last example tends to suggest, much also depends on the types of conflict with which African rulers happened to be confronted at any particular juncture, and in particular on the degree to which a given conflict situation could admit of restructuring. Thus one wonders whether a different kind of leadership could have averted the crises experienced by Rwanda in 1959–60 and Buganda in 1966; in each case the contribution which such a leadership might have made towards the resolution of conflict was largely nullified by the variety of underlying forces pressing in the opposite direction.

In all of the kingdoms discussed in this book major shifts occurred over time in the distribution of political resources, and conflicts developed which could not be handled on the basis of pre-existing formulae. In P. C. Lloyd's words, "any institutionalization in the distribution of power is upset when new sources of power . . . become available for distribution. The contest between the categories of office-holders becomes more intense as established rules do not cover the allocation of new resources".[53] Who the contestants were, what forms of contestation developed among them, and with what consequences for the institution of kingship is what we must now try to elucidate.

PATTERNS OF CONFLICT

As various case studies in this book demonstrate, historical contests have often "spilled over" into modern arenas and fused with conflicts of interest more directly traceable to the legacy of colonial rule, or expectations of its extinction. But if historical dimensions cannot be easily exorcized from the analysis of contemporary forms of conflict and resulting struggles, an attempt must be made to clarify the nature of the options faced by African kings during the colonial and post-colonial periods. With this end in view, one may usefully differentiate among the following types of conflict situations:

(1) Situations characterized by the *persistence or reactivation of historical forms of competition among traditional categories of office-holders*: In this type of situation the legitimacy of the incumbent (king or chief) may be challenged, and the volume of resources at his disposal called into question; yet the legitimacy of the role associated with the occupancy of monarchical office remains unchallenged;

(2) *Structural contradictions between different segments of the social or political systems:* Here the legitimacy of monarchical office is directly threatened by the injection of new resources; the challenge expresses itself in one of two ways: either in the form of extreme value clashes along vertical lines—as in the case of an attempted reversal of established superordinate-subordinate relationships within the same national community (as in Rwanda)—or along horizontal lines—as when conflict over the definition of community boundaries leads to a head-on confrontation between the incorporated kingdom and the wider political system (as happened in Buganda);

(3) *Societal conflicts*, involving varying degrees of incompatibility between the goals and interests of the monarchical establishment on the one hand, and of the newly emergent sectors on the other.

Although these situations are by no means mutually exclusive, they must be kept analytically separate if one is to grasp the nature of the different patterns of interaction which have impinged upon African kingships, and the way in which they have affected the capacity of African kings to adjust to, and work through, new constitutional orderings.

(a) Persistence and Reactivation of Traditional Contests: King *v*. Chief; Chief *v*. Chief

Some of these contests merely tended to reflect the nature of the kingship as an object of competition among potential aspirants. A case in point is the succession struggle released by the death of Griffith in Lesotho, in 1939, which successively pitted his two half-brothers, Bereng and Seeiso, against each other, and ultimately Seeiso's senior wife and Acting Regent, 'Mantsebo, against Bereng. Others, however, involved a conscious attempt to reallocate political resources between traditional sectors—between chief and chief, or king and chief. Illustrative of this type of conflict is the struggle for power that went on in Burundi during the colonial period between the Bezi and Batare segments of the royal family. Expressed in the language of game theory the Bezi-Batare struggle initially partook of the qualities of a zero-sum game in that the amount of resources gained by one party (land, cattle, clients, etc.) implied a corresponding loss for its opponents. A third type of situation is exemplified by Ijebu Ode between 1933 and 1949. Though often cast in a traditional idiom, the opposition between the Awujale and the chiefs was more than a mere continuation of traditional rivalries into a "modern" political arena; it also expressed the conflict of roles and interests that were built into the Native Authority system after 1933. As shown by P. C. Lloyd, the constitutional arrangements devised by the British greatly enhanced the power of the Awujale in relation to the chiefs; but this did not imply a static state of affairs. Conflicts of interests between the oba and the chiefs led them to engage in a perpetual probing to power relationships. "The educated oba wished to assert his power in his town, to achieve substantial wealth and maintain the prestige of his office"—and because "the first and possibly the last of these three goals [could] be achieved only at the expense of his chiefs, the traditional struggle between oba and chiefs [was] thus enhanced in the new situation". Not only was it enhanced but it was transformed through the new resources made available to the oba.

In none of these cases was the legitimacy of the institution of kingship openly challenged. In all three cases, however, significant changes took place in the volume and character of resources available to the incumbent. In Lesotho the result of the succession struggle was, in Weisfelder's words, "to emasculate the kingship for a most crucial twenty-year segment of its evolution". Although the competition was, strictly speaking, over the office of kingship rather than one aiming at a redistribution of resources, the end result was the enthronement of a female regent ('Mantsebo) whose claims to legitimacy were dubious, and skills for leadership almost non-existent. By default, as it were, control over political resources passed from the kingship to the Basotho National Council. Historical trends in Burundi ran in the opposite direction—towards a gradual reinforcement of the monarchy through a concomitant strengthening of the traditional resource-base of the Bezi segment. Although the resource advantage gained by the Bezi meant an enhancement of the position of the *ganwa* (or chiefs) rather than of the monarch, they each came to realize the mutual benefits involved in this relationship. Despite the conflicts of interests which subsequently developed between different generations of ganwa of Bezi origins, the reciprocities between the Crown and the chiefs could not readily be undone.

Far more ambiguous was the situation that developed in Ijebu Ode. Here the interplay of traditional and modern resources created a much wider range of options not only for the monarch but also for the chiefs. As P. C. Lloyd points out, the Awujale could, in theory, opt for one of two roles—that of traditional ruler or Native Authority; or he could segregate these roles depending on the circumstances; or he could work out a half-way role between the expectations of the administrative officers and those of his chiefs; or he could develop an entirely new role.[54] As it happened the Awujale "appeared to play a largely passive role, attempting to maintain his salary and power but not creating any new role". A stalemate situation developed which in turn paved the way for the substitution of party politics for factional politics, meanwhile leaving the Awujale in the position of a rudderless appendage easily manipulated by up-and-coming politicians.

Besides calling attention to the different options made available to African kings through the continuation or reactivation of traditional contests, the foregoing suggests important qualifications to Gluckman's thesis that competition for the kingship, in the form of "rebellion", serves to reinforce the legitimacy of the office.[55] The succession crisis that took place in Lesotho did little to strengthen the legitimacy of the kingship. The accession of 'Mantsebo created a political void which not only encouraged the ascendancy of the National Council but discredited the legitimacy of the office of kingship to an unparalleled extent. Similarly, the fraternal rebellions released by the death of Ntare in Burundi might have strengthened the kingship, but only to the extent that "after a rebellion the strongest prince was in possession of the throne".[56] In fact, Ntare's death was to initiate a process of territorial fragmentation which nearly destroyed the kingship, and in any event drastically constricted its resource base. Or consider again the case of Rwanda: the so-called Rucuncu coup, in 1894, brought a new Mwami to the throne (Yuhi Musinga) and shifted authority away from the Banyiginya to the Bega clan. Ultimately, however, the displacement of Banyiginya chiefs led to a major protest movement in the north. For a while the Rwanda monarchy was effectively deprived of an important segment of its traditional resource base; meanwhile the exigencies of the situation faced by the "rebel" chiefs in the north led to a significant reallocation of wealth and status within the northern region. This initiative was to create new "propensities"—in the direction of an equalization of wealth and status—and hence a major potential for the subsequent activation of revolutionary sentiment and activity.

The legitimacy accorded to the institution of kingship and the legitimacy accorded to the incumbent are of course two different things. Yet both are in some ways affected by decisions concerning the allocation of political resources. Thus to argue that "since rebellions attack the personnel of office and not the office themselves"[57] the legitimacy of the office is not only unimpaired but magnified, is far too simplistic a statement. For one thing the argument makes relatively short shrift of the change of political resources which may accompany the accession of a new dynasty. Different incumbents may opt for different ways of distributing power; and a change in the distribution of power may generate changes in conceptions of legitimacy about the institution of kingship, as well as in the structures through which legitimacy is established and perpetuated. When this happens significant changes are likely to occur in popular attitudes toward the institution of kingship.

Moreover, conflicts which on the surface seem to involve a competition for traditional offices may create the very conditions by which new political resources are injected into the system. Conflicts between traditional descent groups, chiefs, or aspirants to the throne may create a feeling of "status displacement" among the "losers", and this, as Hagen suggests, may prompt them to seek access to new resources in order to make up for this denial of traditional status.[58] What Hagen refers to as "withdrawal of status respect" may thus lead to an accumulation of new resources in the hands of the "traditional" opposition, and indeed to a new conception of monarchical legitimacy. The result may be the emergence of a sort of " 'Whig' political philosophy, whereby the deficiencies of [political] life [are] to be accounted for by the improper increase of the royal power at the expense of that of the aristocratic leaders of the people".[59] The phenomenon has been dealt with in some detail by T. O. Ranger and G. L. Caplan in connection with Barotseland: They both show how the emergence of a "progressive", nationally-oriented Lozi elite within the United National Independence Party (UNIP) tended to reflect, among other things, the persistence within the traditional society of an aristocratic opposition to the paramount. "Since it was impossible to overthrow Mwanawina III from within the traditional system, aristocratic oppositions within Barotseland looked to external agencies to force the changes they desired."[60] A very similar phenomenon occurred in Burundi, in the form of the Batare opposition to Mwambutsa, and in Lesotho, through chief Jonathan. In each case traditional conflict has tended to erode traditional conceptions of legitimacy, while setting important limitations on the options available to the throne.

Finally, Gluckman's contention that "it is a historical fact that these struggles [between rival houses] kept component sections of the nation united in conflicting allegiances about the sacred kingship"[61] omits another type of historical evidence, exemplified by the secession of the component units and the setting up of independent kingships. The history of Burundi during the last decades of the nineteenth century conclusively demonstrates the point.

Where Gluckman's argument acquires relevance is in the distinction it draws between "rebellion" and "revolution": "rebellion" in the sense in which Gluckman uses the term is associated with competition for the status of king. This was clearly the case in Lesotho after 1939; similarly, the Bezi-Batare struggle in Burundi was not only a competition for the status of chief but also, initially at least, for the status of king. Neither type of contest can be subsumed under the label of "revolution". Although the term "revolution" is by no means free of ambiguity, the types of confrontation that took place in Rwanda from 1959 to 1962, and in Uganda in 1966, are obviously much closer to Gluckman's use of the term than any of the contests discussed in this section. In Rwanda as in Buganda structural contradictions developed over the definition of community boundaries which virtually eliminated possibilities of adjustment.

(b) Structural Contradictions: Caste *v.* Caste; King *v.* Nation

In none of the situations we have just described was the legitimacy of the regime called into question: major changes took place in the distribution of resources among traditional sectors, but these did not imply a fundamental threat to legitimizing norms. In Rwanda as in Buganda, however, radical transformations took place in distributive patterns which did not simply initiate new "propensities"; they also introduced entirely new paramenters for the allocation of resources.

Rwanda provides the most extreme example of a sudden reversal of traditional statuses through the injection of new political resources. The advent of independence was accompanied by an abrupt and massive distribution of authority on a *per capita* basis, through the suffrage; citizenship, moreover, conferred equality of status to all, irrespective of caste distinctions, thereby opening new opportunities for the acquisition of wealth to lower-caste elements. Hence a fundamental contradiction developed between the "premise of inequality" of the traditional society and the egalitarian implications of the new constitutional order: the introduction of democracy implied a radically new "commitment" of political resources, and as status and authority shifted from the Tutsi caste to the newly enfranchised Hutu masses there occurred a rapid heightening of social conflict. The reversal of the traditional status hierarchy meanwhile deprived the monarchy of its traditional bases of support. Unable to sustain the costs of a major reconversion, the abolition of the monarchy was the logical consequence of the structural contradictions introduced by the departing colonizer through the extension of the franchise to lower-caste elements.

An altogether different type of contradiction is revealed by the recent history of Buganda. In contrast with Rwanda, where the problem was one of vertical integration, the key dilemma faced by Buganda was to achieve political integration within a wider territorial framework while at the same time preserving its cultural integrity and political autonomy. Here the main obstacle to integration stemmed from horizontal contradictions between the Buganda sub-system and the larger political system of which it had become a part. The privileged status which Buganda had enjoyed during the Protectorate, coupled with "monopolistic" propensities of its traditional political system, made integration within the Uganda-wide system all the more problematic. Moreover, the very ease with which vertical integration was achieved *within* Buganda further contributed to its "staying power". In these conditions encapsulation could scarcely become effective short of a major political surgery.

(c) Societal Conflicts: The Emergence of New Sectors

A third type of conflict—often co-existing with, and indeed reinforcing, the ones we just described—arises from the challenge posed to monarchical regimes by the mobilization of new sectors. Here we are not so much dealing with a competitive struggle for office among traditional aspirants, or with structural contradictions over the definition of community boundaries, as with conflicts of goals and interests between the monarch and his "clients" on the one hand, and a new category of political actors, identified with modern-day politicians, bureaucrats and army men. Although they generally shared the oppositional mentality of educated elites elsewhere in Africa, their opposition to the regime received added impetus from the presumptive conservatism of monarchical structures.

The demands made upon monarchical regimes by these newly emergent sectors varied substantially, both in scope and intensity, as did the responses of African monarchs to these demands. For purposes of analysis, these variations may be examined in the light of the following variables:

1. One such variable refers to the incidence of ethnic, cultural or religious discontinuities on the structure of societal conflict. Where the regime and its beneficiaries were both identified with the interests of a specific ethnic or religious group, socio-economic demands have tended to reactivate historical grievances, or generate fresh grievances, on the part of the "excluded" communities. In this case societal conflict tends to fuse with, and exacerbate, traditional conflicts of loyalty among groups. Thus if the grievances currently directed against the Ethiopian monarchy are in part related to its identification with Shoan interests, the blows struck against the Rwanda monarchy were directly motivated by its ideological links with the Tutsi caste. But as these examples also suggest, the boundaries of conflict may differ substantially from one case to the next. Where the mobilization of one ethnic group triggers the countermobilization of another the point may be reached where the choices open to the regime become extremely limited. This is particularly the case where the structure of ethnic conflict is dichotomous in character and national in scope. Here the options open to the regime are essentially two: the Crown can either cast its lot with one of the contestants (as happened in Rwanda), or it may try to steer a relatively neutral course by avoiding close identification with either camp (as happened in Burundi from 1962 to 1964). Other situations may arise, however, where the locus of interaction among groups is primarily local or regional: the Erytrean separatist movement in Ethiopia, and the "positive protests" of the Tafilelt (in 1956) and the Rif (in 1958), in Morocco, are obvious examples. "In such situations," as D. Horowitz notes, "the centre has some flexibility and can sometimes grant the demands of one group without necessarily injuring the interests of others."[62]

2. Another variable concerns the degree of "relative deprivation" felt by these new sectors as a result of actual or anticipated changes in the distribution of political resources. Shifts in the relative prosperity of one sector as against another may have the effect of directing grievances against the more privileged sector. The monarchy itself, however, may become the source of a deprivation experience, and, ultimately, the target of remedial action, as happened in Burundi. The sudden shift to royal autocracy, in July 1965, immediately after the palace had given unmistakable proof of its intent to restore the legitimacy of parliament was a key element in the decisions of Hutu politicians and army officers to turn against the monarchy. Almost the reverse situation developed in Lesotho, in January 1970: by denying the BNP leadership and its royal allies (affiliated to the Marematlou party) the fruits of their electoral victory, Chief Jonathan exacerbated the frustrations of his "monarchical" opponents to the point where violence became the only resource at their disposal for gaining power.

3. A third variable concerns the incidence of time sequences on the intensification of societal conflict. If temporal space provides a major reference point for understanding the mutations that have affected monarchical roles, this dimension is equally relevant to an understanding of the changes that have taken place over time in elite perceptions of monarchical legitimacy. As several studies in this book suggest, major differences of orientations to monarchical symbols can be noted among different generations of educated elites, reflecting (1) the different types of socializing influences to which they were exposed, (2) the different types of skills and sense of achievement which they acquired, and (3) the variable range of professional opportunities available to each generation. The implication is not that there is a "unidirectional and positive relationship between education and democratic political orientation", a fallacy convincingly refuted by James S. Coleman, but, in Stember's words, that "the impact of education varies in direction and strength with specific issues (and time periods".[63] When nationalism emerged as the key issue of African politics, the tendency of the educated elite was to seek maximum advantage from the manipulation of monarchical symbols in order to strengthen their nationalist claims. Their instrumental view of the monarchy persisted for some time after independence, accepting it as a means of access to power and wealth. Ultimately, however, two related phenomena occurred which together contributed to heighten their sense of alienation: Absorption into the ranks of the Establishment became increasingly problematic as the demand for jobs began to outstrip employment opportunities; moreover, the seeds of protest generated by the constriction of employment opportunities caused the regime to rely increasingly on coercion rather than inducements. At this point the costs involved in the maintenance of monarchical symbols tended to exceed whatever residual gratifications they still had to offer.

As noted earlier, the significance of these variables cannot properly be gauged without taking into consideration the "countervailing pressures" originating from specific policies and initiatives on the part of individual monarchs. What these policies and initiatives were, how they have affected the structure of conflict, and ultimately the destinies of African kingships, is what we shall try to elucidate in the conclusion to this volume.

Processes of change in monarchical settings can be approached from two alternative perspectives. From the perspective of the societal transformations effected through the surge of modernity African monarchies can be treated as a dependent variable; but monarchical structures can also be seen as an independent institutional force affecting the rate and direction of social change. In this case the capacity of African monarchies to come to grips with developmental problems depends essentially on the kinds of policies initiated by the throne. Although the emphasis in this introductory essay has been in large measure on the first of these dimensions, we have also tried to suggest possible connections between the two. In particular, attention has been drawn to the limitations set by environmental constraints upon the range of options available to African monarchs. In pointing to the type of conditions that appeared to inhibit or encourage policy innovation special emphasis has been laid on the character of the traditional polities and their adaptability to the transformative influences introduced under the auspices of colonial rule. In so doing, our aim has been suggestive rather than exhaustive. The chapters that follow further illuminate the processes of change outlined in this introductory essay. Our hope is that they will clarify not only the nature of the traditional parameters within which change has taken place, but also, how, as a result of the initiatives of individual monarchs or through the projection of their own personality traits into their public roles, new social patterns and institutions came into being which either delayed or hastened the demise of traditional monarchies.

NOTES

1 Quoted in Kingsley Martin, *The Magic of the British Monarchy* (Boston: 1962), p. 15.
2 See, for example, Arnold Rivkin, *Nation-Building in Africa* (New Brunswick, N.J., 1969), in which four of the monarchies discussed (Rwanda, Burundi, Ethiopia and Libya) are identified as "special", "very special" or "odd" cases: pp. 189, 194, 199.
3 Rupert Emerson, "Nation-Building in Africa", in Karl W. Deutsch and W. Foltz, *Nation-Building* (New York: 1963), p. 104.
4 See S. Huntington, *Political Order in Changing Societies* (New Haven: 1968), p. 142; and David E. Apter, *The Political Kingdom in Buganda* (Princeton: 1967), p. 84 ff.
5 See D. E. Apter, "The Role of Traditionalism in the Political Modernization of Ghana and Uganda", *World Politics*, Vol. XIII, No. 1 (Oct. 1960), pp. 54–68.
6 Claude E. Welch, "The Challenge of Change: Japan and Africa" in Herbert J. Spiro, *Patterns of African Development* (Englewood Cliffs, N.J.: 1967), *passim*.
7 David E. Apter, "Political Religion in the New Nations", in C. Geertz, *Old Societies and New States* (Glencoe, Ill.: 1963), p. 83.

8 See Ali A. Mazrui, "The Monarchical Tendency in African Political Culture", *British Journal of Sociology*, Vol. XVIII, No. 3 (September 1967), pp. 231–250, and "Nkrumah: The Leninist Czar", *Transition* No. 26 (Kampala: 1960).
9 For a typical illustration of this "reductionist" approach to political phenomena, see S. M. Lipset, *Political Man* (Garden City, N.Y., 1963), p. 64 ff.
10 S. N. Eisenstadt, *The Political Systems of Empires* (The Free Press, New York: 1963), p. 111; for a more recent and systematic discussion of the characteristics and functions of political resources, see Warren Ilchman and Norman Uphoff, *The Political Economy of Change* (Berekley and Los Angeles, 1969).
11 For a further elaboration on this point see P. C. Lloyd, "The Political Structure of African Kingdoms: An Exploratory Model", in Michael Banton, ed., *Political Systems and the Distribution of Power*, A.S.A. Monographs 2 (London, New York, 1965), p. 73 ff.
12 Jan Vansina, "Anthropologists and the Third Dimension ', *Africa*, Vol. XXXIX, No. 1 (January 1969), p. 62.
13 C. Kluckhon, *Mirror for Man* (Greenwich, Conn.: 1960), p. 11
14 Leonard Binder, *Iran: Political Development in a Changing Society* (Berekley and Los Angeles: 1962), p. 63.
15 See Ivor Wilks, "Aspects of Bureaucratization in Ashanti in the Nineteenth Century", *Journal of African History*, Vol. VII, No. 2 (1966), pp. 215–232; cf. David Apter, *The Politics of Modernization* (Chicago: 1965), p. 100 ff.
16 The expression is borrowed from Edmund Leach, "Golden Bough or Gilded Twig?" *Daedalus*, Spring 1961, Vol. 90, No. 2, pp. 371–387.
17 See Claudine Vidal, "Le Rwanda des anthropologues ou le fetichisme de la vache", *Cahier d'Etudes Africaines*, Vol. IX, No. 35 (1969), p. 384–401.
18 C. G. Seligman, *Races of Africa* (London, 1966) p. 100.
19 See J. D. Fage and R. Oliver, *A Short History of Africa* (Baltimore, 1961), and A. J. Arkell, *A History of the Sudan* (London, 1955).
20 J. Goody, "Feudalism in Africa?", *Journal of African History*, Vol. IV, No. 1 (1963), p. 15.
21 J. H. M. Beattie, "Kingship", in *International Encyclopedia of the Social Sciences* (New York, 1968), Vol. 8, p. 386.
22 P. C. Lloyd (personal communication). A further source of confusion stems from the different titles conferred on African rulers by colonial authorities with a view to enhancing or diminishing the status the incumbent, as the circumstances required. In Barotseland, for example, the British South Africa Company saw fit to deprive Lewanika of his right to be called "king" "in order to reduce him to the same status as that of other chiefs of Northern Rhodesia"; yet half a century later, as Northern Rhodesia was about to be come Zambia, the British authorities decided to confer the title of *Litunga* upon the Lozi Paramount—"the supreme title of the Lozi themselves"—in order to soothe the pill he had to swallow for being refused the right to secede from Northern Rhodesia and the Federation. See Gerald L. Kaplan, *The Elites of Barotseland 1878–1969* (Berkeley and Los Angeles, 1970), p. 195.
23 See Jan Vansina, "Anthropologists and the Third Dimension", *op. cit.*; cf. G. Balandier, *Daily Life in the Kingdom of the Kongo from the 16th to the 18th Century*, tr. H. Weaver (London, 1967).
24 For example, Daryll Forde & P. M. Kaberry, eds., *West Afrcan Kingdoms in the Nineteenth Century* (Oxford: 1967); see also P. C. Lloyd's illuminating review article, "The Political Development of West African Kingdoms", *Journal of African History*, Vol. IX, No. 2 (1968), pp. 319–329.
25 A major exception is Samuel Huntington, "The Political Modernization of Traditional Monarchies", *Daedalus*, Vol. 95, No. 3 (1966), pp. 763–788.
26 Leon Bramson, *The Political Context of Sociology* (Princeton, N.J., 1961), p. 146.
27 Maurice Delafosse, *Haut-Sénégal-Niger* (Paris, 1912), Vol. 2, p. 182.
28 For a discussion of how economic and commercial resources have affected the growth of Sudanic kingdoms, see Fage, *A History of West Africa* (Cambridge, 1969), pp. 10–17; for an analysis of the way in which financial and fiscal resources

have assisted the development of a centralized bureaucracy in late 18th and early 19th century Ashanti, see I. Wilks, "Ashanti Government", in D. Forde and P. Kaberry, *West African Kingdoms in the 19th Century, op. cit.*, pp. 206–238; see also L. Mair's discussion of the importance of economic wealth in the building up of centralized states, in *Primitive Government* (Baltimore, 1962), p. 109.

29 Talcott Parsons, "The Distribution of Power in American Society", *World Politics*, Vol. X, No. 7 (1957), p. 140.

30 The term "sector" in this context refers to persons or groups of persons engaged in political exchange (see Ilchman and Uphoff, *The Political Economy of Change* (Berkeley and Los Angeles, 1969), p. 39 ff.). They include chiefs, lineage heads, ethnic groups—as would be the case in a traditional society—as well as the educated elites, parties, armies and bureaucracies.

31 As Eisenstadt argues, "Commodities, services, products of nature . . . are a creation of human culture, and their values are merely symbolic. Within each of these realms there exists not only the possibility of variability of permutations within a fixed universe but also the continuous possibility of the creation or invention of new contents, orientations and symbols." S. N. Eisenstadt, *Essays on Comparative Institutions* (New York, 1968), p. 28.

Although the term "currency" is sometimes used interchangeably with "resource" the distinction between them is usually made clear by the context in which they appear. To avoid confusion, let us emphasize that whereas "resource" is intended to designate wealth, authority, status or coercion, "currencies" refer to the means through which such political resources are acquired, e.g. education, commercialization, popular elections, etc. For a further elaboration on "resources" and "currencies", see Ilchman and Uphoff, *op. cit.*, p. 54 ff.

32 A. Southall, *Alur Society* (Cambridge: 1953), p. 248.

33 P. C. Lloyd, "The Political Structure of African Kingdoms: An Exploratory Model", *op. cit.*, p. 83 ff.

34 J. Goody, "Economy and Feudalism in Africa", *The Economic History Review*, Vol. XXII, No. 3 (December 1969), pp. 393–495; see also, L. Mair, *op. vit.*, p. 107 ff., and R. Gray and D. Birmingham, *Pre-Colonial African Trade* (London, 1970), p. 7.

35 M. Gluckman, "The Rise of a Zulu Empire", *Scientific American* Vol. CCII (1960), pp. 157–168; C. C. Wrigley, "Bagunda: An Outline Economic History", *Economic History Review*, Vol. X, Nos. 1, 2 & 3 (1957), p. 72.

36 Quoted by H. Darley, *Slaves and Ivory* (London, 1926), *passim*.

37 Quoted by C. Young; see *infra* p. 196.

38 B. Malinowski, Magic, *Science and Religion and Other Essays* (New York, 1948), p. 64.

39 Ilchman & Uphoff, *The Political Economy of Change, op. cit.*, p. 73.

40 For an interesting discussion of the incidence of clientage ties on the growth of monarchical power, see B. Davidson, *The African Genius*, (Boston, 1969), pp. 203–211, and Lucy Mair, *Primitive Government, op. cit.*, p. 167 ff.

41 E. Gellner, "The Great Patron: A Reinterpretation of Tribal Rebellions", *Archives Européennes de Sociologie*, Vol. X, No. 1 (1969), p. 64.

42 Clifford Geertz, *Islam Observed* (New Haven and London, 1968), p. 111.

43 Claude Lévi-Strauss, *Structural Anthropology* (Garden City, N.Y., 1967), p. 204.

44 See for example how Archinard defined the functions of the king (*fama*) of the Bambara, after the conquest of Segou, and compare his methods with those adopted by Lord Lugard some thirteen years later in dealing with the Sultan of Sokoto. See John D. Hargreaves, ed., *France and West Africa* (London, 1969); cf. pp. 198–200; cf. A. H. Kirk-Greene, *The Principles of Native Administration in Nigeria* (Cambridge, 1965), pp. 43–45.

45 It was none other than a former CMS missionary, Charlie Stokes, who supplied the Christian Party of Buganda with the firearms that enabled its leaders to capture the Kabakaship in 1890; for further details, see D. A. Low, *Religion and Society in Buganda* (Kampala, East African Studies No. 8, n.d.).

46 The relevance of this phenomenon to the Rwanda situation is ably discussed by

Alison Des Forges in "Kings without Crowns: The White Fathers in Rwanda", *Boston University Papers in African History* (Boston: 1967).

47 James S. Coleman, *Education and Political Development* (Princeton, 1965), *passim*.

48 Phyllis Ferguson and Ivor Wilks, "Chiefs, Constitutionas and the British in Northern Ghana", in Michael Crowder and Obaro Ikime, *West Afriain Chiefs* (New York and Ile-Ife, 1970). p. 326.

49 *Ibid.*, p. 328.

50 In addition to the evidence supplied in this book, important clues in support of this hypothesis may be gathered from John A. Rowe, *Revolution in Buganda 1856–1900* (unpublished Ph.D. thesis, University of Wisconsin, 1966).

51 According to one testimony, Adeona Fusigboye, who held the obaship of Ijebu Ode from 1906 to 1915, was referred to by a British official as "a weak and useless individual", and his successor, Ademolu, as "so decrepit and feeble a personality", that . . . he was "incapable of settling a dispute between two fowls in the backyard". These characterizations are difficult to reconcile with the personality traits displayed by Daniel Adesanya, as they emerge from the descriptions offered by the same commentator, or indeed by Professor Lloyd in his contribution to this volume. See E. A. Ayandele, "The changing position the Awujales of Ijebuland under Colonial Rule", in Michael Crowder and Obaro Ikime eds., *West African Chiefs*, *op. cit.*, p. 238.

52 Fred Greenstein, *Personality and Politics* (Chicago, 1969), p. 42.

53 P. C. Lloyd, "The Political Development of West African Kingdoms", *op. cit.*, p. 322.

54 See P. C. Lloyd, *Kings in Crisis: A Study of the Changing Roles of Yoruba Oba* (unpublished MS.).

55 Max Gluckman, *Custom and Conflict in Africa* (Oxford, 1963), p. 45 ff.
"All sections struggle for the kingship and this unifies them. They seek to place their own prince on the throne; they do not try to become independent from the kingship . . . Rebellions reassert the values of kingship and restore power" . . . "I am aware", adds Gluckman, "that this is a bold suggestion, and it may be teleological. But in practice, when I study the history of African states—or when I read about the War of the Roses—it seems clearly to emerge that the effect of rebellion (as against revolution) was at least temporarily to reunite the nation about the kingship". *Ibid.*
Professor Gluckman s subsequent reappraisal of his "rebellion theory" (in a personal communication to this writer) introduces some major qualifiers to his initial formulation. He notes, for example, that "since we cannot isolate variables and processes in test tubes, but work on reality itself, we have by mental abstraction to isolate some institutional, or interactional processes to analyze how far they would work out through time (what I call their structural duration) if they were not interfered with by other processes. The theory of a cycle of rebellions, or series of rebellions, is such an abstraction. One has to see if given the physical and social environment such a process is likely to be realized in maintaining the legitimacy of the kingship, the claim of the royal family to it, the canalization of ambition of princes and other leaders, grievances of subjects, territorial segmentation and loyalties and autonomies. I believe this to be so as long as the fight is for the kingship—though defeat of one party may weaken the numerical strength of the nation, lead a defeated section to flee, in extreme cases lead to fragmentation. The fragments may then set up new kingdoms based on the old model. There would then be two or more kingdoms, each perhaps smaller than the original, but of the same model." These reservations add an entirely new and important dimension to his original thesis. I am fully aware of the value of abstractions, in that, in Gluckman's own words, "they take one out of the mire of mere description into theoretical appraisal of the complexity of what is occurring". Yet I wonder whether by abstracting out of his analysis such important variables as the ones mentioned above the equilibrium model implicit in his initial formulation does not become exceedingly removed from empirical realities. For further caveats and qualifications,

see M. Gluckman, "The Utility of the Equilibrium Model in the Study of Social Change", *American Anthropologist*, 70 (1968), pp. 219–239.

56 Martin Southwold, "Succession to the Throne in Buganda", in Jack Goody, *Succession to High Office*, *op. cit.*, p. 119.

57 Max Gluckman, *Custom and Conflict in Africa*, *op. cit.*, p. 46.

58 Everett E. Hagen, *On the Theory of Social Change* (Homewood, Ill., 1963), p. 185 ff.

59 Terence O. Ranger, "Nationality and Nationalism: The Case of Barotseland", *Journal of the Historical Society of Nigeria*, Vol. IV, No. 2 (1968), p. 245.

60 T. O. Ranger, "Nationality and Nationalism", *op. cit.*, *loc. cit.*; see also G. Caplan, *The Elites of Barotseland*, *op. cit.*

61 Max Gluckman, *Custom and Conflict in Africa*, *op. cit.*, p. 46–47.

62 Donald L. Horowitz, "Three Dimensions of Ethnic Politics", *World Politics*, Vol. XXII, No. 2 (January 1971), p. 238.

63 James S. Coleman, ed., *Education and Political Development*, *op. cit.*, *passim*.

PART I

A THEOCRATIC
KINGSHIP: ETHIOPIA

1

ETHIOPIA

Christopher Clapham

The Ethiopian Empire has so far been able to overcome the challenges to
monarchical legitimacy to which many African kingdoms have succumbed
in the colonial and post-colonial eras, and has maintained a political
supremacy which must be the envy of its less fortunately placed contemporaries. No other African monarch in recent times has wielded such power
for so long as Haile-Selassie in Ethiopia. We are therefore dealing, comparatively speaking, with a story of success, and part of the purpose of this
chapter must be to examine the means which have enabled the monarchy
to play so dominant a role in modern Ethiopian politics.[1]

Of course, this dominance may be precarious, and the future of the
throne is by no means assured. But its long history, though it provides
no insurance against the future, does at least offer some insight into the
present. As we shall see, Haile-Selassie has achieved his astonishing pre-
eminence in Ethiopia over the last forty years by closely combining his
own personal skills with an office deeply rooted in the Ethiopian past.[2]
Until very recent times, in fact, it would scarcely be too much to say that
the Ethiopian state *was* the Emperor; its shifting territory has been
definable only as the area under the sovereignty, actual or nominal, of the
Ethiopian crown—a definition still retained in the present Constitution—
and the Emperor's authority has been essential for any unified political
system to exist.

The structure of the Ethiopian monarchy reveals many similarities
with other African kingdoms, especially some of those in the interlacustrine area, though even in pre-colonial times it was notable for its
age and the size of the area which it controlled. To this spatio-temporal
continuity it can now add the distinction of being one of very few indigenous monarchies in sub-Saharan Africa to have survived through the
colonial period and beyond as an independent state. Its traditional value
system and decision-making functions have not been undermined—as in
Rwanda—by a long period under colonial supervision, nor its cultural
identity threatened—as in Buganda—by the need to co-exist with a
national government of which it only formed a sub-system. Traditional
and modern forms of government have remained concentric, and at the
time of the greatest recent challenge to the Ethiopian state, in the Italian
occupation of 1936–1941, the crown was able to present itself, with
ultimate success, as the symbol of national independence. This independence has in turn enabled traditional political forms to survive in Ethiopia

without the successive shocks of foreign rule and liberation which they
have had to undergo elsewhere. More even than other kingdoms, then,
Ethiopia's present polity must be approached through its past.

HISTORICAL BACKGROUND

The origins of the Ethiopian state, to which it owes both the monarchy
and the Ethiopian Orthodox Church, lie in the kingdom of Aksum between
fifteen and twenty centuries ago. A millennium later, the Empire enjoyed a
second flowering from the restoration of the Solomonic dynasty in about
1270 until the Moslem invasions of the mid-sixteenth century. By this time,
its main features were already set. Its territory, at its mid-fifteenth century
zenith, stretched some six hundred miles from north to south over the
Ethiopian plateau, and some three hundred miles, at its widest, from east
to west; its population since then has been fluctuating and uncertain, but
can safely be numbered in millions; the Empire's present population, still
uncertain, is over twenty million.[3] The myths still used to legitimate the
imperial power were well-established in the medieval period, and we also
find the distinctive duality between the Amhara/Tigrean core in the
northern highlands, and the surrounding Moslem and animist areas over
which the Emperors claimed control. This duality has persisted.

The core areas are themselves separated by regional rivalries and,
physically, by the sheer difficulties of communication over the ravine-
dissected plateau; but they have in common a social structure and political
culture on which the monarchy ultimately depends. This structure—
broadly speaking, and making allowance for local variation—comprises
a hierarchy of superior-inferior relations held together by powerful
authority figures, in what has aptly been described as a "tough-man
system."[4] A quotation from Donald Levine will make the point:

> The complex of beliefs, symbols and values regarding authority constitute a
> key component of Amhara political culture. Throughout Amhara culture
> appears the motif that authority as such is good: indispensable for the well-
> being of society and worthy of unremitting deference, obeisance, and praise.
> Every aspect of Amhara social life is anchored in some sort of relationship to
> authority figures, and the absence of such a relationship evokes feelings of
> incompleteness and malaise.[5]

This malaise appears in its most extreme form in battle, where Ethiopian
units characteristically disintegrate on the death of their leader,[6] and in
the succession to the throne, when prolonged periods of anomic behaviour
or factional violence may occur until a successful leader has gained
acceptance and recreated the pattern of authority and deference about
himself.

The political culture has both a religious and an economic base. The
Orthodox Church provides a primary focus for national identity against
foreign invaders, and furnishes the monarchy with legitimizing symbols
which will be examined in a later section. The arable highlands are rich
enough to sustain permanent cultivation, chiefly of grains, and to produce
a surplus which maintains a permanent (though little specialized) adminis-

trative and military stratum. In the highlands, this stratum is ethnically homogeneous with the mass of the people (excepting a number of sub-merged groups which include the Falasha or Ethiopian Jews), and main-tains a subculture not fundamentally different from the majority.[7] The agricultural economy generates a strong attachment to land—generalized at the national level in a determination to hold on to territory—and a corresponding network of land-based rights and services to which the concept of feudalism has sometimes been applied.

But it would be misleading to suggest that the political culture auto-matically upholds a united nation and a powerful throne. It cuts both ways. Local magnates, authority figures in their own right, may draw on their own support to take an independent line.[8] The Church is subject to regional and doctrinal rivalries which, in the absence of external threats, make it a source more of schism than of unity.[9] Land, language, locality all separate the highland peoples from one another, at the same time as they distinguish them, as a whole, from outsiders.[10] Centrifugal and centripetal elements in the highland core are delicately balanced and intimately linked.

The Amhara/Tigre core has long regarded itself as an Empire not simply in its form of government, but equally in its right to impose itself upon its neighbours, and it has expanded its territory whenever it has been strong enough to do so. As a result the core is surrounded by peripheral peoples with whom it has enjoyed (if that is the word) a shifting and often uneasy relationship. Sometimes independent and at war with the central Empire, sometimes incorporated within it, sometimes even taking a major role in the central government itself, these peoples add a second dimension of unity and fragmentation to the tensions within the core. In the fourteenth and fifteenth centuries, the Empire extended at least a nominal sovereignty over many surrounding tribes and sultanates, but the sixteenth the process was reversed. Between 1529 and 1542, Danakil and Somali forces under Ahmad Grañ ravaged the central plateau and repeatedly defeated the imperial forces—one of the very few historical events which has burnt its way into the folk historical consciousness. In the wake of this invasion, the great Galla immigration pressed into southern Ethiopia, and eventually settled in a broad arc around the plateau, from the escarpment in the east to the Blue Nile gorge in the west.

Deprived of its hold over the periphery, the imperial power gradually declined in the seventeenth and eighteenth centuries until it lost control even over the highlands, where local dynasties replaced it in each of the major regions. These processes were linked, in that the loss of tribute from his vassal states reduced the Emperor's distributive capacity, and military setbacks weakened his ability to control the regional lords. Finally, after establishing a permanent capital at Gondar, he gradually forsook the ambulatory government which had been necessary—in so large a country with such poor communications—for him to keep a close watch on his subordinates. The resulting "Era of the Princes", 1769–1855, marked the triumph of the centrifugal elements in the Ethiopian political system.

The second half of the nineteenth century, by contrast, saw a still sharper swing in the opposite direction, The fragmented polity was pulled together, its territory was more than doubled, and its independence was assured in the face of European invasion. This process was synonymous with the revival of the emperorship. A Galla and Moslem challenge to the hegemony of the highland peoples provided the initial impulse toward reunification,[11] when the visionary Emperor Tewodros (1855–1868) seized the throne and tried to impose his rule on the regional dynasties. Initially successful, this attempt eventually failed, but external pressures continued to emphasize the Emperor's military role, and evoked the capacity for leadership which was latent in the political culture—or, to put it more bluntly, since succession to the throne was determined by civil war between the leading regional lords, the man who eventually came out on top was likely to be a capable soldier able to draw on considerable support. Hence the Tigrean Emperor Yohanes (1872–1889) defeated Egyptian invasions in 1875 and 1876, and died repelling the Mahdists; his Shoan successor Menilek (1889–1913) routed the Italians at Adwa in 1896, by which time he could put into the field an army 80,000–120,000 strong, armed for the most part with modern rifles.[12]

The retention of independence went hand in hand with territorial expansion, and when Ethiopia's frontiers were fixed by treaty at the turn of the century, a broad ring of peripheral peoples were included within them. The coincidence between the strength of the monarchy, the power of the central government, the extent of the territory, and the capacity to resist outside attack, is complete, though it is impossible to single out any one of these as an independent and determining variable.

Even in the twentieth century, the extent of the territory and its independence have been open political questions—the Italian occupation lasted from 1936 to 1941, and Eritrea was absorbed into the Empire in 1952 and maintains an active separatist movement. But for the most part, these basic issues have been transformed into the need to integrate the diverse territories acquired by Menilek into a viable polity, and to accommodate the modernizing pressures induced by Ethiopia's contacts with the outside world. Menilek's grandson and successor Lej Iyasu (1913–1916) failed on both accounts. His close rapprochement with Islam offended the central Christian elite, his sympathy for the German/Turkish cause in the First World War alarmed the allied legations, and his administrative inability and frequent absence from Addis Ababa enabled his enemies to plan his overthrow. In a successful coup, Menilek's daughter Zawditu (1916–1930) became Empress, and her cousin Ras Tafari, later known as Haile-Selassie, was made Regent and heir to the throne. It took years of intricate manœuvre for him to establish his authority over power groups in the capital and, still more slowly, over the provincial lords; the first of these tasks was achieved by the time of his accession in 1930, the second by the Italian invasion of 1935–6. Meanwhile, he pursued the conscious policy of institutional innovation which Menilek had initiated when he founded the first government ministries in 1907. In 1931, Haile-Selassie promulgated Ethiopia's first written constitution, which established an appointive Parliament. He authorized further changes in government organization after the liberation from the Italians in 1941, and introduced a revised constitution, which among other things made one chamber of Parliament elective, to celebrate his silver jubilee in 1955. New legal codes appeared at intervals between 1957 and 1965.

These innovations have been made with one eye on foreign (western and latterly African) opinion, and the other on internal pressures and the need to equip Ethiopia with the structures appropriate to a modern state, but their modernizing impact has been muted by their place within the existing government. Their long-term effects are antipathetic to traditional modes of operation, even to the emperorship itself, but in the short run it is important that they have been introduced under the traditional authority system, and often with the immediate aim of strengthening it.

Similarly, the social and political changes of the last thirty years—the emergence of a new educated elite, the creation of large specialized armed forces, a measure of economic development—have been marked but rarely spectacular, since their immediate effect has again been softened by coexistence with the imperial regime. Haile-Selassie's presence has imposed its continuity over the whole period, and maintained a fragile balance between the tensions implicit in the system. Dissent is growing, and quite a number of plots have been discovered, but only the abortive Imperial Body Guard coup d'état in December 1960 has yet seriously challenged his supremacy. In a continent where survival is the first test of success, this uneventfulness—equalled only by Liberia—provides at least a negative tribute to the leadership which the monarchy supplies.

LEGITIMACY AND SUCCESSION

The age of the Ethiopian Empire, the written record of its imperial chronicles, and its sporadic contacts with European visitors, make it possible to trace its ups and downs over a much longer period than is available for the kingdoms to the south. During this time, some seven hundred years, the emperorship has survived radically changing conditions, and has been subject to cyclical expansions and contractions in its political role. It has taken on some of the colouring of the eras through which it has passed. A constant awareness of its fluctuating record is therefore essential to alert us both to the dangers of telescoping the centuries into too facile generalizations, and to the actual processes through which the monarchy has developed. This is especially true of political legitimation, since legitimizing symbols very often survive at a formal level long after they have lost any practical effect, and they are then as misleading as guides to the present as they can be illuminating in providing clues to the past.

Another caution is needed. Legitimation is essentially an *official* activity. The appeals which express it are those used by Emperors to justify their rule, and transmitted through the political culture of the court. We have no adequate information on the extent to which they are internalized by the Emperor's subjects. Two points to be borne in mind here are, firstly, that Ethiopia is a non-participant polity in which the great mass of the people have had no part in choosing their rulers but have merely had to accept them—hence the whole issue of legitimacy may be less significant than political scientists trained in other cultures tend to assume; and secondly, that the present Ethiopian empire contains many peoples incorporated only in the last hundred years, for whom the historic myths of the core highland areas can scarcely have much relevance.

Nonetheless, our starting point must be that cluster of religious and dynastic symbols which have been used to express the Ethiopian monarchy's legitimacy in terms of accepted external sources of authority. These date back to the Solomonic restoration, chief among them being the support of God and Church expressed through coronation and anointment:

> By virtue of His Imperial Blood, as well as by the anointing which he has received, the person of the Emperor is sacred, His dignity is inviolable and His power indisputable.[13]

This support gains additional "externality" from the fact that the Archbishop, who alone could perform the necessary ceremony, was until 1948 invariably a foreigner, brought from a Coptic monastery in Egypt; he thus combined a ritual autonomy with a generally very weak position in internal Ethiopian politics. A long-standing requirement that the ceremony be performed at Aksum has now been abandoned.

This religious sanction for imperial power is strengthened by a claim to divine selection—expressed in the imperial title *seyuma egzi'abher*, Elect of God—and by the use of those passages in the Bible which command obedience to the established authorities. It retains considerable operational significance, and has beyond doubt been deeply internalized by Haile-Selassie, who since his accession has seen himself as an agent of the divine will:

> We, Haile Selassie I, Emperor of Ethiopia, having been called to the Empire by the Grace of God and by the unanimous voice of the people; and having the Crown and the Throne legitimately by anointment according to the law, are convinced that there is no better way of manifesting the gratitude which We owe to Our Creator, who has chosen Us and granted Us his confidence, than to render Ourselves worthy of it by making every effort so that he who comes after Us may be invested with this confidence and may work in conformity with the laws according to the principles established.[14]

Nowadays his speeches are written by speech writers, but when checking through a draft he still often adds an invocation for divine assistance at the end. It is a view of his position which not only ties him in with previous conceptions of the monarchy, but also strengthens him in the belief that disloyalty to him is both irreligious and necessarily based on personal vendetta or ambition.[15]

This religious legitimation is obtained at the price of imperial support for the established Ethiopian Orthodox Church, a price which most Emperors have been more than willing to pay. Relations between the temporal and spiritual arms of the state have indeed been so close that only at rare moments of crisis has the Church's authority had to be openly mobilized in favour of the Emperor—or if need be, against him. One such moment was in 1960 Body Guard revolt, when leaflets issued by the Patriarch, condemning the rebels, apparently had great effect. Conversely, the Archbishop in 1916 had a decisive role in excommunicating Lej Iyasu for his adherence to Islam, and in releasing his opponents from their oath of allegiance. In the seventeenth century, Church influence had similarly been used to eject Emperors converted to Roman Catholicism by Jesuit missionaries.

Distinct from the specific links between the Emperor and the Church, there remains a sacral element in the monarchy which is less easy to pin down. The Emperor, we are told,

> is guarantor of peace and prosperity for his entire country. Here the super-human virtue attributed to the sovereign by the Ethiopian royal ideology manifests itself most clearly. It is not so much a question of his administering the country politically as it is that he guarantee order by his very presence and the virtue inherent in him.[16]

Certainly the medieval monarchy had a pronounced sacral character, and possessed several (though by no means all) of the attributes of "African despotisms" indicated by Murdock.[17] The Emperor lived in screened seclusion until the mid-sixteenth century, and could only be approached by his subjects through an intermediary; even in the 1770s much of this remained, and Bruce relates that once when the Emperor's features were accidentally exposed, the local headman and his son were killed to wipe out the disgrace. The Emperor had also to be without physical defect in order to symbolize the wholeness of his kingdom, and for long periods his isolation was increased by imprisoning other male members of the im-perial family. He could only be approached with extraordinary signs of deference, and even his messages were received at a distance with similar ceremonial.

Yet the significance of these traits is now difficult to trace. The Emperor's seclusion, like his physical perfection, could not survive the decline of the monarchy in the sixteenth to nineteenth centuries (the Emperor Bakaffa, 1721–1730, had lost the tip of his nose). The deference accorded to recent Emperors, though great, does not incorporate the earlier hints of superhuman power; the assertion in the 1955 Constitution quoted above, for example, that "the person of the Emperor is sacred", has no equivalent in the Amharic text. At most, the sacral element still indicates, in suitably mystic terms, the very real services which the monarchy performs in preserving the peace and unity of the Empire, and imparts a satisfaction which is consciously lacking when these services are neglected: the characterization of the Era of the Princes as a time when "there was no king in Israel: every man did that which was right in his own eyes", carries an implied reproach.[18]

A related cluster of legitimizing symbols concerns the imperial dynasty. Successive analyses of the monarchy recount the famous legend from the fourteenth-century *Kebra Nagast*, which claims the Emperor's descent from Solomon and the Queen of Sheba, and hence places Ethiopian royalty in a special position as heirs to the house of David. This legend was used to justify Yekuno-Amlak's seizure of the throne in 1270, and helped his descendants to retain it for some five centuries thereafter. Like other founding myths,[19] it established a patrilineal descent group[20] whose members alone were eligible for the throne. Within this group, succession was generally by primogeniture, modified however by the choice of court factions at the time of succession and by rebellions or palace plots thereafter. Analysis of the forty-one successions between 1270 and 1770 reveals that twenty-two were filial, nine fraternal, six avuncular, two by cousins, and one each by usurpation and the subsequent restoration.[21] All the Emperors were sons of previous Emperors, except for two (including the usurper) who were grandsons and one who was a great-grandson, and there is a strong tendency for the non-filial successions to be associated with short reigns and periods of civil disorder.[22]

Hence any revolt which aimed to unseat the Emperor had to call on the leadership (actual or nominal) of a prince of the royal blood, a fact which led to the situation, characteristic of such monarchies, in which the Emperor's close relatives were also his most dangerous rivals. The royal progeny were not so numerous as in some of the kingdoms to the south, but even so it was sometimes necessary to keep them out of mischief by confining the whole lot to one of the vertical-sided mountain tops with which the northern plateau is conveniently provided. Both in the tenth century (according to tradition) and during Grañ's time in the sixteenth, the imprisoned princes were massacred by invaders; but the practice was maintained, with periods of abeyance, until the later eighteenth century, and excited the curiosity of European contemporaries among whom Samuel Johnson is the best known.[23] From the mid-eighteenth century onwards, the Emperors became increasingly the puppets of powerful courtiers or regional lords, who brought suitably pliant nominees from the mountain until the Solomonic dynasty finally guttered out.

With the decline of the Gondarine Empire, the dynasty lost its exclusive legitimizing force, and the imprisonment of its members became unnecessary. The Solomonic legend retains a place in the 1955 Constitution, but in this author's view, too many students of Ethiopia have been led astray by its undoubted picturesque qualities, and its actual importance in the modern era has been much exaggerated.[24] For the last hundred years, it has had no effect on the succession, though Emperors once chosen have claimed Solomonic descent; the four Emperors in the latter half of the nineteenth century were entirely unrelated to one another, and even the twentieth century Emperors, though related, do not form a patrilineal descent group of the earlier kind. The fact that Emperors since 1855 have originated as successful provincial lords, contending for the throne with rivals in much the same situations as themselves, must also have denied them the special prestige attached to an ancient dynasty. It is true that Menilek's heirs have retained the throne since 1889, but this can more easily be explained by straightforward political factors (the siting of the capital in Addis Ababa, the appointment of Shoans to key posts, the weakening of rival dynasties) than by reference to a Solomonic descent to which the Shoan Emperors have no greater claim than other noble families.

The actual succession since 1855, then, has largely been determined by the sources of control. Tewodros, Takla-Giyorgis (1868–1871), Yohanes and Menilek gained the throne through leadership of their personal armies, usually backed by a local base. Haile-Selassie owed his rise to an instructive combination of local and dynastic ties, and personal political skill. He was born in 1892, the son of the governor of Harar province, Ras Makonnen, who was first cousin (through his mother) of the then Emperor Menilek. When he was nineteen, he in turn became governor of Harar. This gave him sources of authority at both local and central levels, and like most governors he moved back and forth between his fief and Addis Ababa. In the capital, he kept in touch with intrigue around the imperial court and sought alliances among other noblemen, so that once Lej Iyasu's capacity began to be questioned, his was one of the first names to be suggested as a successor. In Harar, he administered his governate and maintained his army, which, astride the railway line from Jibuti, could quickly be rushed to Addis Ababa in emergencies. After becoming Regent in the 1916 coup d'état, he seldom returned to Harar, but he kept tight control over appointments there, and several times between 1916 and 1930 he moved troops to Addis Ababa to meet threatened confrontations between himself and other leaders. As an Emperor establishes himself in power, the immediate need for coercion recedes, though the threat of it is never absent, and appointments take its place as the primary means of control. In theory, the Emperor has from time immemorial enjoyed complete control over the appointment of governors, military commanders and court officials. In practice, such powers had to be made good through the Emperor's capacity to enforce them. But in the hands of a strong and dextrous Emperor like Haile-Selassie, they provide a far more important weapon than sheer coercion in the day-to-day management of government.

To summarize, the emperorship initially conformed to a pattern familiar in other African kingdoms, though with many elements which were distinctively Ethiopian. But the final collapse of the medieval monarchy during the Era of the Princes paved the way for the restoration of the throne in a rather different form. It is an emperorship more secular in conception, despite the religious aura which it undoubtedly retains. The Emperor's hold on the nation depends more directly on force in the first instance, and subsequently on his capacity to perform essential leadership functions, rather than on sacral and dynastic symbols which have largely lost their effectiveness, and which serve largely to provide *post facto* legitimacy to Emperors who have acquired their power in other ways.

One result is that recent Emperors have been freer from the restraints imposed by the nature of their earlier role, and consequently readier to innovate in many spheres of the national life. Another has been to re-emphasize the monarchy's dependence on the hierarchical aspects of the Amhara political culture, in which authority is revered only so long as it is effective. Or, to put it another way, it is difficult to make any worthwhile distinction between power on the one hand (seen as the capacity to meet demands and enforce decisions), and authority or legitimacy on the other. Lej Iyasu, for example, lost authority through his incapacity to meet the demands which his position as Emperor made upon him, and through the consequent alienation of important political forces. Conversely, lesser notables have gained authority, partly from birth or imperial favour, but essentially from their ability to call on the potential for leadership implicit in a deferential society; Tewodros, the minor nobleman who became Emperor of Ethiopia, is here the outstanding example.

THE IMPERIAL ROLE

The leadership which the Emperor is called on to provide has been, in a sense, both highly personal and highly institutional—institutional in that it has a stable and recognized place in the social system, personal in that it is vested in a particular individual, and hence very difficult to delegate or to routinize. As a result the Emperor, as the embodiment of the national polity, has been personally concerned with most of the functional requirements which have to be met in any political system:

Protective—the defence of the realm and the maintenance of internal order are the Emperor's most important functions, as evidenced both by the monarchy's actual record and by a wealth of symbols and proverbs. In major wars, he has generally been expected to lead his troops personally into battle, though subsidiary campaigns can be left to other commanders. Haile-Selassie, himself no general, felt it necessary to take the field against the Italians in 1936, in order not to disappoint the expectations attached to his office; even so, he was criticized for not leading the guerilla forces in 1936–1941, and official mythology counters this by identifying the Emperor in other ways with the resistance and the steps which led to the liberation.[25] At other times, the Emperor had to impose the king's peace on potentially rebellious vassals. His own power largely depended on the extent to which he succeeded, and his personal capacities directly affected the peace and order of his empire—hence the reign of the weak Emperor Lej Iyasu, following the powerful Menilek, immediately resulted in conflicts, even civil wars, between provincial lords.

Extractive and Distributive—the extractive capacities of the traditional empire were largely concerned with providing the Emperor and his governors with the means to perform their military functions, and with drawing from the economy a surplus large enough to support the state apparatus. Governors lived off their provinces, exacting from them a tribute proportionate to their rapacity, and transmitting to the Emperor a percentage proportionate to their obedience—a system which has not entirely disappeared even in post-war years. The Emperor, in return, was a source of bounty: he gave feasts for his soldiers, and distributed titles, lands and offices to maintain and extend his support. These expectations, more directly than the military ones, are still met by Haile-Selassie, through personal benefactions which supplement the ordinary state machinery:

he distributes largesse, he makes grants of land to deserving servants and retired soldiers, and he adds to the salaries of favoured officials with gifts of cash or property; any charitable fund feels obliged to call on him for a contribution, and he feels obliged to make one; his visits to provincial areas are generally accompanied by grants of titles to local notabilities, and remission of taxation for the peasantry.[26] These activities still have far more than merely ceremonial significance, and serve as one of the principal means through which Haile-Selassie maintains his prestige, secures support and meets political demands: one of the greatest recent displays of imperial munificence, for example, took place during his January 1967 visit to Eritrea, in an attempt to counter local separatism.

Regulative—the Emperor is the only person whose decisions are binding on the whole political system—on the armed forces, Church leaders, ministers, provincial governors, regional and ethnic groups, and so forth. Any major government action requires his approval. He receives petitions, passes judgments, issues orders and decrees. Until recent times, it would scarcely be possible to separate his executive, legislative, or judicial functions, except for some specialization of the dispute-hearing process. Even with the separation of powers produced by a written constitution, the Emperor received the sole responsibility for the executive, he retains power to legislate on government organization at any time and on most other matters during the parliamentary recess, and he still acts, in person, as a final court of judicial appeal.

Symbolic—the Emperor's symbolic functions as guarantor of national unity and independence have already been sufficiently emphasized. Haile-Selassie has made repeated use of them, while the nation-building symbols familiar in other African states have either been absent in Ethiopia, or else have been strongly associated with the crown. Political parties are effectively prohibited, and the usual communal or populist appeals are markedly lacking; the Emperor appears almost as the country's exclusive representative in foreign affairs, any creditable government activity is ascribed to him in person, and a visitor to Addis Ababa can scarcely fail to be struck by the number of occasions on which the word "imperial" is used.

Until the mid-seventeenth century, the multifunctionality of the Emperor's role was perfectly expressed through his tented capital, comprising at least fifty thousand mules and an unspecified number of persons,[27] which shifted erratically over the plateau during the dry season. In this way the Emperor policed his dominions, displayed his magnificence, and spread the considerable burden of supporting so large a retinue.[28]

In carrying out these functions, the Emperor enjoys great but not unlimited prestige. In theory, his powers are absolute, and until the present reign it has been unthinkable to place any formal restraint upon them. In practice his orders, in the absence of the ability to enforce them, do not automatically command obedience. They are subject both to the administrative machinery at his disposal and to the presence of alternative sources of authority within the Ethiopian polity.

The imperial role also leaves considerable scope for stylistic variation, according to the man and the situation. Some Emperors have been military commanders above anything else, others have taken their religious duties especially seriously; some have enforced their rule with fire and sword, others have been quiet and crafty manipulators; some, especially since 1855, have been innovators, others conservatives. Here too the emperor-ship requires examination in the light of surrounding political structures.

One final point: this account of the imperial role has emphasized the continuity between Haile-Selassie's reign and its predecessors. This emphasis is justified: Haile-Selassie holds an office with established powers and expectations, which can only be understood in terms of its place in Ethiopian history and political culture. But obviously, not everything is still the same. In particular, Ethiopia can no longer be regarded simply as an Empire—as a unity existing only by virtue of the Emperor's integrating presence. It has, by incorporation in the international system, become a *state*, with the appropriate frontiers, governmental institutions, and sense of identity. (It is still too soon to call it a nation.) The very fact that Ethiopia is conceivable in other than imperial terms, and the growth of a state machinery which is governmental rather than specifically imperial, reduce the central role of the emperorship, and pave the way for changes which may, in Gluckman's terms, be revolutions and not simply rebellions.[29]

THE MONARCHY AND THE POLITICAL ORDER

The government of a large territory under primitive technological conditions induces an inevitable tension between the central authority and the rulers of outlying provinces. That much is common to any of the major African state systems. The form which this tension takes in Ethiopia is conditioned especially by the nature of the terrain, the emphasis in the political culture on personal leadership, and the omnilineal descent system.

The terrain, comprising settled agricultural areas divided from one another by formidable physical obstacles, imposes a territorial form of government, in which cross-linkages between different areas are likely to be slight, and regional loyalties are easily evoked. The emphasis on personal leadership impedes the development of bureaucratic norms, whether at the centre or in the provinces, while permitting strong governors to develop personal bases of support. On the other hand, the omnilineal descent system prevents the formation of clan structures,[30] and disperses the initial advantages of birth; patrilineal descent has the greater prestige, but even so it is rare to trace a powerful lineage, father to son, for more than three generations, and Haile-Selassie himself derives his Shoan royal blood through his paternal grandmother.

In the traditional polity, these factors created a situation in which the Emperor's theoretically unlimited appointive powers vied with the need to take account of local political structures partly independent of the throne.[31] In the highlands, provincial dynasties which developed between the sixteenth and nineteenth centuries acquired some distinctive legitimacy in their own areas, and were linked through marriage and patronage to lesser chiefs and governors; other peoples, like the Galla of Walo, were incorporated into the Empire as sub-systems under their own rulers. These linkages could not be ignored—Tewodros' attempts to make sweeping changes in provincial government in the mid-nineteenth century were swiftly nullified by the overthrow of his newly appointed governors, and their replacement by pre-existing dynasties. But equally, the Emperor had important cards in his hand. Even where local loyalties had to be taken into account, he could choose the most amenable among several acceptable candidates, and advance his own nominees to provincial posts where local conditions allowed. His distributive capacities, including the right to grant lands and noble titles,[32] provided him with important pay-offs. And his military strength, especially after the introduction of firearms, brought the *ultima ratio regis* against rebellious vassals. The point of balance between the Emperor and other power centres varied according to the Emperor's abilities, the controls at his disposal, and the nature of dissent; in the twentieth century, despite some setbacks, it has moved decisively in the Emperor's favour.

Regional government was thus in the hands of a shifting elite, recruitment to which was mediated by the Emperor. Some of its members were authority figures by virtue of their royal or noble birth, or their local connections; others were not, for as in many political systems, Emperors promoted personal nominees without ascribed status, in order to weaken the position of the magnates. There was no clear distinction, however, between noblemen and commoners; anyone who reached high office could acquire a title and perhaps marry into an established family, and if he had the personal capacity he could attain a position almost indistinguishable from that of a nobleman born and bred. Though the system was highly inegalitarian, in the sense that it depended almost exclusively on hierarchical relations of authority, there was no "premise of inequality". For example, Dajazmach Balcha, a castrated Galla prisoner of the Emperor Menilek, had by the 1920s established such a powerful position in his southern governate of Sidamo that he was able to defy all the central government's attempts to displace him, and fell only when he overreached himself by marching with his army on Addis Ababa.

Such promotion was only possible because Balcha had become assimilated to the central elite based on the palace, and risen to the command of one of Menilek's armies. The imperial government made comparatively little use of "indirect rule" techniques, and most of the southern provinces were administered by officials and armies sent out from Addis Ababa. The exceptions were mostly in areas, notably Walaga, whose indigenous rulers allied themselves with the advancing Ethiopians, and were therefore admitted to the government on terms approaching those of the highland nobility. The Emperor was consequently much freer to make appointments in the conquered provinces of the south, than in highland areas where he had to take account of a closely textured pattern of local customs and authorities. By the same token, he could grant southern lands without hindrance to his generals and supporters, whereas in the north he would have been restricted by a web of vested interests. Speaking generally, the southern conquests enabled the Emperor to extend his powers by placing greatly increased patronage in his hands, while at the same time they helped Shoa, which was the chief beneficiary of the expansion, to establish its hegemony over the provinces to the north.

Since 1941, the creation of a large standing army and the government's vastly increased control over economic resources have quite outdated the old balance of power between centre and periphery, and Haile-Selassie can now make and revoke appointments almost at will to any of the provincial governorships. But this loss of local autonomy has recreated political tensions, since centralization involves subordination to the central province of Shoa, with which the present dynasty is strongly associated. In some areas, notably in Tigre, Haile-Selassie has judged it expedient to choose the governors from among members of the established ruling house, but the great majority of provincial governors have come from Shoa; sub-provincial governors in the north are generally natives of the province, though often not of their actual governate, while in the south they too are usually central appointees. Inevitably, a reaction has been felt, not only in the south but also in traditional provinces such as Gojam, and most obviously in Eritrea.

The oppositional movements are beyond the scope of this paper. But it is worth noting—since it is symptomatic of changes in the polity as a whole—that at this point the role of the monarchy becomes blurred. The great increase in government power and organization which has enabled Haile-Selassie to extend his control throughout the country, has at the same time reduced the specifically *imperial* element in the process. What was previously a relationship between Emperor and provincial lords has become transformed into a confrontation between national government and regional pressures which is ultimately independent of the fate of the monarchy.

The Emperor's appointive powers in the central administration, under-standably enough, have been less restricted than in provincial governates. A court aristocracy, including the Emperor's cousins and relations by marriage, merges into the provincial nobility, and its members alternate between provincial governorships and military commands in the imperial armies. Posts in the Emperor's immediate entourage, in the secretariat for example, have generally been held by protégés with no independent backing; and as in medieval Europe, these have included a high proportion of churchmen.

Political recruitment in the modern era has continued to be processed through the court—here very broadly defined as that complex of relationships between the Emperor and his entourage through which the traditional government operated and from which the modern government has grown—and the Emperors have taken the chief part in training a new administrative elite.[33] Menilek founded a school in Addis Ababa for the sons of his courtiers (the pupils at which included Haile-Selassie), and sent a few young men abroad to broaden their experience. Haile-Selassie extended this process by consciously building up a group of educated protégés. During the 1920s, he formed a small staff of mission boys and former embassy interpreters, and these were supplemented by graduates returned from foreign universities. Before 1936, some 250 young Ethiopians were sent to schools and universities abroad; most were still alive and available in 1941 and 55 have since occupied middle and high level government posts; even now (1973), they still account for five of the nineteen ministers. Many of them had connections in the pre-war government, either at court or with Haile-Selassie's old retinue from Harar, but none were noblemen or possessed personal bases of political support. By being sent abroad, their ability to exercise leadership functions was, paradoxically, weakened: they incurred the suspicion of traditionalists, they often had a diminished sense of national identity, and they were less able than counterparts trained in traditional skills to manage support structures based on intrigue and manipulation. The Habta-Wald family exemplifies this process. The eldest of these three sons of a church official was Makonnen Habta-Wald, who came to court as a page in Menilek's reign, and attached himself to Haile-Selassie during the Regency. He was a court politician of the most devious kind, but he nevertheless secured scholarships for his two brothers, Aklilu and Akala-Warq, who were sent to France, Aklilu to the Sorbonne and Akala-Warq to a technical institute at Mulhouse. After the Liberation, all three of them reached high rank in the central government; Makonnen as Minister of Commerce and of Finance, Aklilu as Minister of Foreign Affairs and, since 1958, as Prime Minister, and Akala-Warq as Minister of Education.

After 1936 Ethiopian education was interrupted, first by the Italian occupation and then by the war in Europe, so that the next Ethiopian graduates did not start to take up government posts until about 1950. There is a distinct gap between the two generations. The new generation now accounts for twelve ministers and a great many junior officials, but those of its members who have held high political office have mostly risen through personal connections in the government; several have been related to existing officials, and others have gained the Emperor's attention through the imperial secretariat. The whole official class has now reached power under Haile-Selassie's patronage.

The monarchy has thus been closely associated with social stratification and political recruitment in the central and regional, traditional and modernizing, sectors. But the identification is not complete. For one thing, the throne possesses a mystique which enables it to detach itself from other social groups, and stand as an arbiter above them. The Emperor is the final court of appeal for common people seeking protection, and he can take their part if necessary even against his own officials. In this way, he can modify the impact of government measures in particular situations, and preserve his authority intact despite the unpopularity of Government in a more impersonal sense. Haile-Selassie is adept at exploiting this position, as a result of which criticisms of the government tend to be directed (except by his educated and radical critics) at the Emperor's corrupt or self-seeking officials rather than at the Emperor himself. This provides a very useful political safety valve, at the same time as it permits the Emperor to avoid responsibility for his decisions.

For another thing, this merger of modern and traditional recruitment patterns has produced a governing elite not radically different, in many respects, from its equivalent in newer African states. Its members fill much the same positions in the inflated government service, and take their place on international occasions with the suave diplomatic grace at which Ethiopians excel. They enjoy the comfortable style of life which is associated in Fanonesque analyses with the non-productive bourgeoisie. And for all their appointment under Haile-Selassie's aegis, they cannot help but share attitudes which have more in common with their university-educated contemporaries elsewhere in the continent than with their octogenarian monarch. Deprived of Haile-Selassie's animating presence, the recruitment patterns of the Ethiopian elite are distinguished chiefly by its social and ethnic homogeneity and its lack of political supports. The pre-eminence of the palace as a social and political centre, and the complex family relationships which link a high proportion of officials, have given the elite a social cohesion which is perhaps only equalled by that of Liberia. Furthermore, it contains a preponderence of Shoans, who account on average for about two-thirds of the major office-holders; and political socialization for the remainder includes at least some element of assimilation to the court of a Shoan Emperor in the Shoan capital.

The other distinguishing characteristic of the Ethiopian elite, its lack of machinery through which to acquire political supports, is due equally to the Emperor's position, and to the absence of the opportunities which the colonial regimes provided for seeking office through the franchise. There are no political parties, and any ambitious politician has been obliged to look upward to the palace rather than downward to a local base in order to achieve advancement.[34] The Ethiopian elite, then, is highly government-centred. Its factional squabbles (which are considerable) are almost domestic in nature, and are marked by internal rumour and intrigue, rather than by appeals to outside interests. This system has had the result of preventing or (more likely) postponing the conflicts which a more open form of government would automatically have produced; but it has equally meant that the gap between the masses and the elite, already a common-place of African political sociology, is still more marked than usual in the case of Ethiopia.

INSTITUTIONS AND DECISIONS

The administrative and institutional framework of the old Ethiopian Empire still awaits a systematic reconstruction, and in its absence is extremely difficult to typify, beyond the broad outline of the throne itself and the provincial governorships. On the one hand, the court was clearly very closely ordered: the moment the Emperor's tent was pitched, for example, everyone else knew immediately where his own should go in relation to it; and the officials who accompanied it were evidently engaged in administering the many specialized tasks, technical, ceremonial, judicial, military and so forth, to which it gave rise. Over the centuries, moreover, it remained the centre of one of the largest and most enduring states in tropical Africa, a feat which it can scarcely have performed without organizational skills of a very high order. Yet on the other hand, effective institutional or bureaucratic forms are hard to find; there is no equivalent of an office like the Katikkiro in Buganda, let alone of the sophisticated councils and accompanying political theory which Gluckman has found among the Lozi.[35] Margery Perham has gone so far as to say that:

> it is almost unbelievable that a monarchy that can claim some 2,000 years of almost unbroken rule to its credit failed in that period to build up any kind of administrative framework through which to exercise the absolute powers with which, by tradition and consent, it was endowed.[36]

That said, one might go further and suggest that it *is* unbelievable, even though the framework is an elusive one, characterized more by personal relationships centred on a leader than by impersonal relations of office.

Certainly there were offices with defined functions, including the *Tsahafe T'ezaz* or Imperial Secretary, the *Afa-Negus* or Chief Justice, and others concerned with court organization. There were also ranks, such as *Bitwadad*, which carried no specific duties but implied that their holders were important men in the Emperor's confidence. Some late seventeenth- and early eighteenth-century chronicles place all these officials in order of precedence, and several accounts report that advice was formally tendered to the Emperor in ascending rank, with the least important officers speaking first and the most important last, after which the Emperor passed his decision. But the Emperor was never bound by these arrangements and could change them at will. Zara-Yaqob (1434–1468) made several sweeping changes in government organization, as previously appointed officials proved incompetent or untrustworthy, even at one stage apparently entrusting the government to the royal princesses.[37] A comment by the Jesuit visitor Almeida in the early seventeenth century sums up the position:

> Under the Emperor there was formerly a dignitary whom they used to call *Beteudet (Bitwadad)*, which is the equivalent of favourite or confidant, by antonomasia. There were two who had this dignity, one of the left hand and the other of the right. Almost the entire government rested with these two men for the King did not discuss anything with anyone, or give audience or even allow himself to be seen, except by very few people. Those two *Beteudetes* had everything in their hands. It is now some years since the Emperors have been less muffled and have allowed themselves to be seen by and conversed with everybody. They then saw that that office was an undesirable one for the two *Beteudetes* were the Kings and the King was one in name only. So they abolished it and created another in its place which they called *Ras*, which means head, for he who has that position is, under the King, head of all the great men in the empire.[38]

The problems of delegation—and hence institutionalization—implicit in this account are relevant to twentieth century government, which has constantly come up against the difficulty of reconciling the Emperor's

E

highly personalized authority with bureaucratic innovations. The first such innovations were made by Menilek, when towards the end of his reign he set up a Council of Ministers in the hope that it would acquire authority enough to tide over the approaching interregnum. Not surprisingly it failed: some of its members were important generals and courtiers, but the council as a whole lacked the cohesion which, in the Ethiopian system, only an authoritative leader can provide. The Council survived, in one form or another, until the Italian invasion, and rudimentary ministries were also established, but they served as little more than adjuncts to the imperial staff. The universal complaint of visitors and diplomats before the war, that the ministers were always at the palace, reflected the simple fact that the palace was where the decisions were taken, and where their ministerial duties had to be performed. Hence the modern machinery of government has been introduced by the Emperors, within a system in which the emperorship remains the supreme source of political authority.

Immediately after the 1941 liberation, when British advisers were attached to the government, a determined effort was made to provide Ethiopia with a systematic framework of political institutions. The ministries were re-established and their functions codified, and a number of anomalies (to British eyes), like the system under which the *Afa-Negus* was both chief judge and a government minister, were rectified; a government gazette was published and a budget introduced; the 1931 Constitution was reactivated, and Parliament was recalled. These reforms had undoubted beneficial results—they made it possible to discover what the law was, for example—but their effect on the decision-making process was more apparent than real. The old palace government continued to operate, more or less undisturbed, behind the façade which they provided.

The key to this system is Haile-Selassie himself, and the style of government through which he rules. This concept of "style" is hard to define satisfactorily, but certain elements must come into it: the leader's conception of his own position; the way in which he handles the demands which his role makes on him; his relations with subordinates and other leaders; and his capacity either to promote his own ends through his leadership position, or else to adapt to those which are pressed upon him. Here I shall argue that Haile-Selassie has largely retained pre-existing conceptions of the emperorship; that he has used traditional manipulative techniques in order to maintain and extend his personal control; and that since his goals are maintenance ones, he has met the problems of change by adapting himself to developments in his environment, rather than by trying to enforce his own initiatives upon it.

Haile-Selassie has made extensive use of the imperial symbols already discussed. His utterances consistently express his belief that his power derives from God, and his consciously paternalist appeal (he is fond of using family analogies) is strengthened by his age, his benevolent mien, and the fact that most of his people can remember no other ruler. All this may suggest that Haile-Selassie is an apolitical "grand old man", a symbolic source of unity who stands above day-to-day politicking. In fact, he is no such thing. He combines his appeal to divine right with an intense personal grasp of power, in much the same way as symbols and controls are combined in the emperorship itself.

Highly personalized control is the essence of his style. He stands at the head of a hierarchically ordered government, with comparatively weak horizontal communications, and acts so as to hold its diverse threads as closely as possible in his own hands. The methods which he favours maximize the upward flow of demands, decisions and information within the administration. Here it is difficult to distinguish style, as an element personal to Haile-Selassie, from attitudes and organizational forms which characterize Ethiopian administration as a whole. Some comparisons with other Emperors are possible, but Haile-Selassie's methods draw heavily on his upbringing in court and provincial politics, and on attitudes and expectations derived from the political culture. As we should expect of so successful a ruler, his style is closely adapted to its setting.

As an administrator, he has a close and conscientious concern for detail, and in this respect we can contrast him with Lej Iyasu, who gave very little attention to government business, or with Tewodros, a man with great vision but small administrative skills. Haile-Selassie is at home with specifics; blueprints and long-term ends do not much interest him. He has no Grand Design, and he controls the government not by setting out policies and guidelines for his ministers to follow, but by considering the requests brought daily to him by officials and other visitors to the palace. Since the 1960s much routine work has been delegated, but Haile-Selassie still intervenes at any point in the administration which raises his interest. In particular, his personal concern is needed to propel any new initiative through the inertia of the government machinery.

Officials must therefore work through the palace to obtain imperial favour, and so achieve their policy or personal ends. Concern for detail brings with it supervision of personal relations. High on Haile-Selassie's list of essential skills is his ability to play on the aims and characters of others in order to secure their dependence on himself—for example, by appointing antipathetic rivals to complementary posts, or encouraging officials to appeal direct to the palace over the heads of their bureaucratic superiors. Information services work in a similar way, through rival politicians reporting on one another's activities, so that the Emperor stands at the centre of a web of competing intelligence networks, each of which is concerned to maximize the information-flow which it controls. Conflict situations are thus deliberately fostered as a centralizing instrument—a technique which requires very delicate handling. The techniques are old ones—the manipulation of appointments is time-honoured enough to have its own name, *shum-shir*, in Amharic—but Haile-Selassie has carried them to a fine art, and capitalized on the attitudes to authority which make them possible. Important appointments, obviously enough, favour politicians who are prepared to work within this setting, and as a result the most powerful officials are men who have retained their posts for many years, and do not often change; by contrast, officials who are impatient with the conventions under which the system operates, and have tried to claim their own authority for decisions instead of retaining a ritual deference to the Emperor, have shifted more rapidly from post to post and have often found themselves in virtually powerless diplomatic positions.

In practice, authority is not so clear-cut as this account suggests—indeed, it is systematically blurred through techniques which allow the Emperor to reduce his personal commitment to particular decisions. If a minister comes forward with some project or suggestion, for example, he may be invited to go ahead with it on the understanding that the Emperor will not be responsible if it fails; or the Emperor may himself initiate actions at second-hand, through officials who can if necessary be disowned; and if some controversy crops up over which ministers are divided, he keeps his own position ambiguous for as long as possible, shifting his ground according to events. In any event, the result is the same: if all goes well, the Emperor claims the credit; if not, others take the blame. Thus he retains his freedom of action, and avoids responsibility for unpopular or mistaken decisions.

The channels of communication leading to the palace are thus not restricted, fixed and institutional, but on the contrary multiple, fluid and personalized. This gives Haile-Selassie scope for the manipulation and manoeuvre at which he excels, maximizing the information and range of choices open to him. There are several ways in which this style affects his role as Emperor. For one thing, it can be used to weaken the strength and cohesion of alternative power centres which might otherwise challenge the throne. By giving senior officers access to the palace, and by encouraging divisions between formations and individuals, he has helped to prevent the growth of a military hierarchy loyal to internal norms—as was seen when the Imperial Body Guard and the Army took opposite sides in the 1960 revolt. Potential opposition leaders have been "tamed" by bringing them into the government and allowing them to enjoy the benefits of office at the price of subordination to the Emperor—for example Ras Ababa Aragay, the most famous resistance leader against the Italian occupation, who became Minister of War. Among the younger educated elite we might take Dr. Menase Hayle, at present Minister of Foreign Affairs, who when a student in the USA was closely associated with Germame Neway, the radical brain behind the 1960 attempted coup; when Menase returned from the USA in 1961, he was quickly whisked into the Emperor's Private Cabinet as personal adviser on foreign affairs, and thus given a strong personal stake in the existing system. The principles of "divide and rule" are familiar enough to need no further illustration.

This style also enables Haile-Selassie to gain access to a wide range of opinions, and maintain an equilibrium among them. He rarely initiates policies himself or is personally committed to them, and there is very little conception of government policy or co-ordinated direction—individuals with the Emperor's backing can plough furrows of their own, provided always that they acknowledge his authority. Rather, he presides over a changing coalition of interests, tending always to occupy the middle ground, and hence his instinct is to move towards potential opponents rather than away from them. After the 1960 revolt, he appointed an ostensibly reform-minded cabinet, and made speeches favouring administrative

delegation. Increased regional assertiveness has been met by limited concessions—including a western Eritrean Moslem in the cabinet, local
government reforms, the replacement of the Governor of Gojam after
riots against him there in 1968. Individual cases may be dealt with by
coercion, but it is always necessary to maintain a large enough central
base from which to control the periphery—and this is the central concern
of Haile-Selassie's leadership.

Analogously in foreign affairs, he relies chiefly on the USA for arma-
ments and other aid, but tries to reduce his dependence by maintaining
contacts with as wide as possible a range of other countries. He has
received a succession of Eastern European Heads of State in Addis Ababa,
he has diversified his sources of arms by ordering Canberra bombers from
the United Kingdom, and he has had close relations with Tito and (until
his retirement) de Gaulle, stemming back to their common resistance to
Fascist invasion. Characteristically, his diplomacy is conducted through
face to face contacts sustained by a multitude of state visits.

It is a style which favours mediation, and Haile-Selassie's greatest
successes have been gained in processes to which this technique can be
applied. Take his African foreign policy—as a field where coercion and
internal Ethiopian factors are excluded, and the stylistic element is to that
extent isolated. His moment of triumph was the 1963 Heads of State
Conference, where he was able to exploit his detachment from existing
division lines—Monrovia and Casablanca, anglophone and francophone,
black south and Arab north—in order to promote some consensus among
African leaders and so secure his primary aim—that the OAU Charter
should be signed in Addis Ababa under his chairmanship. Similar considerations later enabled him to attract the OAU headquarters to Addis
Ababa (in alliance of convenience with Sékou Touré), and he exploited
other leaders' concern for territorial integrity to ensure that the Somalis
(despite the claims of nationalism and self-determination) were isolated
in the Ethio-Somali frontier dispute. By contrast, he has been ineffective
on issues such as Rhodesia or Biafra, which demanded a positive
initiative—a willingness not to mediate but to take the lead.

For all its congruence with its traditional background, this style is not
unique. Its mixture of balance and manipulation is one of the standard
means of reconciling the plural pressures which any political system has to
meet, with the advantage over other techniques that it tends to favour
longevity among the ruling elite. It has been adopted by several of the
longer-lasting African new state leaders,[39] among whom Haile-Selassie's
chief advantage is that the emperorship gives him a more than usually
stable platform from which to conduct his manipulative operations. Closer
to hand, the factional jockeying in the imperial palace has something in
common with that which Lemarchand indicates as taking place around
the Mwami and latterly the President in Rwanda.[40] Behind his esoteric
trappings, then, the King of Kings is an astute politician of a broadly
familiar kind.

The formal institutions of government in Ethiopia grew up under this
system, and had to adapt themselves to it if they were to exert any

appreciable influence. In fact the main machinery, under the crown, through which the government operated in the post-war years owed nothing to the new institutional order established by the British advisers—even though a Prime Ministership had been created in 1943. Power still lay with the imperial secretariat—the old office of the *Tsahafe T'ezaz*, refurbished under its modern title of the Minister of the Pen. Its holder from 1941 until 1955, *Tsahafe T'ezaz* Walda-Giyorgis, was unquestionably the most powerful man in the government during those years, and he exercised his power chiefly by sending out—and manipulating—the Emperor's orders. Any executive action—any expenditure of government funds, for instance—required the Emperor's personal consent, and an order authorizing it which was taken down by a secretary in attendance on the Emperor, and issued by the Ministry of the Pen. Such orders simply by-passed the Prime Minister, Council of Ministers and Parliament, though the Minister of Finance, another powerful individual, had some control over the financial ones. The access to the Emperor which this system required was formalized through the *Aqabe Sa'at*, a system of weekly appointments at which ministers brought decisions to the Emperor for clearance, thus emphasizing their individual dependence on the throne.

Over the last dozen years, nonetheless, several factors have forced a slow institutionalization of at least the routine work of the administration. The increase in the size of the government is one of them—the Emperor's personal authorization of all spending simply became impractical as government expenditure rose to over $150,000,000 a year,[41] and from the late 1950s onwards a budgetary system controlled by the Ministry of Finance was gradually devised. Another key change was in the rise of educated officials: a turnover in political generations took place between 1955 and 1961, with men like Walda-Giyorgis and Makonnen Habta-Wald, nurtured in the pre-war government, giving way to university graduates among whom Makonnen's younger brother Aklilu Habta-Wald is a central figure. A change, too, has come over Haile-Selassie himself; he was eighty-one in 1973, and even for so remarkable an old man his earlier level of activity is no longer possible; he has neither the time nor the qualifications to supervise new subjects like economic planning or complex legislation, and leaves these with officials who come to him only for essential authorizations, while keeping much closer control over subjects which interest him like foreign affairs; for long periods, he leaves most domestic matters to his subordinates, while he goes on state visits abroad or acts as host to one of the international conferences for which Addis Ababa is now noted.

The Prime Minister and his colleagues have been the gainers from these trends. The old machinery of the imperial secretariat collapsed after Walda-Giyorgis' dismissal in 1955, and since 1958 Aklilu Habta-Wald has been steadily building up the Prime Minister's Office as an alternative executive centre, and one which owes far less to the Emperor's day-to-day management. In 1966, he was formally empowered to select the other ministers himself, and though he has made no violent use of his powers in this respect—and would not be Prime Minister if he had—he has become indispensable to the government as an administrative co-ordinator. The Council of Ministers had taken on a similar co-ordinating role, dealing especially with legislation, allocations of funds, and other technicalities of government. Ministries and government agencies now operate in much the same way as their equivalents in other African states; they suffer from the government's general inertia, but the Emperor's part in their detailed operation is no more than sporadic. However, these bureaucratic changes have scarcely affected the Emperor's more important political functions. Of the ministers to whom he has delegated power, none possesses any appreciable authority in dealing with groups outside the bureaucracy—as for instance the armed forces and the more important provincial governors—either as individuals or by virtue of their offices, except insofar as they gain a borrowed authority through the Emperor's support. The throne is still needed as much as ever to hold together divergent sources of power.

Parliament stands outside these developments. In 1955, the previous embryo legislature was replaced by a Parliament in which one chamber, the Senate, is still directly appointed by the Emperor, while the Chamber of Deputies is elected by adult suffrage. The Senate has served as a place of retirement or disgrace for noblemen, provincial governors, civil servants and even army officers, and despite a few clashes with the government it has generally remained quiescent. The Chamber of Deputies, by contrast, is the only open channel for recruitment and demands in this very closed political system, and the only point, moreover, at which the provinces are directly represented in national political life. Elections to it have been held at four-yearly intervals since 1957. Since there are no parties, and residence requirements for candidates are strict, it serves mostly as a forum for local grievances, and does not articulate national problems in any coherent way; its role is also restricted by the absence of means through which to control the executive, except in legislative matters and through a process of calling ministers for questioning, but it has shown itself prepared to defy the administration on subjects which come within its purview. Its basic weaknesses are that it lacks the means to establish its legitimacy among its rural constituents—still less among the urban intelligentsia, who are unrepresented in it, and tend to regard it, rather unjustly, as a mere assemblage of unlettered rustics—and it lacks the power to deliver the benefits (schools, roads, clinics) which its members are elected to provide. As a result, voter participation has tended to fall off, and considerable difficulties were reported in getting voters to register for the fourth parliamentary elections taking place in 1969. Interest among candidates, many if not most of whom are middle and lower-level government employees, is assured by the chance election offers of a high salary in Addis Ababa, with the prospect of a transfer, at the end of their parliamentary term, to a far higher post than they could otherwise have hoped to achieve. Parliament, then, provides no alternative source of legitimacy to the throne, and does very little to offset the hierarchical pattern of recruitment and decision-making.[42]

INNOVATION AND THE CHALLENGE TO IMPERIAL AUTHORITY

For a touchstone of leadership styles within the system, we could do worse than look at the Emperor's innovatory role. Leadership has been essential to innovation in highland Ethiopia, since in a society so conservative and hierarchical, changes have had to be introduced deliberately from above, and validated by the authority of those who introduced them. In this process, the Emperors since 1855 have taken the leading part. Tewodros started to build roads, and by a personal example in heaving boulders induced others to follow him, though his achievements no more than scratched the surface of his grandiose ideas. Menilek founded the first western-style school, set up government ministries, established the permanent capital in Addis Ababa, and authorized the construction of a railway there from the coast. But it was equally open to Emperors like Yohanes IV or the reigning Empress Zawditu to regard themselves as the custodians of indigenous values, and to look on foreign novelties with a suspicion which most of their subjects shared. Individual Emperors have therefore had a good deal of scope. There are few specific limitations on the monarchy's capacity to innovate, beyond the requirements of religious orthodoxy. But this does not mean that any innovation sanctioned by the Emperor is enthusiastically accepted or automatically put into effect. The Emperor's example is only the first step in overcoming inertia, and it may lead to nothing more than a grudging acceptance which is withdrawn the moment his back is turned. Deference to authority, even imperial authority, is unsufficiently internalized to ensure any basic change in attitudes. It is virtually impossible openly to refuse an imperial order, but it is easy enough to do nothing about it, and imperial proclamations from Tewodros to Haile-Selassie are littered with sweeping changes which have remained dead letters for lack of practical implementation. Though specific limitations are few, there are considerable generalized restraints on innovation, especially perhaps in that complex of attitudes relating to the tenure and use of land.[43] The only valid point to be made by typifying Ethiopia as an instrumental system—and it is an important one—is that political authority is analytically independent of the content of the outputs which it is used to convey.

Haile-Selassie has been far more open to possibilities of change than most Ethiopians of his generation. During his Regency and the first part of his reign (1916–1936), he founded more schools and sent men abroad for education, granted a written Constitution establishing the first Ethiopian Parliament, laid the foundations of a professional army, and did much else besides.

Yet two points are worth noting about these innovations: first, that he modernized cautiously, insuring himself at every step against arousing opposition; and second, that the changes tended to increase his own powers. The leading noblemen were consulted in drafting the Constitution, and represented in the Parliament, though the document as a whole was very strongly centralizing. As Regent, he delayed opening his first school until conservative opponents had been pacified; thereafter, the educational system was used to build up an administrative staff, capable of manning the government machinery but politically dependent on the Emperor. The professional army has decisively undercut the military functions of the nobility, who in 1936 had still raised and commanded their own provincial levies.

Even so, in the pre-war period Haile-Selassie was an active innovatory agent, whereas changes which have taken place since 1941 have been far more markedly the result of the need to keep pace with pressures in the political environment. The spurt of changes which followed the liberation can be ascribed partly to the influence of the British advisers, partly to the need for the Emperor to consolidate his supremacy over the nobility and the Church—a need which resulted in basic reforms in taxation and provincial government. The next spurt, in the mid-1950s, can be correlated with the 1952 reunion with Eritrea and the return of the first post-war graduates. The shock given to the regime by the 1960 coup resulted in further concessions.

In this way, Haile-Selassie's leadership provides some framework within which differences can be accommodated, but the price for this is that it fails to provide any dynamic form of government. Quite the opposite. It is an absorptive polity, which can find room for modernizers on much the same basis as it finds room for other pressures, but which is quite unadapted to any goal-oriented development programme. Its stability and its inertia are two sides of the same coin.

This system is adequate only so long as a central mediating position can be maintained, and there are signs that this task is becoming increasingly difficult. One straw in the wind is that criticism is increasingly directed against Haile-Selassie as the symbol of the government's failings, rather than against officials or policies distinct from the emperorship; as late as 1960, the rebels never once publicly criticized—nor even mentioned—Haile-Selassie, but directed their appeal instead against generalized grievances. Regional consciousness has intensified, both in Eritrea and, though less markedly, in the south. Discontent among students, though not a serious threat to the regime, indicates nevertheless a growing willingness to take to the streets and challenge the government directly, and also the declining employment prospects in a non-productive and now almost saturated civil service. The armed forces have on several occasions had to be bought off by improvements in pay and conditions. These challenges have not yet reached the intensity needed to topple the emperorship, but they do suggest that Haile-Selassie's manipulatory techniques are proving decreasingly effective as a means of controlling social and economic forces.

But only in a contingent sense is this opposition directed against the emperorship. It is fundamentally the same opposition as faces both single-party rulers and military regimes all over the continent—from disgruntled elites, ethnic groups, the unemployed. For another thing, even modernizers in Ethiopia have had to rely on existing forms of leadership, because they have been unable to generate any alternative authority to take its place. The exception here proves the rule: the 1960 rebels proclaimed a new

reforming government, with an active programme for economic development; but they markedly failed to generate any corresponding innovations
in their appeals for support, and accordingly fell back on traditional
ones—the Crown Prince, noblemen, military leadership—in order to
legitimate their seizure of power.[44] The need for authoritarian leadership to
manage the Ethiopian political system is scarcely at issue. Modernizers
are distinguished from traditionalists chiefly by their conviction that new,
more active styles of leadership than that of Haile-Selassie are needed to
confront the problems of development. While Ethiopia is now at a stage,
therefore, where it is easy enough to envisage the overthrow of the
emperorship by rival elites—with some resistance perhaps from the Church
and the countryside—a mass-based social revolutionary movement is
simply not yet on the cards.

The immediate future of the emperorship depends on the capacity of
Haile-Selassie and his advisers to handle intensified demands, and after
that, no doubt, on his son the Crown Prince. A succession conflict cannot
be ruled out. In the slightly longer term, it is not difficult to envisage a
"republican emperorship" in which, regardless of the formal fate of the
monarchy, a similar power structure is maintained by an authority figure
who may be a military officer, or possibly a nobleman or provincial
governor with analoguous leadership training, who is also able to draw on
sources of coercive support. Several elements in the present situation make
for this possibility. The hierarchical structure of the society, and the
absence of alternative means to generate authority, create the basic conditions. The divergence in the emperorship since 1855 between the controls
through which power has been acquired and the symbols through which it
has subsequently been legitimated, suggests that power may be exercised
almost unchanged even though symbols are drastically altered; a new
emperor-figure could draw on a "populist" ideology of national unity
and economic development, of the kind favoured by many new state
leaders, and his claims to power would be strengthened if he had to combat
regional or separatist forces to which the label of tribalism could conveniently be attached. He could take over the Emperor's innovatory role, and
substitute for Haile-Selassie's cautious balancing act that more militant
leadership which is equally present in traditional conceptions of the
emperorship; some such vision, indeed, underlay the aspirations of the
1960 rebels.

All this is speculation. But if it rests on a valid perception of the
Emperor's role, then it is inadequate to typify the emperorship simply as a
"traditional" form of government, which is by implication bound to give
way to something more "modern" or perhaps "transitional." The combination of authority and manipulation, pay-off and coercion, implicit in
the emperorship, represents one of the elemental means of managing those
competing pressures with which government is concerned.[45]

NOTES

1 I wish to thank the editors of *African Affairs* for permission to draw on my article "Imperial Leadership in Ethiopia", *African Affairs* Vol. 68 No. 271, April 1969. I have also enlarged on the role of the monarchy in modern Ethiopia in my book *Haile-Selassie's Government* (London & New York, Longmans & Praeger, 1969).

2 He became Regent and Heir to the Throne in 1916, and Emperor in 1930, when he took his present name; he was previously called Tafari, with the titles *Dajazmach* (to 1916), *Ras* (1916–1928), and *Negus* or King (1928–1930).

3 No full census has yet been taken; *Africa Contemporary Record 1972–73* (ed. C. Legum, New York 1973) quotes an official estimate of 24·3 million.

4 The phrase is from G. L. Steer, *Caesar in Abyssinia* (London, 1936), p. 59.

5 D. N. Levine, "Ethiopia: Identity, Authority, and Realism", in L. W. Pye and S. Verba, *Political Culture and Political Development* (Princeton, 1965), p. 250.

6 See Steer, *op. cit.*, p. 46.

7 D. N. Levine, *Wax & Gold* (Chicago, 1965), pp. 155–167.

8 A point well expressed in a much-quoted Amharic proverb, "a dog knows his master, but not his master's master".

9 See, for example, M. Abir, *Ethiopia: The Era of the Princes* (London, 1968), Chapter 2.

10 Levine, *op. cit.*, expecially pp. 241–242.

11 This appears to be the drift of Abir, *op. cit.*, especially Chapter 7.

12 S. Rubenson, "Some Aspects of the Survival of Ethiopian Independence in the Period of the Scramble for Africa", *Historians in Tropical Africa* (Salisbury, 1960), pp. 253–266.

13 Revised Constitution of 1955, Article 4.

14 Speech promulgating the first Ethiopian Constitution, 16 July 1931; from Haile-Selassie, *Selected Speeches* (Addis Ababa, 1967), pp. 386–387.

15 Pardoning Ras Getachaw, who sided with the Italians during the occupation, he is reported to have said: "I pardon you, but I don't know if God will," Perham, *The Government of Ethiopia*, (London, 2nd ed. 1968) p. 84; and of the 1960 rebels: "The judgement of God is upon them; wherever they go, they will never escape it," Greenfield, *Ethiopia* (London, 1965), p. 433.

16 A. Caquot, "La royauté sacrale en Ethiopie", *Annales d'Ethiopie*, Vol. 2, 1957, pp. 205–219; quoted from Levine, *Wax & Gold*, p. 152.

17 G. P. Murdock, *Africa, Its Peoples and Their Culture History* (New York, 1959), pp. 37–39, suggests eighteen common characteristics of African monarchies, which he claims as evidence of common origin. This is not the place to discuss this argument, but it may be helpful to summarize those attributes which the Ethiopian Emperor did *not* possess: he was not divine, nor did he have unique access to divine powers (for the sacral elements in the monarchy were overlaid by the requirements of Christianity, including an omnipotent God and a ritually independent priest-hood); polygamy and concubinage were limited by the Christian requirements of monogamy, with lesser or greater effect according to the lust or piety of the monarch; Queen-Mothers or their equivalents enjoyed no special institutionalized prestige; advisory roles in the central government were rarely specialized, nor was there any supreme advisory council or committee of ministers with constitutional, electoral powers; and ritual human sacrifice was not practiced. It is also worth noting that some of Murdock's characteristics, including the presence of regalia, royal courts, and territorial bureaucracy, appear almost necessary conditions for a state covering a large territory with poor technology.

18 Judges, xxi: 25; hence the Era of the Princes is also known as the Era of the Judges, in the biblical sense; see Abir, *op. cit.*, p. xxiii.

19 cf: that of the Lozi, in M. Gluckman, *The Ideas in Barotse Jurisprudence* (New Haven, 1965), pp. 27–30.

20 It is thus an exception to the general rule of omnilineal descent; the only other such

exception relates to the rulers of Wag, in the centre of the highlands, who are reputedly descended from the dynasty deposed in 1270.

21   Information taken from E. A. Wallis Budge, *A History of Ethiopia* (London, 1928), Vol. I pp. 285–336, Vol. II, pp. 337–470.

22   The Emperors succeeded by their sons ruled on an average for 19 years, those succeeded in other ways for 4 years.

23   For an outline of the history of the practice, see R. K. P. Pankhurst, *An Introduction to the Economic History of Ethiopia* (London, 1961), Chapter 4.

24   Two examples often used to ascribe operational effectiveness to the Solomonic legend can largely be dismissed. The first is the usurper Yustos (1711–1716), who was a grandson of an earlier Emperor through his mother, and whose celebrated words of self-abasement reported by Bruce ("I have made myself king as much as one can be that is not of the royal family, for I am but a private man, son of a subject") were uttered only to secure himself a peaceful death during his final illness; Yustos' succession, like Bakaffa's nose, is no more than evidence of symbolic deterioration in the early eighteenth century. The second example is Yohanes IV's appeal to Lord Granville in 1872 for the return of the *Kebra Nagast*, "for in my country my people will not obey my orders without it"; this key phrase has recently been shown to be a simple mistranslation from the Amharic (E. Ullendorff & Abraham Demoz, "Two letters from the Emperor Yohanes of Ethiopia to Queen Victoria and Lord Granville", *Bull. S. O. A. S.*, Vol. XXXII Part 1, 1969, pp. 135–142).

25   Emphasis is placed, for example, on Haile-Selassie's 1936 address to the League of Nations; his entry through Gojam in 1941 receives markedly more attention than the decisive battles which took place in Eritrea; and the liberation is celebrated as the Emperor's Triumphal Return to Addis Ababa on May 5, 1941, though the city had then been a month in allied hands.

26   On a visit to Gojam in May 1969, for example, he cancelled arrears of taxation for the previous nineteen years—a benefaction which gives a devastating insight into the effectiveness of the tax-collecting machinery (*The Ethiopian Herald*, May 27 1969).

27   Alvares in the 1520s, quoted from R. K. P. Pankhurst, *An Introduction to the Economic History of Ethiopia*, (London, 1961), p. 138.

28   R. J. Horvath, "The Wandering Capitals of Ethiopia," in *J. Modern African History*, Vol. 10, No. 2, 1969, pp. 205–219, suggests that the moving capital was instituted primarily for external defense, and that administrative and distributive arrangements adapted themselves to it, but the evidence he puts forward is not enough to substantiate this argument. In any case, it is clear both that the military functions were important, and that the movements served other purposes which went well beyond, say, the shifting of the court to a neighbouring hill which accompanied a new reign in Buganda; the equivalent of this last practice is found in the Gondarine Emperors who initially each built a palace of their own.

29   M. Gluckman, *Politics, Law and Ritual in Tribal Society* (Oxford, 1965) especially pp. 137–138, 164–165.

30   The absence of clans and common-ancestor myths among the Amharas and Tigreans is one of the most marked differences between them and most other African peoples, and its political significance may be seen by comparing Ethiopia with, say, Buganda.

31   See especially Levine, *Wax & Gold*, Chapter 5.

32   Titles of nobility, which are military in origin, range from *Negus* or King down through *Ras, Dajazmach*, and several lower levels; they are not hereditary, nor are they accompanied by particular posts or special privileges, though the most powerful governors tend to hold the highest titles. There are also a number of civil titles, generally associated with the imperial court, and a few titles attached to individual offices; see Perham, *op. cit.*, pp. 81–86.

33   See *Haile-Selassie's Government*, especially Chapters 6 and 7.

34   A partial exception, the Parliament, is considered in the next section.

35   See especially Gluckman, *The Ideas in Barotse Jurispurdence*, Chapter 2.

36   Perham, *op. cit.*, pp. 72–73.
37   Pankhurst, *An Introduction*, pp. 120–121.
38   Quoted from Pankhurst, *loc. cit.*, pp. 125–126.
39   For example, the account of Tubman's government in Martin Lowenkopf, *Political Modernization and Integration in Liberia* (unpublished Ph.D. thesis, London University, 1969) especially pp. 95–100, is extraordinarily reminiscent of Haile-Selassie.
40   See Chapter 2.
41   $1 Ethiopian equals 40 U.S. cents; the budget for 1972–73 is $757 million.
42   See, however, Peter Schwab, *Decision-Making in Ethiopia* (London, 1972) for a study of the extent to which Parliament can now influence the legislative process.
43   Schwab, *op. cit.*, provides an excellent case study of opposition to central government land reform measures, both in Parliament and in the provinces.
44   As I have tried to show in "The Ethiopian Coup d'Etat of December 1960", *Journal of Modern African Studies*, Vol. 6, No. 4, 1968, pp. 495–507.
5   The political upheavals of early 1974 took place too late for inclusion in this chapter, and at the time of going to press are still evidently unresolved. Military demands for higher pay and political reform led to an explosion of demands from civil servants, students, trades unions and other groups. In an attempt to meet these, Haile-Selassie dismissed the Prime Minister, promised constitutional reforms, and appointed a government—rather younger than its predecessor but still drawn from the court elite—which has had considerable difficulty in restoring control. These events have demonstrated on the one hand the monarchy's role in maintaining a reference point for political continuity, on the other hand its failure to foster institutions through which to incorporate new social groups in the political structure—a failure which is likely to lead, sooner or later, to its demise.

PART II
STRATIFIED KINGSHIPS: RWANDA AND BURUNDI

2

RWANDA

René Lemarchand

The overthrow of the Rwanda monarchy, at the climax of a sanguinary civil strife, epitomizes the crises of legitimacy that have since confronted other African kingships. Nowhere else in Africa has the transition to republican rule been more brutal, its outward manifestations more typically revolutionary, its social impact more disruptive of pre-established norms. In sharp contrast with the pattern observable in most of the countries discussed in this book, the prospects of independence not only failed to enhance the legitimacy of the throne, but in fact raised those very issues around which antimonarchical sentiment crystallized. Having ceased to be an umpire, the Crown became a political football long before it could alter the rules of the game. A year and a half before the country's scheduled accession to independence Rwanda was a kingdom without a king.[1]

That the last of the Rwanda kings should have been the first in the African continent to be forced from his throne in the name of "progress and democracy" is perhaps not all that surprising when one considers the degree of political centralization and depth of social inequalities that characterized the traditional polity. As one of the very rare examples of a caste society encountered in Africa, Rwanda was uniquely susceptible to the levelling impact of equalitarianism; as one of the most "despotic" its traditional system was all the more vulnerable to the traumas elsewhere engendered by the democratization of indigenous institutions. Though reminiscent in many ways of 1789, the language of the Rwanda revolution also carried strong traditional overtones. The stamp of indigenous institutions and social forces impressed itself deeply upon its rhetoric and actual unfolding. Difficult though it may be to assess the cumulative impact of such forces and institutions, the revolution in Rwanda had a logic of its own, in which the interplay of different historical legacies conspired to both thwart and stimulate revolutionary sentiment and activity.

Not the least of our concerns in this essay will be to analyze processes of change in Rwanda not only in terms of how Belgian policies have conditioned the chances of survival of the monarchy as a traditional institution, but from the reverse perspective as well, namely how the monarchy, as an independent variable, has affected Belgian policies, and ultimately the rate and direction of revolutionary change. An essential starting point for an understanding of this reciprocal pattern of interaction is to delineate the normative underpinnings of the kingship (Mwamiship), taking as a reference point the period immediately preceding the inception of colonial rule.

F

I. THE NORMATIVE UNDERPINNINGS OF MWAMISHIP

Associated as it was with a variety of moral sanctions supportive of the established order, the Mwamiship was ideally fashioned to serve the interests of the dominant oligarchy. But it also harboured a "holy force", to use Caillois's felicitous expression,[2] that gave a sense of purpose and identity to society as a whole. What might appear at first as a supreme inconsistency becomes less of an enigma once we recognize that the concept of Mwamiship incorporated within itself elements of unity and disunity; that these features revealed themselves with greater or lesser saliency depending on the circumstances; and that the responses of political actors to monarchical symbols and institutions have expressed themselves differently over time depending on how the tides of history have affected their image of Mwamiship, and of themselves, in the political system.

For purposes of analysis the concept of Mwamiship involves the following dimensions: (a) a symbolic whole incorporating within itself the sacred characteristics of kingship, (b) an ideological framework providing legitimacy to the ordering of relationships in society, (c) an institutional axis around which revolved the entire political life of the kingdom (see Table I). This three-fold perspective is essential to keep in proper balance the several aspects of monarchical legitimacy. Besides suggesting areas of analysis that help disclose the limitations and potentialities of Mwamiship as an integrative mechanism, it also brings into light the various levels at which patterns of consensus and dissent have operated in recent times.

Belief in the Mwami's (king's) descent from the Deity (*Imana*) and the conscious identification of his personal well-being with the welfare of the realm were critical aspects of the symbolic referent of Mwamiship. As the representative of *Imana* the Mwami served as the supreme integrative symbol through which a sense of corporate solidarity could be achieved in the midst of inequality. "The king was a divine and paternal figure," as Maquet reminds us, "and this association helped create a feeling among the inhabitants of the country of belonging to an entirety that offered certain analogies to the family".[3] But this was by no means a family of equals. Rwanda's official ideology, as conveyed through oral traditions, was perfectly consistent with the workings of a social system that denied status and political participation to the Hutu majority and reinforced the social and political supremacy of the dominant Tutsi caste.

The theme of royal omnipotence was inextricably bound up with a system of beliefs about the proper ordering of human relationships, with a moral universe in which inequality was part of the natural order of things. Rwanda's traditional social structure has elsewhere been described in considerable detail,[4] and thus need not detain us overmuch. At the top of the social pyramid, immediately below the Mwami, stood the Tutsi. Though constituting approximately 15 per cent of Rwanda's total population of about 2·5 million, they held a virtual monopoly of power, wealth and social prestige. Next in rank came the Hutu, representing roughly 84 per cent of the total population, appropriately described by Mecklemburg as "a medium-size type of people whose ungainly figures betoken hard toil, and who patiently bow themselves in abject bondage to the later arrived yet ruling race, the Tutsi".[5] The last group, the pygmoid Twa, stood at the bottom of the heap. Representing less than 1 per cent of the population, theirs was a very marginal position, numerically and otherwise. The overall picture, then, was that of a rigidly stratified society in which the allocation of power, wealth and privilege tended to coincide with, and reinforce, ethnic distinctions, and over which the Mwami stood as the supreme empire.

The extraordinary wealth of oral traditions associated with the monarchy, ranging from historical accounts (*igiteekerezo*) and proverbs (*umugani*) to dynastic and pastoral poems (*ibisigo, amazina y'inka*), bears testimony to the variety of sources through which the official values of the regime were internalized by the dominant caste (see Table I).[6] A major function of oral traditions, as Vansina conclusively demonstrated, was to provide a cognitive map to the past—to perpetuate historical distortions with a view to strengthening prevailing conceptions of dynastic and monarchical legitimacy.[7] The "official" history of Rwanda is thus reducible to a mixture of facts and fiction intended to demonstrate the invincibility of the royal Drum (*Kalinga*) and the superior military skills of the dominant caste. As it emerges from the accredited body of myths and legends, Rwanda's past shares the qualities of a great epic story in which a few exceptional men perform exceptional deeds.

Nonetheless, it is all too facile to extract from official myths only those elements that are best suited to a particular line of argumentation. In the case of Rwanda this type of distortion is liable to obscure not only the inconsistencies inherent in traditional myths but the subsequent opportunities for adaptation or re-interpretation offered by the very existence of such inconsistencies. That the same myths eventually acquired one symbolic meaning for those who sought to overturn the regime and quite another for those who strove to preserve it emerges with striking clarity from d'Hertefelt's interesting discussion of the Rwanda myths of origins.[8]

Because of the different perceptions of their self-interests held by each caste, the masses and the aristocracy tended to "identify" with the monarchy in different ways. Monarchical legitimacy for the Tutsi elites was generally identified with the attainment and preservation of instrumental, secular goals. The political myths fashioned around the Court provided them with an ideological justification for maintaining their supremacy in all walks of life. For the masses, however, monarchical legitimacy conjured up an entirely different vision—that of a unifying whole through which a sense of all-embracing solidarity could be achieved in spite of inequality. The symbolic roots of monarchical legitimacy, in short, made it possible for the masses to endure inequality—and for the ruling elites to enforce it.

As long as it was seen through the prism of its symbolic association with the prosperity of all, as seems to have been the case for the majority of the Hutu peasantry right up until the early stages of the revolution, adherence to monarchical legitimacy positively reinforced the loyalty of the masses to the regime. Only by dissociating the monarch from the monarchy, or by giving it a new ideological meaning, could the masses be

TABLE 1

ASPECTS OF MONARCHIAL LEGITIMACY
IN TRADITIONAL RWANDA

Legitimacy	Object	Source	Scope	Norms
Symbolic	King Kingship*	Symbols Rituals	Transcendent (Hutu-Tutsi)	Sacredness Solidarity
Ideological		Political and Aetiological Myths		
	King	ubwiiru†	Oligarchical (abiiru)	
	Dynasty Kingship	ubucurabwenge ibisigo	Tutsi Tutsi	Sacredness Inequality
	Army	icyiivugo	Tutsi	Military Valor
	Caste	igiteekerezo ubucurabwenge	Variable Tutsi	Sacredness Inequality
Structural	Army chiefs Land chiefs Cattle chiefs	Political Clientelism	Tutsi	Reciprocity and protection
	Patron-clients	Buhake‡	Transcendent (Hutu-Tutsi)	Reciprocity and protection

* The term kingship is here taken as synonymous with Mwamiship, and refers to the traditional constitutional order. It is analytically distinguishable from both the Crown (or, perhaps more appropriately the Drum [*Kalinga*]), as the symbol of the Mwami's secular and religious authority, and the Court. The latter may be defined by reference to (1) a specific category of officials whose functions were specified by tradition— essentially the Court historians (*abacurabwenge*) and custodians of the Esoteric Code (*abiiru*); and (2) the conclave of courtiers who formed part of the Mwami's entourage and who generally belonged to high-ranking Tutsi families and held chiefly positions.

† The *ubwiiru* was the Esoteric Code of the monarchy, that is the ritual and legal code of the Mwamiship; its custodians were the *abiiru*. The *ubucurabwenge* were historical accounts memorized by court historians (*abacurabwenge*). The *ibisigo* were eulogies or "propaganda poetry for exalting the powers of the king." The *icyiivugo* were either "of a popular variety enjoyed by the whole population on account of their artistic merits," or less widely known accounts "derived from the court and more particularly from the abacurabwenge." For further information see J. Vansina, *Oral Tradition: A Study in Historical Methodology* (Chicago, 1965), p. 167.

‡ The *buhake* was the institution sometimes referred to as "cattle contract" through which an individual (*umugaragu*) commended himself to a patron (*shebuja*); in exchange for specified services or dues in kind the client enjoyed the protection and support of his patron, as well as usufructuary rights over the patron's land and his cattle.

effectively mobilized against the incumbent authorities. Hence the efforts ultimately made by Hutu and Tutsi intellectuals to reinterpret oral traditions so as to create new justifications for political action—the first by deliberately calling attention to the role played by the monarchy in perpetuating a situation of social, economic and political inequality, the second by emphasizing the unifying bonds of kingship and imputing most of the responsibilities for social injustices to the Belgian authorities. The normative ambivalence involved in the concept of Mwamiship made it possible for each set of protagonsits to extract from the traditional arsenal of the monarchy the ideological weapons they needed for the realization of their political objectives.

Broadly speaking, the calling into question of the monarchical order involved a drastic transformation of popular perceptions of legitimacy. It involved a fundamental alteration not only of its ideological underpinnings, along the lines suggested above, but of its symbolic content and structural bases. The redefinition of the ideological underpinnings of kingship by Hutu intellectuals was bound to threaten its legitimacy among Westernized Hutu; similarly, the desacralization of the symbols of kingship operated under the joint-sponsorship of the Catholic Church and the Belgian Residency (of which more later) paved the way for a secular, jacobin brand of revolutionism. Moreover, just as one needs to distinguish between the symbolic and ideological statements of the reality expressed by the Crown, both must in turn be distinguished from the men and institutions gravitating around the throne. Loyalty to the regime, after all, did not necessarily imply loyalty to the chiefs or to the Mwami's person. Historically, conflicts among competing aspirants to the throne did not seriously threaten the legitimacy of the constitutional order; nor indeed did the resentment of which the chiefs became the object in past and recent times automatically spell the rejection of the monarchy as a form of government. As in the case of the ideological and symbolic transformation noted above, the weakening of the structural bases of monarchical legitimacy (i.e. essentially of the chieftaincy) must in part be viewed as the inevitable consequence of European policies and practices. But it also reflects the survival of structural incompatibilities rooted in specific historical circumstances. As a corrective to the somewhat static picture we have drawn of the monarchy, it may be useful at this stage to look at it from the perspective of the processes of change that have taken place in pre-colonial times.

II. MWAMISHIP IN TIME-SPACE PERSPECTIVE

Historical depth discloses discontinuities in the strength of monarchical sentiment that cannot be properly grasped simply by way of synchronic analysis; in Rwanda it reveals the existence of a political space in which Tutsi rule had only recently penetrated, thus bringing into sight categories of political actors and social structures which might otherwise remain hidden behind the more visible uniformities of caste and ethnicity.

Stripped to its essentials, much of the history of monarchical Rwanda is reducible to chronic spurts of territorial expansion, followed by periods of more or less peaceful assimilation. It is the story of how successive waves of Tutsi or Hima pastoralists, under the leadership of a royal clan of Banyiginya origins, gradually spread their hegemony over the indigenous Bantu (i.e. predominantly Hutu) societies, whose customs and traditions they then proceeded to assimilate into their own.[9] What was involved here was nothing less than an indigenous form of imperialism, bolstered by a superior military apparatus and an equally strong conviction of cultural superiority.

It is difficult to see how these twin processes of territorial expansion and consolidation could have occurred in the absence of a strongly centralized state system—of a reliable corps of centrally appointed chiefs and an efficient military organization—to replace the more or less autonomous kinship and clan structures on which the monarchy had initially relied to establish its rule. When and how this major structural transformation occurred is something of a mystery; all one can do here is to infer the general nature of the processes involved from the better known records of other interlacustrine societies. As happened in Buganda, where the authority of the clan heads (*bataka*) was gradually curtailed in favour of chiefs appointed by and responsible to the Kabaka, the Rwanda kings consolidated their powers by suppressing the autonomy of local hereditary chiefs and replacing them with a group of loyal retainers of Tutsi extraction.

By the end of the nineteenth century the Rwandese polity had achieved a remarkable degree of centralization. Yet, no matter how starkly centralized the powers of the Crown were not unlimited. The religiously sanctioned ritual from which Mwamiship drew its legitimacy imposed significant restraints upon royal behaviour, the nature of which is nowhere more clearly suggested than in the name given by Western observers to the *ubwiiru*, the so-called "esoteric *code* of the monarchy". This code, of which the *abiiru* were the guardians, formed the principal corpus of traditions associated with the exercise of royal authority. Because of the limitations attached to such a ritualized code of conduct some observers have not hesitated to compare it to "a constitution in a modern state", and the collective role of the *abiiru* to that of a "Supreme Court judging whether a new rule is compatible with the fundamental charter of the country".[10] Even though the comparison calls for possible reservations, there can be little doubt that the guardians of the esoteric code did play an important role in the preservation of dynastic legitimacy and in specifying the conditions under which legitimacy could be transferred and perpetuated. Yet their influence in Court politics, that is in "power politics", was almost nil. Instances can be cited of cases where the usurpation of the throne by a rival pretender gained subsequent legitimacy through a calculated lapse in the *abiiru's* memory: the name of the evicted Mwami was purely and simply dropped from the records.

As this last point tends to suggest, royal authority did not remain blissfully unchallenged throughout history. Although the tensions faced by the monarchy were never so deep and persistent as to seriously threaten its legitimacy, they nonetheless introduced considerable instability into the system. These tensions were of two kinds. While some were internal to the system itself, rooted as they were in the cyclical emergence of competitive claims among rival aspirants to the throne, others were external or at least peripheral to its boundaries, originating from the periodic attempts of exogenous elements to resist incorporation into the Tutsi imperium. Very different were the implications carried by each type of challenge, for if the first can readily be identified with "rebellion", in the sense in which Gluckman used the term—in that it involved a struggle for the control of Mwamiship rather than a conflict over the legitimacy of the office itself[11]—the second was clearly more in the nature of a war of independence waged by a culturally distinct community against a foreign invader.

As one might expect, the more recent the conquest, the wider the gap between monarchical power and legitimacy. It is not a matter of pure coincidence therefore if, on the eve of the European penetration, the legitimacy of the Crown was particularly shaky in the northern and northwestern regions.[12] Tutsi control over these regions was not firmly established until the 1920s, and the Tutsi drive to the north did not really get under way until relatively late in the nineteenth century, under Mwami Rwabugiri. This does not mean that these areas had no previous contacts with Tutsi pastoralists. The annexation of indigenous Hutu communities was more often than not preceded by a generous infiltration of Tutsi elements. What it does suggest is that the formal annexation of the peripheral areas of the north is a fairly recent phenomenon when one considers the total span of Rwanda's historical evolution.

Continued territorial expansion meant an almost perpetual displacement of cultural discontinuities from the centre to the periphery. Absorption of the Hutu communities into the caste structure of the monarchy was an endless process, involving a partial loss of cultural identity for the absorbed group and its reintegration into a new social system. Yet the rate of assimilation inevitably tended to lag behind the pace of territorial expansion. Hence the persistence of a conspicuously high degree of cultural autonomy and selfconsciousness among the more recently incorporated Hutu (or Kiga) communities. The pride which some take in referring to themselves as Kiga[13] rather than Hutu, in pointing out variations of speech and culture between themselves and their southern kinsmen, in declaring their continued allegiance to the descendants of local ruling families, in affirming their identity through references to past traditions—these and other factors (such as the survival of autonomous kinship ties and a *sui generis* clientage structure, the *ubukonde*) provide abundant proof of the cultural split which to this day separates the northern Hutu populations from those of central Rwanda.

In this consciousness of themselves as a separate subculture also lies a critical element in the background of the primary resistance movements which from time to time have swept across the northern region. Whatever feelings of regional unity developed in the north must be credited to no small extent to the solidaristic ties created among otherwise unconnected

communities by the upsurge of messianic activities directed against the
Rwanda monarchy—and this long before European colonizers had appeared
on the scene.[14]

The dynamics of revolutionary change in northern Rwanda stemmed in
large part from a carry-over into the modern period of cultural tensions
which the monarchy had never been able to resolve. Just as these tensions,
at the turn of the century, provided the "seedbed" for the growth and
flowering of messianic protest movements, the psychological impact of
these movements upon the northern populations constitutes an important
element in the background of "modern", secular revolutionism. Although
relatively little in the way of a direct interchange of ideas can be detected
between the Nyabingi as a protest movement and the kind of political
upheaval brought to light in the late 1950s, the affinity of their revolutionary appeals is undeniable. Where the situation in the late 1950s
differed conspicuously from what it was half a century earlier is that much
of the rebellious bent of the northern sector could now be communicated
to the previously inert peasant masses of central Rwanda. What led to this
transformation is what we must now examine.

III. MWAMISHIP UNDER COLONIAL RULE: THE SYSTEM REDEFINED

Given the nature of its traditional polity, indirect rule was perhaps the
only viable formula for administering the country once it had been
brought under the tutelage of the European colonizer. Even so, the con-
sistency with which European policies conformed to this formula is striking
when one considers the changes of international status that have accompanied Rwanda's recent historical evolution. Not until 1959, when
suddenly confronted with wholesale rural violence, did it finally dawn
upon the Belgian authorities that their own version of indirect rule was
no longer in harmony with the "spirit of the times". By then they had no
choice but to drastically revise their options, which in practice meant the
abrupt and total repudiation of those very principles which in the past had
been regarded as sacrosanct.

Indirect rule in Rwanda meant essentially two things: Recognition of
the Mwami and the chiefs as the sole legitimate rulers of the country,
and, as a corollary, the strict maintenance of Tutsi supremacy in every
walk of life.[15] The success of indirect rule as a political formula was
believed to depend upon a systematic avoidance of all initiatives likely to
upset the traditional social order. The rationale initially underlying the
official thinking of European authorities in Rwanda was a simple one: all
that was really necessary to administer the country was to use the principle
of monarchical legitimacy as a device through which to enlist the cooperation of "native authorities". The assumption was that the legitimacy
of monarchical rule would somehow survive its own structural transformations while at the same time making possible further transformations in the political system. By lending the prestige of his name and
authority to the measures decreed "from above" the Mwami would act as
the prime legitimizer of European policies—or, to quote André Ryckmans,

"as the familiar décor which permits us to act in the wing without alarming the masses".[16]

But how far could one tamper with the political superstructure without at the same time endangering the basis of the consensus from which stemmed the "premise of inequality"?

(a) The Secularization of Mwamiship

If there can be little question that Christianity served as a major vehicle for the diffusion of egalitarian values, and hence as one of the most explosive forces to which the system could possibly be exposed, this has not always been the case. One of the more remarkable features of the early history of Christian missions in Rwanda is the extent to which they have positively contributed to reinforce the group-conscious and self-interests of the dominant caste.

We have seen how, in the traditional society, the sacredness of Mwamiship tended to reinforce or at least guarantee the viability of the stratification system. With the introduction of Christianity, however, monarchical legitimacy became increasingly divorced from the forces now about to shape the stratification pyramid. Since Christianity threatened to drain the monarchy of its supernatural powers, the response of the incumbent Mwami—Yuhi Musinga—to the spread of missionary activities was understandably hostile; for the Tutsi as a group, however, Christianity was soon identified with Western technology and educational achievements, and because they fully sensed the significance of the new social forces that lay behind it they naturally felt that the preservation of their traditional privileges was intimately linked to their endorsement of the new creed. Out of these conflicting orientations a major source of disharmony developed between the Crown and the aristocracy. Not until the investiture of a new Mwami, in 1931, did the system move into a more stable, if only temporary, equilibrium. Musinga had never been able to adjust himself to the implications of Christianity. Despite his grudging acquiescence to the demands of his entourage that he should allow Christian missionaries into Nyanza, Musinga continued to entertain a strong feeling of suspicion towards all Christian missionaries, and Catholic missionaries in particular. As he once reportedly told one of his *biru:* "The Catholics are the most dangerous because they have adopted the practice of making sacrificial offering to God, unlike the Protestants who recognize the authority of a supreme chief."[17] With the transfer of Rwanda to Belgium his hatred of Christian missions reverberated even more intensely upon the Residency. Where the Germans had merely contended themselves to act as *amici curiae* in the recurrent quarrels between Musinga and the Catholic clergy, the Belgians moved with far greater determination. In 1917 Musinga's powers of life and death over his subjects were abolished; having deprived the Crown of its *jus gladii* the Belgian administration proceeded to further limit its powers through what amounted to a re-enactment of the Edict of Constantine: Religious discrimination was declared illegal, particularly in matters concerning appointments to chiefly office; royal powers were curtailed even more drastically in 1923. From then on all dismissals from office required the preliminary approval of the Residency. In these conditions one can perhaps better understand Musinga's complaints to the administration—"since he was no longer able to kill anyone, or even retain any of his followers into the traditional cult, he had lost all his powers, and the missionaries were now more powerful than himself".[18] One can also appreciate the reason for this growing surliness towards those elements of his entourage who had become converted to Christianity. For Musinga adoption of the new faith by the Tutsi elites was seen as nothing short of a betrayal of his authority.

On a number of counts Musinga's dismissal in November 1931 marked a watershed in the evolution of the Rwanda monarchy. First and foremost, his removal from office by the Residency formalized the "desacralization" of Mwamiship. Not that the monarchical institution *ipso facto* lost all traces of legitimacy; all it meant was that from now on the secular and religious spheres were to be kept separate—at least from the standpoint of the European authorities and educated Tutsi elites. By enforcing this latter-day version of the Gelasian doctrine upon the monarchy the Residency decisively weakened the authority of the Crown: no longer was the monarch identified with the deity; no longer could his person claim "a holy force that creates prosperity and maintains the order of the universe".[19] Yet it is a question whether this secularized image of Mwamiship was really understood by the masses. Where the secularization of Mwamiship held significant implications was at the elite level: the "sloughing off" of its sacredness brought about a partial shift of allegiance on the part of the educated Tutsi elites, in the sense that the ties of affection and awe that once linked the Mwami to the aristocracy were now in the process of being supplanted by the feelings of loyalty which the latter felt towards the Church. The Church, in other words, began to act as an alternative source of "patronage"—and indeed, in a way, as a surrogate monarchy.[20] Yet the loyalty attendant upon this new "client-patron" relationship was clearly conditional: only to the extent that it remained "loyal" to the interests of the dominant caste could the Church expect the reciprocal loyalty of its new "clients".

Musinga's deposition also coincided with a significant change in the kind of political resources available to the Tutsi aristocracy. No longer was birth their sole justification for claiming ascendency over the peasant masses; they could also invoke their superior education and technical competence to strengthen their supremacist claims. By providing them with Western skills and knowledge, with the literary media necessary for the elaboration of their own traditional culture, and, above all, by formally acknowledging their innate superiority, the Christian missionaries gave the Tutsi aristocracy the means and opportunities to reinforce their sense of group identity and cultural superiority.

Musinga's abdication introduced a new heir to the throne—a man whose personality was in some respects very similar and in others very different from that of his predecessor. Rudahigwa had no more sympathy towards Europeans in general than Musinga, and his attachment to tradition often impelled him to act in the same arbitrary fashion as his predecessor. Yet his *modus operandi* was infinitely more subtle than Musinga's. Where Musinga openly challenged European missionaries and administrators Rudahigwa had a special knack for underhand manœuvrings, for working within the confines of the established superstructure rather than against it—for playing one administrator off against another, and in some cases the clergy against the administration. Having come of age at a time when European rule was already firmly established, Rudahigwa was better able to comprehend and accept the norms of the emergent system. More important still, being himself a product of mission schools, he shared with the up-and-coming group of Tutsi elites the Western training and education which his predecessor so conspicuously lacked. All this, together with the fact that his accession to the throne carried none of the stigma attached to the circumstances of Musinga's usurpation, and then coincided with the decline of the old-guard conservatives, at first made it possible for the new Mwami to work out a remarkably close relationship with the incipient "class" of Western-educated Tutsi chiefs and subchiefs. At a time when the whole structure of chieftaincy was about to give way to a new system, this relationship proved to be a major asset in the hands of the administration.

(b) The "Streamlining" of Chieftaincy

As noted earlier, a major feature of the *capitis diminutio* suffered by the Mwamiship after the inception of the Belgian mandate was the limitation placed in 1923 upon the royal powers of dismissal, a limitation paralleled by the enforcement of a similar measure upon the chiefs. The result, was to inaugurate a regime in which the "feudal lords" were about to transform themselves into functionaries. But this was only a beginning. Not until the thirties came to a close did this process of bureaucratization reach something approximating a point of completion.

The over-all picture which emerges from the record is one of a series piecemeal reforms adopted at different intervals and in response to the exigencies of specific situations. The main trends can be identified as follows: first, a conscious attempt was made by European administrators to expand the geographical scope of Tutsi authority, through the appointment of Tutsi chiefs to areas where they had never before exercised any real power. Second, for the trinity of powers previously associated with cattle chiefs, land chiefs and army chiefs was substituted a system in which authority was concentrated in the hands of a single chief. Third, the functions of chief were specified in the form of elaborate rules and regulations designed to meet the requirements of bureaucratic norms. Although the general intent of the European administration was clearly to accelerate the trend towards bureaucratization, the end result was to bring into being a "streamlining" of chieftaincy which, in addition to modifying the structural contours of the political system, produced a much sharper delineation of its geographical and ethnic boundaries.

The expansion of the scope of Tutsi authority came first, chronologically, and, oddly enough, as one of the unintended consequences of the factional strife ushered by the "palace revolution" of 1896. There is no place here for a detailed discussion of the historical events that led the representatives of the evicted royal faction (Banyiginya) to seek refuge in the north. Suffice it to note that the struggle for the Mwamiship rapidly converted itself into something like a civil war. With the arrival into the northern region of "queen" Muhumusa, one of Mwami Rwabugiri's wives, and her son Bilegeya, swells of "nativistic" unrest spread through the entire area, culminating in 1911 with a major rebellion.[21] Since by then the northern region happened to be the main target of missionary activities, the threat which the situation posed to the Catholic clergy could not be taken lightly. Following the murder of Father Loupias, in April 1910, by one of Muhumusa's "men", the German Residency decided to launch a major punitive expedition against "the insubordinate regions, their peoples and their chiefs", which, after it had been carried out, led to the appointment of a number of "loyal" Tutsi chiefs to rule over the northern marches.[22] What had begun as a measure of political convenience, to help resolve a localized problem, was later converted into a more systematic policy: with few exceptions, one after the other the local Hutu rulers were dismissed from office and replaced by chiefs of Tutsi origins. In this the European Residency merely accelerated an expansionist drive begun under Rwabugiri, towards the middle of the previous century. Yet the circumstances under which the Tutsi thrust to the north was now being conducted were undoubtedly more brutal than would have been the case had the process been allowed to run its "natural" course, free of European proddings and firearms. Furthermore, the changes about to be introduced into the structure of chieftaincy were to significantly increase the constraints of the caste system for the peasantry.

As long as power remained divided among several chiefs within the same province it was relatively easy for the Court to follow a policy of "divide and rule" to enhance its influence, and this even when it no longer had formal authority to unilaterally dismiss the incumbents. But even more determining as a motive for doing away with the previous hierarchy of cattle chiefs, land chiefs and army chiefs is that few administrators understood the nature of the functions attributed to each of these categories; and even if they did, this in no way lessened the strength of their argument in favour of a simplified system of administration. Thus in 1926 the Belgian Residency decided to eliminate purely and simply the trinity of power on which chiefly rule heretofore rested and substitute for it the rule of a single chief, thereby preparing the ground for the emergence of a far more starkly authoritarian system.

Not only did the bureaucratization of chieftaincy threaten to undermine the normative understandings that once governed the relationships between rulers and ruled; the additional burdens thereby imposed upon the masses made the perpetuation of traditional obligations all the more difficult to endure. Whatever benevolence and self-restraint used to enter into the traditional pattern of relationships between Hutu and Tutsi gave way to a system almost exclusively geared towards the exploitation of the peasantry.

A mere glance at the variety of customary taxes (so-called "*prestations coutumières*") levied upon the populations is enough to dispel all illusions about the leniency of the traditional system: no less than seven different kinds of tribute (collectively referred to as *ikoro*) were paid to the Mwami by the chiefs and the subchiefs—"as a token of submission and gratitude for the mercies which he designed bequeath upon them".[23] All these, of course, were levied upon the masses. In addition came a host of dues in kind or labour owed to the chiefs and subchiefs—involving the compulsory cultivation of the chief's land (*butaka*), and delivery of agricultural produce at harvest time (*rutete*, or *ipfukire*), keeping watch over the chief's hut at night (*kurolira*), etc.—and the "gifts" which traditionally accompanied the payment of tribute in kind. Coming on top of these customary obligations, the introduction of a capitation tax, levied by the chiefs on behalf of the European administration, sharply increased the demands made upon the masses. Moreover, the expression *"prestations coutumières"* came to serve as a magic label under which a multitude of additional *corvées* were thrust upon the peasantry—the assumption being that custom somehow conferred "automatic" legitimacy upon all forms of labour.

The dominant impression conveyed by the record is that most of the reforms adopted by Belgium in the name of administrative efficiency and financial viability have tended to substantially deepen inter-caste cleavages. Just as the Tutsi oligarchy derived an additional sense of corporate solidarity from its exposure to Western education and technology, the Hutu as a group were made all the more conscious of their cultural and economic separateness by the ruthless enforcement of *corvée* labour and other types of *prestations*. Cohesiveness and solidarity were infinitely more developed within the dominant stratum. Being generally exempt from *corvée* labour and other customary dues, the Tutsi as a group were able to assume the status of a "leisure class" to an unprecedented extent; and because they remained (at least until the early fifties) the sole beneficiaries of Western educational facilities, they were able to "objectify" their elite status through a markedly Western style of life, including Western patterns of household behaviour and more than occasional traces of "conspicuous consumption". More important still, their "supremacist" claims were openly recognized as legitimate by the Church and the administration, and acted upon accordingly. As a result of all this they became more and more visibly differentiated from the "lower orders", culturally, socially and economically.

In their readiness to engage in a radical institutional transformation of the traditional order, the colonial authorities profoundly undermined the structure of norms, statuses and roles that once held society together. Fundamental incompatibilities were bound to develop between the bureaucratic demands of the monarchy and the normative image of the monarch as the supreme embodiment of impartiality and goodness. Similar tensions were likely to arise between the position of the chiefs as civil servants and the traditional expectations of their people, and, more generally, between the growing "class consciousness", in Marx's sense, of the Tutsi aristocracy and the corresponding "impoverishment" of the plebeian masses. But before something even remotely resembling a "class consciousness" could develop among the Hutu, a new source of leadership had to emerge from the lower rungs of society. Not until the mid-fifties was this condition finally satisfied.

IV. THE BIRTH OF EQUALITARIANISM: THE SYSTEM ON TRIAL

The men who eventually led the fight against the monarchy may be divided into two broad categories—they either belonged to a small coterie of *anciens séminaristes* who once studied together for the priesthood (until 1956 the only avenue to higher education, and in any event the only field of human endeavour relatively free of caste discrimination), or to a category of potential "native" administrators collectively referred to as *Astridiens*, after the *Cercle Scolaire d'Astrida*, founded in 1921 under the auspices of the Church for the training of chiefs, subchiefs and subaltern functionaries (*agents auxiliaires*). While the former claimed a distinctly higher level of education (which also helps to explain their higher leadership positions in the revolutionary movement), they both had intimate connexions with the Catholic Church. And through their corporate membership in the Church they both had acquired a whole new set of ideas about human nature—a deep commitment to the principle of equal rights and opportunities for all regardless of caste distinctions, as well as the skills and education which enabled them to articulate their claims to equality.

Yet in seeking to communicate their aspirations to the Hutu masses they were initially confronted with several major obstacles. In the first place there were major disagreements among them over the nature of their ultimate political goals, which in turn raised further disagreements over matters of tactics and strategy. Should their attacks be primarily directed against the governing elites (i.e. the chiefs and the subchiefs) or against all Tutsi without distinction? Should the monarchy be preserved as a form of government, and if so how much power should be left to the Crown? How much reliance should be placed on existing institutions and procedures for affecting change, and how much on "extra-constitutional" means? How much emphasis should one place on reform and how much on revolution? If the answers they finally gave to these questions were characteristically uncompromising, this was more by the force of circumstances than by deliberate choice. At first nothing like a common consensus seemed to exist among them. Even though the lines of cleavage between *Astridiens* and *anciens séminaristes* tended to correspond to a broad division of opinion between "moderates" and "extremists",[24] the situation was further complicated by the persistence in their midst of individual tensions reflective of sub-cultural and regional differences. To mitigate the resulting strains and stresses the stolid opposition of the dominant oligarchy proved barely sufficient: the rift between *Astridiens* and *anciens séminaristes* was never really healed; had it not been for the increasing obduracy of the incumbent Tutsi elites sibling rivalries among the Hutu leaders might easily have deteriorated into an open struggle.

A second handicap stemmed from the absence of strong connecting links between them and the masses other than those supplied through their common ethnic origins, and these at first proved totally inadequate.

Not only were the ties of ethnicity often superseded by the continuing strength of clientage relationships across caste lines; even where anti-Tutsi sentiment was strongest and most widespread this was not always enough to eliminate altogether the divisive pulls of regional and kinship loyalties. This was particularly true of the northern region, for reasons already explained. The social distance between the Hutu intelligentsia and the peasant masses was really a measure of the gap between the new system of values and ideas internalized by this intelligentsia and those of the traditional society.[25]

But perhaps the most crippling handicap facing the Hutu elites stemmed from the overwhelming predominance of Tutsi elements at every level of the indigenous power structure. As late as 1959, 98 per cent of the chiefs and 95·5 per cent of the subchiefs in office were of Tutsi origins; similarly, 94 per cent of the membership of the *Conseil Supérieur du Pays* consisted of Tutsi elements, and the same disparities could also be observed in the lower and middle-rungs of the administration and the police. Denied the minimum of participation through which they might have acquired a sense of political efficacy as well as the means through which to initiate changes from within, the Hutu elites had really no choice but to resort to violence to achieve their social and political goals. Even so, as long as the police and other agencies of external control remained predominantly in Tutsi hands, the chances of organizing a clandestine revolutionary movement were virtually nil; moreover, as long as the scale of social change remained limited, and the system reasonably stable, the incumbent elites could presumably use their repressive capacities with maximum efficiency, that is with expectations of minimum interference from the trust authorities.

Ironically, chiefly intransigence in the end created the very conditions through which a revolution "from below" could be engineered. For if the so-called "revolution" of November 1959 was really a *jacquerie* directed at the chiefs in the name of the Crown, the forces of protest thereby set in motion could now be activated and channelled into a revolutionary movement aimed at the monarchy. Granting that the presence of an alienated counter-elite was a precondition to the release of the revolutionary potential inherent in the caste system, this alone would not have been sufficient to bring it down. Before this could happen a point of rupture had to be reached within the system that would make possible the "detachment" and mobilization of its own resources against itself. The initial rupture, as we shall see, did not occur at the top but at the base of the political structure—not through a frontal assault delivered from "above", but in response to the exactions, short-sightedness and self-estrangement of the regime's most dedicated supporters—the chiefly elites.

If chiefly intransigence was certainly a major element in the background of the events of November 1959, this does not mean that the chiefs were objectively more brutal or demanding in 1959 than they had been at any time in the past—only that by 1959 the structural bases of monarchical legitimacy could no longer be reconciled with the normative image of the Crown. There occurred, in other words, a distinct lowering in the threshold of tolerance of the masses to chiefly rule. What contributed most to the emergence of a potentially explosive situation were the conditions of stress originating, on the one hand, from the joint efforts of the Mwami and the chiefs to reassert their legitimacy in the face of recurrent threats to their authority, and, on the other hand, from the adoption by the Mwami of policies that ran precisely counter to what he sought to achieve.

Few initiatives carried more potentially disruptive consequences than the Mwami's decision, in 1952, to abolish the clientage institution (*buhake*) —a decision justified on the grounds that "(as a result) of the profound transformations that have occurred in all walks of life, the institution had in many respects lost its imperative and regulatory character".[26] In the absence of a chiefly patron from whom they could expect protection, the Hutu peasants became less and less beholden to their chiefs. Their sense of isolation increased accordingly. They felt alienated and adrift in an environment that seemed increasingly hostile. Nor did this in any way improve their economic status. Not only were they sometimes obligated to indemnify their former patrons by a cash payment for the cattle which they now possessed, but since in many cases the patrons insisted on claiming ownership rights over the pasture lands (*ibikingi*) they were now faced with virtually all the inconveniences of the clientage relationship while being deprived of the advantages it once offered. With the formal abolition of clientage ties disappeared one of the most powerful bonds of solidarity between the masses and the elites; moreover, with the severance of this link economic antagonisms between Hutu and Tutsi loomed increasingly larger, causing what little solidarity still survived between them to evaporate.

Meanwhile the responses of the Crown to the repeated attacks launched against the regime by the Hutu elites contributed to further intensify inter-group tensions. Under the pressure of these threats the Mwami felt increasingly drawn towards the more conservative wing of the chiefly stratum, thus pushing the more "liberal" chiefs in a position of political isolation from which they could only extricate themselves by either joining their opponents (which they naturally refused to do) or veering over to the side of the conservatives. Though admittedly few of the chiefs would have qualified as "liberals" in the sense of being wholeheartedly committed to majority rule, there were notable differences between the old "die-hard" conservatives and the younger generations of Tutsi chiefs educated at Astrida. While the former were as unswerving in their loyalty to the Crown as they were intolerant of any move likely to alter their traditional privileges, the latter recognized the need to adapt traditional institutions to the requirements of democracy. As time went on, however, the conservative faction emerged as the more favoured of the two. When in 1958 a group of ultra-conservative chiefs, referring to themselves as "the Mwami's clients" (*bagaragu b'imwami bakuru*), issued a statement to the effect that "there could be no basis for brotherhood between Hutu and Tutsi", Mutara did not even feel the need to issue a disclaimer.[27] Fortified in their belief that the Mwami was tactily supporting their claims, the conservatives showed increasing confidence in their capacity to hold on to their traditional privileges.

Thus as the Hutu intelligentsia stepped up its efforts to mobilize the peasant masses on an ideological basis, new sources of resistance were activated in support of and through the Establishment (i.e. the Court and the chiefs). Parallelling the opposition of the Mwami to the demands formulated by the Hutu intelligentsia, the attitude of the chiefs was one of stolid indifference in the face of changing conditions in the countryside. Whether as a reaction to the shift in the balance of power in favour of the conservatives, or because their expectations were no longer in harmony with political realities, the peasantry displayed an increasing antagonism towards all chiefs in general. Meanwhile the conflict between the forces supporting the Establishment and those opposing it became more intense. Just as the liberal chiefs were gradually eclipsed or mobilized by the conservatives, the more moderate of the Hutu counter-elites felt increasingly drawn over to the side of the extremists. The result was a situation of growing ethnic polarization, and a corresponding intensification of the potential for inter-caste conflict.

V. THE PRECIPITANTS OF VIOLENCE

In addition to what might be referred to as "potential *jacquerie* conditions" a number of factors have contributed to precipitate the occurrence of violence which cannot be inferred simply from the type of "multiple dysfunctions" described above. While tending to intensify existing conditions of stress, these factors were for the most part the product of fortuitous circumstances.

One concerns the situation of political uncertainty created by the visit to Rwanda, in April and May 1959, of a Belgian parliamentary study group (*Groupe de Travail*) to investigate the political problems of the trust territory, and determine the conditions under which a peaceful transfer of authority might be accomplished. Already considerable excitement had been generated by the official announcement by the Belgian government, in January 1959, that the Congo would at some future date become independent, and since the declaration was apparently based on the recommendations of a similar study group which had toured the Congo in August 1958, expectations of a forthcoming pledge of independence for Rwanda made the political climate even more volatile. For if independence now had an appearance of near ineluctability, the crucial question in almost everybody's mind—which of the two contending groups would independence ultimately enthrone?—remained unanswered. In short, the feelings of doubt raised by the arrival of the *Groupe de Travail*, together with the atmosphere of political ferment and mutual suspicions surrounding the *prise de contact* of Belgian parliamentarians with their informants, led to a further questioning of traditional loyalties and political identifications.

Another and even more potent source of destabilization stemmed from the crisis situation and consequent political transformations ushered by the death of Mwami Mutara Rudahigwa, on July 25, 1959. The circumstances of Mutara's death were sufficiently ambiguous to make it possible

G

for the monarchists to accuse the Belgian administration of duplicity and thus lay the entire onus of responsibility for his death upon the *tutelle*. That Mutara was said to have passed away shortly after an exchange of views with Belgian officials, in Bujumbura, and only two days before he was scheduled to issue what everybody expected to be an important policy statement, made the accusation all the more plausible. The name of his successor—Jean Baptiste Ndahindurwa, son of Musinga and half-brother of the deceased Mwami—was revealed to the public before the Mwami's burial, by the head of the *abiiru*, in the course of an improvised ceremony during which the audience was pointedly reminded that "only the *abiiru* have authority to appoint the Mwami's successor . . . and (that) custom prescribes that the Mwami shall not be buried until a successor has been chosen".[28] Nor was any departure allowed from the utter secrecy prescribed by tradition: The administration was left in complete ignorance of the *biru's* choice, and apparently even of their decision to assure the succession. After recovering from the initial shock the Belgian authorities had little choice but to recognize Ndahindurwa as the new Mwami. In so doing the administration not only seemed to be knuckling under to the pressures of the "kingmakers", but conveyed the impression that real power was now in the hands of the chiefs.

The man who had been called upon to assume the succession seemed singularly unfit for the burdens and responsibilities of his office: only twenty-one years old at the time of his accession to the throne, Ndahindurwa—from then on better known as Mwami Kigeli—had none of the personal ascendency and authority of his predecessor. Besides being largely unfamiliar with the arcana of Court politics, and surprisingly unaware of the realities of power that lay behind the relationship of the Court to the Residency, Kigeli's intellectual gifts proved sadly inadequate to compensate these handicaps. Neither able nor really willing to fill the vacuum left by Mutara's death, Kigeli looked increasingly as if he had become the captive of the younger chiefs. Where Mutara had been reasonably successful in preserving the illusion that the Crown was above chiefly politics, Kigeli'a behaviour made it all the more apparent that the fortunes of the Crown were now entirely dependent upon the chiefs.

A comparative glance at two of the more recent crises suffered by the monarchy—that which led to the dismissal of Musinga in 1931, and that which followed Mutara's death in 1959—reveals some interesting contrasts in the evolving pattern of interaction between the chiefs and the Mwami, and between them and the European authorities. The main source of tension in 1931, it will be recalled, was between the Mwami on the one hand, and the educated Tutsi chiefs and the European clergy on the other. What was involved here was essentially an intra-elite conflict, reflecting a deliberate effort on the part of the more educated chiefs to accommodate the political system to their changing status in society. Their target was not the monarchy as an institution but the monarch himself. It was the fear that the resistance of the Mwami to the demands of Westernized chiefs might in the end compromise the future of the monarchy as an institution that led the Residency to intervene. Very different was the situation in

1959: the conflict was essentially between Hutu and Tutsi, moving rapidly
in the direction of a fundamental ideological clash between monarchists
and republicans, with the trust authorities increasingly drawn to the
latter's side. No longer was the monarchy regarded by the *tutelle* as a
guarantee of social stability and political progress but, rather, as a major
obstacle to both. No longer were the chiefs turning against the monarch in
order to preserve their traditional privileges; both the monarch and the
symbols of the monarchy were now consciously manipulated by the
chiefs to assure the maintenance of the status quo. Yet never before had
the status quo been subjected to greater strains. By mid-1959 peasant
apathy or helplessness threatened at any moment to give way to a violent
reaction against the traditional elites.

VI. THE PEASANT UPRISINGS: NOVEMBER 1959

What came to be officially referred to by the Residency as a "revolution"
was little more than a peasant revolt triggered by a localized incident, and
motivated, like all such manifestations, by a belief that the system had been
betrayed by its elites.[29] Though primarily directed against the chiefs, the
peasant uprisings of 1959 eventually served as a "carrier movement" for
a type of political protest whose goals and implications were much more
typically revolutionary.

The revolutionary energies released by the uprisings varied widely
however, both in character and intensity, carrying the anti-Tutsi crusade
in strange and sometimes conflicting directions. At least two separate
strands can be identified: one, reflective of the situation of latent unrest
created in the north by the carry-over of messianic influences, has tended
to impart to the northern rebellion some of the qualities of a millenarian
movement—"the hope of a complete and radical change", along with a
"fundamental vagueness about the actual way in which the new society
will be brought about".[30] The millenarian thrust behind the uprisings was
extremely short-lived, however. Its energies were at once absorbed into a
very different type of movement—localized, anarchistically-oriented, and
exhibiting a very high quotient of pre-Tutsi traditionalism. The rapid
disintegration of the Tutsi-implanted superstructure in the north cleared
the way for the partial resurgence of pre-Tutsi institutions and the re-
establishment of the old *bagererwa-bakonde* type of clientelism.

The second strand, confined to the central region, revealed the
restorative-egalitarian element common to all *jacquerie* situations. Unlike
the former, which initially sprung from a collective quest for the millenium
and rapidly transformed itself into a nostalgic search for a pre-Tutsi
identity, its aim was to appeal to the legitimacy of the monarchical order
against the illegitimacy of chiefly exactions—in short "to purge the regime
of its violators and, so to speak, to set it back on the tracks".[31]

However barren ideologically, the peasant revolt in central Rwanda
brought to light the "levelling instinct common to all such occasions which
prompts the poor to seek a degree of elementary social justice at the
expense of the rich, *les grands* and those in authority". This, adds Rudé,

is the "common ground on which the militant *sans-culottes* meets the 'Church and King' rioter, or the peasant in search of his millenium".[32] This is also where a convergence of aspirations occurred between north and south. As contrary as it may have been to the norms operative in the traditional society—as transient, too, as its manifestations proved to be— the egalitarian impulse released through the act of rebellion served as a major stimulus to ethnic solidarities, thus helping the transformation of more or less atomistic communities into a "disposable" revolutionary mass. Yet, if only because of the unstable and ephemeral character of peasant movements in general, it is difficult to see how these bonds could have been activated into an effective revolutionary nexus in the absence of further changes in the existing power structure.

By causing a widespread disorganization of the existing institutions of local government, the revolt made possible the release and channelling of fresh energies into the revolutionary movement, while at the same time creating the conditions through which further unrest spread into the countryside. The most devastating mutation took place in the north. In a matter of days most of the chiefs and subchiefs were forced out of office or massacred by the local populations. In subsequent weeks the area was almost totally deserted by the Tutsi civilian population, resulting in the establishment of what one might call a "liberated area". Besides providing temporary protection and security against Tutsi-led retaliatory raids, the "liberation" of the northern region decisively weakened the position of the regime. Not only did it offer a kind of "privileged sanctuary" from which new recruits could be enlisted into the revolutionary movement, and new attacks mounted against the remnants of the old order, but the sudden influx of thousands of refugees from the north into the central and southern regions confronted the Belgian authorities with a major resettlement problem, for which no immediate solution could be found. The result was an immediate resurgence of political unrest among both the refugee and the host communities. Meanwhile the interim appointments made by the administration to fill the positions vacated by the incumbents gave the northern populations their first taste of local "self-government".

Among the measures taken by the *tutelle* to cope with the sudden breakdown of chiefly rule, one of the most consequential refers to the substitution of "interim authorities" of Hutu origins for those chiefs and subchiefs who had either been physically forced out of office or whose maintenance in office no longer seemed desirable. Between November 1st, 1959 and March 1st, 1960, 22 chiefdoms out of a total of 43, and 297 subchiefdoms out of 559, had passed under the control of "interim authorities"; of these approximately 50 per cent were appointed in the northern region. The local Hutu leadership was thus presented with a unique opportunity to consolidate its hold over the local institutions of government, and to expand its influence to areas where popular support for their ideas had yet to be awakened.

The next officially-inspired move in the direction of an institutionalization of revolutionary change came with the communal elections of June and July 1960. The aim, in essence, was to substitute popularly elected local executives (burgomasters) for the interim authorities that were still in office, and in this way initiate an institutional transfer of power that would presumably restore a modicum of stability to the political system. In one respect at least the operation proved eminently successful: the elections brought a radical shift in the distribution of power at the local level. Of the 229 communes set up under the terms of the decree of December 1959, 210 ended up being headed by Hutu burgomasters. (Of these, however, only 160 were members of the *Parmehutu*.) Whether this in itself could be taken as a proof of stability is an entirely different matter. Although the evidence varies from one locality to another, the remark of a Belgian administrator that "neither the burgomasters nor the councillors knew the exact limitations of their powers"[33] provides a fairly suggestive, if somewhat euphemistic, summary of the conditions that prevailed in the weeks following the elections. Although the outcome of the electoral process made it technically possible for the burgomasters to achieve virtually unlimited control over local affairs, in many cases the handing over of executive responsibilities to Hutu politicians led to a situation bordering on anarchy. Sheer administrative incompetence, a tendency to use violence as a substitute for authority, latent fears of a monarchical reaction, and a host of miscellaneous personal motives and rumours combined to create a climate of insecurity in the countryside and generate new conflicts among the insurgents.

Since the goals of the insurgents were not immediately attainable through legally available means, the Residency, already heavily committed to the cause of the Hutu intelligentsia, felt that the only realistic course at this stage was to extend to the revolutionary leadership whatever sources of support were deemed necessary to accelerate and legitimize the process of political transfer. These supportive moves took a variety of forms, ranging from concerted efforts to ensure "peace and order" to restrictive measures against Tutsi chiefs and politicians. The underlying objective was basically the same, however: to impart cohesiveness, structure and viability to a movement which, initially at least, seemed conspicuously lacking in each of these qualities.

Of all the initiatives taken by the administration to aid the insurgents, none has been more decisive in ensuring the success of the revolution than the assistance they received from the Residency in planning and executing the so-called "coup" of Gitarama, on January 28, 1961. Not only did the coup place the Hutu elites firmly in control of the provisional organs of government, thus enabling them to discipline and coordinate the action of the revolutionary subgroups in the countryside; by extending immediate *de facto* recognition to the republican government formed at Gitarama the trust authorities in effect sanctioned a double breach of legality: that which led to the formation of a provisional government in flagrant violation of the timing and procedures laid down by the UN resolutions of November 20, 1960; and that which, on the very same day, led to the *de facto* abolition of the monarchy.

The events of Gitaram marked a turning point in Belgian policies: after decades of efforts directed at consolidating the secular authority of the Crown, the *tutelle* had now reached the point where it felt it had no other choice but to turn against it. In another sense Gitarama also marked the ultimate stage in a long series of missed opportunities. There can be little question, for example, that the sheer stringency with which the "social corollaries" of indirect rule were applied carried the seeds of its own undoing, and indeed of the monarchy's. Nor is there any doubt about the general lack of foresight and initiative displayed by Mwami Mutara Rudahigwa and his successor. Partly through their own ineptitude, partly through their unswerving commitment to the supremacist claims of their kinsmen, in a few years the last of the Rwanda monarchs probably did more to discredit the monarchy than the Belgian authorities in the course of the previous decade. Their stubborn refusal to face the issues raised by the prospects of independence, their unwillingness or inability to use what was left of the sanctity of their office to exercize a moderating influence, and, in the case of Kigeli, a conspicuous lack of leadership qualities, are certainly important elements in the background of Gitarama. Given the normative constraints of the traditional environment, however, one wonders whether in the long run different colonial policies would have yielded different results. By the same token one may also wonder whether different personalities from those of Mutara and Kigeli would have produced a substantially different outcome. In the conditions of ethnic strife unleashed by the November revolt it is indeed a question whether more gifted monarchs would have succeeded where lesser ones failed.

VII. CONCLUSION: TRADITIONALISM AS A SOURCE OF REVOLUTIONARY CHANGE

From the perspective of the internal contradictions generated by the impact of radically new ideas, techniques and forces upon the traditional Rwanda society, the fall of the Rwanda monarchy appears as a classic example of the inability of traditional institutions to handle the new political resources introduced under the aegis of the European colonizer. Viewed from the standpoint of traditionalism as a source of revolutionary change, however, the institutionalization of republican rule is perhaps better seen as an attempt to redefine Hutu-Tutsi relationships through the resources of the indigenous society. Our argument, briefly stated, is that for the majority of the Hutu peasants the shift of power to the republican elites did not signify the substitution of Western democratic norms for those prevailing in the traditional society, but the redefinition, or rehabilitation, in a new guise of certain traditional norms and institutions.

In a fundamental sense the *jacquerie* of November 1959 was the last in a long series of cyclical attempts by the northern populations to evade the constraints of Tutsi hegemony. In seeking to evict Tutsi elements from all positions of authority the rural *sans-culottes* of the northern marches were following in the paths of their predecessors, taking up the cudgels where Ndungutse and other social bandits of the turn of the century had laid them down. Rather than seeking to ameliorate the system within the framework of established norms, as in the more typical instances of

"Church and King" revolts, the aim was to partially restore the legitimacy of the pre-Tutsi past.

A somewhat different orientation can be detected in the pattern of violence of the central and southern regions, a pattern more clearly reminiscent of a *jacquerie*-type phenomenon than of a millenarian or anarchistic movement. Characteristically, the attack against the agents of monarchical rule was conducted in the name of monarchical legitimacy. Violence was resorted to as a means with which "to purge the regime of its violators and, so to speak, set it back on its tracks".[34] More specifically, revolutionary activity in these areas received its initial impetus from efforts at mitigating the disparities between "perceived" and "expected" images of monarchical legitimacy. Whereas the "ideal" image of the Mwami had always been that of a supreme and impartial arbiter, by 1959 this image could no longer be reconciled with the actual role of the chiefs in the political system. Not only were the chiefs acting as though they were the sole interpreters of monarchical legitimacy, but their blatant favouritism towards their own group of origin was enough to cast further doubts on the capacity of the Mwami to perform his expected functions. But this did not imply a rejection of monarchical legitimacy. It merely invited a redefinition of the bases of monarchical authority. What the Hutu elites claimed to be evidence of a passionate commitment of the peasant masses to democracy was in fact a groping for a new kind of monarchical legitimacy, identified with the peasant's own conception of their ethnic self-interest. Though possibly apocryphal, stories of Kayibanda going about the countryside saying that the aim of the revolution was to give the Hutu a Mwami of their own seem perfectly consistent with the exigencies of the situation we just described.

The crystallization of ethnic solidarities, in the form of a vertical Tutsi-Hutu split, certainly played a major part in bringing together these separate strands, and in temporarily obfuscating their different orientations. As the scope of ethnic interaction widened, and the quotient of ethnic violence increased, regional and clan affiliations within the Hutu stratum were rapidly superseded by ethnic solidarities. The point was eventually reached where ethnicity emerged as the only meaningful referent in the stratification system, in the end substituting a sharply dichotomous conception of status differences for the multiplicity of ethnic and social rankings in existence in the traditional society.[35]

Yet ethnicity alone does not suffice to explain the enlistment of the peasant masses into the revolutionary crusade. As I have elsewhere argued,[36] the really critical factor behind processes of revolutionary mobilization lies in the dissolution of the vertical patron-client relationships that once tied the Hutu peasants to their Tutsi overlords, and the recasting of the patron-client nexus within the Hutu stratum. As they were allowed to gain access to an increasingly wide range of political resources, including authority, status and wealth, the insurgents were placed in an ideal position to act as surrogate patrons to the peasantry, and to appropriate for themselves the role of benevolent protectors heretofore assumed by their oppressors. Once redefined along ethnic lines the patron-client nexus could serve both as an instrument of political mobilization and as an additional source of ethnic solidarity. This relationship, however, could nòt have materialized as long as the insurgents were barred from legitimate access to political resources, including force. Only through a deliberate choice of the *tutelle* could these resources be made available to the insurgents.

A major consequence of the coup of Gitarama has been to create the conditions for the extension of clientage ties from the top to the base of the political structure, and thus to make possible the establishment of control mechanisms with which to further accelerate the shift of loyalties to local Hutu patrons. Support from the centre was essential to the consolidation of local patronage networks. In order to acquire political "weight" at the local level the burgomasters had little choice but to cast themselves in the role of client vis-à-vis the central authorities. Only at this price could they appeal to the influence of their patrons in the capital to enhance theirs in the communes. The expansion of clientage ties from the centre to the countryside has everywhere tended to facilitate the recruitment of new revolutionary cadres, to create new vested interests in the success of the revolution, and more generally to promote new forms of group identifications in which ethnic identities were further emphasized and inter-ethnic divisions sharpened.

The paradox, then, is that although the relationship of clientage, as once practiced by the Tutsi oligarchy, may well be seen as the germ from which the monarchy developed its power and territorial base, it was from a very similar type of relationship that the revolutionary movement which formally destroyed the monarchy derived its sustenance and structural configuration. One is reminded in this connection of Toynbee's comments on the potential destructiveness of cultural strands detached from their original social moorings:

> A loose strand of cultural radiation, like a loose electron or a loose contagious disease, may prove deadly when it is disengaged from the system within which it has been functioning hitherto and is set free to range abroad by itself and in a different milieu . . . In escaping from its original setting, the liberated particle, bacillus or culture-strand will not have changed its nature; but the same nature will produce a deadly effect, instead of a harmless one, now that the creature has broken loose from its original associations. In these circumstances, "one man's meat" may become "another man's poison."[37]

Toynbee's law of "cultural radiation" holds a dual relevance to the Rwanda situation: from the standpoint of the motivations operative at the elite level, it focuses attention upon the revolutionary potential carried by the spread of Western egalitarian norms among lower-caste elements; viewed against the backcloth of peasant involvement in the revolutionary process it throws into relief the nature of the processes by which the subordinate group managed to extract from the cultural arsenal of the dominant oligarchy the weapons which enabled it to break loose from its traditional links. This is not to deny the effectiveness of ethnic violence as a source of revolutionary cohesion. Violence and the resurgence of clientage ties went hand in hand in the unfolding of the revolutionary struggle, violence creating the very conditions of insecurity that made possible, indeed necessary, the transference of clientage solidarities from one ethnic group to the other.

NOTES

1 Although the overthrow of the monarchy had already been a *fait accompli* since January 1961, following the so-called "coup of Gitarama", not until the UN-sponsored Referendum of the Question of the Monarchy, in September 1961, was the Rwanda monarchy formally abolished. Between January and September 1961 the country remained technically a monarchy, but power was in fact in the hands of the Republicans. For further information see my *Rwanda and Burundi* (London, 1970), pp. 84–89.
2 R. Caillois, *Man and the Sacred* (Glencoe, 1959), p. 91.
3 J. J. Maquet, *The Premise of Inequality in Rwanda* (London, 1961), p. 152.
4 *Ibid.*
5 A. Frederick, Duke of Mecklemburg, *In the Heart of Africa* (London, 1919), p. 47.
6 See J. Vansina, *De la Tradition Orale* (Tervueren, 1961), translated in English as *Oral Tradition: A Study in Historical Methodology* (Chicago, 1965).
7 *Ibid.*, see also J. Vansina, *L'Evolution du Royaume du Rwanda des Origines à 1900* (Bruxelles, 1962), by far the best available source on pre-colonial Rwanda.
8 M. d'Hertefelt, "Mythes et Idéologies dans le Rwanda Ancien et Contemporain", in J. Vansina, R. Mauny and L. V. Thomas, eds., *The Historian in Tropical Africa* (London, 1964), p. 224 ff.
9 See J. Vansina, *L'Evolution du Royaume du Rwanda des Origines à 1900, op. cit.*, *passim*.
10 J. J. Maquet, *The Premise of Inequality, op. cit.*, p. 127.
11 Max Gluckman, *Custom and Conflict in Africa* (Oxford, 1963).
12 As Hans Meyer wrote in 1916: "The king of Ruanda must constantly worry about the border regions of his empire, for the Bantu populations there tend to rebel against Tutsi officials, and killing and murder is the rule rather than the exception. In the north, in the region of the Virunga volcanoes, especially in the Mulera, and in the west, there are scarcely any Tutsi and the rule of King Musinga there is not very well established." Hans Meyer, *Die Barundi* (Leipzig, 1916), p. 159.
13 A substantial proportion of the northern "Hutu" are indeed ethnically related to the Kiga of the Kigezi District of southern Uganda; but unlike their kinsmen in Uganda, described by M. Edel as possessing a "basically anarchic structure", the Kiga of Rwanda developed fairly centralized political structures, a process which must have developed in opposition to the threats of the Tutsi monarchy in the south; there is some evidence that this was also the tendency in Uganda at the turn of the century. I am grateful to Rachel Yeld for drawing my attention to each point. Cf. M. M. Edel, *The Chiga of Western Uganda* (Oxford, 1957).
14 This heritage of messianic activity is directly connected with the history of the Nyabingi movement, a spirit possession cult which developed partly in response to the threats posed by the expansion of the Rwanda monarchy to the indigenous populations, and partly as a result of the concomitant extension to northern Rwanda of millenarian beliefs which first appeared among the neighbouring people of Karagwe, in northern Tanganyika. For a general discussion of the origins and character of the Nyabingi movement, see J. E. T. Phillips, "The Hyabingi", *Congo*, Vol. 1 (1928), p. 316 ff., and M. J. Bessel, "Nyabingi", *Uganda Journal*, Vol. VI, No. 2 (1938), pp. 73–86. For archival references, see T. O. Ranger, "Connexions between Primary Resistance Movements and Modern Mass Nationalism in East and Central Africa", *Journal of African History*, Vol. IX, No. 3 (1968), p. 452.
15 Richard Kandt, *Caput Nili* (Berlin, 1905) *passim*; *Rapport sur l'administration Belge au Ruanda-Urundi en 1925* (hereafter cited as *Rapport*). (Bruxelles, 1926), p. 64.
16 See *Congo*, Vol. I, No. 3 (1925), p. 407.
17 A. Kagame, Yuhi Musinga: "Un Règne Mouvementé" (unpublished MS.).

Consider also the revealing comments made in 1934 by a certain Thaddée Gishoma, presumably a Christianized Tutsi: "(Although) Christianity is the basis of civilization . . . Musinga abhors it. Being superstitious and polygamous, Christianity goes against his grain, annoys him, humiliates him, deprives him. He therefore hates the religion of the Europeans. This is why he regards every Tutsi convert as a personal enemy . . . Musinga is a renegade in his words and in his actions . . . There is nothing good in him, no trace of Christianity whatsoever . . . Meanwhile Christianity, or better Catholicism, marches forward, along with civilization and peace, that peace which the Angels wish all men of good will to enjoy. As for Musinga, captive of his own incapacity, victim of his superstitions, he is slowly fading away like darkness before dawn." Thaddée Gishoma, *La Chute de Musinga* (typescript, n.p., 1934), from the Derscheid Collection).

18 De Lacger, *Rwanda* ((Kabgaye, n.d.), p. 467.

19 R. Callois, *op. cit., loc. cit.*

20 This, at least, is what can be inferred from Thaddée Gishoma's interesting comments: "Every man endowed with high qualities can use them to influence the people and raise himself to the highest station. I recall that when the first White Fathers came and settled in the Bugoyi they were called 'Bami'—'kings'. The youngest among them, Father Classe, was called 'Kamigato'—'young king'. Whenever a palaver of some sort arose, people would say to each other, 'Tuj'ibami', that is 'Let's go and see the king'. On their way back one could hear them say 'Umwami arararuchiye'—'The king settled it'. Thus Musinga and the chiefs were ignored by the people. The qualities of the true king were inexistent in him." Thaddée Gishoma, *op. cit.*

21 See Roger Louis, *Ruanda-Urundi 1884–1919* (Oxford, 1963), pp. 145–160.

22 *Ibid.*, p. 156.

23 *Rapport* . . . 1926, p. 51.

24 This cleavage tended to reflect the very different career opportunities to which each category could aspire by virtue of his training: Whereas the Astridiens had every reason to expect access to administrative positions after completion of their studies, the *séminaristes* were, by statutory regulations, denied such opportunities. Having no professional vested interest in the maintenance of the *status quo* their attitude was understandably less compromising.

25 This is clearly revealed by the outcome of the 1953 and 1956 elections to chiefdom, subchiefdom, and territorial councils: Fifty-two per cent of the seats in the sub-chiefdom councils fell into Tutsi hands in 1953 and 49 per cent in 1956, with the Tutsi gaining an increasingly larger share of the seats at each ascending step in the hierarchy. Thus at each election over 90 per cent of the seats in the territorial council (*Conseil Supérieur du Pays*) went to Tutsi elements. See J. J. Maquet and M. d'Hertefelt, *Elections en Société Féodale* (Bruxelles, 1959).

26 *Circulaire No. 33/52 du Mwami du Ruanda: Projet de Suppression de l'ubuhake* (Nyanza, April 10, 1952). See also, R. Bourgeois, *Banyarwanda et Barundi: L'évolution du contrat de bail à cheptel au Ruanda-Urundi* (Bruxelles, 1958).

27 *Ruanda Politique 1958–1960* (Bruxelles, 1961), p. 35–6.

28 For a more detailed account of these events, see *UN Visiting Mission to Trust Territories in East Africa, 1960: Report on Ruanda-Urundi*, T/1551, p. 20 ff.

29 See Chalmers Johnson, *Revolution and the Social System* (Stanford, 1964), p. 31 ff.

30 E. Hobsbawm, *Primitive Rebels* (New York, 1965), p. 57, 58.

31 Chalmers Johnson, *op. cit.*, p. 32.

32 G. Rudé, *The Crowd in History, 1730–1848* (New York, 1964), p. 224.

33 *Réunion des Administrateurs de territoire,* September 2, 1960 (unpublished document).

34 Chalmers Johnson, *Revolution and the Social System* (Stanford: 1964), p. 32.

35 For a further elaboration of this theme, see R. Lemarchand, "Status Differences and Ethnic Conflict: Rwanda and Burundi", unpublished MS.

36 R. Lemarchand, *Rwanda and Burundi* (London, 1970), p. 480 ff. also, "La Relation de Clientèle comme moyen de contestation", *Civilisations*, XIX, 1 (1969), 1–27.

37 Quoted by Leo Kuper in *Passive Resistance in South Africa* (New Haven, 1957), *passim,*

3

BURUNDI

René Lemarchand

With characteristic craft and tortuousness, the recent history of Burundi unfolds on a seemingly repetitious checkerboard of dynastic intrigues, factional struggles and ethnic violence. It is a story punctuated with crises, the most recent one accompanied by the eruption of ethnic violence on a scale approaching the dimensions of a genocide. In the orgy of counter-terrorism triggered by the abortive, Hutu-led uprising of April 29, 1972, an estimated 80,000 Hutu men, women and children lost their lives. The assassination of ex-Mwami (king) Ntare V, in Gitega, on the very same day, approximately five and a half years after the formal aboli-tion of the monarchy, calls to mind yet another crisis, which, though bloodless, is not entirely unconnected with the 1972 killings. On November 28, 1966, shortly after being formally installed as Mwami Ntare V, the teenage pretender to the throne, Charles Ndizeye, was peacefully ousted from the Mwamiship through an army coup. Thus ended the shortest interregnum ever recorded in the annals of the kingdom, and a form of government whose roots reach as far back as the seventeenth century, if not earlier.

In retrospect the fate suffered by the Burundi monarchy may seem like a logical extension of the similarities it once shared with Rwanda, its neigh-bour to the north: whether looked at in terms of their respective cultural traditions, ethnic make-up and social structure, they bore an unmistakable likeness to each other, including a sense of inner political unity which, for centuries, belied the diversity of their ethnic components. Even though the historical record suggests a rather different type of relationship, it is not without reason that they were once referred to as "les royaumes frères".[1]

Yet to see in the passing of the Mwamiship a re-enactment of the events that led to the demise of its northern analogue would be an oversimplifica-tion, masking the differences of social structure and political organization that lay behind their apparent uniformities. To the dual challenge of political modernization and popular participation the Burundi monarchy at first responded with an air of national self-consciousness unmatched by its Rwanda counterpart. Monarchical symbols encompassed a feeling of national identity, indeed of nationalism, from which they derived a signifi-cantly greater "staying power", and which, for a while, made it possible for the Crown to act as a major unifying bond among the various ethnic segments of society. Although the surcease accorded to the Burundi monarchy may not seem all that generous, that it should have lasted long enough to allow the institution to be carried over into independence is nonetheless a noteworthy achievement. More intriguing still, when the moment of truth finally came the ultimate blows were delivered not by the peasantry, nor by its spokesmen, but by a mixed assemblage of army officers and civil servants comprising in their midst a substantial proportion of those very elements who, in Rwanda, posed as the staunchest supporters of monarchical institutions. Although both countries have experienced ethnic violence on a terrifying scale (and Burundi even more so than Rwanda), the eruption in Burundi occurred some twelve years later than in Rwanda, at a time when the monarchy had long ceased to exist as an institution; the immediate result, furthermore, has been precisely the opposite of what happened in Rwanda, i.e. to virtually eliminate all Hutu elements from positions of influence and responsibility and to place the levers of power in Tutsi hands.

Behind these contrasting patterns of development lie fundamental variations in the traditional authority systems associated with each state With its multiplicity of competitive and semi-autonomous power centres, leading to recurrent fragmentation, Burundi differed from Rwanda to the same extent that a pyramidal system differs from a hierarchical one.[2] Its traditional system was like most pyramidal systems, "essentially a system of compromise and accommodation, flexible in its internal policies . . . (yet) given to crisis, fission and recombination as part of its natural history".[3] The dominant trend in recent years, however, has been in the direction of an increasingly hierarchical pattern of authority, accompanied by a sharp polarization of intergroup conflict. The key to this mimetic transformation, as we shall see, lies in the interworkings of social structure and monarchical authority. Just as in recent times the forces of social change released by modernity have set in motion a fundamental restructuring of monarchical authority, this process of institutional transformation has had a direct impact on the shape and direction of intergroup conflict, and ultimately on the stability of the kingship.

TRADITIONAL ASPECTS OF MONARCHICAL LEGITIMACY

What from one perspective might be regarded as an element of strength may, from another perspective, appear to be a major source of disability. The "despotic" character of the Rwanda monarchy was an element of strength for the Mwami in the traditional context of Rwanda politics, but a fundamental handicap in the democratic-egalitarian context of the post-war years. Precisely the reverse situation can be observed in the case of Burundi. Those very features which in the past conspired to weaken the power of the monarchy turned out to be its most valuable drawing cards when independence finally came into sight. The paucity of reliable traditions concerning the nature and scope of monarchical legitimacy; the recurrent struggles among princely factions over the occupancy and privileges of Mwamiship; the absence of mutually supportive links between the Crown and either of the two major ethnic groups in society (Hutu and

Tutsi)—these were some of the elements that have both circumscribed and enhanced the legitimacy of the monarchical authority.

Nowhere is this paradox more clearly evidenced than in the elusiveness of the traditions from which the Mwamiship derived its legitimacy: not that the legitimacy of the office did not rest on widespread consensual agreement, but the form and content of this consensus were sufficiently vague to impart to the nation of monarchical legitimacy a distinctive malleability. The metaphysical underpinnings of Mwamiship are, of course, fairly well established. More than a symbol of national unity, the Mwamiship was a source of religious sanctions which served as a powerful deterrent against possible threats to its legitimacy. Even though the incumbent might have been regarded as unworthy of holding office, the office itself conveyed an image of virtue which clearly transcended the realm of human contingencies.

Beyond this, however, the picture is one of extreme vagueness. The problem in part, lies in the near absence of institutionalized communication channels for perpetuating the traditional norms of the system. Official court historians were unknown in Burundi, and while many of the types of traditions encountered in Rwanda are also found in Burundi, these are of limited usefulness for the historian. As Vansina points out, "the political system of Burundi was not of the kind that favoured historiography . . . There was nothing to foster the rise of oral traditions: . . . no fixed provincial boundaries, and so, little likelihood of local traditions arising; no important families apart from that of the king, and so, no family histories, or hardly any. Lastly, there was no central government which might have given rise to official historians such as the *abiiru*."[4] Vansina's conclusion that "there was a strong bias against history in Burundi" finds an interesting echo in the observations made by Resident Oger Coubeau, in 1935: "It is extremely difficult to obtain any sort of reliable information about the kings of Burundi. Even those natives who gravitated around Mwezi Kisabo ignore the feats of his predecessor . . . How much easier would our work be, including the tracing of genealogies, had the Court in Burundi had anything like the *ubucurabwenge* of Rwanda!"[5]

In these circumstances any attempt to specify the legitimizing norms of kingship, whether as a symbol, an institution, or a framework of aspirations, becomes extremely hazardous. Even the tersely evocative royal motto, *Sabwa Ganza*—roughly translatable as "The Mwami reigns and rules"—conveys a totally misleading picture of the nature of royal authority. For if one can entertain legitimate doubts as to the scope and structure of royal authority at any given point in time, that royal power was anything but despotic, but in fact rested in the hands of a traditional oligarchy which ruled in the name of the monarch, or in spite of himself, is a point on which most observers seem to agree.

The most plausible explanation for this lack of "official" communication networks lies in the extreme competitiveness of the political system. From about 1850 onwards traditional Burundi came as close to the ideal "pyramidal" model as any other African state. Not only was authority decentralized, more often than not gravitating in the hands of rebellious princes, but the struggle for power among the princes of the blood (*ganwa*) often led to an extremely high rate of turnover among provincial office-holders. This in turn created strong disincentives to perpetuate oral traditions. Since most of the incumbents owed their tenure in office in large part to the application of force—and to their success in maintaining a favourable balance of power between themselves and their nearest opponent—no special effort was made to cultivate antecedent traditions. Inasmuch as these tended to confirm the legitimacy of their rivals' claims, the incumbents had indeed a vested interest in fostering oblivion. Again to quote Vansina: "It was in everybody's interest to forget about history, whether it were the chief in his province, the subchief who had been dismissed, or the king himself, who relied now upon one faction, and now upon another . . . Even the guardians of the dynastic tombs or of the royal drum were no more expert in traditions than their fellow countrymen."[6] Unencumbered by the petrified mould of narrow rituals and elaborate traditions, the legitimizing "myth" of the Burundi monarchy exhibited to an exceptional degree those very qualities of pliancy and adaptability that were so conspicuously lacking in the case of the Rwanda monarchy.

If the ambiguity surrounding the legitimizing norms of the Burundi monarchy is directly traceable to the occurrence of princely rebellions, the latter were equally instrumental in depriving the Mwami of the substance of power. Rather than reinforcing the power base of the monarchy through a strengthening of popular commitment to the legitimacy of the office, as might be gathered from Gluckman's "rebellion theory",[7] the evidence shows that princely rebellions did in fact impose serious limitations on the exercise of monarchical power. Indeed the position of the Mwami on the eve of the European penetration has often been compared to that of a *primus inter pares* among the princes of the blood. In the long run, however, the loss of effective political power suffered by the kingship proved far less detrimental to its staying power than might be inferred from the foregoing. If anything it was the structural weakness of the Burundi monarchy which, at the time of independence, proved its strongest source of legitimacy. Unlike what happened in Rwanda, where royal absolutism made the adoption of effective constitutional reforms virtually impossible without at the same time challenging the legitimacy of the Crown, in Burundi the monarchy's relative impotence for a while operated to insulate it from the main arenas of political involvement. One finds here partial confirmation of the phenomenon discussed by E. Shils and M. Young: "Whereas the lands where personal or absolute monarchy prevailed were beset by revolution, countries of constitutional monarchy became politically stable and orderly . . . When protected from the full blast of destructiveness by its very *powerlessness*, royalty is able to bask in the sunshine of an affection unadulterated by its opposite."[8]

Besides contributing to the powerlessness of the kingship, another consequence of princely rebellions has been to perpetuate in the guise of modern political parties a type of competition which not only tended to deflect the focus of conflict away from the kingship but temporarily relegated to the sidelines the really important issues raised by independence.

The issue of monarchical vs. republican legitimacy did not intrude itself on the political scene until *after* independence, and, characteristically enough, not until the monarchy had again shown tendencies toward absolutism. Until then Burundi politics were primarily centred upon the resurgence of dynastic feuds between the descendants of princely families. Whatever opposition the Crown might have otherwise attracted unto itself was thus automatically deflected against the spokesmen of these families, or the parties with which they became identified.

Finally, the very nature of competitive relations among princely factions produced a much higher degree of inter-group cohesion than might have been the case otherwise. Simmel's observation that "conflict may also bring persons and groups together which otherwise have nothing to do with each other" gives us a clue to an understanding of the changing pattern of inter-group relations created by princely rivalries.[9] Cyclical competition among the princes, as well as between them and the Mwami, brought together under the same banner groups of supporters which under different circumstances would have remained much more strongly demarcated by the barriers of caste and ethnicity.

As in Rwanda the basic social cleavages below the *ganwa* stratum were between Twa, Hutu and Tutsi, with the latter claiming highest rank. Although the numerical strength of each caste varied substantially from one region to another, the overall percentage is roughly the same as in pre-revolutionary Rwanda, with the Tutsi representing between 12 and 15 per cent of the total population, and the Hutu approximately 84 per cent. Yet the element of differential moral valuation which entered the caste structure was infinitely more flexible than in Rwanda. The Tutsi of Burundi never assumed the status of a "squirearchy" in the sense in which the term might have applied to Rwanda. Nor did they display the kind of haughty arrogance and self-conscious superiority which so often characterized the attitude of their northern kinsmen. They lacked the latter's exclusivist, patrician ways as well as the value system associated with such typically aristocratic behaviour.

One's chances of gaining access to wealth and privilege did, of course, depend in some important ways upon ascriptive criteria, such as membership in a specific caste or lineage group. But this was by no means the sole determinant of economic and social status. The social structure allowed for a considerable measure of social climbing across caste lines, in particular through the favours and "benefices" offered by the clientage system. Ethel Albert's statement that "the dynamics of the social system make provision for political and economic mobility by which all but the most wretched Burundi know how to profit" is fully corroborated by Albert Trouwborst's illuminating discussion of the built-in capillarity of the clientage system.[10] Thus within the limits of the existing opportunity structure it was not uncommon for an ordinary Hutu to acquire wealth and political influence through his own personal resourcefulness, or what the Burundi refer to as *ubgenge*. Whether defined as "successful cleverness", the art of obtaining favours from a superior, or, more crudely, "getting away with murder", the possession of *ubgenge* was clearly a prime condition of social mobility. *Ubgenge*, however, was by no means the exclusive privilege of the well-born. "The specific manifestations of *ubgenge* are numerous and diverse: The cleverness of a rogue; the industriousness of a virtuous man whose overlord gives him a cow as a reward for virtues; the skill of a good psychologist-rhetorician in persuading a generous, impulsive—or thoroughly inebriated—superior to give him a cow although he had done nothing to earn it; the skills of a medical curer; the success of a practical joker who has victimized some simple-minded peasant . . . are all equally good examples of *ubgenge*—for they all succeed in bringing something good to their designers."[11] Status differences based on personal achievement thus significantly blurred the contours of the formal hierarchy associated with the caste system.

Besides exhibiting a comparatively high degree of intercaste mobility, Burundi society was also characterized by a multiplicity of *intracaste cleavages* for which there was no equivalent in Rwanda. Quite aside from the fact that the *ganwa* came to be regarded as a distinct caste, towering far above all others socially, economically and politically—and bearing in mind the presence of certain ethnic groups (like the Mosso) which simply did not fit into the conventional caste structure,—one finds an amazing number of intergradations within each of the major castes.[12] There is, to begin with, and important line of cleavage within the Tutsi caste between the Tutsi-Banyaruguru and the Tutsi-Hima, a cleavage coincident with, and reflective of, major social and ethno-cultural differences between the two segments; secondly, reference must be made to the differences of status pertaining to the various patrilineages (*imiryango*) within each caste. The literal translation of the Kirundi term for patrilineage—"door" —nicely conveys the significance of such substructures for gaining entry into the political system. Recruitment to political roles had often less to do with caste differences than with lineage ties. Although chiefly roles were generally filled by *ganwa* elements, recruitment patterns below this level were never so strongly biased against Hutu aspirants as to deny them access to the political arena. Many were the Hutu who served as chiefs or subchiefs in the royal domains, the so-called *ivyibare*; even more numerous were those who served as *bashigantahe*, or councillors, at the local or provincial levels; then a number of Court offices were traditionally held by Hutu elements recruited from high-ranking patrilineages. The incorporation of Hutu office holders into various sectors of the political system thus stands in sharp contrast with the hegemonic position assumed by Tutsi elements in the traditional Rwandese polity—and so does their remarkably close association with monarchical institutions. The symbolic and institutional links once existing between the Crown and the Hutu peasantry made it possible for the Burundi monarchy to perpetuate the belief, or the illusion, that the existing constitutional order was the only legitimate one even after it had ceased to be so regarded by the newly-emergent elites.

Despite the potential for ethnic strife inherent in Burundi's pluralistic structure, ethnic polarization along Hutu-Tutsi lines was significantly delayed by the presence of a multiplicity of intermediate cleavages. As long as they were allowed to persist, the cleavages constituted, in Huntington's words, "a series of breakwaters which divided society and permitted the political mobilization of one group at a time".[13] Momentarily sheltered from the full blast of political competition by the fences of its own social environment, the Mwamiship was able to bear the initial strains of political mobilization with apparent equanimity.

FACTIONALISM OLD AND NEW: BEZI *v.* BATARE

The impression conveyed by much of the official literature on Burundi is that political instability was part of an immutable cycle of chronic frag-mentation and reconstruction. The causes of instability, according to this view, were embedded in certain structural uniformities which inevitably produced the same results. An official source elaborates the point as follows: "The functioning of political institutions (in Burundi) is con-ditioned by three factors . . . 1. The designation of an infant-king, leading to a long regency; 2. The partial turnover of royals, each generation eliminating one branch of the royal family and replacing it by another; 3. The gradual parcelling out of chiefdoms by way of successive in-heritance. Under the combined influence of these three factors the history of Burundi *unfolds and renews itself with all the rigour of natural phenomena*" (my italics).[14] Conflict in this sense is part of a structural competition which periodically recurs without ever fundamentally upsetting the system's equilibrium.

A major difficulty with this kind of interpretation is that it tends to formalize into patterned regularities a set of historical events which, in retrospect, seem far less neatly structured.[15] Specifically, it overlooks the capacity of "royals" (i.e. *ganwa*) to capitalize upon new resources, and through the use of such resources, to alter the distribution of power around the throne. As will be seen, one of the most significant consequences of the colonial interlude is that it created the conditions for a major redistribu-tion of power among the *ganwa*, with the Bezi branch of the royal family emerging as the major beneficiary of administrative and social reforms. This, of course, is not meant to imply a concomitant transformation of the political system from a pyramidal to a hierachical one. Only after independence did the monarchy emerge as the central pivot around which power and authority revolved. But this could scarcely have happened in the absence of a fundamental reallocation of political resources among the *ganwa*. If the Bezi were able to make an effective use of power for the defence of their patrimony *qua* royals, this was due to no small extent to their ability to turn to their advantage the symbolic resources of the monarchy.

Nor is this interpretation really adequate to account for the changes that took place in factional processes. A major common denominator of factions, as Nicholas points out, is that they divide the community along vertical rather than horizontal lines.[16] Instead of "representing the interests of superordinate against subordinate stratified groups",[17] as is generally the case with "caste" and "class", factions can better be described as

H

quasi-groups founded on vertical and essentially personalized relationships between a leader, his clique, and their supporters. But this is not to imply that the political aggregates involved in factional struggles must necessarily remain identical. Factions, as J. M. Bujra has argued, are dynamic phenomena: "Factional processes are in a dialectical relationship with other social and political processes going on both within and outside the community."[18] This dialectical relationship is nowhere better illustrated than in the changes that have affected the scope and structure of factional politics in Burundi during the colonial period. Whether looked at from the perspective of the recruitment processes associated with each of the main factions (Bezi and Batare), the character of the process of political competition between them, or their relationship to the wider political system, the physiognomy of Burundi politics on the eve of independence differed in some important ways from what it was at the inception of colonial rule.

(1) Historical Roots of Factional Strife

The specific historical issues and events that lie behind the emergence of *ganwa* factions are in large measure a matter of conjecture. Yet enough is known of Burundi's precolonial past to suggest that factionalism in this sense did not arise until a comparatively recent date (i.e. *circa* 1860), and then as a consequence of the sudden enlargement of the kingdom's original boundaries. This process of territorial expansion reached its peak under the reign of Mwami Ntare II (*circa* 1795–1852), whose reputation as a "great conqueror" is well established. From a relatively small entity, bounded on the north by the Buyenzi and in the south by the Nkoma and Butusi regions, at Ntare's death Burundi had expanded into a kingdom twice its original size, roughly co-terminous with present boundaries. Control over the newly-acquired territories was assumed by Ntare's sons who, from then on acted as the Mwami's deputies in the peripheral marches. With the accession of Ntare's youngest son to the throne, in 1852, the stage was set for a bitter struggle for supremacy between the new Mwami, Mwezi II Gisaabo, and those of his brothers who refused to surrender their newly acquired positions. Thus, from about 1860 until his death in 1908 Mwezi's main preoccupation was to evict his brothers (Batare) from their entrenched positions and replace them by his own sons (Bezi). The reconquest started in 1860, with the defeat of Mwezi's elder brother, Ndiivyaariye, at the battle of Nkundo, near the royal capital of Muramvya, and continued unabated throughout the colonial period, albeit in a more or less muted form.[19]

"If a prince of the blood is sent to govern a distant province," writes Audrey Richards, "what more likely than that he should try to develop a local dynasty of his own? . . . Established as a governor for the king some fifty or hundred miles away, what more likely than that the pince should strive to become a kinglet?"[20] Burundi is obviously a case in point. The new political resources rendered available to the rebellious (i.e. Batare) princes through conquest enabled them to successfully challenge the authority of the central government. These resources, however, included more than just royal militias or tribute. In seeking to assert their independence from the throne the Batare princes also used their traditional claims to legitimacy, as royals, to build up support for themselves among the local populations. The legitimacy of the kingship was thus converted into a weapon directed against the legitimacy of the king. To counter these moves the Bezi princes were led to adopt a somewhat similar strategy, meanwhile reducing the kingship to a relatively minor element in the political system. As in most other African states where power tended to gravitate to unilineal descent groups, political competition took the form of a factional struggle among the representatives of the different dynastic segments of the royal line. The extreme fluidity of political alignments within each of the segmenting branches of the royal line, the centring of all political action on *ganwa* elements, and the relative impermanence of the supportive links between the faction leaders and their followers, such in brief, were the key characteristics of Burundi politics on the eve of the European penetration.

The basic parameters of the system were not fundamentally altered by the establishment of colonial rule. *Ganwa* rivalries, whether intra- or inter-dynastic, continued as before to form the axis around which the political life of the kingdom revolved; and to the built-in limitations previously faced by Mwami were added those enforced by the presence of the European colonizer. Yet the transformations inaugurated under the aegis of the imperial powers were of lasting consequences for the monarchy. Although in the end Westernization sowed the seeds of the discontents that eventually led to the collapse of the monarchy, before this happened colonial rule created the conditions that made it possible for the monarchy to acquire a new basis of legitimacy—and a new power base.

(2) Ganwa Politics Under Colonial Rule (1899–1957)

It was perhaps inevitable, given the logic of the internal situation, that the Germans should have resorted to a policy of "divide and rule" to establish their hegemony over the kingdom. The immediate result, in any event, was to carry political fragmentation to the point where the means defeated the end. By 1903, four years after the founding of the *Militärstation* in Bujumbura, Burundi was, for all intents and purposes, split into three seperate kingdoms, two of which were under the control of pro-German (i.e. Batare) elements (Kilima and Machoncho); the independent status claimed by the two leading figures of the Batare branch soon led a number of smaller chiefs, mostly of Batare origins, to claim a similar status for themselves; meanwhile Mwezi's Kingdom had shrunk to approximately one third of its original size. Not until half a century later would the Bezi be able to recoup their losses.[21]

How, from a position of near impotence, the Bezi eventually managed to rise to a position of virtual supremacy in relation to the Batare, is not easily explained. Certainly, the immediate consequences of the German pacification proved sufficiently detrimental to the long-range objectives of the Residency—i.e. to find "a basis on which to build in Burundi an authority as strong and effective as in Rwanda"[22]—to dictate at least a partial reversal of previous policies. Yet at no time during the colonial period was a conscious effort made by European administrators to systematically eliminate the Batare from the political scene. Whether because of a tacit sense of obligation to their former allies, or because of a commitment to a notion of democracy that presupposed the existence of a "healthy opposition",[23] European Residents were generally predisposed to acknowledge the legitimacy of the Batare's claims in their respective fiefdoms. That a major change did in fact occur in the territorial distribution of power between Bezi and Batare is indeed a tribute to the skill with which the former were able to exploit the latent opportunities of the situation created by colonial rule.

The strategies through which the Bezi were able to consolidate their hold over the country must be viewed against the background of the changing position of the kingship in the political system. As a symbol of legitimacy the kingship emerged in a new light from its trial of strength with the German colonizer; as an institution it gained new prerogatives from its incorporation into the administrative scaffolding later on erected by the Belgians; and as the crucial link in the network of patron-client relations radiating from the royal capital it also derived added influence from the new resources made available through European rule. Out of these transformations a new set of mutually supportive relationships developed between the throne and the Bezi which in the end decisively strengthened the latter's position vis-à-vis the Batare elites.

However detrimental it may have been, initially, to the powers of the Bezi chiefs in general, and of the King in particular, the ultimate result of German "pacification" was to substantially reinforce the symbolic legitimacy of the throne. There is no point here in re-emphasizing the innumerable inconsistencies and contradictions which so prominently figure in the record of German colonial rule in Burundi—how, from a policy of non-intervention, the Residency abruptly shifted, in 1903, to a posture of active military intervention against the old Mwami, Mwezi Kisabo, and how, after recognizing the independence of Kisabo's enemies —Machoncho and Kilima,— the Germans eventually turned against those who had once been their strongest supporters in their fight against Mwezi. Not until 1905 was Mwezi Kisabo finally recognized by Resident Von Grawert as *Oberkoenig des Urundireiches*—"Supreme King of Burundi". The term was strangely inappropriate to describe the fledgling authority of the ageing Mwami: drained of what energies he had left by his incessant fights against the *Schutztruppe*, his court riven by internal dimensions, his domains splintered by the play of dynastic feuds, Mwezi was in no position to make a constructive use of the powers which the German Residency had so belatedly—and grudgingly—conferred upon him. Yet there can be little doubt that Mwezi's efforts to resist foreign domination added a further element of legitimacy to the Mwamiship. The evidence even suggests a strengthening of the Mwami's own authority among the masses.[24] In any event, much of the nationalist aura which in later years surrounded the public image of the Bezi is traceable to the active resistance of their forefathers, and of Mwezi Kisabo himself, against the repeated onslaughts of the German colonizer. In time the cause of national unity and monarchical legitimacy became indissolubly linked with the cause of Bezi.

Having learned the lessons of the German experiment, the Belgians went much further than their predecessors in recognizing the authority of the Mwami. "The cooperation of the Mwami," states an official report for 1925, "constitutes an indispensable element of progress and civilisation . . . Without him the problem of government would remain insoluble . . . Legitimacy is a moral factor of incalculable importance."[25] Pierre Ryckmans, Belgium's first Resident in Urundi, unambiguously stressed the cardinal importance of the king's "presence" in mediating and legitimizing governmental policies: "The presence of the king, the only one capable of conferring a legal, customary investiture upon a candidate of our choice, makes it possible for us to go forward without running the risk of being faced with a fatal impasse, without having to make an impossible choice between a rebellious legitimacy and an impotent submission . . ."[26] Ryckman's emphatic recognition of the legitimizing function of the Crown offered the Bezi a fresh opportunity to use the Mwamiship as a lever with which to consolidate their hold over the country. But their ability to take advantage of this policy was itself conditioned by other factors.

Mwambutsa's minority (which lasted until 1930) not only enhanced the influence of the Bezi chiefs over the Crown, but justified the creation of a Regency Council through which they were able to further increase their leverage vis-à-vis both the Crown and the Residency. At Ryckman's request three prominent Bezi chiefs, Ntarungera, Nduwumwe and Karabona, were to serve as Regents. Shortly after Ntarugera's death, however, in 1921, his seat on the Regency Council went to a prominent Mutare, Mbanzabugabo, son of Ntare, and the membership of the Regency Council was simultaneously enlarged to include seven additional *ganwa* of different origins, among whom figured another prominent Mutare, Baranyanka, descendant of Birori, son of Ntare. Although the inclusion of Mbanzabugabo in the Regency Council was bitterly resented by Nduwumwe and Karabona, the latter had already had ample opportunities for formalize their claims to authority, and, through the pressure they were able to exercise upon the Residency, to tip the scales in their favour: Nduwumwe, in particular, emerged as the most powerful figure in the entire kingdom, and retained his pre-eminent position until about 1943–44; furthermore, following Mbanzabugabo's submission in 1920, a sizeable portion of his "fief" was turned over to Ntarugera. Moreover, though weakened by the admission of Batare elements to the Regency Council, the Bezi still held a clear majority of the seats. In brief, while "the reorganization of the Regency Council had . . . as its immediate consequence a reinforcement of the ties between the Crown and the chiefs",[27] the Bezi chiefs were clearly in a better position to draw advantage from this "special relationship".

Not until the 1930s, however, were the Bezi able to make significant additions to their territorial domains. These gains were the unintended consequence of the initiatives adopted by the Residency in the interest of "administrative efficiency". Beginning in 1929–30, and in line with the directives of Vice-Governor Voisin, a conscious effort was made by the Residency to achieve a territorial regroupment of the smaller chiefdoms into larger and hence more viable administrative entities. The aim, to quote Voisin's words, was "to regroup chiefdoms in such a way as to suppress the dispersion of fiefs and make the administration easier and more efficient".[28] In part because the Bezi knew how to manipulate the Crown to their advantage and because of the lack of familiarity of European administrators with local issues and their consequent inability to cope with the manoeuverings that went on behind the scenes, the implementation of the Voisin directives brought about the dismissal of a number of hitherto semi-independent chiefs of non-Bezi origins; simul-taneously, the consolidation of Bezi holdings into fairly large, contiguous blocs of territory led to a substantial aggrandizement of their territorial jurisdiction. With the transfer of new resources—primarily in the form of tribute and taxation—in the hands of the Bezi chiefs, there also occurred a concomitant increase of their potential leverage upon the Crown.

Contrary to what has often been alleged, by the early thirties the Crown was anything but a passive instrument in the hands of the old Bezi feudatories. As Mwambutsa reached the age of adulthood his powers of appointment were formally recognized by the Residency. From about 1931 onwards all subchiefs were appointed by the Mwami, a function which had hitherto been the sole prerogative of the *ganwa*. After the promulgation of the decree of July 14, 1952, a whole new range of prero-gatives were devolved upon the Mwami, ranging from the delineation of the chiefdom's boundaries to decisions concerning policemen's salaries and taxes (*centimes additionnels*). By then, however, the Crown had already emerged as a significant factor in the play for power that went on among the *ganwa*. As a result of the expansion of political resources available to the Mwami the palace became increasingly vulnerable to "pressure politics", and the political dividends that might accrue from such pressures all the more attractive to the Bezi chiefs.

The relationship of *ganwa* factionalism to the wider political system changed drastically in the years preceding and following World War II. Rather than being exclusively focussed on autonomous cliques operating within fairly narrow boundaries and more or less independently of the throne, factionalism became increasingly tied up with palace politics. Given the nature of such politics, and the covert character of factional behaviour, much of the substance of this relationship remains beyond the pale of scholarly investigation. Yet what little evidence there is available suggests that if the Bezi chiefs were able to recoup their losses[29] this was due to no small extent to their adroitness in enlisting the support of the throne in their struggle against the Batare. This relationship entailed mutual advantages. Just as the status and authority of the Bezi chiefs came to depend to a considerable extent on the mediation of the Crown, the legitimacy of the Mwami as well as his ability to get its "fair share" of tribute and taxes was contingent upon the continued support of the Bezi faction. Behind this pattern of reciprocities one can discern the familiar contours of the clientelistic networks so ably described by Albert Trouwborst.[30] But if the new resources introduced under the auspices of the Belgian colonizer continued to be handled on the basis of an age-old formula, the arena and scope of factional politics were nonetheless substantially different from what they were at the inception of colonial rule.

So, also, were the patterns of recruitment associated with the Bezi and Batare factions. Although the resources they were able to extract from the Crown were in part the consequence of the prerogatives which the Residency had devolved upon the Mwami, the resulting links of dependency can easily be exaggerated. New resources eventually became available which were not directly controlled by the throne. Beginning in 1921, with the creation of the *Cercle Scolaire d'Astrida*, new educational opportunities came into being, accompanied by the emergence of a new wave of young Bezi chiefs, trained at Astrida, whose administrative skills and personal dynamism were ideally suited to meet the objectives of the Residency—"to achieve the gradual replacement of old or incapable chiefs", and "relentlessly pursue the adaptation of 'native chiefs' (*le cadre dirigeant indigène*) to modern ideas of progress and to the economic evolution of the country".[31] New groups and individuals thus became involved in factional politics whose outlook and behaviour were decidedly more "modern" than that of their predecessors. As the elder generations of Bezi chiefs (i.e. *ganwa*) saw their position threatened by these young "upstarts", a new line of cleavage developed *within the* Bezi faction which substantially altered the previous pattern of factional competition.

From a straight Bezi-Batare struggle, factional politics in the forties and fifties thus moved in the direction of an intra-dynastic competition between different generations of *ganwa*. The most serious of the crises occasioned by this situation occurred during World War II, when, in an attempt to curb the growing ascendency of his nephew Nyawakira, Nduwumwe entered into a tactical alliance with Baranyanka, then leading spokesman of the Batare family. In an unpublished memorandum Resident Schmidt summed up the elements in the background of this "reversal of alliances" in the following terms: "One (Nduwumwe) wished to hold on to his ranks as the Mwami's 'First Councillor'; the other (Nyawakira) wanted to rob him of this privilege and use it for the benefit of his favourites . . . After World War II . . . Nyawakira's intrigues succeeded in rallying the Mwami to his cause: Nduwumwe found himself progressively insulated from everything and everyone (at the Court) . . . Nduwumwe became Baranyanka's great friend, and brought along into his camp a segment of the Bezi family. Among these some continually switched sides, now supporting Nduwumwe, now Nyawakira. It was no longer a matter of Bezi *v.* Batare. These tergiversations were to create a troubled, subterranean atmosphere rendered even more unpleasant by Baranyanka's blunders."[32] What Schmidt neglected to mention, however, is that by 1953 Baranyanka had become the protégé of the Residency. The conflict between the Nduwumwe-Baranyanka and the Mwambutsa-Nyakira factions rapidly took on the qualities of a proto-nationalist struggle between supporters and opponents of the Belgian administration.

By casting his lot with the Nyawakira faction Mwambutsa immediately exposed himself to the suspicions and criticisms of the administration. "By confining his role to that of an arbiter," wrote Schmidt, "the Mwami could have had a preponderant influence. He refused to follow my advice and openly supported the Nyawakira faction, against which I had no choice but to defend Nduwumwe and Baranyanka. By identifying himself with the interests of Nyawakira, the latter's enemies or opponents became his (Mwambutsa's), and these were from then on referred to (by the Crown) as 'rebels'."[33] Although Schmidt never explicitly admitted his own personal preference for the Baranyanka faction, his partiality for the Batare comes out with striking clarity from his strongly opinionated characterization of the personalities involved, including Mwambutsa, the latter said to be interested in only two things: "la femme, et faire plaisir à un entourage de favoris dont la plupart ont une vie privée quelque peu déréglée".[34]

Trivial as they may seem in retrospect, these comments have more than an anecdotal interest. Besides calling attention to the potential influence of the throne, they also cast a revealing light on the "pro-Belgian" stigma from then on attached to the Batare, and on the element of "nationalist" respectability which the Residency unwittingly imparted to the Bezi's political image. Although Resident Schmidt may not have gone so far as to openly recommend the dismissal of Mwambutsa and his replacement by one of Baranyanka's sons, this is precisely what many Barundi had come to believe, and still believe. It is not difficult to imagine, in these conditions, the tremendous prestige gained by the Bezi in their quarrels with their domestic opponents: were they not the staunchest supporters of the Mwami against his internal foes, in the best tradition of the *abadasigana*?[35] Were they not the ones who suffered most from European indignities, prejudices and animosities? And in the end was it not to the Bezi's own efforts and resourcefulness that the Mwami owed his political survival in the face of the combined assaults of his enemies both from within and from without?

Ironically, the Residency's blatant favouritism towards the Batare faction was largely responsible for dissipating whatever residual animosities still existed among Bezi elements. By the mid-fifties factional politics had again swung back to a straight Bezi-Batare confrontation. But the ties of reciprocity previously established between Mwambutsa and his younger courtiers survived long after their initial *raison d'être* had disappeared. Mwambutsa's indebtedness to Nyawakira found expression in the total trust which he later displayed towards Nyawakira's son, Germain Bimpenda, and Léopold Bihumugani, one of the leading personalities of the Nyawakira faction. Temporarily severed by Prince Rwagasore's meteoric rise to power, immediately before independence, these ties were quietly re-established after his death, in 1961. From then on the Crown was drawn into an ever closer relationship with the Bihumugani-Bimpenda tandem, a relationship entirely consistent with the "parton-client" ties which traditionally existed between the Mwami and his princely supporters and persisted virtually unchanged throughout the colonial interlude. The political debts contracted during this period were easily carried over into the next phase.

(3) Ganwa Politics in a New Guise: Uprona *v.* PDC. (1957–1961)

No sooner did the vision of independence enter the political consciousness of the Barundi than factional cleavages reasserted themselves with renewed vigour, this time in the guise of new associational groupings. Modern party politics in Burundi were from the outset dominated by the struggle between the *Parti de l'Unité et du Progrès National*, better known as *Uprona*, and the *Parti Démocrate Chrétien* (PDC), whose leaders were associated, respectively, with the Bezi and Batare branches of the royal family.

How far pre-independence party politics have tended to reflect the carry-over of precolonial divisions is easily seen from the bases of support, political symbols and leadership patterns associated with each of the major contestants. While the *Uprona* was at once identified with Bezi interests, and was indeed founded by a leading Bezi personality, Léopold Bihumugani (better known as "Biha"), the PDC became the exclusive articulator of Batare interests. The initiative to launch the PDC came from Baranyanka, leading spokesman of the Batare family; and two of the most prestigious figures associated with the PDC were Baranyanka's sons, Joseph Biroli and Joseph Ntitendereza. The Kirundi appellations adopted by each party also contributed to the perpetuation of political affects based on historic cleavages: while the Kirundi term for *Uprona* (*Abadasigana*) conjured up memories of Mwezi Kisabo's followers, the name adopted by the PDC (*Amasuka U'mwami*) carried political connotations more clearly associated with the reign of Ntare Rugaamba. But perhaps even more symptomatic of their presumptive links with the past was the absence of fundamental ideological cleavages discernible in the parties' platform. Both were openly committed to the perpetuation of the monarchy as a constitutional form of government, and only marginally concerned about substantive ideological issues.

The element of historical fixity conveyed by these characteristics needs to be corrected in the light of the new social forces in gestation behind the façade of *ganwa* politics, of the new issues raised by the approach of independence, and of the new personalities about to emerge on the political scene. Once these factors are taken into account party politics are no longer exclusively reducible to a straight Bezi-Batare struggle.

Just as the emergence of the Nyawakira-Bihumugani faction, in the early forties, expressed the dissatisfaction of a younger generation of Bezi chiefs (for the most part *Astridiens*) with the power and privileges of their elders, the challenge faced by the survivors of this faction in the late fifties and early sixties stemmed from the threat to their interests posed by the rise of a younger and better educated generation of chiefs, most of whom were of Bezi origins. In each case the success of the younger faction resulted from its ability to draw advantage from the political resources of the monarchy.

The effect of generational cleavages on intra-party competition can best be understood by looking at the political fortunes of the *Uprona* between 1957 and 1961. Founded in early 1957 by Léopold Biha, shortly before the arrival of the UN Visiting Mission, the *Uprona* was initially intended to dramatize the opposition of the Bezi chiefs to the decision of the administration to extend to Kitega, Nyanza Lac and Rumonge the system of *centres extra-coutumiers* (CEC) already in existence in Bujumbura since 1941.[36] Because the initiative was so patently prejudicial to the interests of the chiefs, and of the Bezi chiefs in particular, it was at once denounced by these chiefs as a wholly unwarranted attempt on the part of the Residency to interfere with the traditional prerogatives of the Crown. Although the issue which precipitated the creation of the *Uprona* was evidently new, the interests at stake were basically the same as in the early forties. At this stage of its history the *Uprona* was but the latest in a series of moves taken by the Nyawakira-Bihumugani faction to defend their *positions acquises* against the encroachments and prejudices of the Residency.

Less than a year after its foundation, however, the leadership of the *Uprona* had passed to younger hands. With the return of Prince Louis Rwagasore from Belgium, in 1958, the party underwent a major transformation. Though never officially associated with the *Uprona* otherwise than in a purely advisory capacity, Rwagasore quickly asserted himself as the driving force behind the party. Nor is this too surprising considering the nature of his credentials: as the Mwami's eldest son, Rwagasore was in an ideal position to deflect upon the party the aura of legitimacy surrounding the Crown; as a Western-educated intellectual, Rwagasore was deeply sensitive to the claims of the newly-emergent, Westernized elites, and in any event more conscious than most *ganwa* of Bezi origins of the need to adapt the socio-political structures of the kingdom to the requirements of political modernization. On both counts Rwagasore was uniquely qualified to implement the twin objectives of "Unity and Progress" to which the *Uprona* claimed to aspire. But if the goal of unity was still identified with the preservation of monarchical symbols, Rwagasore's conception of "progress" was obviously very different from that held by Biha and his clique in 1957. "Progress" for Rwagasore did not mean the preservation of chiefly privileges but the substitution of a popularly-elected government for chiefly rule, the organization of a broadly-based party representative of the "general will", the setting up of auxiliary associations destined to mobilize the energies of peasant masses and, above all, emancipation from colonial bondage. His nationalist stance, rendered all the more suspect in the eyes of the Residency by his "populist" leanings, earned him the reputation of a dangerous crypto-Communist among Belgian administrators; his commitment to democracy that of a malevolent upstart among the elder generations of Bezi chiefs; and his royal origins that of an ancestral foe among the Batare chiefs. Despite or because of these handicaps, Rwagasore emerged as the most prestigious leader Burundi had known since the days of Mwezi Kisabo.

By 1958, then, the *Uprona* was no longer the exclusive preserve of Bezi elements. Its leading spokesman was in fact a Mwambutsa (i.e. Rwagasore), and while many younger Bezi elements joined the party after

Rwagasore's take-over, by 1961 many of the "old guard" Bezi aristocrats had founded their own separate organizations. Equally noteworthy was the Mwami's withdrawal from involvement in the party struggle. Despite allegations to the effect that the *Uprona* was Mwambutsa's party, there is nothing in the record to suggest that such might have been the case. The irony, however, is that for the majority of the Barundi the *Uprona* could not be anything but the party of the monarchy.[37] Was not Rwagasore the Mwami's elder son? Did he not consciously seek to exploit his royal parentage to strengthen the appeal of his party among the masses? Did not the PDC time and again attack Rwagasore for trying "to officialize his activities under the cover of his princely status"?[38]

The identification of the *Uprona* with the Crown was decisively strengthened by the decision of the Residency, in September 1960, to abolish all chiefdoms and replace them with provinces headed by provincial administrators appointed by the Residency. Not unnaturally, the political void created by the elimination of the chiefs was in time filled by the *Uprona*, the only remaining symbol identifiable with monarchical authority. As Ghislain observed, "the chiefdoms having been suppressed . . . the Barundi felt completely disoriented (*désemparés*) and they all rallied around the Mwami's person . . . like castaways around the mast of a sinking ship".[39] And how could the masses better express their loyalty to the Mwami than by voting for the party headed by his son?

This sudden upsurge of popular fervour for the Mwamiship, in many ways reminiscent of the populist enthusiasm surrounding the Kabakaship in the early phase of Buganda nationalism, is of critical importance for an understanding of subsequent developments. The key to post-independence politics in Burundi lies in the combination of two inter-related phenomena—the emergence of the Crown as the main focus of popular loyalties, and the continued structural weakness of political parties. While the former must be seen as a conjunctural phenomenon, expressing the sense of emotional disarray of the peasant masses in the face of a totally new political situation, the latter must be attributed to the inability of party leaders to overcome the fluidity, expediency and relative impermanence of factional alignments. Assuming that "factions" and "parties" stand at the opposite poles of a logical continuum—ranging from a relatively simple to a more complex political structure, from a relatively informal to a more formal and institutionalized relationship to the wider political system, and from a more or less personalized type of leader-follower relationship to a recruitment pattern based on common interests or ideological affinities[40]— one can scarcely avoid the conclusion that neither the *Uprona* nor the PDC really qualified as political parties. They both stood as half-way houses between "factions" and "parties". Lacking the minimal conditions of a stable party organization, neither was as yet in a position to substitute more durable organizational links for the leader-clique, or clique-follower nexus around which traditional politics tended to revolve.

In these conditions one can better understand why, in spite of its sweeping victory at the polls during the 1961 general elections, the *Uprona*

only met with limited success in its effort to achieve a modicum of integration among its supporters (both Hutu and Tutsi); why, after Rwagasore's death on October 13, 1961, the party almost immediately fell prey
to ceaseless internal bickerings among its presumptive leaders; and why, in
the face of this chaotic situation, the Crown emerged as the only legitimate
arbiter of intergroup conflict.

The Displacement of Conflict: Hutu *v.* Tutsi

The sheer rapidity with which the focus of inter-group conflict moved
away from factional feuds to centre almost exclusively upon Hutu-Tutsi
rivalries is one of the most perplexing phenomena brought to light by the
advent of independence. The shift from dynastic to ethnic antagonisms
inaugurated a period of chronic governmental instability. As the polarization of ethnic feelings began to penetrate governmental structures, and as
the pressures from below became more intense, the attractions of
monarchical absolutism became all the more difficult to resist—and the
legitimacy of monarchical rule all the more fragile.

Though in part rooted in the pluralistic nature of Burundi society, the
origins of the Hutu-Tutsi problem are in part traceable to the "demonstration effect" of the Rwandese revolution upon the attitude of certain
Hutu elites.[41] As early as 1960–1961, a number of Hutu politicians, at
first mostly outside the *Uprona*, began to feel the contagion of republican
ideas. They grew increasingly sensitive to the implications of majority
rule. By identifying their political aims and aspirations with those of their
Rwandese kinsmen, they imputed to the Tutsi of Burundi motives which
they (the Tutsi) at first did not possess but to which they eventually gave a
substance of truth. Furthermore, with the transition from trusteeship to
self-government important changes were introduced in the existing
structure of career opportunities which served to further exacerbate ethnic
feelings. Because of the discriminatory implications of indirect rule in the
field of secondary and higher education,) the majority of the newy-created
bureaucratic posts went to Tutsi elements (See Table I), thereby creating a
whole new set of vested interests among the educated Tutsi elite. The

TABLE I

ETHNIC DISTRIBUTION OF HIGHER CIVIL SERVICE
Posts (as of July 1st, 1965)

Administrative Positions*	Ethnic Background				Total
	Ganwa	*Tutsi*	*Hutu*	*Other*	
Directeurs Généraux		12	7		19
Directeurs	3	36	14	1	54
Directeurs Adjoints		35	22	3	60
TOTAL	3	83	43	4	133

*The grades listed under this heading are borrowed from the classification used in
Belgium (and France), and are roughly comparable in the United Kingdom to the three
top grades of the administrative "class"—namely (and in descending order) those of
permanent secretary (*directeur général*), deputy secretary (*directeur*) and under
secretary (*directeur adjoint*).

advent of independence, in other words, by opening a new range of career opportunities both in the public and private sectors, led to an unprecedented competition between Hutu and Tutsi.

But the really decisive element behind the crystallization of ethnic conflict stemmed from the struggle for power, both within and outside the *Uprona*, released by Rwagasore's death. The first signs of conflict occurred in January 1962 six months before independence, when the youth wing of the *Uprona*—the *Jeunesses Nationalistes Rwagasore* (JNR)— launched a series of armed raids against trade-union leaders and politicians of Hutu origins, most of them associated with Christian Trade-Unions. From then on the rot rapidly spread to the directing organs of the *Uprona*. By August 1962 the struggle for power between Hutu and Tutsi *Upronistes* had brought the entire party apparatus to the verge of collapse. What had begun as an intra-party struggle now threatened to assume wider dimensions. The incidents of August 1962, marked by Paul Mirerekano's[42] abortive attempt to resolve the party crisis through an improvised plebiscite of the rank and file of the *Uprona*, signalled the beginning of a deepening split along ethnic lines which, by contagion, spread to the National Assembly and eventually permeated the entire bureaucratic governmental machinery.

Less than a month after independence the kingdom faced a situation of ethnic stalemate in almost every sector of its political life. No other independent African state had so little to offer at a comparable juncture of its history in the way of effective leadership; and no other African state— save perhaps Zaire—suffered from such extraordinary weakness of its party apparatus. That in spite of these handicaps the country nonetheless managed to maintain a semblance of political cohesion is where the role of the monarchy takes on crucial significance. With the government and the legislature reduced to impotence by their own inner contradictions, the constitutional restraints which the monarchy had grudgingly imposed upon itself lost their *raison d'être*. As the only remaining structure still free of ethnic stigma the Crown quickly emerged as the single most important stabilizing element in the political system.

THE INTERVENTION OF THE CROWN

Traditionally, as we have seen, the most effective restraints on the Mwami's whim stemmed from *ganwa* opposition to his rule. To these were in time added the bureaucratic limitations imposed by the *tutelle*. With the elimination of the Batare as an active political force, almost immediately followed by the eviction of the colonial bureaucracy, these restrictive influences at once disappeared.

This situation led between 1962 and 1965 to an unprecedented concentration of powers around the throne: from a pyramidal system, characterized by the co-existence of separate sovereignties, the monarchy evolved into a distinctly more centralized polity, perhaps closer to the hierarchical pattern in existence prior to 1850 than had been the case at any other point in the recent historical past.

Conscious as he was of his obligations as an "impartial arbiter", Mwambutsa quickly realized the need to act when the circumstances required. Whether or not Mwambutsa took an active part in the creation of the PDR as some have intimated presumably in order to set up a "third force" against the PDC and *Uprona*, is difficult to say. But there can be little question that it was Mwambutsa, and he alone, who took the initiative in determining the composition of the interim government set up prior to the 1961 legislative elections; it was Mwambutsa who, in August 1962, suggested that a new executive committee of the *Uprona* be elected by the rank file of the party when the leadership crisis threatened to deteriorate into open violence; and it was again Mwambutsa who in June 1963, personally intervened to obtain the release of Thaddée Siryuyumunsi, President of the National Assembly, after his arrest by the Muhirwa government for his suspected involvement in a plot against the regime. Thus, when Prime Minister André Muhirwa finally tendered his resignation to the Mwami, on June 7, 1963, it was, as one commentator observed, "largely out of disgust . . . for being publicly made to look like a fool by the Mwami and his close advisers".[43] Muhirwa's resignation was more than a symptom of the rising aspirations of the Court; it also marked an incipient shift in the centre of gravity of the political system. From then on the machinery of government became increasingly subject to the veto of the Court.

For purposes of analysis this process of "escalation" may be seen as falling into two distinctive phases: (1) from June 1963 to July 1965: a period of covert, indirect and intermittent intervention on the part of the Crown, during which power tended to gravitate in the hands of an oligarchy of Court officials and civil servants; (2) from July 1965 to October 1965: a period of overt and direct intervention, with the monarch and his courtiers now playing "an active, efficient political role in the governing process".[44] (A third phase, lasting from October to November 1966 can best be characterized as involving a process of forced de-escalation or disengagement. Inaugurated by the abortive coup of October 18, 1965 this phase ended with the seizure of power by the army on November 28, 1966, and the overthrow of the monarchy.)

Following Huntington's terminology, passage from phase (1) to phase (2) may be said to correspond roughly to a transition from an "oligarchical" to a "ruling" monarchy; with the inception of phase (3), leading to the exercise of royal authority by remote control, the system moved in the direction of a "nominal" monarchy, with authority now in the hands of the army and the bureaucracy. (See Table II, p. 122.)

(1) Strategies of Oligarchical Control

In order to accentuate the force of its own gravity in the political vacuum that followed independence, the court went to great lengths to ensure a proper balancing of ethnic interests in government. Each of the five consecutive governments appointed by Mwambutsa between 1963 and 1965 contained an almost even proportion of Hutu and Tutsi, all of them chosen because of their presumptive loyalty to the Crown; moreover, following the appointment of Ngendadumwe, in June 1963, each Prime

Minister of Hutu origins was inevitably succeeded in office by a Tutsi. Not only did this conjure up a vision of monarchical impartiality ideally suited to ward off the criticisms of Hutu or Tutsi against the monarchy, but the stalemate which this situation produced within the government gave the Crown additional justification for further emasculating what little power was left in the hands of the Cabinet.

Next, a deliberate effort was made to neutralize actual or potential opponents to the regime by incorporating as many of them as possible within the bureaucracy. Hence the phenomenal expansion of civil service posts between 1962 and 1964. By mid-1964 the central administration comprised 1,239 functionaries, over half of whom belonged to the upper ranks of the civil service (the so-called *cadres de collaboration*). Approximately 72 per cent of the national budget for 1964 was spent on personnel expenses. While some of these appointments undoubtedly helped silence the voices of the opposition against the monarchy, it did relatively little to abate the stridency of ethnic recriminations. Since the principle of ethnic parity was rarely observed in the allocation of lower administrative posts— in part because the Tutsi were generally better qualified than the Hutu for manning these posts—Tutsi elements continued to predominate in virtually every sector of the bureaucracy, both at the central and provincial levels.

Finally, much of the stability temporarily achieved by the Crown, and indeed much of its political influence, stemmed from its ability to exploit the resources of "political clientelism". The resurgence of patron-client ties around the throne was in fact little more than the adaptation of an age-old relationship to the exigencies of the post-independence situation. Just as in the past "to be a subordinate was tantamount to being a client",[45] the subordination of the administration and the government to the Palace expressed itself through the establishment of clientelistic links between the Mwami and his courtiers on the one hand, and the ministerial and bureaucratic elites (both Hutu and Tutsi) on the other. By 1964 these ties of reciprocity tended to produce a far greater centralization of authority than had normally been the case in previous times.

Clientelism was itself contingent upon specific tactical moves on the part of the Crown. First of all, by gradually bringing under its jurisdiction a variety of functions and prerogatives heretofore assigned to the government, Mwambutsa made it clear that from then on the regulation of political resources—and favours—belonged to the Palace. Thus on June 7, 1963, the Army and the Gendarmerie were made directly answerable to the Mwami; in February, 1964 the Mwami served notice to the Minister of Interior that no Provincial Governor could be appointed to office or dismissed without prior consultation with the Palace; subsequently the Ministries of Planning and Justice, along with the Ministry of Information and Immigration, were all converted into Secretariats of State under the direct supervision of the Crown. Secondly, in order to be really effective, clientelism required the appointment of reliable intermediaries at various levels, in the government, the central and provincial administration, state enterprises (*parastataux*) and banks. And since the most prestigious and trustworthy patrons around the Mwami were of *ganwa* blood, criteria of reliability were generally identified with *ganwa* ties. Thus, along with this drastic curtailment of governmental powers noted above, the tendency from 1963 onwards has been to entrust key posts within and outside the government to members of the royal family, that is, in most cases to *ganwa* of Bezi origins. As it happened, no sooner was Pierre Ngendadumwe appointed Prime Minister than he found himself besieged with a pleiad of former chiefs, or sons of chiefs, nearly all of whom had gained access to their new positions under the protective wing of the Court. This sudden infusion of *ganwa* blood into the sinews of the government and the administration meant, first of all, that an increasingly large segment of public life took on the characteristics of a "patrimonial" polity: in the Weberian sense, with a substantial portion of civil servants and cabinet members forced into the roles of personal retainers. To paraphrase Weber, "those subject to the authority (of the Mwami and his men) were not 'members' of an association but either their traditional 'comrades' or their subjects' ".[46] Moreover, as the tentacles of clientelism began to expand to the outer reaches of the bureaucracy an increasingly large proportion of the national wealth was mobilized to satisfy the demands for personal favours made upon the Mwami by his clients. Which brings us to yet another tactic involved in the gamesmanship of clientelism, i.e. the dispensation of "prebends", more often than not through the diversion of public funds, to ensure the continued loyalty of subordinates to their superiors. Fiscal and commercial policies were thus overwhelmingly geared towards the preservation of particularistic loyalties, rarely towards the attainment of developmental goals.

The fragility of the system stemmed in part from its inability to generate the technical, economic and administrative resources necessary for the tasks of modernization, and in part from its inability or unwillingness to provide more than a palliative to the Hutu-Tutsi problem. The financial and economic resources of the kingdom were evidently too limited to meet the "prebendary" requirements of clientelism and at the same time implement the developmental goals to which the Westernized elites generally aspired. Since the demands for favours generally exceeded the resources available, whatever initial "slack" existed in the system quickly disappeared. With the flow of prebends getting thinner and thinner, and official sinecures increasingly scarce, the survival of the Mwamiship hinged on its ability to keep the animosities of each ethnic group against each other at a constantly higher level of intensity than the animosities of either group against itself. By 1965, however, the policy of ethnic counter-balancing, helpful as it may have been at the beginning, had become a meaningless ritual. As ethnic pressures from below steadily built up—as much as a result of the circumstances noted above as because of the incidence of external stimuli—the policies of the Crown became self-defeating.

Although the clientelistic structure of the system proved reasonably effective for a while in muting the criticisms of those Western-educated elites who happened to be on the receiving end of the line, some nonetheless refused to go by the rules of the Palace, and eventually joined the

ranks of the opposition. Undercurrents of resentment against the "absolutism of the Court" persisted even among those who stayed in office.
Regardless of ethnic origins, the consensus of opinion among these newly-
emergent elites was that the Court was essentially made up of retrograde
and obscurantist elements who were neither willing nor able to bring the
country into the twentieth century.

Yet no matter how widely shared, propensities to call into question the
legitimacy of the regime varied substantially from one ethnic group to
another, depending on the political conjecture. When the policies of the
Court seemed to favour the interests of the Hutu, either by the award of
the Prime Ministership to a Hutu, or because of its temporary receptivity
to the marginal demands of their spokesmen, inclinations to challenge the
legitimacy of the system were strongest among the Tutsi—and vice versa.
This "see-saw" game could not go on forever without creating its own
inconsistencies. Indeed the most serious threat to the legitimacy of the
Crown came from the very inconsistency of its responses to the demands
for political participation voiced by the representatives of the masses (i.e.
the Hutu), demands which it had initially encouraged but subsequently
failed to acknowledge. By creating false expectations to begin with, and
then moving further away than ever before from the realization of expected
goals, the monarchy, in effect, created the seeds of its own destruction.

(2) From "Oligarchical" to "Ruling" Monarchy

Viewed from a broad perspective the passage from "oligarchical" to
"ruling" monarchy, in mid-1965, was the logical outcome of the inner
contradictions that had developed within the system between 1963 and
1965. As the scope of governmental and administrative autonomy gradually atrophied, ethnic competition became all the more intense over those
few sectors of political life that were still immune from royal intervention.
Moreover, if the policies of the Palace were sufficiently authoritarian to
invite a reaction of protest on the part of Westernized elites, they were
never so constrictive as to prevent these elites from enlisting the support of
outside forces, or indeed of their own ethnic constituents in the countryside,
in order to increase their leverage on the Court. Although the Court was
sufficiently receptive to ethnic pressures to allow bargaining, parleys and
petitions, it also proved obdurate enough on specific issues to invite violence or threats of violence against its protégés in government.

In short, the methods of oligarchical control adopted by the Palace were
permissive enough to make possible the mobilization of ethnic interests,
yet never so tolerant as to allow the representatives of either group to
gain effective control over the system. Part of the animus entertained by
each ethnic group against the other was in time deflected against the
Crown.

By early 1965 the polarization of ethnic feelings threatened to deteriorate
into open violence. At this point two possible courses of action were open
to the Court: Either to follow a policy of "ethnic disengagement" through
popular elections, or else operate a further limitation of governmental
and administrative authority and resolutely assert the primacy of

I

monarchical powers. While the first raised the possibility of further ethnic violence in the countryside, the second could well have provoked an equally violent reaction against the Crown. As it happened the Palace opted for the worst possible course: having at first decided to hold legislative elections, thus making it possible for the Hutu to gain a solid majority in the National Assembly, the Mwami almost immediately thereafter proceeded to deny the victors the opportunity to make good their claims to power. In July 1965, shortly after the elections, the Mwami publicly indicated that "although it was not (his) intention to rescussitate certain obsolete customs, (he) refused to subscribe to a subterfuge of language that would deprive (him) of all control, of all authority, and of all possibility to extend (his) protection to (his) subjects."[47] Thus, no sooner had an alternative structure of legitimacy been set up than the Crown immediately proceeded to reduce it to a sham, at the same time dispelling all possible doubts as to where, from now on, power was to lie.

What otherwise might seem like an inexplicable attitude on the part of the Court becomes less of an enigma once we remind ourselves of the extraordinarily improvised character of the decisions made by the throne; of the absence of clearly-defined centres of power around the Mwami; and of certain unforeseen developments that took place shortly after the elections. As noted earlier, the *ganwa* certainly had vested interest in perpetuating the situation of oligarchical control in existence prior to the elections. Yet none of them seemed to have realized the implications of a possible Hutu victory at the polls. If they did, their counsels must not have been taken very seriously by Mwambutsa. Only after realizing the extent of the Hutu victory, and, more specifically, only after realizing the implications of the inflammatory speech delivered by Gervais Nyangoma—a Hutu civil servant of left-wing proclivities who had once served as *Directeur Général* in the Prime Minister's Office—did it suddenly dawn upon the Palace that, in Nyangoma's words, "a new party, a new economy, and a new State" might indeed come about as a result of the triumphant showing of the Hutu.[48] This, however, neither Mwambutsa nor his courtiers were prepared to accept. At this point the stage was set for a trial of strength between the Crown and the Hutu leadership.

The explosion came on October 18, 1965, when a group of Hutu army and gendarmerie officers, acting hand in hand with some civilian Hutu elites, unsuccessfully tried to take over the royal Palace, presumably as the first step toward the establishment of a Hutu Republic. Even though the coup failed to achieve its long-run objectives, it can best be described, in Gilles Bimazubute's words, as a "coup partiellement manqué".[49] The insurgents came as near to attaining their immediate political goals as if they had actually succeeded. Although they failed in their attempt to forcefully abolish the monarchy, the "whiff of grapeshot" was enough to persuade the Mwami at once to flee the country. With Mwambutsa in Switzerland, and the Prime Minister, Léopold Biha, temporarily hospitalized in Belgium for treatment of injuries received in the course of the attempted take-over, the kingdom was literally without a king, and with only a semblance of a government. Moreover, after the summary execu-

tion of virtually every Hutu leader of any standing, exactly ten days after
the abortive coup, the system was, for all intents and purposes, purged of
all meaningful opposition. Not until November 20 did the Mwami restore
the Biha government, momentarily suspended during the emergency; yet
there was really no government to be reinstated. The army and the
bureaucracy had taken the law into their own hands. Since the wounded
Prime Minister was physically incapable of discharging his functions, the
Mwami at first tried to reign and rule from a distance, only to discover the
shortcoming of government by remote control. Partly for this reason, but
mainly because the attractions of power no longer matched the enticements
of life in Europe, he decided on March 24, 1966 to issue a royal decree
entrusting to Prince Charles, his heir apparent, "special powers to coordinate and control the activities of government and the Secretariats of
State". By then it was clear that the Mwami did not wish to return.

From a ruling monarchy too ephemeral to really assert its rule, the
system, moved back into an almost total political void. By default, as it
were, power passed into the hands of a mixed assemblage of army officers,
civil servants and youth leaders, most of them of Tutsi extraction; more
than ever the conduct of government became a matter of improvisation. It
is against this background of institutional vacuousness, at times verging on
anarchy, that one must view the fresh rivalries, intrigues and manoeuvrings
which this situation at once released among the new set of aspirants.

THE POLITICS OF SUCCESSION: FROM NOMINAL MONARCHY TO ARMY RULE

The crisis of succession inaugurated by Mwambutsa's precipitous flight
to Europe brought to a head a crisis of legitimacy that had been in the
making ever since the Mwami decided to reign and rule. We have seen how,
in trying to restore legitimacy to the Crown, first through the application
of a proper ethnic dosage of governmental posts, then through an overt
and categorical assertion of his "traditional" prerogatives, Mwambutsa
was led into situations which violated the very values which he was
supposed to uphold. The abortive coup of October 1965 dramatically
revealed the loss of legitimacy incurred by the monarchy among the Hutu
elites; by then however, the Mwamiship had also suffered considerable discredit among the Tutsi elites. The value of the monarchy for the Tutsi
elites, was function of its perceived utility in furthering their own ethnic
self-interests. As it happened the monarchy served as a kind of "trip wire"
device, setting off the explosion that caused the shell-shocked Mwambutsa
to seek refuge in Switzerland, destroyed the Hutu elites as a political
force, and at the same time enabled their Tutsi opponents to move into the
breach. The resultant breakdown of authority, together with the sudden
disintegration of the power structures built around the throne, provided
the Tutsi elites with a unique opportunity to redefine the position of the
Crown in the political system, and to invest it with a new conception of
legitimacy: by October, 1965, the aim was no longer to settle for the
monarchy as the lesser of two evils but to convert it into a positive
institutional asset for the furtherance of Tutsi interests.

The transfer of the Crown from Mwambutsa to his son, Prince Charles Ndizeye—formalized by the ceremonies of September 1, 1966—expressed an attempt at a total restructuring not only of the monarchy but of society as a whole, with the Crown intended to serve as the most important supportive symbol behind this task of national renovation. This, however, proved infinitely more arduous than had been anticipated by the "king-makers". For one thing they had to contend with the residual opposition of the old *ganwa* elements, whose interests were inextricably linked to Mwambutsa's claims to the monarchy; in addition, they apparently under-estimated the capacity of the "new" monarchy to generate its own power base once its *de jure* legitimacy had been secured. Thus as the Mwamiship painfully negotiated its way into a new era, the pattern of conflict created by the circumstances of the succession was curiously reminiscent of the rivalries generated by the approach of independence.

The difficulties involved in this process of institutional reconversion are best understood in the light of the changing definition of the ethnic context in which it occurred. The contest between Hutu and Tutsi, as we have seen, was not only a contest between themselves but a kind of game being played against the limitations imposed by the Court. During the initial phase of the contest each group tended to evaluate its chances of success against the other in terms of its ability to influence the decisions of the Court. With the elimination of the Hutu elites, however, following the abortive coup of October, 1965, what until then had looked like a triangular contest evolved into an increasingly polarized field of tension in which the key protagonists were the Mwami and his elder courtiers on the one hand, and the Mwami's son and his young Tutsi (and *ganwa*) supporters on the other. Although at first neither Mwambutsa nor his entourage had seriously considered the possibility of an unconditional surrender, in the end they had no choice but to reliquish power—Mwambutsa to his son, and the "king's men" to the new "king-makers". With the benefit of hindsight it is difficult to see how it could have been otherwise: not only did Mwambutsa lack the power necessary to reassert his rule (assuming that this was really his intention and not his courtiers'); the conditions of ethnic stalemate which until then had precluded any meaningful cooperation among the Westernized elites against the Crown were no longer present, at least at the elite level. The situation was made to order for the new generation "king-makers".

Though predominantly of Tutsi origins, the "king-makers" were in fact much more diversified, ethnically, socially, and politically than the fore-going might suggest. Among the civilian elites the main line of cleavage ran between the Tutsi-Hima and Tutsi-Abanyaraguru on the one hand, and the younger *ganwa* elements of Bezi origins on the other (the latter represented by Leon Ndenzako, Mwambutsa's son-in-law and Provincial Governor of Kitega; Joseph Mbazumutima and Gaspard Nkeshimana). Unlike the old *ganwa* group who would have been content to restore things as they were, these younger elements had some interest in economic and social modernization; while the former tended to distrust the young "hotheads" in the army and the civil service the latter seemed more willing to get along, if not go along, with the "Young Turks". In short, these younger generations of *ganwa* saw a distinct advantage in dissociating themselves from the stigma of the old monarchy; yet they also realized the opportunities offered by the investiture of the Prince: a new structure of power might be erected around the throne which would enable them to make good their traditional claims to authority.

Although the non-*ganwa* were generally in agreement on the need to limit the powers of the Crown, even among them certain major differences of attitude could be discerned. Among those who were the least favourable to the perpetuation of the monarchy as a form of government the youth leaders were certainly the most vocal. They also stood as a group apart because of their pronounced radicalism and because their ideology was and still is typically structured along "mobilization" lines. Another group was represented by those junior civil servants who served as *directeurs généraux* in various ministries before and after the coup. Though deeply critical of the methods and style of the *ancien régime* they felt that their authority would continue to depend in large part on their ability to manipulate the symbols of kingship. Their aim was to extract from the symbols of Mwamiship the sanctions that would give legitimacy to their modernist aspirations. Finally there were the army men—the young army officers who, however ruthlessly, managed to restore a semblance of order to the kingdom after the events of October 1965.

Although the overwhelming majority of army officers were and still are of Tutsi origins, until then the troops were predominantly Hutu. So far from being a monolithic entity, socially and ethnically undifferentiated, the Burundi army, like most other African armies, comprises within itself a variety of factions, clans and ethnic interests, all of which have contributed to shape the political leanings of its officers as well as their responsiveness to the political environment.

As long as the army understood its role to be that of a docile and primarily decorative instrument in the hands of the Mwami its tendency was to align itself with the Royal Establishment; but when the circumstances made it necessary for the army to serve as an instrument of political coercion its relationship with the Crown underwent a major change: not only was the army forced into the unenviable role of a repressive agent, causing Hutu troops to move against Hutu civilians; the state of near paralysis created by Mwambutsa's flight to Europe, coupled with his subsequent decision to recruit West German mercenaries for the establishment of a personal militia, were powerful inducements for the officers, if not as yet to abolish the monarchy, at least to lend their support to the civilians to bring a new dynasty to the throne.

If the government which came to power on July 8, 1966, represented a fairly accurate cross-section of the new elites already described, the personality of the Prince—his very youth and apparent dynamism—seemed wholly in keeping with the style of the new regime. For the time being the incipient tensions between the government and the Palace were concealed by the enthusiasm for the change. Yet behind this apparent solidarity a relentless manoeuvring for position was already going on among the civilian elites. The manoeuvring suggested the ancestral feuds which in the old days pitted the young *bami* and members of their entourage against dissident chiefs. The youthfulness of the Prince and his consequent obligations to the "king-makers" created a situation ripe for social and political intrigue. His position recalled the state of affairs which Hans Meyer witnessed in 1912, when Mwambutsa's predecessor on the throne, Mutaga, then only a year older than the Prince, found himself utterly dependent on the princes of the blood. "Since the present king is a youngster," Meyer wrote, "approximately 20 years of age, and totally lacking in will-power, he is entirely under the influence of some of his elder brothers who live in the vicinity (of the royal capital), and who, along with their followers, are the true rulers of Urundi."[50] In 1966, however, the "true rulers of Burundi" were no longer the *ganwa* but a mixed consistory of remarkably youthful, Westernized elites. Their psychological commitment to the symbols of kingship was far from unconditional, and their power infinitely greater than that which the old *ganwa* once possessed. Strange as it may seem, the behaviour of the Court (i.e. of the Prince and the younger *ganwa*) in 1966 reflected little awareness of the changes that had taken place since the days of Mutaga.

By resurrecting the powers which the civil servants and the army officers had recently taken away from the Court, the latter paved the way for its own undoing. By mid-August tensions were becoming apparent between the Prince's men represented by Leon Ndenzako and Remy Nsengyumva, and the government. When in September of the same year, the Mwami tried to force the issue, first by insisting upon the resignation of the Foreign Minister, Pie Masumbuko, and subsequently by creating three new Secretariats of State for the Army, the Gendarmerie and Justice—which, of course, implied a corresponding transfer of jurisdiction from the government to the Palace—a definitive parting of the ways seemed to have come.

The trial of strength between the Palace and the government stemmed from the same kind of open defiance of the executive powers of the cabinet which occurred in 1963, when Mwambutsa and his "men" deliberately tried to arrogate to themselves the constitutional powers entrusted to the government. By then, however, the army was unprepared to pay the costs of renewed royal intervention, unwilling to abdicate its share of power to the Court, and understandably reticent to be once again forced into the role of a repressive instrument at the disposal of the Palace. Rather than allowing the Court to undermine their corporate solidarity, directly or indirectly, the army officers decided to bring the game to a close. On November 28, as the Mwami journeyed to Congo-Kinshasa as President Mubutu's guest at the first anniversary celebration of Mobutu's military takeover, Micombero deposed the Mwami and proclaimed the birth of the Republic. Mwami Ntare and his men—or should the order read Ntare's men and the Mwami?—apparently fell prey to a series of miscalculations. They miscalculated their chances of winning out against the combined strength of the army and the bureaucracy. They miscalculated the amount of support they could reasonably expect from the masses.

Above all, they overlooked the determination of the army to strike at monarchical institutions once these appeared to have out-lived their usefulness.

MWAMISHIP IN PERSPECTIVE: AN OVERVIEW OF "SYSTEM TRANSFORMATIONS"

On the basis of the model outlined in Table II the Burundi monarchy appears to have gone through roughly six different phases of "system transformations" between 1850 and 1966. The transformations have been (1) from a hierarchical (i.e. centralized) to a pyramidal (i.e. decentralized) monarchy (1850–1958); (2) from a pyramidal monarchy largely under Bezi control to a constitutional monarchy (1958–1962); (3) from a constitutional to an "oligarchical" monarchy in which substantial control was vested in the hands of *ganwa* elements operating behind the throne (1962–1965); (4) from an "oligarchical" to a "ruling" monarchy in which the king reigned and ruled (July 1965–October 1965); (5) from a "ruling" monarchy to a "nominal" monarchy, with control theoretically exercized by the king from abroad but in fact by army officers and civil servants on the spot (October 1965–July 1966); (6) from a short-lived attempt at centralized monarchical control (under Ntare) to the abolition of the monarchy both as a symbol and as a form of government (July 1966–November 1966).

Phase 1, involving a shift from a hierarchical to a pyramidal system, requires little elaboration: the emergence of autonomous centres of power, in the form of ganwaships, and the concomitant restraints imposed on royal powers, has already been discussed at length here and elsewhere. Phase 2, leading to the emergence of a constitutional monarchy, was in a sense the logical outcome of the environmental challenges that had arisen in Phase 1: although the effect of a party competition has been to institutionalize the Bezi-Batare conflict, on surface the struggle for power between the PDC (Batare) and the Uprona (Bezi) was being conducted according to the rules laid by the Belgian administration. The Mwami, in other words, was expected to act as a constitutional monarch. The substitution of ethnic for *ganwa* rivalries led to Phases 3 and 4. The main stimulus behind the intervention of the Crown between 1962 and 1965 originated from the total deadlock of governmental institutions caused by the sudden politicization of ethnic ties. The abortive coup of October 1965, while testifying to a major reorientation of environmental challenges, led to Phase 5—to a situation where the king and his courtiers now operated by remote control (from Geneva). By now, however, the dialectic of intergroup competition produced a new crystallization of interests, reflective of a struggle for power between the Mwami and the old *ganwa*, on the one hand, and the younger generations of *ganwa* and Tutsi bureaucrats on the other, the latter seeking to gain access into the system through the installation of a new dynasty. This led, in July 1966, to the inception of Phase 6, marked by the abdication of Mwambutsa and the accession to the throne of Charles Ndizeye. The next and final phase of the dialectical process saw the emergence of a new pattern of

TABLE II

MONARCHIAL SYSTEM TRANSFORMATIONS IN BURUNDI (1850–1966)

Chronology	Principal Sources of Legitimacy	Environmental Challenges	Monarchical Responses	Political Outcomes	System Transformation
Phase I: 1850–1958	Mwamiship	Ganwa Rivalries (Bezi v. Batare)	Coalition-building with selective ganwa support	Feuding and Factionalism	From Hierarchical to Pyramidal Monarchy
Phase II: 1958–1962	Parties & Mwamiship	Party Struggle (Uprona v. PDC)	Withdrawal	Displacement of chiefs (ganwa) accompanied by emergence of new elites	Constitutional Monarchy
Phase III: 1962–July '65	Parliament & Mwamiship	Ethnicity: Hutu v. Tutsi	Limited Intervention	Ethnic stalemate in party & Parliament	Dispersed control Oligarchical monarchy
Phase IV: July '65– Oct. '65	Parliament & Mwamiship	Ethnicity: Hutu elites v. Mwami and the Court	Overt Intervention	Trial of Strength between Hutu deputies & Palace leading to abortive Hutu-sponsored coup of Oct. '65 and flight of Mwami to Europe	Centralized control: Ruling Monarchy
Phase V: Oct. '65 July '66	Army, bureaucracy and Mwamiship	Ethnicity: Tutsi elites v. Mwami and the Court	Government by remote control (from Geneva)	Effective Tutsi control of government and administration; investiture of heir apparent (Ntare) as Mwami, followed by mixed, civilian-military rule	Remote control: Nominal Monarchy
Phase VI: July '66–	Army, government	Sectionalism: Mwami and younger ganwa (Bezi) v. Tutsi elites, civilian & military	Coalition-building with ganwa support	Trial of strength between government & palace	Attempts at centralized control: Abolition of Monarchy in Nov. '66

conflict between the army and the bureaucracy on the one hand, and the Prince and the younger *ganwa* on the other, leading in November 1966 to the abdication of the monarchy.

The loss of legitimacy suffered by the Crown was the logical outcome of the institutional transformations it underwent in its attempt to cope with environmental challenges, both internal and external. We have seen how the exigences of ethnic strife caused the monarchy to redefine its position in the political system, and in time to transform itself into a ruling monarchy. By then popular conceptions of monarchical legitimacy were no longer reconcilable with monarchical despotism. The trend towards royal autocracy was widely regarded as a violation of both modern and traditional conceptions of legitimacy.

Ironically, while monarchical centralization did cause substantial disaffection towards the symbols and institution of kingship, at no point in its recent evolution did the monarchy acquire a sufficient concentration of effective power to make possible the implementation of modernizing objectives. "Modernization," writes Huntington, "frequently requires not only a shift in power from regional, aristocratic, and religious groups to central secular national institutions, but also the concentration of authority in a single individual within these institutions."[51] Despite the initial trend toward centralization, at no time since independence did the Burundi monarchy meet these conditions. The fragile edifice built around the Court could scarcely serve as an instrument of modernization: its institutional base was virtually non-existent; its efficiency limited by the very nature of its clientelistic underpinnings; and its political orientation overwhelmingly geared toward the preservation of vested interests. By resurrecting the claims of the old *ganwa* in order to counteract the conflicting demands of the Westernized elites, Hutu and Tutsi, Mwambutsa sacrificed the requirements of modernization to the imperative of stability; by falling prey to the enticements of the younger *ganwa* Ntare reasserted the primacy of family and kinship ties over the secular claims of the army and the bureaucracy, in effect sacrificing both stability and modernization to the demands of his blood-brothers. Ultimately the dilemma could only resolve itself at the expense of the monarchy.

The final act in the unfolding drama of the monarchy also marks the opening of the most radical of all system transformations ever experienced by Burundi society. It began with a helicopter flight, and ended with a regicide. There is no room here for a detailed discussion of the circumstances surrounding the return of ex-king Ntare to Burundi, in March 1972, followed by his subsequent execution in Gitega on April 29. Suffice it to note that it was as an ordinary citizen that Ntare had asked to return to Burundi; by then the monarchy had long ceased to exist as an institution. But if the survival of the monarchy was no longer at issue, ethnic conflict was even more of a reality now than ever before. As it became evident that neither the government nor the army had the capacity to resolve the impending crisis, Ntare must have seen in this situation a unique opportunity to stage a come-back. Just how, exactly, he intended to carry out his plans, through what tactical alliances, and whether or not he actually entertained the thought of restoring the monarchy, will probably never be known. Assuming that he did intend to restore the Mwamiship, subsequent events soon demonstrated how illusory his hopes were.

His return to Burundi was negotiated between President Idi Amin of Uganda and Micombero shortly after his arrival in Kampala on March 21. On the strength of the verbal and written assurances given by Micombero, Amin allowed Ntare to return to Bujumbura on March 30. No sooner had the ex-king's helicopter landed in Bujumbura, however, than he was immediately taken to Gitega under military escort and placed under house arrest. The news of his death reached Bujumbura via an official radio broadcast announcing that the ex-king had been killed in the course of rebel attacks against his residence. Later, however, Micombero admitted that he had been tried for plotting against the government and executed on the night of the attacks, on April 29. Official allegations were that Ntare tried to invade the country with the aid of foreign mercenaries.

That Ntare happened to be shot on the very same night that the Hutu rebellion started, as a prelude to the most appalling bloodbath ever recorded in the annals of an independent African state, represents the ultimate nemesis of the Burundi monarchy. If the news of his death caused so little commotion this is because the monarchy had become utterly irrelevant both as a symbol and an institution. However instrumental it may have been in the past in mitigating ethnic conflict, by the time the crisis erupted it had long outlived its usefulness. Although the threats imputed to citizen Charles Ndizeye must have had something to do with his status as ex-king, there was in fact very little he could do to reactivate his claims to traditional authority among Tutsi or Hutu. Neither group had any reason to give the monarchy another chance. Ntare's assassination was not so much a settling of accounts between monarchists and republicans as a mere precaution, if not an after-thought. As he lay dying, in his old rococo-style residence, a far more serious settling of accounts was already taking place, in the form of an ethnic strife of unprecedented proportions, nourished by the very same forces which the monarchy had once tried to contain. Regicide at this point was only a footnote in the history of ethnocide.

NOTES

1 The expression is borrowed from Mgr. Gorgu, *Face au Royaume Hamite du Ruanda: Le Royaume Frère de l'Urundi* (Bruxelles: 1938).
2 See David Apter, *The Political Kingdom in Uganda* (Princeton, 1967), p. 20 ff.
3 *Ibid.*, p. 24.
4 J. Vansina, *Oral Tradition: A Study in History Methodology*, trans. by H. M. Wright (Chicago: 1961), p. 166.
5 From a personal communication to J. M. Derscheid (Derscheid collection).
6 Vansina, *op. cit., loc. cit.*
7 Max Gluckman, *Custom and Conflict in Africa* (Oxford, 1963).
8 E. Shils and M. Young, "The Meaning of the Coronation", *Sociological Review*, Vol. 1 (1953), p. 79.

9   G. Simmel, *Conflict*, trans. by K. H. Wolf (Glencoe, Ill.: 1955), p. 98.
10   See R. Albert, "Women of Burundi: A Study of Social Values", in Denise Paulme, *Women of Tropical Africa*, (Berkeley and Los Angeles, 1963), p. 180; Albert Trouwborst, "L'organization politique et l'accord de clientèle au Burundi", *Anthropologica*, Vol. IV, No. 1 (1962), pp. 10–43, and "L'organization politique en tant que système d'echange au Burundi", *Ibid.*, Vol. III, No. 1 (1961), pp. 1–17.
11   Ethel Albert, " 'Rhetoric', 'Logic' and 'Poetics' in Burundi: Culture Patterning of Speech Behaviour", *American Anthropologist*, Special Issue, Winter 1964–65, pp. 39.
12   See J. Keuppens, *L'Urundi Ancien et Moderne* (mimeo., n.p., 1959).
13   Samuel Huntington, "Political Development and Political Decay", *World Politics*, Vol. XVII, No. 3 (1965), p. 419.
14   *Rapport sur l'Administration Belge du Ruanda-Urundi* (Bruxelles: 1921), passim.
15   See J. Vansina, "Notes sur l'Histoire du Burundi", Aequatoria No. 1 (1961), pp. 1–10.
16   R. Nicholas, "Structures of Politics in the Villages of Southern Asia", in B. S. Cohn and M. Singer eds., *Structure and Change in Indian Societies* (Chicago, 1968), p. 264.
17   *Ibid.*
18   Janet M. Bujra, "Factions and Factionalism: A Reappraisal" (unpublished MS., 1970), p. 22.
19   For further information see J. Vansina "Notes sur l'Histoire du Burundi", *op. cit.*
20   Audrey Richards, "Social Mechanisms for the Transfer of Political Rights in some African Tribes", *The Journal of the Royal Anthropological Institute*, Vol. 90, part 1 and 2 (Jan.-Dec. 1960), p. 143.
21   For further information on the early phase of the colonial period see Roger Louis, *Ruanda-Urundi: 1884–1919* (Oxford, 1963); also Pierre Ryckmans, *Une page d'Histoire coloniale: L'occupation allemande dans l'Urundi* (Bruxelles, 1953).
22   Roger Louis, *op. cit.*, p. 115.
23   See Robert Schmidt, *Abatare et Abezi* (typescript, Kitega?, 1953; Derscheid collection).
24   In 1904, for example, a year after Von Beringe's devastating campaign against Mwezi Kisabo, Resident Von Grauwert toured the interior and reportedly "made it a point to ask the Hutu with whom he met what their relation was with Kisabo. 'Everywhere,' wrote Von Grauwert, 'there was a real awareness that he was their real Sultan . . . Everywhere it came to light that they feared subjection to the greatly increasing power of the smaller chiefs (Kilima, for example)' "; cited in R. Louis, *op. cit.*, p. 119.
25   *Rapport sur l'Administration du Ruanda-Urundi, 1925* (Bruxelles, 1926), p. 63.
26   Pierre Ryckmans, "Le Problème politique au Ruanda-Urundi", *Congo*, Vol. 1, No. 3 (1925), p. 410.
27   *Ibid.*
28   For the full text of the Voisin directives, see *Historique et Chronologie du Ruanda* (Kabgaye?, n.d.), p. 25.
29   By 1959 the Bezi controlled 17 chiefdoms out of a total of 37, and the Batare 9; but the total area controlled by the Bezi was more than twice the size of that held by the Batare. Moreover a number of chiefs and subchiefs whose origins were neither Bezi nor Batare were in fact committed to the Bezi cause. For further information see R. Lemarchand, *Rwanda and Burundi*: (London and New York, 1970), p. 309 ff.
30   A. Trouwborst, "L'organisation politique et l'accord de clientèle au Burundi" *Anthropologica*, IV, 1 (1962), p. 35 ff.
31   *Rapport Annual, Urundi* (Kitega 1946), p. 53.
32   R. Schmidt, *Abatare et Abezi* (typescript, Kitega?, 1953).
33   *Ibid.*
34   R. Schmidt, *Repercussions politiques de la vie privee de Mwambutsa* (typescript, Kitega?, 1953; Derscheid collection).
35   Meaning, roughly, "the Mwami's followers", a term used specifically in reference to Mwezi Kisabo's "loyal supporters".

36   The CED formula provided for an appointed advisory council representative of local interests, and a chief appointed by the administration after consultation with the councillors. Both were in fact closely supervised by the European administration. See Guy Baumer, *Les Centres Extra-Coutumiers au Congo Belge* (Paris, 1939). Curiously enough, this effort to revive the CEC as an administrative device came about at a time when Belgian administrators in the Congo were almost unanimous in recognizing the failure of the experiment.

37   For a descriptive account of party politics in Burundi before independence see Jean Ghislain, *Chronologie Politique du Burundi* (mimeo., n.p., n.d.); see also Michel Lechat, *Le Burundi Politique* (Bujumbura, n.d.).

38   The phrase is from a PDC tract entitled *Le Climat Politique à la Veille des Elections* (mimeo., Bujumbura?, 1960).

39   J. Ghislain, *op. cit.*

40   See J. Bujra, "Factions and Factionalism: A Reappraisal", *op. cit.*, p. 24.

41   For further elaboration of the factors leading to ethnic polarization see my *Rwanda and Burundi*, *op. cit.*, p. 343 ff.

42   It is sadly ironic that Mirerekano, a Huto who, through his writings, did more than any other modern day Murundi politician to legitimize the Mwamiship, was later shot for his alleged complicity in a plot against the monarchy. His *Mbwire Gito Cane . . . (Listen, my son . . .)*, though written in the form of a paean to the monarchy, represents the closest approximation we have of what the symbols of Mwamiship meant for the Hutu masses. For further information see my *Rwanda and Burundi*, *op. cit.*, p. 306 ff.

43   Anon., "Le Burundi à la recherche d'une stabilité", *Présence Africaine*, No. 47 (1963), p. 237.

44   Samuel Huntington, "The political Modernization of Traditional Monarchies", *Daedalus* (Summer 1966), pp. 763–88. "In an *oligarchical* monarchy the monarch reigns but does not rule; yet the monarchy remains the principal source of legitimacy in the political system . . . In a *ruling* monarchy the Crown is the principal source of legitimacy and the king rules as well as reigns . . . The efficient powers of government may be shared with other institutions, but in all cases the monarch also plays an active, efficient political role in the governing process", *Ibid.*, p. 763–4.

45   Albert Trouwborst, "L'organisation politique et l'accord de clientèle au Burundi", *op. cit.*, p. 33.

46   Max Weber, *The Theory of Social and Economic Organization* (New York, 1957), p. 341.

47   Quoted in *Infor-Burundi*, July 1965.

48   *Ibid.*

49   G. Bizamubute, *Remarques Africaines*, Nov. 3, 1965.

50   Hans Meyer, *Die Barundi* (Leipzig, 1916), *passim*.

51   Samuel Huntington, *Political Order in Changing Societies* (New Haven and London: 1968), p. 156.

PART III

ETHNIC KINGSHIPS: SWAZILAND AND LESOTHO

4

THE NGWENYAMA OF SWAZILAND:
The Dynamics of Political Adaptation

Christian P. Potholm

Seen against the backdrop of turmoil and violent upheaval experienced by most other African monarchies, the recent history of the Swazi King emerges as a story of success. On April 25, 1967, Sobhuza II, Ngwenyama (king) of the Swazi, was sworn in as King of Swaziland, and on September 6, 1968, when the kingdom formally recovered its independence, Sobhuza added to his traditional titles that of Head of State. His party, the Imbokodvo, controls every seat but three in the House of Assembly; his personal selections occupy every seat in the Senate; and his handpicked choice, Prince Makhosini, is the Prime Minister. All Swazi national land and mineral wealth is vested in the King's person in trust for the Swazi nation. From all appearances, the legitimacy of the Crown remains beyond challenge.

How this traditional Swazi authority became King of all Swaziland rather than just the Paramount Chief of the Swazis, and emerged as the prime mover of the entire country when the rest of the political landscape of Africa is strewn with the wreckage of traditional rulers is a complex and convoluted story.[1] The success of the Ngwenyama commands attention not only because of its continuing influence upon the course of politics in Southern Africa but because of the amendments it offers to much of the current theorizing on the relationships between traditionalism and modernity.[2] Examples of situations where traditional authorities were able to use the intrusion of modernity to bolster or at least maintain their positions in the existing political system are not totally uncommon in Africa;[3] there have been few political successes of the magnitude registered by the Ngwenyama, and few as enduring. The Kabaka of Buganda, the Sardauna of Sokoto, the Mwamis of Rwanda and Burundi, the Moro Naba of the Mossi and the Litunga of Barotseland were all traditional rulers who, after some initial successes, failed in their attempts to attain, or retain, hegemony over the larger political systems or subsystems of which they were a part. With the qualified exception of Ethiopia, Swaziland is the only independent state of sub-Saharan Africa where the status of the monarchy seems assured.

In view of the formidable constellation of forces arrayed against the throne in the early '60s, survival of the monarchy appears all the more impressive. The Ngwenyama saw his position threatened, first, by the

British colonial authorities, determined as they were to institute a one-man, one-vote constitution which would have presumably undermined the centrality of his role and political efficacy; second, by a series of Pan-African-oriented political parties which would have made him a mere figurehead in the newly-emergent polity; and third, by the European settler oligarchy who would have liked to use the prestige and symbolic credibility of the monarchy to entrench themselves in the commanding heights of economic and political power within Swaziland and Southern Africa.

In the face of such opposition, the Ngwenyama saw his options clearly. He could either challenge these political forces on their own terms or he could fade back into tribal remotemess, enjoying the trappings but not the substances of national political authority. Sobhuza II chose the former course and, in a series of triumphant manoeuvres, he held off those members of the British administration who threatened him, worked in consort with the Euorpean settlers to crush his "modern" political adversaries and, ultimately, turned on his ertwhile allies to emerge as the central political figure in Swaziland, enlarging the scope and power of the monarchy until it embraced the entire country.

In order to explain the nature and extent of Sobhuza's triumph attention must be drawn to the following set of variables: (1) the position of the institution of kingship in Swazi political life, and the underlying social and economic values radiating therefrom; (2) the personality and operational skills of Sobhuza; and (3) the political ecology of the arena in which the struggle occurred. From these perspectives one can perhaps better identify which of the various situational "givens" made possible the survival and indeed the reinforcement of the monarchy, which hindered its thrust, and which ultimately contributed to its overwhelming political success. Only by separating out these various strands can one establish the relevance of the Swazi phenomenon for an understanding of political systems elsewhere in Africa.

HISTORICAL PERSPECTIVES

Some historical overview is required in order to see the institution of Swazi kingship in its proper frame of reference with regard to the Swazi community and the larger, national political arena. As is the case of many of the Bantu-speaking groups of Southern Africa, the early history of the Swazis is somewhat obscure.[4] It now appears that members of the Nguni cluster moved south from central Africa reaching southern Africa during the fifteenth and sixteenth centuries. One of these groups, centred around the Nkosi-Dlamini clans, gradually expanded during the seventeenth century in the area around Delagoa Bay in present-day Mozambique. Led by a vigorous chieftain, Ngwane III, this group coalesced into a larger unit and became known as *Bantfu Baka Ngwane*, the people of Ngwane. They eventually crossed the Lubombo escarpment and entered the area now known as Swaziland. Two kings, Ndungunya and Sobhuza I, attempted to consolidate their hold over this area but their position was always tenuous owing to the strength of the neighbouring Zulu and Ndwandwe.

Faced with increasing pressure on their southern borders, the people of Ngwane moved north about 1820, defeating in the process and subsequently incorporating within their own political system the local Sotho and Nguni populations. Despite the successes of Sobhuza's warriors, they avoided pitched battles with the stronger Zulu forces who occasionally appeared and only once, in 1838, did they defeat a Zulu army already weakened by skirmishes with the Boers. Sobhuza died the next year and was succeeded by Mswati in 1840. Mswati (1840–1868), perhaps the greatest of the Swazi warrior kings, gave his name to his people and to their language (siSwati) and further expanded their nation. He introduced the highly effective Zulu age-set system (called by the Swazis lifbutfho) and many of their military tactics, spurred political integration and enhanced the position of the monarchy. Under his leadership, the Swazi warriors ranged far and wide, defeating such peoples as the Pedi and the Shangana. Nevertheless, the Swazis were still subject to Zulu incursions and after a particularly vicious Zulu raid in 1854, Mswati appealed to the British Agent General in Natal, Sir Theophilus Shepstone, for protection. The British were unwilling to take on additional responsibility in Southern Africa although Shepstone did use his influence to curtail the Zulus.

Mswati was the last of the truly independent Swazi kings for during his reign the situation in Southern Africa changed markedly owing to the expansion of the British in the cape and the formation of the various Boer republics. In the words of T. V. Bulpin:

It was the European whose footprint, as the Swazis say, was the footprint of the elephant, for it remained in the ground.[5]

In addition to the encroaching European powers, individual Europeans soon appeared and sought grazing, mining, manufacturing and commercial concessions from the local African rulers.

Upon the death of Mswati in 1868 and the murder of his twelve-year-old successor, Ludvonga, Mbandzeni (1874–1889) became king and during his reign, the Swazis were reduced to international pawns. Concessions for mining, manufacturing and commerce were extended to Europeans and covered the Swazi area, often three or four deep until over half the land of present-day Swaziland was alienated, reserved for the exclusive use of Europeans. Further, Great Britain was unwilling to protect the Swazis from either the settlers or from the Boer republics and signed a series of conventions with the South African Republic in 1881 and 1884. Although these agreements guaranteed the "independence" of the Swazis, they actually allowed the South African Republic to incorporate three-quarters of the land initially claimed by the Swazis. Subsequent conventions acknowledged Boer control over the Swazis despite their vigorous but essentially peaceful objections. Boer hegemony was short-lived, however. Following the outbreak of the Anglo-Boer war in 1899, they withdrew and the Swazis were left to themselves until 1902. Upon the death of Bhunu (1894–1899), a period of internecine strife followed and the matter was not settled until the Queen Mother, and her son, Malunge, acted as regents for the young prince Mona who was to be crowned in 1921 as Sobhuza II.

K

With the conclusion of the Anglo-Boer war, Great Britain placed Swaziland under the juridiction of the provincial government of the Transvaal but after the Transvaal received self-government in 1906, the British assumed direct control over Swaziland as one of the three High Commission Territories in Southern Africa (along with Basutoland and the Bechuanaland Protectorate). Of considerable import for the future political development of Swaziland was the fact that for most of the next sixty years the British did not practice their classical form of indirect rule with the Swazis. Legislative and executive authority was vested in the High Commissioner for the three territories. However, since the post of High Commissioner was often simply a second hat worn by the British High Commissioner in the Union (and later, Republic) of South Africa, effective power actually devolved to each of the three Resident Commissioners.[6] Although episodic contact did occur between the traditional hierarchy and the European administration, the British colonial authority generally issued proclamations directly and enforced them by means of their own bureaucracy and a national police force. In effect, this meant that while being denied widespread participation in the colonial super-structure, neither the Ngwenyama nor his chiefs were sullied by too close or willing a cooperation with the British as Swaziland languished during the 1920s and 1930s.

It was not until 1944 and Proclamation No. 44 of that year that the Ngwenyama was given formal power "to issue to natives in Swaziland legally enforceable orders on a sizable number of subjects".[7] Even then, the Ngwenyama was not rescued from the limbo into which the events of the nineteenth and twentieth centuries has thrust the monarchy for it was not until proclamations Nos. 79, 80 and 81 of 1950 that the British government officially recognized the right of the Ngwenyama to appoint chiefs, to establish a system of Swazi courts (criminal jurisdiction had been with-drawn from Bhunu by the South African Republic and never returned) and to set up a Swazi National Treasury. Subsequent British policy toward the monarchy during the 1950s and 1960s was marked by some ambiguity. On one hand, some British officials such as the Resident Commissioner Brian (later Sir Brian) Marwick accepted the notion that the future lay with "modern" political forces and that in terms of meaning-ful political power, the monarchy would eventually be by-passed. At the same time, there were countervailing influences within the Colonial, Commonwealth relations and Foreign offices which sought to rehabilitate and support the Ngwenyama. R. P. Stevens has quite rightly pointed to the importance of this factor in providing the Ngwenyama with an opportunity to maximize his political advantages during these critical years.[8]

KINGSHIP IN TRADITIONAL SWAZI SOCIETY

During the decolonization struggle, then, the Ngwenyama was able to capitalize on the monarchy's tradition of independence and on differing British views as to the future of that monarchy. More important, Sobhuza

II had a most solid base of support within the Swazi nation. Despite the fact that the British referred to the Swazi leader as "Paramount Chief", in the eyes of the Swazis, he was always the Ngwenyama, or king. The Swazi monarchy was not as, for example, the Litunga of Barotseland, a recent creation but traced itself back through the reigns of twenty-five kings.[9] The long tradition of kingship was highly supportive to the Ngwenyama's struggle for political hegemony. If Sobhuza II has to contend with a host of opponents and hostile forces, he was nonetheless bolstered by the homogeneous ethnic composition of Swaziland and the pervasive hold of the traditional authority on that population. Presently there are over 400,000 Swazis in Swaziland and only 9,000 Europeans and 25,000 non-Swazi Africans and Eurafricans.

In our analysis of the traditional Swazi authority structures, we are most fortunate to have a wealth of detailed information on the role of the monarchy in traditional Swazi politics, the nature and scope of the political socialization process and the system of values which encouraged the cultural unity of the Swazi people.[10] Although most investigations of Swazi political life were completed in the 1930s and 1940s, they have been updated and offer a strikingly rich portrait of the traditional Swazi political system. We can thus speak with some assuredness about those factors in Swazi tribal life which seem to have influenced the course of politics in Swaziland. As matters turned out, the institutions, processes and values which had held the Swazis together through the vicissitudes of partition, occupation and colonial rule proved to be both persistent and highly resilient when confronted with the holistic thrust of modernity and the concomitant rise of numerous hostile political forces.

At the very heart of Swazi traditional life lies the institution of kingship which serves as the linch-pin of the entire socio-political system. From early in the nineteenth century the Ngwenyama has stood at the centre of the political system which was, and remains, a powerful, centralized monarchy with universal membership in the tribe through one's direct allegiance to the king. In this regard, the Swazi political system is close to that of the Zulu but differs markedly from those of the Xhosa, Pondo, Bemba and Ashanti where political participation at the tribal level and, indeed, membership in the tribe is predicated on allegiance to a local ruler who in turn pledges himself to the central political authority.[11] Because the Swazi monarchy permitted individuals to join the tribe and encouraged their participation in it, the traditional political system was endowed with extensive absorptive capabilities and provided the mechanisms for a continual process of systemic rejuvenation. In exchange for fealty to the Ngwenyama and the Ndlovukazi (or Queen Mother), new members of the tribe were entitled to their protection, the use of land and political participation. As will be indicated, this feature of Swazi traditional political life enabled the monarchy to extend its authority over non-Swazi Africans and Europeans alike during the 1960s and eventually, to re-absorb the "detribalized" Swazis who had temporarily renounced the traditional political structure.

For over two hundred years, the monarchy has been the central feature in the life of the Swazis and the Crown has remained the symbolic focal point of the nation. It provides the major symbolic referents for the Swazi masses and the element of cohesion so critical to the maintenance of that nation. The Ngwenyama is the "Lion", the "Sun", the "Milky Way". He is the repository of Swazi law and custom and a religious-magical figure. Although the Swazis believe in a "Great One" (*Mkhulumng Qande*), he is a supreme being far removed from the life of the nation.[12] As there is neither a religious class nor a sacred literature among the Swazis, it is the Ngwenyama who is the central character in the cosmic metaplay, linking the Swazis beyond the commonsensical world. He is the bringer of the life-giving rains, and the national welfare of the tribe is intrinsically tied up with his health. He cannot, for example, come in contact with a dead body, even that of a close relative.

In short, the Ngwenyama is the personification of the Swazi nation and its primary representative. Nowhere is this relationship seen more clearly than in the *Incwala*, the yearly ceremony which brings the Swazis together.[13] At this time, the people focus their attention on the king while he, in turn, draws his substance and strength from them. The *Incwala* is many things. It is a harvest celebration and a first-fruits ceremony. It is at one and the same time a metaphysical drama in which the line between the sacred and the profane is demarcated and a morality play. But most importantly, it is an act of political solidarity designed to perpetuate the glory of the Ngwenyama and reaffirm the unity of his people. There are no *Incwalas* during the minority of the king, and the Ngwenyama alone can begin and end the full ceremony. Of crucial importance is the activity on the fourth day of the so-called "big" *Incwala* when the Ngwenyama symbolically distrusts his Dlamini rivals for the throne and banishes them, along with all non-Swazis, from the royal kraal. Only his loyal subjects remain behind to revitalize the king and share in his renewed glory. The Ngwenyama is thus rejuvenated by his people and prepared to lead them in the coming year.

In terms of the political life of the nation, the importance of the Crown as a symbol of unity for all Swazis cannot be overlooked. Whereas many contemporary African political systems are characterized by a search for efficacious national symbols, the Crown in Swaziland has already demonstrated its functional utility during the nineteenth and twentieth centuries. Faced with considerable exogenous intrusions and pressures, the Swazis did not become a broken tribe, but retained their sense of nationhood and cultural identity by means of their attachment to the Crown. In fact, so strong was the people's attachment to the monarchy and to its symbols that in the first exercise of national voting in January 1964, 102 per cent of the eligible voters chose the symbol of the lion, the royal crest. Some have argued that traditional symbols inhibit political development and that over time the entire set of beliefs and values associated with traditional Swazi social and political life may well prove dysfunctional to the attainment of a modern, achievement-oriented society. At the same time, however, these traditional patterns have proven to be major sources of national unity to date. As Daryll Forde has written:

These may indeed appear, from one point of view—and one especially apparent to the outsider—to block obvious and important opportunities for general economic advance or social reorganizations; but from another, they can be seen as preserving patterns of activity and social relations which are felt by the people to be of intrinsic and over-riding value and so may in fact be indispensable to the preservation of their social cohesion and solidarity.[14]

In this study, we are less concerned with the long-term implications of such a traditional pattern of allegiance to national symbols than with their relevance to an understanding of the contemporary assertion of the monarchy. As the acknowledged leader of a recognized and cohesive cultural, linguistic and territorial entity, the Ngwenyama was aided in his fight for political hegemony by the existing levels of structural and value integration within the Swazi nation and its commitment to national symbols. From this tribal base, the Ngwenyama expanded the traditional Swazi political system to the entire country, encompassing the non-Swazi Africans and Europeans alike. This was no minor accomplishment for the forces opposed to his political power and the very nature of the modernization process placed significant obstacles in his path.

The Ngwenyama also stands at the apex of the social structure for the social order of Swaziland is directly conditioned by the institution of kingship. There is a rough hierarchy discernible in the more than seventy clans found in Swaziland, culminating with the royal Dlaminis at the top. Since the early migrations into what is now Swaziland, the Dlaminis have been the royal clan and they have enjoyed a monopoly over the lines of kingly succession. Yet, despite the ascriptive importance of one's lineage, it should be noted that this arrangement is ". . . neither precise nor static. While some clans have risen in rank through diplomacy or loyalty, others have been degraded through conquest or the treachery of their representatives".[15] Although the web of kinship is not immutably spun and there are substantial channels of social mobility and political advancement, social stratification continues to exist among the Swazis. During July 1968, for example, Polycarp Dlamini, Swazi Minister of Public Works and Communications, was accused of running over and killing a policeman while under the influence of drugs. His chief defence was that, despite his governmental standing, he was obligated to answer the summons of one Simanga Dlamini, his social superior, and had to drive her to the hospital in spite of his condition.[16]

Because the Ngwenyama is regarded as a special person, his belongings and pets, likewise, have special names.[17] He is expected to have more cattle than anyone else in the nation and the largest number of wives. His fields are the most productive and his generosity the most pronounced. All mineral wealth and all Swazi national land are vested in his office for the Swazi nation. He allocates the land to his subjects through local chiefs and princes who actually assign the land (grazing land is held communally, land for cultivation is utilized on an individual family basis). Non-Swazis must be accepted by the Ngwenyama before they can acquire land.[18] The importance of the Ngwenyama has not decreased in recent years and he presently serves as an agent of modernity in the socio-economic system. His demonstration plots near the royal homestead at Lobamba, where maize and other vegetables as well as cash crops such as cotton are grown scientifically, serve as models for his people. He is also the principal owner of stock held in trust for the Swazi nation, in many of the major industrial projects (such as Usutu Pulp Ltd.).

In the political realm, the issue is somewhat more complex. The Ngwenyama stands at the head of the traditional political structure. Yet the monarchy is a dual one, with the Ndlovukazi ruling jointly with the Ngwenyama. She enjoys considerable prestige and power in her own right. Her village is the ritual capital of the nation and as the "She Elephant" and the "Mother of the Nation", she stands both as a check on the Ngwenyama's action and as a complement to it. In the event of his death, she may play an important role in the choice of his successor and act as regent for the new king. Her position is of such importance that in case of her own death, a substitute "mother" is found to fill the position of queen mother from among the surviving widows of the Ngwenyama's father. In the nineteenth century, most Swazi kings died relatively early so that the Ndlovukazi was a figure of political importance during the subsequent interregnum. In the case of Sobhuza II, however, he has already outlived his own mother and one substitute queen, her sister. The present Ndlovukazi is old, infirm and not politically active and her primary function is social.[19]

The Ngwenyama is not an absolute monarch. He is expected to take advice from his senior male relatives and from his advisers. In addition, he is responsible to the Swazi inner council or *Liqoqo*. Swazi national land is divided into districts, each headed by a chief, each with considerable authority over his "own" area. Each chief has his own council and responsibility for the people in his area although they may appeal his judgments to the Ngwenyama and Ndlovukazi. These local tribal leaders are either Dlamini princes, hereditary leaders of other clans or direct appointees of the king. In theory, the Ngwenyama chooses new chiefs each time one dies although in fact, the family council of each chief most often selects a successor which the Ngwenyama confirms. The *Liqoqo* consists of a small group of twenty to thirty chiefs and commoners, the *Liqoqo* advises the Ngwenyama on both political tactics and strategy and he regularly consults with its members. The *Liqoqo* should not be confused with the *Libandla laka Ngwane* or Council of State which is often referred to as the Swazi National Council. In contrast to the *Liqoqo*, the *Libandla* is a meeting of all adult males in the Swazi nation. It is essentially an unstructured opportunity for discussion and no formal votes are taken. It is seldom convened and its large size and diverse membership militate against its playing a preeminent political role. It is thus the *Liqoqo* which is the main institution offering a potential check on the Ngwenyama although there are other social and magical religious checks on the arbitrary use of kingly power.[20]

A word of explanation is necessary at this stage to illuminate the process of decision-making in the traditional Swazi political system. During both its periodic and *ad hoc* meetings, the *Liqoqo* interacts with the Ngwenyama.

During its sittings, the Ngwenyama puts aside his pre-eminent position and debates with its members on a more or less equal basis, often deferring to his advisers on specific issues. Generally, his plans and suggestions are subject to their approval. No formal votes are taken but a general consensus emerges after hours or days of discussion. Once the issue is decided, the decision is announced to the Swazi nation as a command from the King and carries with it the full force of his office.

From an analysis of the decolonization period therefore, it would appear that Sobhuza's crucial role in the Swazi decision-making process did not (and does not today) derive solely from the eminence of his office but from his own persuasive skills and ability to generate consensus (later reinforced by the cumulative effect of his political successes). The force of his personality, his college education and his intimate knowledge of Swazi law and custom, the oral constitution which is such an intrinsic part of Swazi political life, have combined to make his wishes generally prevail over those of the *Liqoqo*, although during the period under review, his views seem to have met little strong opposition from the *Liqoqo*. Although he is ageing (born in 1899) and conservative, Sobhuza II nevertheless has demonstrated a quick and resolute mind and a willingness to experiment and remain flexible in the face of challenges to his position and that of the Swazi nation. Moreover, his willingness to accept commoners and even former opponents into his circle of advisers had the net effect of strengthening the position of the monarchy. As in many other political systems, the traditional ruler often had to deal with "overmighty vassals". In the nineteenth century, Swazi kings moved militarily against powerful or recalcitrant chiefs; in the twentieth, Sobhuza co-opted them by convincing them that the entire traditional system would endure or collapse together.

In keeping the nation together, and maintaining his power, the Ngwenyama of Swaziland made excellent use of two aspects of traditional Swazi political life, the right of royal appointment and the *lifbutfho* or regiment system. Traditionally, the Swazi kings created their own bureaucracy in order to keep a check on local chiefs and Dlamini princes located far from the capital. Included in this bureaucracy were many princes without chieftaincies of their own and royal *tindvuna*, the *tindvuna* being the appointed representatives of the king and directly responsible to him. Their ranks include many commoners and they are similar in purpose and action to the *hommes du roi* of the Capetian kings of France. There are also the ritual blood brothers of the Ngwenyama called *tinsila* who are commoners chosen to protest the monarch. The use of commoners in positions of authority, on condition of their loyalty and expertise, has provided important channels of upward mobility—both social and political —which have in turn given pliancy to the social system as well as durability to the monarchy. Together with the absorptive capabilities noted above, the process of utilizing talent irrespective of its source has greatly aided political integration. Because of the asynchronous and asymmetrical nature of the modernization process, many Swazis, both commoners and members of important clans, became estranged from the tribal structure during the 1950s and 1960s and moved away from the authority of the local chiefs and their tribal superiors. With the reassertion of the monarchy as a major political force, the creation of a mass-based party, i.e. the Imbokodvo National Movement, and the gradual extension of these renovated political structures to encompass all of Swaziland, this periodic absorption of exogenous elements proved of enormous consequence in aiding national unity. Given the alienation of these detribalized Swazis and the need for their professional skills, these had to be re-absorbed if the system as a whole was to avoid fragmentation. The same is true of the European entrepreneurs whose capital and economic skills were necessary if economic development was to take place rapidly. The re-absorption of the detribalized Swazi and the inclusion of many Europeans and non-Swazi Africans occurred by means of an updated version of the traditional process. Loyalty to the Ngwenyama became the crucial ingredient and once that was demonstrated, past failings, even past opposition, were held to be of minor significance.

In addition to careers open to talent based on loyalty to the Ngwenyama, the Swazi nation has also made extensive use of the *lifbutfho* or regiment system. Historically, all adult males were brought together in a series of age-sets which cut across kinship groupings, exposed their members to Swazi law and custom and socialized them politically. As Hilda Kuper has noted:

> Little formal education is given in the regiment, but it is the main training school of conservatives. It continues and extends the work of the kinsmen who enforce the authority of age and seniority. Throughout life the position of a man is fixed in and by his age class which defines his rights over those who are junior to him and his obligations to those who are senior.[21]

Sobhuza II made excellent use of this nineteenth century innovation to aid in the process of political socialization long after its military utility had been eliminated. In addition to learning discipline and the nature of the social order, the initiate is inculcated with a deep sense of pride in belonging to the Swazi nation and of loyalty to the Ngwenyama. Each age-set experiences a strong corporate life and provides the individual with bonds which remain with him all his life. Formerly, the age groups had a military basis. Today, they are seldom called upon once the regiment is dismissed (when a majority of its members become married) except during important national ceremonies such as the annual *Incwala* festival. They are available, however, for national service and during the outbreak of foot-and-mouth disease in 1965, several regiments were used to cordon off the stricken areas and enforce a ban on the movement of stock.

According to some, the regiment system arose as a mechanism to de-energize the tensions created by polygamous "diluted" marriages and represents an attempt to counteract the strong mother-child axis which develops in such societies.[22] Without judging on the validity of such psychocultural interpretations, the age-set as an institution is certainly a political factor of considerable magnitude; traditionally, age-sets have provided powerful integrative bonds among the Swazis. It may well be that over time, some "modern" institution will assume the functions now fulfilled by the regiment system, but for the present, it continues to be of importance. Even the less formal age-sets for women (together with such ceremonies as the Reed dance) are instrumental in the development of pride and cohesion among the Swazis.

Thus the Ngwenyama, when faced with the thrust of modernity, could rely on the cohesion of the Swazi nation and its general allegiance to him, a set of political institutions which would enable him to marshall his people behind him and the confidence of his princes and chiefs. Neither he nor they had been closely allied with the colonial authority and both saw in the changes of the 1940s and 1950s, threats to their existence and political figures. One can make a case that for all his operational skill, Sobhuza II enjoyed a great advantage over his Pan-African and European rivals in the cohesion of his nation and the structural advantages which he enjoyed in the traditional political system. He was to need both.

THE THRUST OF MODERNITY

For modernity did impinge on Swaziland following World War II as a series of exogenous inputs, some economic, some political, led to a substantial alteration of Swazi life and threatened to undermine the pre-eminent position of the monarchy and the personal influence of Sobhuza II. Most prominent of the phenomena during the post-war period was the quickening pace of economic life. The once-stagnant economy was stimulated by the introduction of large-scale agricultural, mining and, eventually, industrial projects. During the late 1940s, major forest product plantations were introduced into the Piggs Peak and Usutu areas; in the 1950s, a series of irrigation schemes involving sugar, cotton, rice and citrus were developed near Mhlume, Big Bend and the Malkerns valley; in the 1960s, the asbestos mining facilities at Havelock were expanded, iron ore mining was begun north of Mbabane, and an industrial complex was opened at Matsapa. During the latter two decades, over $69 million worth of economic aid was provided by the British Colonial Development and Welfare Corporation (later renamed the Commonwealth Development and Welfare Corporation)..

This infusion of public capital, when coupled with substantial amounts of private investment, greatly expanded the cash sector of the economy, led to a vastly improved physical infrastructure, and stimulated urbanization. Indirectly, the process reduced the importance of the tribal authority even in rural areas as many Swazis moved from subsistence agriculture to participation in the modern sector of the economy. As age-old socio-economic patterns were altered and urbanization increased, demographic changes were considerable.[23] The first trade union, the Pulp Timbers Union, was formed in March 1962 and the first strike occurred the next month. Labour difficulties with major political ramifications took place during May and June of 1963 and one of the most prominent of the new political parties, the Ngwane National Liberatory Congress (NNLC) of Dr. Ambrose Zwane, developed a strong base in the union movement.

International political events also had an important impact on the situation in Swaziland. It is most difficult to quantify or measure, but the growing numbers of independent African states after 1960 and the surge and rhetoric of de-colonization elsewhere seem to have stimulated political activity in Swaziland. Several of the early political parties, the NNLC and the Swaziland Progressive Party (SPP) of J. J. Nquku, were strongly Pan-African in orientation and the recipients of financial, educational, and logistical support from Ghana. More importantly, due to their perceptions of the way in which the winds of change were blowing, some colonial authorities sought to interject into the Swaziland situation a political structure which would be conducive to the development of modern political forms and party politics. The imposition of the 1963 constitution did, in fact, irrevocably alter the course of politics in Swaziland and had far-reaching and widespread consequences for the process of political development in Swaziland. Finally, both the economic aid and political stimulation were conditioned by contemporary events in Southern Africa. The establishment of a republic in South Africa (1960) and its withdrawal from the British Commonwealth (1961) significantly altered the politics of the area, especially when it was accompanied by gradual British disengagement from Southern Africa. The approaching independence of Bechuanaland (as Botswana) and Basutoland (as Lesotho) and the implementation of a forward strategy of international relations by the South African government all contributed to the turbulence and change which washed over Swaziland during the 1960s.

In this dynamic context, the Swazi experience offers an interesting and substantial amendment to the widely-held theory that economic and political modernity are inimical to the maintenance of traditional authority. This seems to have been the case during the early stages of the period under review. By the early 1960s the Ngwenyama and his closest advisers in the Swazi National Council felt that their political power was being eroded. The interpenetration of the modern and traditional milieus had already produced a situation in which the Ngwenyama was forced to act if the monarchy was to emerge from decolonization with meaningful political power. Having operated in the political backwater of Swaziland for forty years, the traditional authorities suddenly found themselves faced with major challenges to their political position within both the tribal nexus and the latger national arena. Initially they were fearful and hesitant, and over-estimated the potency of their opposition but, eventually, led by the Ngwenyama, the Swazi traditional authorities used the very intrusions of modernity and modern political techniques to enhance their position and to emerge victorious in a protracted struggle against the British, the Pan-African parties and the Europeans.

This is not the place for a detailed history of Swaziland during the 1950s and 1960s. That has already been done.[24] At the same time, some recapitulation of events is necessary if the reader is to grasp the significance of the Ngwenyama's triumph and to ascertain whether his success was ultimately due to his advantages and political expertise, the mistakes of his opposition, the factors inherent in the international subsystem of Southern Africa, or a subtle combination of all three. Looked at with the benefit of hindsight, the political history of Swaziland during the 1960s may be broadly divided into two parts. The first, running from 1960 until 1965 forms a period of challenge to, and response from, the monarchy while the second, from 1965 until the present, is characterized by the triumph and consolidation of the political power of the Ngwenyama. There is, however, one event, the formation of the reconstituted European Advisory Committee, which predates these periods and which must be mentioned for it was at once a source of major inputs into the political system of Swaziland and a result of a century-old pattern of political life within the territory.

Since the days of the concessionaires, the European community in Swaziland had always enjoyed a special, privileged position. Often, this position was institutionalized. In 1888, for example, the British and Boer settlers obtained a charter of self-government from Mbandzeni. The European Advisory Council was subsequently formed and played an important role in the development of the European community and in the process by which Europeans secured control over half the land in Swaziland. Racked by internal difficulties and reduced in importance with the arrival of British colonial rule, however, the Council fell into disuse. As part of the growing political awareness after World War II, it was reconstituted in 1949:

> . . . to advise the Resident Commissioner on matters directly affecting Europeans in the Territory and in other matters specifically referred to the Council by the Resident Commissioners.[25]

The ten elected members of the Reconstituted European Advisory Council (REAC) were all Europeans and from its inception until it was superseded by the territorial Legislative Council in June 1964, it served as the spokesman for European interests and as a vehicle for their political and economic advancement. The interest of the European community in gaining political power coincided with the movement on the part of the tribal authorities to regain some of their prerogatives lost during the nineteenth and twentieth centuries. Both sections were stimulated by the belief that if they did not gain control during decolonization, other groups would. In an attempt to forestall these other forces, the members of the REAC and the Ngwenyama called for a territorial-wide legislature, equally divided between Europeans and Swazis. More importantly, the Swazis declared that their representatives were to be chosen by the regional traditional authorities by means of the *tinkhundla* method of local acclamation. This meant, in effect, direct nomination by the traditional hierarchy. The Ngwenyama put the matter quite simply:

> . . . the European public should elect representatives according to its established system of elections and that the Swazis should select theirs in the manner which was most familiar and suitable to the Swazi people.[26]

Because such an arrangement would have prevented the newly emerging, detribalized Swazis from achieving political prominence, British officials refused to accept the European and Swazi demands as stated. Instead, they initially proposed a constitutional arrangement based on universal suffrage and on modern political processes with a gradual devolution of power from the British administration to the national politicians. Because of its threatening implications for their political power, the British proposal was bitterly opposed from its inception by the Europeans and traditional Swazi leadership. During the period 1960–1964, a major struggle occurred over the form of the constitution with all sides seeing its institutional framework as critical to their hopes for triumph. There is, of course, significant dramatic irony in the cooperation between the European settlers and the Swazi traditional authorities for, eventually, it was the very Swazi traditional leaders whom the Europeans had encouraged that would outmanœuvre them and short-circuit their drive for political hegemony. All of these developments lay in the future, however. Faced with the informal British proposals and threatened by the spectre of political eclipse, the Swazi hierarchy and the European community believed that they must cooperate if they were to emerge with meaningful political power during the decolonization process.

THE BEGINNINGS OF PARTY POLITICS

The rise of the "modern" opposition to the tribal authorities, to the Europeans and the British colonial administration is an interesting phenomenon in itself. Led for the most part by "detribalized" or non-Swazis, the political parties which sprang up during the early 1960s proved, without exception, to be small in size, poorly organized and splintered by personality and ideological conflicts, generally wasteful of their scant human and capital resources and needlessly antagonistic to the Swazi authorities and the British colonial administration. It is true that many of their programmes and policies were actualized after 1964 and that the political culture of Swaziland is undoubtedly richer for their existence. At the same time, the inability of their leaders to cooperate amongst themselves, their predilection for attending international conferences instead of concentrating on grass roots organization and their gross exaggeration of their ability to apply political techniques borrowed from other parts of Africa to the Swazi situation, drastically reduced their cumulative impact and ultimately prevented them from attaining political power.

The first such party to appear was the Swaziland Progressive Party (SPP) of J. J. Nquku. Formed out of the old Swaziland Progressive Cultural Association in 1960, the SPP (Nquku) advocated a non-racial society and a one-man, one-vote constitutional arrangement without reserved seats for any group. Although Nquku was not a Swazi but a Zulu, many detribalized Swazis, including Dr. Ambrose Zwane and Dumisa Dlamini, joined the party and it gained some territorial-wide status. Nevertheless, from its inception, the SPP (Nquku) was beset by internal difficulties including an almost continuous power struggle for control of the party apparatus and funds, and recurrent charges of embezzlement and "bigmanism". Dr. Zwane eventually broke away from the organization in February 1962, taking with him the bulk of the membership. After a somewhat confused period during which the Zwane group was also referred to as the Swaziland Progressive Party (Zwane), it was renamed the Ngwane National Liberatory Congress (NNLC) in April 1963. The original SPP was further splintered in August 1962 when another anti-Nquku faction, led by O. M. Mabuza, broke away and formed another Swaziland Progressive Party (Mabuza). This miniscule group subsequently fell heir to the grand title of the Joint Alliance of Swaziland Political Parties in June 1964. Its hard-core strength never exceeded a dozen.

In an attempt to reconcile the various political viewpoints, the British called for constitutional talks which began in November 1960. The proposals for a modern constitution were so stubbornly resisted by the Ngwenyama and the settlers that the talks dragged on inconclusively until 1963 notwithstanding two special conferences in London during December 1961, and January 1963. Agreement was never reached during these deliberations and the British were eventually forced to impose a constitution which pleased no one. The more the administration sought to compromise the different positions, the more they lost the initial faith of the political parties and convinced the Europeans and Swazi traditional authorities that whatever framework was initially agreed upon, the British would eventually work for a diminution of their political power.

In attempting to oppose the settlers and the Swazi tribal hierarchy, the political community which called itself "modern" became increasingly fragmented. In addition to the splits already described within the Swaziland Progressive Party, the strength of these elements was further dissipated by the formation of the Swaziland Democratic Party (SDP) led by Simon Nxumalo and Vincent Rozwadowski in March 1962. The SDP was essentially a moderate coalition of Swazis and some Europeans who, while they opposed the 50–50 sharing of power by the Europeans and the traditionalists, also were concerned over the Pan-African orientation and quasi-socialist jargon of the various branches of the SPP. Initially, the SDP favoured a constitutional monarchy with the Ngwenyama as head of state and symbol of unity but with political participation based on a qualified franchise. By steering a mid-course between the opposing poles of public opinion, the SDP could not develop much in the way of national support. On one hand, most Europeans and the conservative Swazis found their proposals "extreme" while, on the other, the more urbanized, detribalized Swazis and many non-Swazi Africans found their position too "conservative". Although the SDP probably offered the most realistic compromise formulation for reconciling the different political forces in Swaziland, few in either camp accepted the need for that compromise.

Further splintering of the modern political forces occurred in May 1962 when three new parties sprang up. Winston Madlala formed the Swaziland Freedom Party, Clifford Nkosi created the Mbandzeni Party and Dr. George Msibi the National Convention Party. Although these groups never amounted to much (despite an amalgamation of the Nkosi and Msibi forces into the Mbandzeni National Convention), they further accelerated the proliferation of political parties and helped to discredit the notion that the modern political forces would be instrumental in attaining the unity of all Swaziland. With seven or eight sets of party leaders racing around the country issuing proclamations and manifestos and claiming to have thousands of supporters, whatever opportunities originally existed for the "modern" forces to gather momentum rapidly vanished.

In addition, the Europeans and the forces of the monarchy began to take the offensive when the Constitutional Committee proposed that a Legislative Council be established with four officials appointed by the Resident Commissioner, twelve Europeans and Eurafricans elected on a common roll and twelve Swazis chosen by the *tinkhundla* system. As soon as the British officials raised serious objections to this plan, the Ngwenyama began to cast about for allies. This was particularly obvious after the meetings in June 1962, between the leaders of the political parties and a select committee of the *Liqoqo*. The various politicians were interviewed at the royal village at Lobamba and subjected to lengthy cross-examination. Convinced that the parties and the British colonial authorities were out to undermine their position, the traditionalists called a meeting of the full *Libandla* during July. At that time, spokesmen for the Ngwenyama explained the nature of the threat to the Swazi nation and obtained pledges of support in the coming struggle (although there was some internal opposition to the proposed alliance with the Euroepan settlers). After the *Libandla* meeting, the Ngwenyama met with the then Minister of Justice for South Africa, B. J. Vorster. At that time, he apparently received a promise of unofficial support, including legal assistance. He also ascertained that many of the large, European-owned firms such as the Anglo-American Corporation were prepared to come to terms with the monarchy after the British granted Swaziland independence.

The Ngwenyama and the Swazi National Council emerged from these exploratory talks greatly encouraged by the promises of support. None of the sources of support in and by themselves guaranteed the eventual success of the monarchy but taken together they enabled Sobhuza II to continue his opposition to the British proposals and to press for the implementation of the recommendations of the Constitutional Committee. This is not to suggest that the Ngwenyama could totally ignore British officialdom or isolate himself completely from the growing numbers of detribalized Swazis; rather, secure in the knowledge that he had considerable support from those individuals and forces which would remain operative in the Swazi context after the British departed, the Ngwenyama could play for time and resist those proposals which threatened the monarchy's position. In this regard, one should not read too much into the Ngwenyama's tactical cooperation with the South Africans and local Europeans. Sobhuza II did not, and does not, favour apartheid nor was he willing to share power with the European settlers over the long term. His cooperation with these two forces meant rather that he felt so threatened by the likely course of events in Swaziland that he was willing to accept support regardless of its source. In terms of the expediency of the moment, the Ngwenyama made a realistic assessment of the current directions of Swazi politics and his need to change those directions if he as an individual and the monarchy as an institution were to survive as viable political forces.

When the British learned of the continuing obstinacy of the Ngwenyama and the Europeans in support of the constitutional proposals based on a sharing of power, they called for a second conference to be held in London during January 28 to February 1, 1963. In addition to members of the REAC and the Swazi National Council, representatives from the SPP (Nquku), SDP and Mbandzeni National Convention attended the constitutional conference. Despite their misgivings about the nature of the other political parties, the leaders of the SDP decided to join with them to form a united front, the Constitutional Alliance. In order to bring their position on the suffrage into line with that of the other parties, the SDP dropped their demands for a qualified franchise and espoused the principle of one-man, one-vote.[27] The Constitutional Alliance struck the first blow when Dr. Allen Nxumalo joined forces with the Alliance, later becoming the president of the SDP. This defection, however spectacular, failed to alter the position of the tribal authorities and with both groups sticking to their original proposals, the proceedings soon degenerated into unproductive sessions marred by name-calling and vicious personal attacks.[28]

The British Colonial Office continued to oppose the 50-50 sharing of power proposed by the settlers and the traditionalist but now recognized that these two groups could not be ignored in any settlement and that the political parties' demand for one-man, one-vote was premature. The British thereupon suggested a compromise scheme which included a 34-member Legislative Council with 4 official members chosen by the Resident Commissioner, 10 Swazis elected by the *tinkhundla* system and 20 members, 10 Africans and 10 Europeans, elected by all adults on a national roll. These proposals were later amended so that half of the European seats were selected by a purely European roll and formed the basis for the so-called Sandys Constitution released in May 1963, and officially set forth in the Order in Council of December 1963. At the time of the London conference, the British arrangement was unanimously rejected by all sides and the conference broke up without agreement. It may seem that the conference was fruitless and in the sense of finding a compromise solution which the various groups would embrace, it was. At the same time, by exhausting the patience of the British government the talks were highly functional in that they led rather inexorably to the imposition of a constitution which, however unpopular, eliminated the widespread uncertainty which was affecting both the political and economic life of Swaziland and forced the opposing groups to get on with the business of reconciling their differences.[29]

During the conference and directly after it, the Swaziland Progressive Party (Zwane) set about increasing its strength in the trade union movement and using the fledgling unions as a political base. Excluded from the London talks partially because of the legal technicalities inherent in the situation (the SPP (Nquku) retained the official title of the organization) and the growing estrangement between Dr. Zwane and the British authorities, the SPP (Zwane) renamed itself the Ngwane National Liberatory

Congress and sought to place itself in the vanguard of the modern forces. A series of small strikes at Ubombo Ranches and the Big Bend sugar plantation in March and a "sour porridge" disturbance in the African market of Mbabane during April encouraged the NNLC to utilize its new-found power to engage the Europeans and the British colonial authorities. When a strike broke out during May at the Havelock Asbestos mine, representatives of the NNLC including MacDonald Maseko and Dumisa Dlamini took charge of it and spread the work stoppage to the timber concerns around Piggs Peak and the sugar-growing area around Big Bend, ultimately calling a general strike in the capital, Mbatane.

Yet the very successes of the NNLC isolated it. The SPP (Nquku) and the SDP worked against the strikes. The British became alarmed and rushed in troops and the Ngwenyama refused to protect the strikers from the colonial authority. Despite its oratorical skill and its ability to galvanize public opinion over specific issues, the NNLC lacked staying power and the ability to turn its latent power into political advance. Once the British flew in a contingent of special police from the Bechuanaland Protectorate and the 1st Gordon Highland Brigade from Kenya early in June, the strike was broken. Bogged down in a series of lengthy post-strike trials and harrassed by the government, the NNLC was unable to develop the organizational strength necessary to maintain its momentum and its importance diminished thereafter.[30]

In the midst of these disorders, the British released the details of the new constitution on May 31. The Legislative Council of Swaziland was to consist of four official members plus a speaker and twenty-four elected members. Eight of these were to be Swazis chosen by means of the *tinkhundla* system, eight were to be Europeans, four of whom were to be chosen by a European roll and four by the national roll, and eight were to be members of any race elected by all voters on the national roll.[31] In addition, the post of Resident Commissioner was to be replaced by that of Her Majesty's Commissioner for Swaziland and elevated in status to the rank of colonial governor.

THE RESPONSE OF THE MONARCHY

At this juncture, Sobhuza faced the most important political decision of his reign. The Ngwenyama could have accepted the one-third allocation of seats on behalf of the Swazi National Council and probably preserved his position in the traditional community, at least for the duration of the new constitution, even though his chance for national political hegemony would be greatly diminished. Instead, encouraged by his closest advisers within the Swazi National Council and some Europeans in Swaziland and South Africa, Sobhuza II decided to enter the national political arena and contest the modern parties on their own terms. If, in retrospect, that decision proved to be the correct one from the standpoint of monarchical interests, at the time, there was the very real danger that Sobhuza's personal involvement in national politics might discredit the monarchy and cost it both power and prestige. There was also the possibility that the traditional forces might turn out to be ineffectual in dealing with modern parties. Once the decision was made to compete with these parties, the Europeans and the Swazi tribal hierarchy worked together to circumvent the spirit of the constitution even though they had failed to change its form. By accepting the realities of the situation and attempting to derive maximum advantage from the imposed political framework, the Ngwenyama and the traditional authorities proved to be more realistic and resourceful than the leaders of the political parties. The monarchy, it is true, enjoyed significant advantages in the struggle, inasmuch as it could capitalize upon the cultural and linguistic cohesiveness of the Swazis, their loyalty to the Ngwenyama and the financial and organizational strength of the traditional network. But, beyond that, the traditionalist worked harder to insure their triumph and were able to adduce political issues which had greater relevance for the voters of Swaziland than those raised by the modern political parties.

Once the Ngwenyama decided to enter the national political fray, the leaders of the SDP, NNLC and SPP (Nquku) engaged in a great deal of wishful thinking, looking for some last minute *deus ex machina* to extricate them from their dilemma by insisting upon a one-man, one-vote election. Instead of organizing on the grass roots level, raising issues of importance for the average Swazi (as opposed to the new elite) and above all, earnestly cooperating among themselves, the parties continued to dissipate their energies in factional disputes. Even when the Prime Minister of South Africa, Dr. Hendrik Verwoerd, stated that South Africa could lead the three High Commission Territories "to independence and economic prosperity far more quickly and more effectively than Great Britain", and the extent of the collaboration between the European settlers and the Swazi National Council became known, the political parties could not capitalize on these issues.[32]

Having reluctantly decided to contest the national elections in June 1964, the political parties formed a paper alliance, the Swaziland African National Union. It was of no consequence. Each of the Alliande parties, the NNLC, the SDP, the SPP (Nquku) and SPP (Mabuza), nominated its own candidates for all seats, ran against each other in the crucial urban and peri-urban districts, published manifesto after manifesto (on fine points of socialist thought and in English rather than siSwati) and avoided any serious campaigning in the countryside. As matters turned out, once the Ngwenyama decided to confront them, the political parties could not entirely have defeated his political thrust, but, with unity and hard work, as well as a realistic appraisal of their position, they could have, at the very least, assured themselves some representation on the Legislative Council. In terms of political payoffs, the Europeans (at least initially) and the traditionalists proved themselves better able to handle modern political techniques and processes than the leaders of the "modern" political parties.

The Ngwenyama's first significant response occurred in January 1964, when the Swazi National Council announced that it would hold a national plebiscite to prove how the Swazis felt about the new constitution and the

L

directions of Swazi politics. The aim of the plebiscite was two-fold: to in-dicate to the colonial administration that the wishes of the Swazi people ran counter to the British vision for the political future of Swaziland; and more importantly, to galvanize public opinion, test voting and mobilization procedures and engage in positive political socialization. The Ngwenyama chose the symbol of the royal house, a lion, to stand for a rejection of the constitution while a reindeer, an animal unknown in Swaziland, stood for the constitution and, in the minds of many, con-tinued colonial status. In addition, the Swazi tribal organization mounted an intensified campaign to get out the vote as a sign of support for the monarchy. They were spectacularly, if somewhat dubiously, successful. Despite a boycott of the elections by all the political parties who rightly feared that the people, once having voted for king and country would do so again, 102 per cent of the eligible voters chose the lion.

When the British ignored these surrealistic figures (as they had the results of an earlier European referendum in which 98 per cent of those voting expressed support for the 50–50 sharing of power proposed earlier), the Ngwenyama and the European settlers formed a working alliance to capture the eight European seats and the eight at-large positions on the national roll. For the Europeans, their major political vehicle was the United Swaziland Association (USA). Formed late in 1963 as a "club", the USA group took on a formal political character early in 1964. Led by an Afrikaner farmer, Willie Meyer, and an English-speaking businessman, R. P. Stephens, the USA party stood irrevocably for the continued privileged status of Europeans in Swaziland and the containment of African nationalism. In public the party leadership stood for racial partnership. Privately its members talked about their ability to control the tribalists and "keep the kaffirs in their place". Clothing their racial views under a cloak of staunch anti-communism, the USA leaders quickly gained the support of most of the European residents of Swaziland.[33] The USA group was opposed within the European community, however, by the somewhat more moderate Swaziland Independence Front (SIF) which sprang up in April 1964. Led by the English-speaking farmers and ranchers, Frank Corbett and R. J. Lockhart, the SIF was composed primarily of those Europeans who not only opposed the demands of the SDP and NNLC, but also resented what they took to be South African involvement in the affairs of Swaziland and the reactionary attitudes of the USA party. Small and disorganized, it sought only to contest the European reserved seats and made no pretensions of African support.

In April 1964, the Ngwenyama and the Swazi National Council an-nounced the formation of their own party, the Imbokodvo National Movement. Nominally under the leadership of Prince Makhosini, the Imbokodvo was in reality an extension of the monarchy and under its direct control. Sobhuza II envisioned that the Imbokodvo would contest the national roll seats and, in cooperation with the USA forces, prevent the other political parties from attaining political power. Although the Imbokodvo had a constitution, local chapters and many other trappings of a mass party, it was based primarily on the traditional bureaucracy in the districts and the local authority of the chiefs. Because of the size and societal depth of that structure, it was more than a narrowly based "patron-party", but no national conventions were ever held and decision-making, principally by the Ngwenyama and the Swazi National Council, was always hierarchical rather than polyarchal in scope. It was the Imbokodvo leadership rather than the rank and file which developed a close working arrangement with the USA settlers and with the sympathetic elements in South Africa. Although the Swazi hierarchy was careful to play down the extent of cooperation, it was considerable.[34] The common-roll constituencies were divided up among the Imbokodvo and USA candidates and both groups avoided any conflict during the pre-election debates. The Imbokodvo encouraged the Swazis to vote for the USA candidates on the national roll and the USA party obtained the use of Radio South Africa for its candidates and those of the Imbokodvo.

With the resources available to it and the funds from the Swazi National Treasury, the prestige of the monarchy and the in-place bureaucratic organization, the Imbokodvo was a most formidable force and it probably did not need the support of the USA group to emerge victorious. At the time, however, the tribal authorities perceived that they needed the backing of the Europeans if they were to defeat the other political parties. Until the last minute, the traditional authorities were concerned over the outcome of the elections. Nowhere is this seen more clearly than in the way in which the Imbokodvo approached the nomination process for the various types of seats. Instead of concentrating their most well-known and important figures in the national roll contests, the Imbokodvo nominated Polycarp Dlamini, D. Hlophe, John Mfundza Sukati, Dr. George Msibi, George Mabuza and Prince Makhosini for the safe *tinkhundla* seats, thus assuring their membership in the Legislative Council. Such a strategy hardly made sense if the Imbokodvo was confident of a national victory.

As it happened, the Imbokodvo leadership need not have worried. They and their European allies swept the June elections. While the monarchy was controlling the *tinkhundla* seats, the USA party was taking every European seat by a wide margin. More importantly, the Imbokodvo-USA alliance won all the national roll seats by margins ranging from 4–1 to 11–1. The other political parties were swamped. Even Dr. Zwane of the NNLC who ran the best of all the Pan-African leaders was beaten by 6,000 votes in a 10,000-vote constituency. Other leaders were also humiliated. For example, Dr. Allen Nxumalo received 200 votes and J. J. Nquku 67. All told, the Imbokodvo- USA alliance took 84·6 per cent of the vote while all the other parties combined totalled 15·3 per cent.

Clearly, the issues of Pan-African unity and African socialism, even charges of collaboration with the European settlers, were of little consequence when measured against the symbolic integrity of the monarchy and the preservation of traditional Swazi life. The victory was of major consequence in determining the future course of politics in Swaziland for the Imbokodvo had emerged as the most significant political organization in the country and the Ngwenyama could regard its success as his personal triumph. The electoral sweep was accompanied by a signal that the British government was prepared to acknowledge the primacy of the Ngwenyama. Francis Loyd replaced Brian Marwick as Her Majesty's Commissioner and soon demonstrated great sympathy for the monarchy. After the Swazi hierarchy and the Imbokodvo broke with the European settlers, he allowed them to have considerable say in the drafting of a new constitution, one which would give maximum advantage to the Imbokodvo's rural strength.

The defeated political parties were severely shaken by the results of the election. Although they filed petitions against the results of the elections and created yet another "common" front, this time entitled the Joint Alliance of Swaziland Political Parties, their power was markedly reduced as the people of Swaziland were better able to judge the depth of their support. The members of the United Swaziland Association rejoiced in the magnitude of the defeat suffered by the Pan-African parties. Their joy was short-lived. No sooner had the Legislative Council met in September 1964 than the Imbokodvo called for a new constitution, without reserved seats for any ethnic group, and pressed for "immediate" independence. Having crushed the Pan-African opposition to the monarchy, the Ngwenyama now turned to disengage himself politically from the European settlers and so to emerge as the only dominant force on the political scene. This new tact, carefully planned and deftly executed, had a twofold objective: to defeat those Europeans who felt that they should share in the national political power and to re-absorb those detribalized Swazis who were now willing to acknowledge the primacy of the Ngwenyama. In a spirit of national reconciliation and unity and exuding a new-found confidence, the Imbokodvo opened its political arms and accepted back into its fold those opponents who now pledged their loyalty to the Ngwenyama. In the process, the Imbokodvo itself underwent substantial ideological alteration and ended up espousing many of the ideas previously championed only by its opponents. The election results in any event showed that the monarchy and the Imbokodvo had little to fear from the previous hostile forces and could compete with them on their own terms. All of this had a cumulative impact, for as the more the Imbokodvo accepted these ideas, the more detribalized Swazis accepted its primacy and joined its ranks.

Simon Nxumalo was the first to do so, resigning from the SDP in October 1964. The next April, Dr. Allen Nxumalo merged the SDP with the Imbokodvo and during the following year, Arthur Khoza, Dumisa Dlamini, Frank Groening, Sam Khumalo and other prominent members of the NNLC resigned and joined the Imbokodvo. Dumisa Dlamini, perhaps the single most exciting politician in the country, appraised the new political realities:

It is left for us to grow up and rid Swaziland of this ridiculous situation (having five warring political parties) by joining hands with the majority organization, and there is no doubt that the majority organization here in Swaziland is the Imbokodvo National Movement.[35]

The USA party was stunned by the turn of events, but slow to appreciate their full import. The matter should have been clear as early as October 1965 when the Imbokodvo members of the Legislative Council called the constitution "racist" and rejected a USA motion to give those South Africans resident in Swaziland the right to vote beyond the British-imposed citizenship deadline of December 31, 1965. Prince Mfanasibili, later Minister for Local Government, spoke for the Imbokodvo and reacted in mock surprise to the USA proposals. He declared that such a motion would indeed indicate cooperation with the forces of apartheid. If it were a matter of money, suggested the Prince, the Imbokodvo would offer to pay the cost of applying for British citizenship.[36] European concern grew when, at the new constitutional conference, the Imbokodvo pressed for the abandonment of the separate European roll. The European community had been led to believe by the USA leadership that the Swazi traditionalists were politically docile and easily manipulated. In the face of the Imbokodvo's growing militency, many now realized with a sense of frustration that what the Imbokodvo had done to the Pan-African parties, it could now do to the United Swaziland Association.

Some Europeans responded by withdrawing from politics altogether. Others, including Frank Corbett, Jerry Bordihn and Leo Lovell, formed a "Committee of Twelve" which declared that they were willing to acknowledge the primacy of the Ngwenyama and accept the dictates of African majority rule. The Twelve refused to demand minority representation and thereby undercut the premise that the USA spoke for the European community. Such political realism was well rewarded for the Swazi monarchy proceeded to use the talents of those Europeans who accepted the hegemony of the Ngwenyama. Leo Lovell, for example, became Finance Minister in the Independence cabinet. The USA leadership responded to the trauma of defeat by fixating on demands for a 50–50 sharing of power, an anachronistic position which was untenable two years earlier. With an amazing lack of finesse, the USA members continued to press for such an arrangement even after the new self-government constitution was announced in March 1966. When the formal vote on the constitution was taken in the Legislative Council, the USA members proposed an amendment which would have created a separate roll for Europeans with equal representation in parliament. When this motion was decisively defeated, the USA was spent as a political force. It had lost its struggle to preserve the once-privileged political position of Europeans in Swaziland, partially because it had encouraged the very forces strong enough to defeat it. The USA party did not contest the April 1967 national elections and faded into oblivion.

The 1966 constitution, formally issued on February 22, 1967, was the result of a British-Swazi agreement and embodied a non-racial Parliament based on universal suffrage. It also signalled the political paramountcy of the Ngwenyama. It recognized Sobhuza II as king of all Swaziland and vested all Swazi national land in his office (and, after a prolonged debate, the mineral wealth as well). The Ngwenyama emerged with maximum executive power, obtaining the right to appoint the Prime Minister and

Cabinet and to nominate six members of each house. With the promulg
tion of the new constitution, only the national elections of April 1967
stood between the forces of the monarchy and their control of an independent Swaziland in September 1968. The Imbokodvo seized the
initiative and put forth a holistic platform, seeking to undercut the appeal
of the remaining political parties. It promised "independence now", a
non-racial society, maximum economic development, a free and democratic
spirit of national unity, universal welfare services and international neu-
trality.[37] With the USA, SDP and SIF out of existence, the Imbokodvo
faced only the NNLC and two fragments of the old Swaziland Progressive
Party led by Nquku and Mabuza. The NNLC alone made a credible
showing as the Imbokodvo won every seat in the 24-man House of
Assembly by margins of over 4–1, gathering nearly 80 per cent of the popular vote to 20 per cent for the NNLC, one-third of one per cent for the
Mabuza forces and one-tenth of one per cent for those of Nquku. There is
a good deal of validity to the NNLC contention that the eight three-man
constituencies penalized its urban strength by insuring heavy rural
majorities for the Imbokodvo. On balance, the NNLC gathered what was
in essence a protest vote, running best in those districts such as Mbabane
and Mphumalanga which had significant non-Swazi African and
Eurafrican populations.[38] The NNLC remains an important ingredient
in the national political life as a vibrant opposition but is not it a serious
threat to the hegemony of the Imbokodvo.

THE NGWENYAMA TRIUMPHANT

With the attainment of internal self-government and later, independence,
the Ngwenyama and his supporters emerged overwhelmingly triumphant.
The institution of kingship in Swaziland, personified by Sobhuza II,
significantly expanded its scope and increased its power. No longer is the
Ngwenyama simply king of the traditionally-oriented Swazis, he is now
King of Swaziland as a whole, and all people who would participate in the
political system must be recognized as "Swazis". The monarchy has
emerged both as a symbol of national unity and a force for it. It has
developed new modes of conflict resolution and through its absorption of
non-Swazi Africans, detribalized Swazis and Europeans into the political
system, enriched the political culture of the country.
    Not that the system is flawless. The Imbokodvo must continue to develop
internally if it is to embrace the growing numbers of politically aware
Swazis. As more and more of them receive education and move into the
modern economic sector, increasingly they will want a greater measure
of political responsibility and a greater voice in the policy-making organs
of the party apparatus. As time goes on, one can well expect that there
will be increasing tension within the Imbokodvo between the new bureaucrats and the older tribal authorities. The next interregnum may well bear
witness to major structural strains and stress as competing forces within the
Imbokodvo and the Swazi National Council struggle to assert themselves.
At that time, both institutions may well attempt to expand their power at

the expense of the monarchy and, depending upon the nature of the new Ngwenyama, there could be a three-way struggle for political primacy in Swaziland. All of this lies in the future, however, for as long as Sobhuza II remains healthy and vigorous, it is he who will dominate the political landscape of Swaziland. He remains the political prime mover in the country.[39]

Looking back over the recent political history of Swaziland, one is tempted to view the rise of the Ngwenyama as inexorable. This is misleading. As strong as the monarchy was in 1960 and as resilient as the institution of kingship proved to be, a great deal depended on the operational skill of Sobhuza II. His political dexterity and his superb use of the instrumentalities of statecraft were important contributory factors to his success as a political actor. Observers have pointed, and rightly so, to the sources of traditional legitimacy which supported the Ngwenyama. But a great deal also depended on his "modern", pragmatic ability to get things done. At several critical junctures, Sobhuza II guessed, and guessed correctly, choosing courses of action which in addition to securing a pre-eminent position for the kingship, helped to unite the country. It is he who enlarged the power of the political centre at the expense of a series of potentially dysfunctional elements which could have fragmented the political life of Swaziland.

The formation of the Imbokodvo and the commitment of the full weight of the monarchy to the national political fray dramatically altered the political context of Swaziland. Despite the risks, Sobhuza II was correct in ascertaining that if he left the national political arena to others, the power of the monarchy would surely decline. The nature of the Imbokodvo and his choice of its leader were also politically astute for they enable the Ngwenyama to operate behind several screens, to preserve his political techniques and reserve his freedom of action. One could also argue that the Ngwenyama's marriage of convenience with the European settlers was a clever strategy for it enabled him to defeat his more serious rivals without interference and gave the members of the Imbokodvo time to gain political expertise. Here again, there was considerable risk that the alliance would damage the prestige of the monarchy. Certainly in other parts of Africa, European support of a traditional ruler would have been seized upon a *cause célèbre*. In the Swazi case, the traditionalists were careful to indicate privately that such an alliance was merely a tactic:

> We are entitled now to use the white man's legal devices to do to them what they did to us, to get our land, to chase them out of it . . .[40]

The swiftness with which the Imbokodvo moved against the USA party once it gained confidence indicates just how transitory was the nature of that alliance.

The Ngwenyama was also skilful in the use of delaying tactics. By declaring, which was only partially true, that he could not act without long deliberations with the *Liqoqo* and the *Libandla*, the Ngwenyama was able to drag out his negotiations with the British until they conceded the need for a compromise. By playing for time over the 1963 constitution, he was able to build slowly to a political peak while the political parties, particularly the NNLC, were overplaying their hand and gaining the enmity of the colonial authority. Inaction and delay immeasurably aided the monarchy, not only over the 1963 constitution but over the entire question of the status of the Ngwenyama and also his relation to the national mineral wealth. With the tide of decolonization running on his side, Sobhuza II derived maximum advantage from careful, exhaustive negotiations and outright stubbornness.

The foregoing recapitulation of the political events which led to the present situation in Swaziland was meant to throw into relief the strength of the monarchy and the skill with which the Ngwenyama operated politically. At the same time there is little doubt that the Ngwenyama was greatly aided by the nature of the national political arena. Its size, ethnic composition and its location, in fact, its entire ecological setting, all supported the monarchy's drive for political hegemony. The enclosed situation of Swaziland and the constellation of forces operative in Southern Africa during the 1960s presented Sobhuza II with a substantial opportunity to enhance his own position and to make maximum use of his advantages. It is not by chance that the then Secretary-General of the Organization of African Unity, Diallo Telli, remarked in Accra on October 15, 1965:

> In Basutoland, Bechuanaland and Swaziland, where we note with concern that the political parties which have won the recent elections, organized in *vase clos* and which took place in conditions of which we are aware and under pressures that we can well imagine, are all favourable to cooperation with the fascist, racist government of South Africa, the situation is no less alarming.[41]

That Swaziland was a *vase clos*, or sealed system, is clear. Small in size (6,705 square miles) and population (400,000), it consists of a single tribal-nation, the Swazis. It is relatively isolated, surrounded on three sides by South Africa and on the fourth by the Portuguese territory of Mozambique. Until independence, its contacts with Black Africa were superficial and sporadic. Swaziland has been bound up in the context of Southern Africa for so many years that when political and ideological intrusions occurred their impact was markedly reduced.[42] As exogenous forces impinged on Swaziland, their political impact was muted both by the insulation of the surrounding European-controlled areas and by the nature of Swazi traditional society in which 87 per cent of the population was encapsulated in its rural, tribal milieu and 97 per cent of the population was illiterate.[43] These factors helped to prevent the Pan-African-oriented parties from rapidly gaining support and there seems little question that the more or less controlled environment which prevailed in Swaziland during the 1960s aided the traditional forces in their thrust for political power.

The constellation of forces operative in the 1960s in Southern Africa also helped. Until 1960, for example, each of the three High Commission Territories was vulnerable to incorporation into South Africa should Great Britain agree. After 1961, however, with the British decision to develop the territories for eventual independence, there was far more room for political manœuvre. The Ngwenyama could thus use the South Africans and the European settlers against the Pan-African parties and the British, and having defeated them, use the British against the European settlers. At the same time, the nature of the arena did not, in and by itself, guarantee the triumph of the monarchy. Certainly in nearby Lesotho where an analogous situation existed, the King of Lesotho, Moshoeshoe II, was far less successful in attaining political power. On balance, then, it would seem that the vibrancy of the Swazi tribal structure and the nature of the arena, particularly its homogeneity and isolation, made possible the triumph of the monarchy, but it was the political expertise of Sobhuza II which accounted for its magnitude.

Faced with the intrusion of modernity, the Ngwenyama used its impact to enhance his standing within the tribal community and extend the power of the monarchy over non-Swazi forces in the country. In the process, his actions led to significant levels of political development. This is not to say that Sobhuza II deliberately set out to lead his people to modern political life or to induce them to participate in political development. This he did not do. But in reacting to the threat to his political power and by elevating the monarchy to a position of pre-eminence which it had not enjoyed for over a hundred years, the monarchy increased the linkage between the political centre and the population of Swaziland and generated meaningful levels of political integration. The monarchy then, partially by default, partially by design, led to a greater sense of national unity and community in Swaziland until the Crown is now the main symbolic referent on the national political level. Nowhere else in sub-Saharan Africa has a traditional ruler emerged so powerful or with greater functional utility for the political integration of the nation-wide political system.

In Swaziland the small number of non-Swazis within the larger, trans-Swazi political system and the generally coterminous nature of the Swazi state and kingdom greatly aided the Ngwenyama.[44] It was the size and the nature of the arena which enabled the monarchy to best utilize its advantages of a traditional political system receptive to elite-sponsored change and centralized political authority. This cluster of advantages gave the monarchy a basis for its drive toward political hegemony which few other political systems in sub-Saharan Africa could offer a traditional ruler.

At the same time, it should be pointed out that even with all these advantages, the Ngwenyama might still have been defeated and his power curtailed if he had not played his hand carefully and well, utilizing his advantages to maximum impact. In nearby Lesotho where many similar ingredients were present, the king lost, not gained, power. Thus it would appear that on balance, the type of traditional political system, the historical importance of the institution of kingship and the nature of the political arena made feasible the Ngwenyama's bid for political hegemony but his skill insured its success.

POSTSCRIPT

On April 12, 1973, the King of Swaziland, Ngwenyama Sobhuza II, scrapped that country's constitution, calling it "un-Swazi". He then took personal command of the government and the civil service, and organized a paramilitary force loyal to him to "preserve order". In addition he abolished political parties and similar organizations, which he said had "cultivated dissension"; and he instituted a sixty-day detention law. In September 1973, on the fifth anniversary of Swaziland's independence, the seventy-four-year-old King announced that he was going to set up a royal commission to draw up a new constitution for the country. This new constitution, he declared, was to embody "the Swazi national character" and to "harmonize" Swazi tradition with modern principles of constitutional and international law. Since members of the commission were selected personally by the Ngwenyama and serve at his pleasure, there seems little doubt that the eventual constitutional report will further entrench the king's power.

As of today, however, the commission has not reported its findings and there is every indication that the promulgation of a new constitution lies a good way in the future. Sobhuza II is not unhappy with this interlude. Although he had considerable power under the old constitution, and expects to have more under the new, ruling without a constitution has not proved to be burdensome. There was little overt opposition to his complete takeover last year (although some opposition politicians, including Dr. Ambrose Zwane, leader of the Ngwane National Liberatory Congress, have been jailed under the sixty-day detention Act); and there was widespread support among the more traditional members of the government for his action.

At the same time, the present political system, which so clearly bears the stamp of Sobhuza II, faces a time of testing when he departs; and it remains to be seen whether the new King and the leadership of the Imbokodvo are prepared or able to handle the challenges of the post-Sobhuza era. The new constitution, when and if it appears, may offer some important clues as to the outlines of the future, but it will in no way ensure that the subsequent interregnum period will be without both trial and turbulence for the political system and the nation.

NOTES

1 The author is indebted to the many valuable comments of Absalom Vilakazi, John Grotpeter and Dr. Msindazwe Sukati, Ambassador of Swaziland to the United States and High Commissioner for Swaziland in Canada.
2 For a fuller examination of these facets, the interested reader should consult C. P. Potholm, *Swaziland: The Dynamics of Political Modernization* (Berkeley: University of California Press, 1972).
3 David E. Apter, "The Role of Traditionalism in the Political Modernization of Ghana and Uganda", *World Politics*, Vol. XIII No. 4 (1960), pp. 45–68 and *The*

Political Kingdom in Uganda (Princeton: Princeton University Press, 1961); C. S. Whitaker, Jr., "A Dysrhythmic Process of Political Change". *World Politics*, Vol. XIX No. 2 (1967), pp. 190–217, and Norman N. Miller, "The Political Survival of Traditional Leadership", *The Journal of Modern African Studies*, Vol. VI No. 2 (1968), pp. 183–198. See also Lloyd Fallers, "The Predicament of the Modern African Chief: An Instance from Uganda", *American Anthropologist*, Vol. LVII (1955), pp. 290–305 and Peter C. Lloyd, "Traditional Rulers", in James S. Coleman and Carl G. Rosberg, Jr. (eds.), *Political Parties and National Integration in Tropical Africa* (Berkeley: University of California Press, 1966), pp. 382–412.

4   Hilda Kuper, *An African Aristocracy: Rank Among the Swazis* (London: Oxford University Press, 1947), Chapter II; A. T. Bryant, *Olden Times in Zululand and Natal* (London: Longmans, 1929); T. V. Bulpin, *Storm over the Transvaal* (Capetown: Standard Press, 1955); J. D. Omer-Cooper, *The Zulu Aftermath* (Evanston: Northwestern University Press, 1966), Chapter III. For the vital last decades of the 19th century, the reader should consult N. G. Garson, *The Swaziland Question and the Road to the Sea 1887–1895* (Johannesburg: University of Witwatersrand Press, 1957).

5   Bulpin, *Storm over the Transvaal*, p. 125.

6   In 1963, the post of High Commissioner for Swaziland, Basutoland and the Bechuanaland Protectorate was abolished and each of the Resident Commissioners, now known as Her Majesty's Commissioners, were formally elevated to a status roughly equal to that of a colonial governor.

7   Government of Great Britain, Colonial Office, *Swaziland 1946* (London: His Majesty's Stationery Office, 1947), p. 50.

8   R. P. Stevens, *Losotho, Botswana and Swaziland* (New York: Frederick A. Praeger, 1967), pp. 174–254. Stevens sees the appointment of Francis (later Sir Francis) Loyd in 1964 as Her Majesty's Commissioner as particularly indicative of this latter trend.

9   Kuper points out, however, that the Swazis themselves agree upon only the last eight. See her *The Swazis: A South African Kingdom* (New York: Holt, Rinehart and Winston, 1963), p. 7. The Litunga makes a most interesting comparison and the reader is urged to consult Gerald L. Caplan, "Barotseland: the Secessionist Challenge to Zambia", *The Journal of Modern African Studies*, Vol. VI No. 3 (1968), pp. 343–360.

10 In addition to *An African Aristocracy* and *The Swazis: A South African Kingdom* (cited above), she has written *The Uniform of Color* (Johannesburg: University of Witwatersrand Press, 1947); *The Swazis* (London: Oxford University Press, 1952); and "The Swazis of Swaziland", in J. L. Gibbs (ed.), *Peoples of Africa* (New York: Holt, Rinehart and Winston, 1965). Her novel, *Bite of Hunger* (New York: Harcourt, Brace and World, 1965) also offers an illuminating insight into the impact of modernization on the Swazi tribal fabric as does her more recent play, *A Witch in My Heart* (London: Oxford University Press, 1970). Allister Miller has also written a novel about the Swazis, *Mamisa: The Swazi Warrior* (Pietermaritzburg: Shuter and Shuter, 1953). In addition, Brian Marwick has done extensive work on the Swazis, including *The Swazis* (Cambridge: Cambridge University Press, 1940) and *Abantu Bakwa Ngwane* (Capetown: University of Capetown Press, 1939). Dorothy Doveton has a shorter monograph, *The Human Geography of Swaziland* (London: George Philip and Son, 1937).

11 S. N. Eisenstadt, "Primitive Political Systems: A Preliminary Comparative Analysis", *American Anthropologist*, Vol. LXI (1959), pp. 200–220. For a comparison of these two generic types, see Max Gluckman, "The Kingdom of the Zulu of South Africa", and Audrey I. Richard's "The Political System of the Bemba Tribe—North-Eastern Rhodesia", in M. Fortes and E. E. Evans-Pritchard (eds.), *African Political Systems* (London: Oxford University Press, 1960), pp. 25–55 and 83–120, respectively. Additional comparative material is to be found in I. Schapera, *Government and Politics in Tribal Societies* (London: C. A. Watts and Company, 1956) and Max Gluckman, *Politics, Law and Ritual in Tribal Society* (Oxford:

158   AFRICAN KINGSHIPS IN PERSPECTIVE

Basil Blackwell, 1965). See also the discussion of these strands in C. P. Potholm, *Four African Political Systems* (Englewood Cliffs: Prentice Hall, 1970), pp. 62–89.

12 Kuper, *The Swazis*, p. 59.

13 Kuper, *African Aristocracy*, pp. 197–223. See also G. M. Carter, "Sacred Fertility Festival", *Africa Special Report*, Vol. II No. 4 (April 1957), p. 5.

14 Daryll Forde (ed.), *African Worlds* (London: Oxford University Press, 1954), viii.

15 Kuper, *African Aristocracy*, p. 113.

16 *Times of Swaziland*, Vol. LXVI No. 29 (July 19, 1968), pp. 1–6. In this regard, we should perhaps remember that social organization as stated often differs from social organization as practiced: Claude Levi-Strauss, *Structural Anthropology* (New York: Basic Books, 1963), Chapters VII, VIII.

17 Schapera, *Government and Politics*, p. 98. For the Swazis, it is the office which gives the symbols efficacy and not vice versa. They thus differ quite markedly, for example, from the Anuak and the Shilluk, among whom the mere possession of royal emblems makes a noble a king.

18 Kuper, "The Swazis of Swaziland", p. 494.

19 Marwick, *The Swazis*, p. 65 and Kuper, *African Aristocracy*, p. 60.

20 John Beattie, "Checks on the Abuse of Political Power in Some African States: A Preliminary Framework for Analysis", *Sociologus*, Vol. IX No. 2 (1959), pp. 97–115. Beattie applies these to his analysis of the *Bunyoro: An African Kingdom* (New York: Holt, Rinehart and Winston, 1960). Another prominent example of institutional checks on the political power of traditional African leaders is found in K. A. Busia, *The Position of the Chief in the Modern Political System of Ashanti* (London: Oxford University Press, 1951) and E. M. Smith, *The Golden Stool* (London: Halloran Publishing House, 1927).

21 Kuper, *African Aristocracy*, p. 127. For a complete synopsis of the age-sets among the Swazi, see pp. 117–133 of that work.

22 James W. Fernandez, "The Shaka Complex", *Transition* No. 29 (March, 1964), pp. 11–14 and "Filial Piety and Power: Psychosocial Dynamics in the Legends of Shaka and Sundiata", paper delivered at the Dartmouth College faculty seminar, April 1968. Francis L. K. Hsu has pioneered work in this area. See his *Psychological Anthropology* (Homewood, Illinois: The Dorsey Press, 1961).

23 J. F. Holleman (ed.), *Experiment in Swaziland* (Capetown: Oxford University Press, 1964).

24 R. P. Stevens, "Swaziland Political Development", *The Journal of Modern African Studies,* Vol. I No. 3 (1963), pp. 327–350; C. P. Potholm, "Changing Political Configurations in Swaziland", *The Journal of Modern African Studies*, Vol. IV No. 3 (1966), pp. 313–322, and "Swaziland in Transition to Independence", *Africa Report* Vol. XII No. 6 (June, 1967), pp. 49–54; R. P. Stevens, *Lesotho, Botswana and Swaziland* (New York: Frederick A. Praeger, 1968); and Jack Halpern, *South Africa's Hostages* (Baltimore: Penguin Books, 1965). See also John J. Grotpeter, *Political Leadership and Political Development in the High Commission Territories* (unpublished Ph.D. thesis, Washington University, 1965).

25 Government of Great Britain, Colonial Office, *Swaziland 1946* (London: His Majesty's Stationery Office, 1950), p. 25.

26 Government of Great Britain, Commonwealth Relations Office, *Swaziland 1960* (London: Her Majesty's Stationery Office, 1961), p. 3.

27 Swaziland Democratic Party, *Minutes 10/11/62* (Mbabane: mimeographed, 1962), p. 9.

28 Government of Great Britain, Colonial Office, *Minutes of the Swaziland Constitutional Conference January 28–February 1, 1963* (London: mimeographed, 1963).

29 *Times of Swaziland*, Vol. 60 No. 26 (June 29, 1962), p. 9 and the *Swaziland Recorder* No. 8 (September–December 1962), p. 5.

30 The Gordon Highlanders were later replaced by a battalion of the North Lancashire Royal Regiment (1964), who in turn were replaced by the Gloucester Regiment (1965) and the Royal Irish Fusiliers (1966). The presence of these troops gave Great Britain a strategic reserve in southern Africa and was widely regarded as a firm British commitment to the area until they were withdrawn in November 1966.

31 Government of Great Britain, Colonial Office, *Command Paper No. 2052* (London: Her Majesty's Stationery Office, 1963).
32 *Johannesburg Star*, September 4, 1963, p. 7; *Rand Daily Mail*, October 1, 1963, p. 1; Ngwane National Liberatory Congress, *Press Release*, January 26, 1965, p. 2.
33 *Times of Swaziland*, Vol. 62 No. 23 (June 5, 1964), p. 13.
34 The initial draft of the Imbokodvo constitution, for example, refers to close "cooperation with other political movements, especially European organizations with similar policies". (Imbokodvo National Movement, *Imbokodwe Embalala Constitution* (Mbabane: mimeographed, 1964). In the text finally made public, however, the words "political" and "European" were deleted.
35 *Times of Swaziland*, Vol. 64, No. 49 (December 4, 1966), p. 1.
36 *Times of Swaziland*, Vol. 63, No. 44 (October 29, 1965), p. 1.
37 *Times of Swaziland*, Vol. 65, No. 14 (April 7, 1967), pp. 1–2.
38 C. P. Potholm, "Swaziland in Transition ', p. 53.
39 This is in no way jeopardized by the ability of the NNLC, as demonstrated by the April 1972 election, to win a number of seats in the House of Assembly if the political system is so constructed that the Ngwenyama remains firmly in control.
40 Swaziland Democratic Party, *Minutes 16/4/63* (Mbabane: mimeographed, 1963), p. 1.
41 *Joint Memorandum by the Leaders of the Elected Governments of Basutoland, Bechuanaland Protectorate and Swaziland to the Heads of African States* (Accra: mimeographed, October 25, 1965), p. 2.
42 C. P. Potholm, "The Protectorates, the O.A.U. and South Africa", *International Journal*, Vol. XXII, No. 1 (Winter, 1966–1967), pp. 68–72; Larry Bowman, "The Subordinate State System of Southern Africa", paper delivered at the African Studies convention meeting (November, 1967); and Peter Robson, "Economic Integration in Southern Africa", *The Journal of Modern African Studies*, Vol. IV, No. 4 (December 1967), pp. 469–490. For an overview of the entire southern African context, see C. P. Potholm and Richard Dale, *Southern Africa in Perspective: Essays in Regional Politics* (New York: The Free Press, 1972).
43 *Swaziland Recorder* No. 4 (September–December 1961), p. 21. The rate is now down to 75 per cent.
44 We are not concerned with the large numbers of Swazis who live outside the present borders of Swaziland in the Republic of South Africa for they did not play any role in the development of the present political system.

5

THE BASOTHO MONARCHY[1]

Richard F. Weisfelder

On March 31, 1970, the King of Lesotho, Mosheoshoe II, was abruptly whisked out of the country for what Prime Minister Leabua Jonathan called an extended vacation.[2] The King's unexpected excursion was precipitated by the acute constitutional crisis, economic uncertainty, and sporadic violence which followed Chief Jonathan's eleventh-hour decision to retain power despite the defeat of his National Party in the General Election on January 27, 1970.[3] Many observers perceived Moshoeshoe II's departure to be the culmination of a protracted series of confrontations with the National Party regime and the beginning of an exile which would last for at least as long as Chief Jonathan remained in power.

Throughout his tenure as "Paramount Chief" from 1960 to 1965 and as "King" under the independence constitution, Moshoeshoe II has consistently resisted being relegated to the role of a passive Head of State in the mould of the British constitutional monarchy. At every stage of constitutional advance, he has argued against thoughtless mimicking of foreign political institutions. Instead, he advocated a synthesis of parliamentary democracy with the Basotho political tradition in order to preserve executive functions for the King as the ultimate "protector" and "arbiter" of the Basotho national heritage. After reluctantly participating in independence celebrations on October 4, 1966 under a constitution of which he thoroughly disapproved, the King continued to demand the revisions and amendments that he deemed appropriate. His actions, both before and after independence helped to precipitate a political melée superficially reminiscent of Gilbertian farce.

The roots of conflicts involving the Basotho monarchy lie in an ambiguous historical legacy, an unresolved institutional format and a paradoxical basis of legitimacy. Kingship, like almost all "traditional" Basotho patterns, is a relatively recent innovation. Its existence derives from the creativity and political genius of Moshoeshoe I, the founder of the ruling Koena dynasty in the early nineteenth century. Since that time, Moshoeshoe's successors have been engaged in a continual process of adapting the kingship to the circumstances of British colonial rule in Basutoland, to the impact of the economic, political and social transformations occurring in Southern Africa and recently, to the processes of constitutional evolution toward independence. The rapidity and regularity of significant changes in the functioning model of the monarchy meant that no format was ever fully institutionalized or generally accepted as a normal standard. Virtually all Basotho groups recognize that the identity and survival of their nation has been rooted in the monarchy, but each has excerpted divergent elements from this brief history of kingship in formulating its conception of those arrangements that are genuinely "traditional".

To unravel and understand the predicament of the monarchy in Lesotho, it is not sufficient to rely upon the usual dichotomies offered by way of explanation. Far more is involved than just a clash between the traditional legitimacy of a hereditary monarch and the popular mandate of a democratically selected Prime Minister and Parliament. Moshoeshoe II's battle with Chief Jonathan is not merely a longstanding personal feud, an uneven match of a canny politician against a political dilettante, or a factional struggle within the royal family. The underlying issues should not be obscured by stereotyping the protagonists as either dupes of Moscow and Peking or proponents of apartheid and Bantustans. Similarly, Chief Jonathan's actions only superficially vindicate those who see an unbridgeable gap between indigenous African political systems and "modern", "Western" forms of government such as constitutional monarchy or parliamentary democracy. In Lesotho, contemporary battles between competing ideologies and interests have taken on the protective colouration of efforts to define an appropriate modern role for the monarchy. Moreover, the paradox of pervasive conflict in one of the few ethnically and linguistically homogeneous African states lends added significance to efforts at penetrating this tangled political thicket.

The elements which seem most crucial in studying kingship in Lesotho are the sources of its legitimacy, the institutional framework, the impact of individual personality factors, and the intrusion of developments from South Africa.[4] Primary referents in discussing institutions and legitimacy are (1) the substantive and symbolic functions and purposes of the monarchy, (2) the extent, efficacy, and types of popular participation, (3) the structure of supportive and opposing groups, and (4) the amount and location of power in the political system. Since virtually every political issue in Lesotho is distorted and complicated by the harsh realities of its being a tiny enclave state totally surrounded by South Africa, special emphasis must also be placed on the interaction of domestic and international dimensions.

EMERGENT KINGSHIP

Observed in broad historical perspective, the development of kingship among the Sotho represented a sharp break with earlier political patterns.[5] During the sixteenth through eighteenth centuries, fragmented groups of Sotho peoples had gradually expanded into the high veldt portion of Southern Africa between the Vaal River and the Drakensberg mountains. Although these dispersed segments, primarily of ascendant Koena and Kgatla lineage-clusters, dominated and often assimilated the earlier inhabitants of the area, they retained a decentralized, small-scale pattern of political organization. Fission within existing communities was a frequent occurrence.

A trend toward amalgamation of separate Sotho political units began to occur in the late eighteenth and early nineteenth centuries, probably as a result of increasing population density and the emergence of new trading patterns with distant European settlements. The unifying catalyst dramatically reinforcing this rudimentary state-building process took the form of a devastating series of wars known as the *Lifaqane*. Throughout approximately fifteen years of recurrent struggle against a series of intruders dispossed by Chaka's expansionist Zulu state, the Southern Sotho suffered a degree of social and physical dislocation that substantially altered their territorial distribution, ethnic composition, and political and economic life. The desperate search for security engendered by this protracted chaos provided the opportunity for Moshoeshoe, the son of a minor chief from the junior branch of the Bamonaheng Koena, to preside over the creation of a new state out of the many Sotho and Nguni remnants.

Moshoeshoe's rise from obscurity during the 1820s resulted from his exceptional capacity to counteract anarchic trends precipitated by the *Lifaqane*. Almost all commentators have acknowledged the courage, flexibility, and sagacity with which he mobilized the physical and human resources at his disposal. Moshoeshoe was, first and foremost, a consummate politician whose genius lay in the breadth of his vision, in his ability to balance and retain viable options, and in his mastery of the art of persuasion. The charismatic qualities ascribed to his leadership rested upon an essentially empirical underpinning, namely, his sustained ability to achieve improbable and spectacular results.

According to Eugene Casalis, the basis of political and social cohesion among the Sotho was the principle that "sovereigns, instead of being supported by the community, are the chief supporters of it".[6] The Sesotho word *morena* inadequately rendered as chief or king in English is in fact derived from a verb meaning to be prosperous or to be tranquil. Its figurative meaning—he who watches over the public safety and welfare— emphasized the obligations and responsibilities of a ruler which are ignored in the standard translation. Moshoeshoe's unusual effectiveness as a *morena*, or protector and provider, can be attributed to his fortunate choice of the secure hilltop fortress, Thaba Bosiu, as a refuge after setbacks in the early years of the *Lifaqane*. To this defensive capacity he quickly added the economic inducements of resources in cattle taken from distant Thembu peoples in deft raids across the Drackensberg.

In drawing together individuals and groups of divergent origins, Moshoeshoe adjured the luxuries of avenging old grievances, of indulging parochial prejudices, or of imposing ascriptive criteria of kinship and class. Protection, land, cattle and other rewards of membership in his expanding community were extended to all who would simply swear allegience to himself or one of his subordinates, regardless of whether they were Sotho or Nguni, longstanding allies or former enemies, or even former cannibals who had devoured his own grandfather, Peete. Moshoeshoe shrewdly legitimized his style of rule by identifying it with recognizable elements of prior Sotho governmental patterns. However, his readiness to adopt a host of agricultural, educational, military and political innovations minimized the risks of untimely defeat or ill-fortune.

To cope with stronger, hostile neighbours he repeatedly aligned himself with distant, still more formidable forces whose assistance would tip the balance of power in his favour. Hence Moshoeshoe sent tribute of ostrich plumes and animal skins to Chaka to secure Zulu support against local enemies. Later in his career he entered into numerous arrangements with the British rulers of the Cape Colony to try to forestall the aggressive Boer trekkers who, after 1836, sought to displace him from choice positions of his country. From the late 1840s to the mid 1860s, he made Thaba Bosiu a major centre of diplomatic efforts to create a unified African defensive arrangement against white territorial expansion. When forced into large-scale hostilities, Moshoeshoe typically fought cautious, defensive battles on his own ground. Even then, he was content to reap a limited harvest from partial successes without pressing for total victory or preventing his enemies from saving face and retiring gracefully.

No doubt Moshoeshoe's diplomatic and persuasive skills had been honed by the fact that his domestic political power was contingent upon his ability to secure consent through regular consultation with his sub-ordinates and with his people at large. The frequently cited Sotho maxim, "A chief is a chief by the people", is especially applicable to Moshoeshoe. To determine the tenor of public opinion on controversial issues and to mobilize support for his policies, he regularly convened a national or local gathering of his adult male adherents, known as a *pitso*. Although ecstatic foreign observers have unduly idealized these deliberative assemblies as pure reincarnations of classical direct democracy, they are quite correct in portraying them as meaningful political forums where a wide range of viewpoints was freely and intelligently articulated by ordinary citizens with minimal fear of reprisal. To be sure, the chiefs retained a dominant influence through control of the agenda, recognition of speakers, applause for favoured ideas, and the right to formulate any final decisions. But, for Moshoeshoe the *pitso* served as a primary basis of support in lieu of traditional hereditary legitimacy and as a medium of political socialization for inculcating a sense of cohesion among his polyglot following. Moshoeshoe could rarely afford to disregard either his subordinate chiefs or the common people. His public statements that *pitsos* "constituted his power and he was their servant"[7] have a distinct ring of authenticity.

When it was not possible to consult the nation at large, Moshoeshoe relied upon the wisdom of subordinate chiefs, close kinsmen, and other prominent members of the community. This small, informal core of national leaders tended to be responsive to grass-roots attitudes and desires because of their intimate face-to-face contacts with ordinary citizens in the daily parley at their local village meeting place or court (*lekhotla*). The abundance of good land meant that despotic chiefs might lose their following if they failed to represent local interests in the highest councils of state.

Much of Moshoeshoe's own influence and prestige emanated from his even-handed control of the distribution of cattle to worthy retainers and of the allocation of land which he held in trust for the nation. His prerogatives

M

of summoning communal labour, levying taxes in cattle (*sethabathaba*), and demanding a share of agricultural produce and wild game allowed him to mobilize the economic resources necessary to carry out military and administrative responsibilities, to pay tribute to enemies, to provide hospitality for strangers, and to care for the indigent. While comprehensive governmental functions were concentrated in Moshoeshoe's hands his ubiquitous powers implied heavy obligations and responsibilities, not the absence of restraints.

Adherents of the Basutoland Congress Party (BCP) perceive these underlying egalitarian, consensual, and cooperative elements to be central to the Basotho tradition. Indeed, the BCP contends that Moshoeshoe's historic role as unifier and protector of the Basotho might serve as a prototype for contemporary "African Socialism" and for black liberation struggles against alien domination and white racism. However, the substantial germ of truth within the BCP image should not be permitted to obscure the prescriptive dimensions within Moshoeshoe's political system.

Several Sotho phrases, such as "A man without a chief is an animal", imply that the fabric of society depended upon obedience to authority and suggest that the "body" of the people must necessarily have a "head", commonly legitimized by right of birth. The acquisition of power was clearly restricted to near kinsmen within the Koena lineage. Hereditary prerogatives, combined with comprehensive chiefly functions, gave chiefs the wherewithall to employ telling sanctions against opponents, to reward supporters handsomely, and to treat communal wealth or services as personal perquisities. In spite of the economic, political, and social advantages accruing to the Koena elite under Moshoeshoe, clan or lineage relationships did not create impermeable caste barriers or preclude development of more comprehensive national loyalties. Since virtually all of the pre-national components fused in Moshoeshoe's state were themselves heterogeneous, a new political identity transcending narrow kinship ties and based upon broader cultural, historical, and linguistic communalities was quite feasible. Thus the relationships between the rulers and the ruled embodied not only reciprocity of duties and functions but also a complex dual basis of political legitimacy summed up in the aphorism "A chief is a chief by the people; the people are a people through the chief".[8]

Moshoeshoe's following, which between 1827 and 1848 had increased from a few thousand adherents to approximately 80,000 persons, continued to expand rapidly because of an influx of refugees displaced by white settlement. As a result, existing political institutions required constant adaptation, in particular the development of mechanisms appropriate for asserting central direction over a much more complex and physically dispersed polity. Chiefs allied with or subordinate to Moshoeshoe fulfilled the same multiplicity of functions and responsibilities as their superior. They also retained ultimate control over the men, arms, food, and other resources within their respective jurisdictions that were required to implement central decisions. Hence, there was still a rich potential for local autonomy, and more ominously, for separatism and schism.

To cope with such tendencies, Moshoeshoe and his successors instituted the practice of placing their sons, brothers, and most trusted retainers as subordinate chiefs or headmen over segments of the country that were sparsely settled or where the loyalty of the local ruler was suspect.[9] The uncertain hereditary or popular legitimacy of a newly placed chief within his designated area generally compelled him to support the central authority upon which his own political survival so obviously depended. Shrewd placings, coupled with strategic royal marriages, abetted the process of political unification, accentuated the trend toward a more hierarchical, centralized system of government, and further justified Moshoeshoe's right to be considered as *morena e moholo*, *i.e.* a great chief or a king. However, placing by no means guaranteed central control or destroyed the entrenched segmentary principle that encouraged local autonomy. Chiefs with a prior hereditary right to rule a given area usually retained much of their land, local following, and influence as they were downgraded rather than deposed by having a superior placed over them. Similarly, members of the royal lineage frequently took advantage of poor communications with the central authority to build their own local power bases and to assert maximum discretion and independence *vis-à-vis* their senior kinsmen. Allowing for substantial internal variations, the structure of role approximated what Apter and Southall have described as a "pyramidal system" of authority, where a decentralizing, "segmentary" principle co-existed with its centralizing "hierarchical" opposite in a rather delicate balance.[10] This mixed pattern, while permitting a measure of local autonomy and continuity, at the same time offered ample opportunity for the monarch to assert his power in local matters by placing a person of his choosing as the pre-eminent chief of a given locality.

No formalized governmental bureaucracy, apart from the structure of chieftainship, existed to enforce central decisions upon each of the subordinate units comprising the state. Moshoeshoe and other senior chiefs were assisted by various ad hoc officials who helped them to fulfill public obligations and responsibilities. This rudimentary bureaucracy included (1) the commander of a chief's personal regiment, (2) a "town crier" responsible for security and public information within a chief's village, (3) "messengers" who were knowledgeable persons regularly entrusted with missions to domestic and foreign leaders, and (4) an informal cadre of councillors. Despite growing structural complexity and differentiation of roles, all of these functionaries served the monarch exclusively and lacked independent legitimacy of their own. It is precisely on this point that King Moshoeshoe II has attempted to mobilize popular sentiment against the Lesotho Independence Constitution and the incumbent Prime Minister. Specifically, the King has drawn invidious comparisons between his own stormy relationship with Chief Jonathan and the allegedly harmonious, supportive bonds linking his ancestor Moshoeshoe I, with Makoanyane, the leading warrior and councillor of that period.

Contemporary political controversies aside, it is clear that in the absence of a structured bureaucracy Moshoeshoe I himself bore the brunt of responsibility for conducting the affairs of the state and protecting its tenuous national unity. His personal political organization was remarkably effective and workable given the serious challenges with which it was confronted. His system, delicately balancing oligarchic and democratic facets, embodied a series of reciprocal duties, functions, and obligations shared by the rulers and the ruled. Indeed, the need for constant adaptation and adjustment in a particularly uncertain environment guaranteed that both leaders and ordinary citizens could wield effective options for influencing each other's behaviour. Nevertheless, the future of that political system remained particularly uncertain because its basis was so intensely personal rather than institutional. The declining physical powers and eventual death of the now aged nation-builder coincided with the increasing inability of the Basotho system to withstand the competing Boer and British powers in Southern Africa. At the very moment when his successors were vying among themselves to redefine and maximize their own roles, they were also forced to cope with the transformation of Basotho society within the confines of colonial rule.

THE RESTRUCTURING OF KINGSHIP UNDER COLONIAL RULE

It is impossible to avoid ambiguous conclusions when assessing the effects of white encroachment on the processes of Basotho state-building and national integration. The missionaries of the Paris Evangelical Mission Society (PEMS) to whom Moshoeshoe had extended his protection in 1833 were utilized to enhance his political power and influence. Virtually all commentators are agreed on the importance of their roles as advisors on foreign affairs, secretarial aides, interpreters, educators, and loyal arbiters between the Basotho and their adversaries. The arrival of missionaries was not an unmixed blessing since the new ideological cleavages between Christianized and traditional Basotho, and later, among adherents of competing Christian denominations, complicated the fashioning of a common national purpose. Rival missionary groups established among Moshoeshoe's neighbours and vassals often reinforced separatist tendencies and undermined efforts at further political consolidation.

In Moshoeshoe's era, as at present, the appropriate strategy for dealing with the white menace was a matter of controversy, augmenting and complicating dynastic struggles and other political antipathies. So long as Moshoeshoe's diplomacy and military might could gain grudging Boer and British respect for his supremacy, check armed assaults, and maintain the economic assets of the community, he was able to exert a modicum of control over his brothers, sons and other subordinates. Simultaneously, he used the ominous presence of the whites to justify greater unity and centralization of authority. But when the balance of power began to swing in favour of the Orange Free State Boers, these subordinates increasingly asserted their autonomy by making war or peace in accordance with their own economic and political interests, even at the expense of the national cause.

In one instance, Moshoeshoe's second son, Molapo, consented to the draconian peace of Mpharane that (temporarily) incorporated his lands and people, comprising the northern portion of Lesotho, into the Free State, The memory of this alleged treachery has been resurrected by opponents of Lesotho's Prime Minister, Leabua Jonathan, a grandson of Molapo, whose dealings with the South African regime are portrayed as reminiscent of his ancestor's "sell-out". To be sure, this absence of coordinated policy and strategy among the sons, brothers and retainers of the royal house in crisis situations reflected personal rivalries and the acute fissiparous potential in Moshoeshoe's political framework. Yet these domestic divisions and conflicts must also be perceived as expedients in a frantic diplomatic game which aimed at preserving the maximum options for the nation or at least the chance to survive. Like the leaders of the present-day Lesotho, Moshoeshoe and his subordinates found it impossible to sustain national cohesion while forced by military and economic weakness to choose among unsatisfactory, dependent political relationships with the white power structure.

Extension of British protection to the defeated and demoralized Basotho in 1868 prevented the complete dismemberment of the nation by the Orange Free State Boers, but did not immediately permit Moshoeshoe's eldest son and successor, Letsie, to regain the pre-eminence of his father. The government of the Cape Colony, which had assumed administrative responsibility for the Basotho, imposed an unpopular pattern of direct rule by colonial magistrates that circumscribed the roles of chiefs by removing such critical functions as the allocation of lands and the adjudication of criminal cases. Among the Basotho, Letsie was recognized as the legitimate head of the royal family. He was, however, *primus inter pares* since his brothers, Molapo and Masupha, were also treated as "great chiefs" and his political authority within their domains was virtually nil. Cape officials sought to exploit these divisions to forestall re-emergence of a central Basotho power that could prove inimical to their control. Nevertheless, the real autonomy among supposedly subordinate chiefs made it impossible for the colonial magistrates to affix responsibility upon Letsie for the strenuous Basotho opposition to Cape rule.

A remarkable prosperity and military resurgence, based on the earnings of Basotho migrants at the Kimberley diamond diggings enabled the nation to resist successfully the ill-advised Cape plans for disarmament and alienation of the Quthing district for white settlement. These struggles, known as the Gun War (1880-1), were a complex amalgam of civil strife and rebellion against colonial authority. Domestic cleavages occasioned by factionalism within the polygynous royal family, pitted Basotho ostensibly loyal to the colonial regime against rebellious brothers. Throughout this period Letsie adroitly played a difficult double game that led the white administrators to consider him vacillating, indecisive, and ineffectual. By feigning submission in order to retain the favour of the colonial administration, he sought to preserve both the status of the monarchy and British protection against the Free State. Nevertheless, his tacit encouragement to the rebel cause could be inferred from the vigorous part that his heir, Lerotholi, played in the resistance. Thus Letsie and his successors found it necessary to temper overt antagonism toward British colonial rule with the realization that subjection to the Free State, or later to South Africa, could be the unwanted outcome of trying British patience too severely.

Letsie's strategies received overwhelming vindication when Britain resumed direct responsibility for the Basotho in 1884 and reversed the policies of the Cape administration.[11] In the hope that "peace could be better kept under one chief than three",[12] the new colonial authorities emphatically defended the authority and central position of the monarch, or in British jargon, the Paramount Chief, against all challenges. The Paramountcy was deprived of jurisdiction over foreign affairs and judicial cases involving capital punishment but was permitted virtually complete freedom of action on most domestic matters. Lacking any distinctive philosophy of economic and political change, the colonial regime declined to interfere in matters of "national custom" so long as a balanced budget and law and order were maintained. This *laissez faire* approach allowed a total, if unintentional, recasting of patterns of authority and responsibility in Basutoland by making it possible for successive monarchs to transform the responsive, "pyramidal" structure of chieftainship into a more authoritarian, "hierarchical" format. The *pitso* and *lekhotla*, institutions geared to the earlier interdependent, reciprocal relationships between the rulers and the ruled, became less significant when popular demands for the redress of grievances could be treated as illegal disruption of the political fabric.

The capacity of the monarch to intervene regularly in local affairs was still limited by (1) the absence of a specialized royal bureaucracy able to enforce central decisions throughout the country; (2) reliance on subordinate chiefs, whose comprehensive administrative, economic, and social functions allowed them ample opportunity to pursue independent policies; (3) the privileged, hereditary position of descendents of Molapo and Masupha in the northern districts; and (4) the extraordinary difficulty of physical communications given the rugged terrain. Clearly, this revised colonial strategy, based on a minimal expenditure of force and money in Basutoland, could not rapidly or efficiently facilitate the institutionalization of a new political pattern. Thus the Basotho system of kingship remained a variegated patchwork, full of anomalies. But the fact that the monarch now had the option of intervening in select situations slowly created a more oligarchic framework which gave subordinate chiefs a greater interest in having the ear and favour of their superiors than the respect and support of their subjects.

These authoritarian trends were strongly reinforced by a host of other economic, political, and social factors. Rapid population increases doomed the *pitso* as a viable deliberative assembly and raised the economic and social costs of abandoning a despotic chief. Massive migration of Basotho to jobs in South Africa destroyed the face-to-face communication and sense of communal participation in the *lekhotla*, leaving the villages to the aged, the infirm, and those least able to resist ambitious chiefs. The monetization of relationships meant that chiefs were no longer the sole providers for the community and were tempted to disregard their obligations to the citizenry. Extensive use of the technique of placing by polygynous chiefs at all levels of the hierarchy resulted in a proliferation of new chiefs without grass roots support, who nevertheless asserted "traditional" prerogatives. Such placings, interposing layers of subordinate chiefs between the Paramountcy and the people, created administrative chaos and stymied the articulation and communication of popular interests and grievances.

Obviously, the bases of legitimacy of the monarch and of the chieftainship had changed in practice, if not in theory, from Moshoeshoe's era. Great emphasis was now placed on prescriptive dimensions such as hereditary rights to rule and the necessity of obedience to any legally established authority. Popular support no longer rested upon active participation in decision-making processes but on respect for the monarchy and the chieftainship as symbols of national identity. Although the monarchy appeared at a zenith of prestige and influence, its primarily defensive stance would prove a serious obstacle to its capacity for future leadership.

KINGSHIP LOSES THE INITIATIVE

Surprisingly little attention and research has been devoted to the brief reign of Lerotholi's son, Letsie II (1905–1913), or the long tenure of Letsie II's brother and successor, Griffith (1913–1939). No doubt the unaccustomed tranquility and prosperity that prevailed in Basutoland during the first three decades of the twentieth century fostered a lack of interest in what seemed to be a static political milieu, adapted and reconciled to colonial rule. Neither the Basotho chieftainship nor the British colonial authorities appeared to comprehend how the awesome expansion of the white South African economy was transforming Basutoland into a dependent rural backwater and perpetual reservoir of unskilled migrant labourers. Similarly, the visible power of the Paramount Chief in most domestic administrative matters concealed weaknesses in the capacity of the monarchy to promote economic progress and to exert a constructive influence over the tiny enclave's crucial external relationships.

Since the South Africa Act of 1909 had anticipated the transfer of Basutoland from British to South African sovereignty, the struggle to preserve separate Basotho statehood remained the central preoccupation of Kingship during the reigns of Letsie II and Griffith. By equating national survival with maintenance of their own expanded "customary" powers, prerogatives, and status, these monarchs were able to channel and transform intense Basotho aversion to the prospect of South African rule into broadly based support of the Paramountcy. Confronted by this Hobson's choice of colonial masters, the monarchy expressed its loyalty to the British Crown and its satisfaction with the "many and great benefits"[13] of the existing administrative arrangements that conveniently upheld the position of kingship. Thus, the spectre of incorporation into South Africa provided the Paramountcy with a plausible justification for embracing the dubious status quo under British protection.[14]

Even if Letsie II and Griffith had been cognizant of the political and social costs of increasing economic dependence, they could not have easily overcome the many barriers to modernization of the Basotho economy. Placing pressure on Britain for development assistance would not only have risked compromising the favoured political position of Kingship, but would have accentuated British eagerness to be rid of this unprofitable and troublesome territory. Indeed, the inducement used to justify incorporation into South Africa was the alleged economic advantage of such a transfer for Basutoland. Furthermore, projects undertaken in cooperation with the British authorities invariably had the unwanted effect of augmenting the influence of colonial administration at the expense of indigenous political structures. An influx of development capital or personnel would have created strong pressures for alienation of land and resources to foreign interests which could not readily be displaced thereafter. So acquiescence to economic stagnation, relieved only by stopgap palliatives, was the price that the monarchy had to pay for the constricted survival of Basutoland as a separate political entity.

Adverse circumstances account for only a part of the growing rigidity of the monarchy under Griffith. Fleeting glimpses of his career show a strong-willed individual, ready to gain his objectives on his own terms. Shortly before his accession to the throne, Griffith was converted to Roman Catholicism. The Paramount Chief was probably attracted by the Catholic missionaries' emphasis on notions such as hierarchy and deference to authority and by their manifest eagerness to work through the traditional institutional framework. This close association of Griffith and his royal successors with Catholicism buttressed the authoritarian political tendencies already stimulated by colonial rule. Far from planning comprehensive innovations, Griffith struggled with the routine problems of consolidating central power in the midst of bitter religious cleavages occasioned by his own conversion and of discontent over controversial new placings.

The initial stirrings of several rudimentary groups outside the framework of chieftainship must be interpreted as a response to both the declining innovative potential and narrowing responsive capacity of the monarchy. Political consciousness began to grow among a predominantly PEMS educated elite of clergy, teachers and laymen and was strongly reinforced by the development of similar African organizations in South Africa. Both the Basutoland Progressive Association founded in 1907 and Lekhotla la Bafo (Commoner's League) created in 1919 vigorously attacked abuses of power within the chieftainship. However, each would have preferred the rejuvenation of responsive traditional institutions to the substitution of a new African nationalist leadership. Because the monarchy had adopted a cautious, defensive posture, the achievement of more effective representation of popular opinion became their highest priority.

The Basutoland National Council, established in 1903, rapidly emerged as the principal focus of activity for politically-mobilized Basotho groups.[15] Composed of the British Resident Commissioner as President, the Paramount Chief as Chief Councillor, ninety-four nominees of the Paramount Chief, and five appointees of the Resident Commissioner, the Council was dominated by the "Sons of Moshoeshoe", that is, by the major descendants of the Moshoeshoe lineage plus the few remaining chiefs of non-Koena segments of the nation. In the short run, this advisory body reinforced the dominance of the monarch and the hierarchy of chiefs, since its members could pose as the legitimate spokesmen for the nation and act as staunch defenders of traditional interests. However, a number of lesser chiefs, headmen, and commoners, including such outspoken individuals as Josiel Lefela, the founder of Lekhotla la Bafo, were able to gain nomination to the Council. The chiefly contingent was factionalized and far from monolithic. Thus, the National Council gradually emerged as a distinctive institution, a counterpoise to both royal and colonial power and the logical vehicle for the promotion of political and social change.

After 1936, the British administration accepted and sought to implement Sir Alan Pim's dubious conclusion that social ills in Basutoland could be remedied by a restructuring of chiefly administration and courts after the Nigerian or Tanganyikan model of "indirect rule".[16] Confronted with this sudden determination to impose reform from above, Griffith attempted to soften the blow by giving his consent to the proposed measures only when he had secured concessions delaying their implementation. The resultant Native Administration and Native Courts Proclamations (Nos. 61 and 62 of 1938) asserted the predominance of the colonial authorities over the Paramountcy and the Chieftainship by making the right to rule contingent upon recognition from the British High Commissioner, in addition to meeting customary hereditary requirements. Although the ostensible purpose of these edicts was to regularize the existing system and to restrict further proliferation of chiefs and courts, the proclamations also accentuated the centralization of power in the monarchy. Armed with authority to issue orders and rules promoting good government and with the right to be consulted on the recognition of subordinate chiefs, the Paramountcy had gained telling levers for intervening in local politics. A strong monarchy could have reaped advantages from such innovations, while mobilizing the nationalist sentiments shared by chiefs and commoners against those reforms thought to compromise royal interests. The death of Griffith in 1938 led to a radically different outcome.

Two strong-willed half-brothers, Bereng and Seeiso Griffith, claimed the throne.[17] In designating his favourite son Bereng as his heir, the late Paramount Chief had ignored Seeiso's more senior rank. Reluctant to endorse this apparent breach of custom the British High Commissioner convened the Sons of Moshoeshoe to reconsider the issue of succession. At this meeting Seeiso's claim to the Paramountcy was upheld by a majority, presumably because it was congruent with established precedents. No doubt, the Sons of Moshoeshoe were also influenced by Seeiso's" strong and attractive personality"[18] and demonstrated political and administrative acumen. Despite continued rancor between the royal adversaries, Seeiso appeared to have restored a modicum of national unity and to have taken auspicious steps toward rationalizing the weak royal bureaucracy before his untimely death in December 1940 after only one year in power.

Seeiso's senior wife, Amelia 'Mantsebo Seeiso, was appointed Acting Paramount Chief and Regent for Constantine Bereng Seeiso, the two-year-old heir to the throne.[19] As the ranking adult male relative of the deceased monarch, Bereng Griffith had seemed the logical candidate to assume this role. He almost certainly had the support of the Sons of Lerotholi, that is, of the immediate royal family. However, Chief Gabashane Masupha, who had been Seeiso's principal councillor, and other members of the Sons of Moshoeshoe convinced the British authorities that the decision was a national one in which they should be permitted to participate. 'Mantsebo had received the support of a majority of the leading chiefs at a meeting of this more comprehensive descent group. Most probably, her supporters disregarded Bereng's compelling claims to be Regent out of fear that he would usurp the throne or in the hope of reaping political benefits from the reign of a weak and inexperienced female.

In a society where women were considered incompetent to manage their own affairs, any female Regent would have been hard pressed to command respect or exert purposive leadership. 'Mantsebo proved unable to cope with the intense social conflicts unleashed by (1) recrimination over the succession; (2) dissatisfaction with the 1938 administrative alterations; (3) pressure for further reforms; and (4) recruitment of 22,000 Basotho for overseas service during World War II. Indeed, the ineptness of the sickly and uneducated Regent caused rifts and disillusionment among her strongest supporters, some of whom, like Chief Gabashane Masupha, became aligned with Bereng's faction. 'Mantsebo's divisive impact permitted the British colonial regime to push ahead with hitherto delayed administrative revisions. More importantly, various groups of commoners and factions of chiefs seized the opportunity to advance their own political interests through the National Council to the detriment of the monarchy.

Bereng was embittered at twice being denied the throne and by Justice Lansdowne's unfavourable High Court verdict which rejected his attempt to secure judicial reversal of 'Mantsebo's appointment. He and his supporters continued their battle against the Regent by other means that apparently included medicine murder (*liretlo*) whereby the flesh of an innocent victim was used to prepare medicines believed to advance the interests of persons for whom the killing was performed.[20] The execution in 1949 of Chief Bereng Griffith and Chief Gabashane Masupha, two of the highest ranking and most renowned chiefs in the land, for complicity in such a crime dealt a grave blow to the standing of the Paramountcy and the entire Chieftainship. Although there was speculation that the Regent was involved in this unsavoury practice, there was more general agreement that her incompetence had contributed to the outbreak of medicine murder and to the hesitancy of remedial action. Thus, the Basotho Kingship was both literally and figuratively emasculated for a critical twenty-year segment of its political evolution. A glance at the Swazi monarchy, which during the same period sustained a unified defence of royal interests under the experienced leadership of a single ruler, Sobhuza II, suggests the unusual importance of personality, health, and the timing of succession in determining the fate of kingship.

The pervasive insecurity and restiveness within the chieftainship was not difficult to comprehend. Virtually all administrative changes promulgated between 1938 and 1950 strengthened the hand of the ranking chiefs, known as "principal" or "ward" chiefs while making the position of lesser chiefs and headmen more tenuous. Major chiefs gained patronage and prestige from the power to nominate the personnel of the restructured central courts within their jurisdictions. In lieu of income from the collection of fines or from compulsory communal labour, all authorized chiefs were now paid salaries from a National Treasury. However, the short-handed British administration was compelled to rely upon the advice of the principal and ward chiefs in determining who ought to be recognized and what, if anything, he should be paid. While the monarch and major chiefs received satisfactory sums, lesser chiefs were grossly underpaid.

Despite the theoretical rationalization of the structure of the chieftainship, a host of unrecognized and uncompensated chiefs continued to perform judicial roles and were expected to carry out such crucial functions as the allocation of land. Ordinary citizens were caught between the conflicting demands of legally constituted chiefs and of *de facto* authorities tolerated by superiors unwilling to disrupt the status quo. It takes little imagination to understand the confusion and demoralization of lesser chiefs or headmen whose status and economic position had been degraded or who stood in constant jeopardy of arbitrary actions by their superiors. Medicine murder provided an illusory outlet for frustration while more positive redress of grievances was sought through the Basutoland National Council.

During the 1940s and early 1950s, most elements in the National Council, including ranking chiefs, minor headmen and commoners, joined together in efforts to check the authority of both the monarchy and the colonial government. The Regent Paramount Chieftainess not only failed to turn administrative innovations to her advantage, but in an incredibly brief period surrendered important prerogatives to other bodies. By 1944 she was persuaded to promise that she would always consult the National Council before using her powers to make rules or issue orders. The inclusion of forty-two indirectly elected representatives in the National Council by 1950 diluted royal influence over its membership. Opportunities for the monarchy to control the purse strings and to establish a strong royal bureaucracy faded when 'Mantsebo permitted dominion over the judicial and administrative structures of the new National Treasury to devolve upon the National Council. Her acceptance of advisers nominated by the Council signalled the right of that body to be consulted and the rapid metamorphosis of the kingship from an institution having comprehensive executive powers into one playing a limited, "constitutional" role. These trends would not easily be reversed.

Despite the deadly seriousness of internal Basotho rivalries and divisions, these conflicts were reminiscent of a play within a play, ultimately refocussing attention upon the larger national struggle against colonial rule and South African racialism. British efforts to legitimize the administrative reforms through consulting and even securing the prior consent of the Paramountcy and the National Council did little to stem growing Basotho concern that their leaders had been deceived and pressured into hasty acquiescence to very questionable proposals. A youthful generation of militant leadership, associated with the ANC Youth League in South Africa and inspired by the Lekhotla la Bafo at home, was instrumental in providing a comprehensive explanation of what had gone wrong and in regrouping the disgruntled Basotho for a renewed struggle toward common objectives.

The Basutoland African Congress (BAC),[21] formed by Ntsu Mokhehle in 1952, interpreted the sequence of British-initiated reforms as a deliberate attempt to introduce the South African pattern of native administration in preparation for the ultimate transfer of the Basotho to the Union Government. Furthermore, the BAC portrayed the supposed "outbreak" of medicine murder as a trumped-up effort to weaken the nation by destroying the chieftainship and dividing the people into hostile and fearful segments. To be sure, the Regent and senior chiefs also criticized discriminatory colonial employment practices, British reluctance to permit constitutional advance toward internal self-government and the callous appointment of a white South African as Resident Commissioner. But it was the BAC, rather than the monarch or the National Council, which became the dynamic force articulating national grievances and creating a broad coalition to press for rapid constitutional change.

Whether a modern political movement could have flourished and eventually have seized the initiative under a stronger monarch cannot be proven either way. The difficulties experienced by Dr. Zwane's Ngwane National Liberatory Congress in Swaziland may provide a relevant example of partisan weakness in challenging a vigorous king. Certainly the rapidity of the BAC rise to prominence and of Basotho identification with competitive political parties was an important outcome of the leadership vacuum during the Regency. Ntsu Mokhehle implied as much in his comments upon 'Mantsebo's death in 1964 when he said, "I always wonder whether our Party could have survived if she had not reigned at the time of its inauguration."[22]

A SECOND MOSHOESHOE?

Throughout its recent history, the Basotho kingship has been plagued by the fact that few of the king's partisans at any given moment are men for whom the enhancement of the role and status of the monarchy is the fundamental objective.[23] Thus the king has constantly wrestled with the perplexing problem of how to convert the enormous popular enthusiasm for his person and office into an effective political base for achieving his specific objectives. From the start, Moshoeshoe II remained heavily dependent upon the support of partisan forces.

Chief S. S. Matete was the first leader to call for the Regent's retirement in favour of the youthful heir to the throne. Because of the constitutional deliberations occurring in Basutoland from 1956 through 1958, Matete felt that the Paramountcy required "a fresh, clear and diligent brain . . .

at a time when many great and painful changes are taking place".[24] To promote the installation of the new monarch and to facilitate unity between chiefs and commoners, he organized the Marematlou Party in 1957.

Following British and Basotho acceptance of constitutional arrangements that accorded the Paramount Chief the right to appoint fourteen members in a reconstituted National Council and one member of the new Executive Council, the timing of Bereng Seeiso's accession became more critical. A majority of the ranking chiefs supported Marematlou efforts to have him installed prior to the promulgation of the new constitution, so that he would make these appointments which could determine the balance of power in the legislature. Predictably, the primary resistance came from the Regent and her advisers, who argued that he should complete his education at Oxford and marry before assuming the Paramountcy. In 1959, several of 'Mantsebo's staunchest defenders, led by Chief Leabua Jonathan, formed the Basutoland National Party which aimed at defending traditional patterns of life and basic Christian values against the alleged, radical challenge of Mokhehle's movement.

From its inception, the BNP was associated with Catholicism and covertly supported by the resources of that Mission, whereas Marematlou had no clear religious affiliation though its leadership had a decidedly PEMS cast. The BNP utilized its ties with the Regent and with Catholic mission stations to gain access to the lesser chiefs and headmen at the village level; whereas Marematlou developed links with the influential principal and ward chiefs. The Marematlou forces emphasized images of national unity under an effectual monarch; whereas the BNP articulated the needs of lower segments of the chiefly hierarchy. Hence, the existing economic and status differentials within the chieftainship gained new expression through the medium of modern political parties. Chief Jonathan's desire to prolong the Regency can be interpreted as a rearguard action against the great chiefs as well as a straightforward effort to produce a monarch whose educational achievements would be beyond reproach. Much of the personal hostility between Moshoeshoe II and his cousin, Leabua Jonathan, originated in this complex generational and socio-economic conflict.

The Basutoland Congress Party (formerly the BAC) remained cool to the idea of Bereng's installation before he finished his BA degree, but maintained a hands-off attitude on the succession issue and concentrated its energies upon winning the 1960 election. Since Mokhehle had been successful in coping with the Regent, he preferred to postpone the problems of dealing with a well-educated Paramount until the BCP had had time to adjust to the new constitutional pattern.[25]

In September 1959, Bereng Seeiso entered the fray by requesting the Regent to arrange for this accession without delay. 'Mantsebo was forced to capitulate when the immediate royal family and the Sons of Moshoeshoe supported his demand. His official installation as Paramount Chief and the formal opening of the restructured Basutoland National Council on March 12, 1960, marked a new epoch of Basotho history. However,

Bereng Seeiso has not yet succeeded in recapturing the political initiative of his ancestors although he was permitted to assume the name Moshoeshoe II, symbolic of a recrudescence of Basotho nationhood.

The 1959 Basutoland Constitution embodied a triumph for the National Council over royal power and proved to be a difficult, if not insuperable obstacle to Moshoeshoe II's dreams of playing a consequential executive role. The monarch retained discretion in making certain appointments, the right to be consulted, and his traditional supervisory role over the allocation of land. However, his authority to delay or force reconsideration of legislative and executive decisions was an insubstantial shadow of former royal prerogatives. The disbanding of the National Treasury and devolution of many of its functions to district councils deprived the Paramount Chief of direct access to any modern bureaucratic structure. Moreover, his influence upon the chieftainship was shaken by the transfer of the powers of disciplining subordinate chiefs, of adjudicating jurisdictional conflicts, and of arbitrating disputes over succession to a College of Chiefs dominated by the principal and ward chiefs.

Despite the isolation of the royal headquarters at Matsieng from the new centres of Basotho political power in Maseru, Moshoeshoe II had little choice but to work within the existing institutional framework. Although the BCP had won most of the elected seats, the new National Council was controlled by a majority composed primarily of *ex-officio* chiefs and nominated members not unfriendly to the monarch. Following shifts in party affiliation, the Basotho component of the Executive Council was firmly in the grasp of proven royal allies like S. S. Matete. If Moshoeshoe II had attempted to create a new political base of his own, he would have compromised and embarrassed some of his most vocal supporters. The young King's political inexperience, lack of organizational roots, and sense of the dignity of his office compelled him to rely upon these established politicians.

Moshoeshoe II's effort to seize the initiative from the BCP and to place himself in the forefront of constitutional evolution toward responsible government found expression in several speeches before the National Council. His most noteworthy presentation contained a scathing attack on British "empiricism" as a "hand-to-mouth" policy that had produced authoritarian administration and a stagnant economy.[26] The remedy, he argued, could be found only by adapting traditional institutions to changing circumstances in accordance with an ideology which would provide a thorough analysis of the economic, political, and social milieu and a plan for attaining shared objectives.

While his advocacy of "comprehensive programming and planning"[27] by the central government gave evidence of constructive attitudes toward social change, Moshoeshoe II's statements also reflected improved prospects that a revitalized monarchy might supplant the BCP as the dominant political influence. The new Constitution Commission appointed by the monarch gave heavy representation to those likely to advocate an enhanced role for kingship. Moreover, the BCP became embroiled in an enervating series of internal ideological and power struggles. In December 1962 a merger of organizations led by S. S. Matete and B. M. Khaketla created the Marematlou Freedom Party, a broadly based group which seemed particularly sympathetic to the Paramount Chief.

Moshoeshoe II's expectations were rudely shattered when the Commission unanimously decided to deny him broad powers and cited Bagehot's argument that "a ruler of sense and sagacity would want no other" right than "to be consulted."[28] The overwhelming weight of public testimony supporting a "constitutional" Head of State had neatly buttressed the reluctance of these experienced politicians to sacrifice their own ambitions by conceding decision-making capacities to a hereditary monarch. Men like Khaketla and Matete now seemed to feel that ministerial responsibility and royal freedom of action were inherently incompatible.

A more compelling explanation of their apparent change of heart was their determination, in concert with other politicians, to prevent Basotho domestic squabbles from foreclosing rapid advance toward independence. During the tricky constitutional negotiations in London in 1964, differences regarding the role of kingship were muted to permit unanimity on such absolutely fundamental issues as British economic assistance and future Basotho relationships with South Africa. Despite his displeasure with the eventual agreement, Moshoeshoe II was unwilling to appear to be a barrier to national independence and reluctantly agreed to sign the Constitutional Conference Report. However, the Paramount Chief hoped that an enhanced royal role could still be attained via a massive electoral triumph by the MFP.

Many observers believed that the combination of experienced politicians, major chiefs, association with the Paramountcy, and external funding had turned the MFP into the front-running electoral contender. Such prognostications failed to take into account how the MFP's individualistic leadership, lack of programmatic coherence, and chimerical organizational apparatus would make the party vulnerable to abrupt variations in its fortunes. Thus a split between factions led by Seth Makotoko and S. S. Matete and a violent clash between MFP and BCP partisans at Rothe caused unexpected electoral defections possibly to the BNP which had attempted to identify both of these rivals with communism and disorder.

Although MFP supporters agreed that Moshoeshoe II would have a "central role to play" as a focus of national identity, this so-called "royalist" group consisted of persons who had embraced the cause of kingship for quite different reasons. Some MFP stalwarts were committed either to the person of Moshoeshoe II or to the institution of monarchy as an energizing force capable of resolving national problems. For many of the principal chiefs, the MFP not only offered the best available counterpoise to the militant, commoner-based BCP and to the dissatisfied lesser chieftainship in the BNP, but also became a ready source of vehicles, supplies and cash. Some recruits from the BCP, fearing the possible excesses of a Mokhehle regime patterned after Nkrumah's Ghana, perceived monarchy to be a plausible buttress for a competitive democratic system. Other former BCP politicians who were closely aligned with ANC politics in South Africa entered the MFP alliance with the monarchy as an expedient in their battle against the Africanist-oriented BCP. Hence the image of the MFP as non-dogmatic and middle-of-the-road reflected less a consensus on monarchy than a delicately poised balance, approximating the centre of the broad political spectrum included in the party.

The distribution of MFP votes in the general election of April 29, 1965, neatly illustrated the supportive effects of Moshoeshoe II's not-so-covert preference for that party. However, the MFP array of glittering personalities proved no match on a national scale for the radical ideological appeal and grass-roots organization of the BCP or for the "bread-and-butter" policies and conservative Catholic alliance of the BNP.

Following the promulgation of the pre-independence constitution on April 30, 1965, Moshoeshoe II moved into the official dwelling in Maseru formerly occupied by the British Resident Commissioner. This symbolic act masked the transfer of real political power over domestic matters to the government formed by the victorious National Party. To be sure, Moshoeshoe II could exercise some discretionary powers of appointments. But in the majority of his roles the monarch was compelled to act in accordance with British constitutional conventions, many of which were explicitly written into the 1965 text. The Paramount Chief's right to be informed of Cabinet decision-making processes was vitiated at the outset by the history of political and personal enmity between himself and Prime Minister Jonathan. Furthermore, the development of even a cool working relationship was precluded by the narrowness of the BNP majority in the National Assembly and tenuous plurality in the country at large which made Jonathan appear deceptively vulnerable and kept the political pot boiling.[29]

Prior to independence, Moshoeshoe II embarked on a series of stratagems to attain his constitutional demands for a voice in the areas of foreign affairs, defence, internal security and the public service. Initially, he hoped that the MFP-oriented majority of *ex-officio* chiefs and royal appointees in the Senate would block the motion for independence, permitted after one year of self-government, and thereby force the Prime Minister to compromise. When Chief Jonathan's skilful use of patronage cracked this MFP phalanx while maintaining BNP solidarity in the National Assembly, the King attempted to utilize a constitutional loophole to replace five Senators who had abandoned his cause. Rebuffed by the High Court of Basutoland in this effort to restore the royalist majority in the Senate, Moshoeshoe II received unexpectedly vigorous support for his position from the BCP. The King recognized Mokhehle's new-found affinity for the royal cause to be a product of adverse circumstances, but hoped the BCP would become too committed to reverse its position. Meanwhile, BCP organizational capabilities were instrumental in assembling huge crowds at meetings addressed by the monarch. This joint effort to convince the British not to permit independence under the existing constitution and the allegedly unpopular BNP regime failed, since it was perceived as an opportunistic attempt to escape the consequences of electoral defeat.

Moshoeshoe II's refusal to initial the independence agreement of June 1966 with Britain and Mokhehle's withdrawal from the conference signalled genuine fears that Jonathan might rule arbitrarily and betray Basotho interests to South Africa unless the monarch gained viable options to check his power. Political tension was exacerbated by the Prime Minister's repeated warnings that the Paramount Chief must refrain from political activity or else abdicate. To avoid the debilitating effects of royal obstructionism, the British unilaterally inserted a new constitutional provision authorizing the Prime Minister to act on behalf of the King if the monarch refused to perform the duties required of him. Despite this final blow to royal pride and influence, Moshoeshoe II felt obliged to join in independence festivities and to receive the Constitutional Instruments from Princess Marina on October 4, 1966.

Far from promoting reconciliation of the monarch with his government, King Moshoeshoe II's carefully-worded speech contained a warning "that the act of independence, by itself, is not necessarily a solution to all these stresses and strains".[30] The King's oath to "preserve, protect and defend" the constitution seemed compromised by his earlier statement that his participation would reflect acceptance only of independence and not of the "totally unsuitable and thoroughly unpopular constitution".[31] These events foreshadowed Moshoeshoe's equivocal, precariously balanced role since independence. While the King has allowed his political ambitions to bring him to the brink of disaster, he has invariably drawn back at the last instant, preferring to accept temporary humiliations rather than risk the loss of his hereditary permanence and security in office.

Moshoeshoe II's underlying caution was demonstrated by his behaviour during a confrontation between royalist sympathizers and police on December 27, 1966, and throughout the subsequent political crisis. The King had decided to proceed with a national "prayer" meeting at the grave of Moshoeshoe I in spite of the banning of the gathering by Chief Jonathan on the grounds that political speeches by the monarch were unconstitutional. Although Moshoeshoe II, Mokhehle and Makotoko believed that "peaceful disturbances" were now the appropriate method of pressing their demands, they showed little inclination to persevere once violence occurred. Their hesitance reflected genuine aversion to bloodshed, mistrust of each other's motives, and fear that an attempted coup might precipitate South African intervention to preserve the BNP regime. All believed that it was more crucial to live for another day than to take daring and probably futile action.

While forestalling pressures for his immediate abdication, Moshoeshoe II signed a bizarre document which placed his tenure as King at the complete discretion of the BNP government and made him a virtual prisoner in his palace.[32] The monarch was unreconciled to this fate and subsequently declined to perform his symbolic roles, to give speeches prepared by his ministers, or to otherwise function as a political cipher. In a wide-ranging interview given in July 1967, Moshoeshoe II protested the restrictions upon his activities, the January agreement with its "suicide clause", his lack of meaningful access to the decision-making process, and his

N

inability to fulfil his "traditional and vital role as the national leader of the Basotho".[33]

From 1967 through to 1969 tension between the King and Prime Minister frequently threatened to reach crisis stage and precipitated talk of forced abdication and exile. If Chief Jonathan had deposed Moshoeshoe II, he would have risked alienating his own supporters because both the principal and lesser chiefs depended on retention of the traditional principles of hereditary legitimacy. However, the Prime Minister further emasculated the kingship by enacting legislation which transferred residual royal powers over chiefly discipline and land tenure to the government. Adding insult to injury, Moshoeshoe II was also deprived of direct administrative control over the royal wards of Matsieng and Mokhotlong.

Chief Jonathan's contention that the King's unconstitutional intervention in politics was the primary cause of the stunning BNP setback in the 1970 General Election was a little ingenuous. To be sure, the long confrontation with the King was a major factor in undermining BNP popularity. However, Moshoeshoe II resisted the temptation to abdicate and to challenge Chief Jonathan at the polls. Such an act would have been irrevocable, necessitating a long interregnum and relegating the King to the not-so-tender mercies of public opinion. With the BNP control of the electoral machinery, of the news media, and of the resources of the state and with the BCP also experienced and well-organized, Moshoeshoe II would have risked sacrificing his throne only to be outmanœuvred or to find himself contesting an election that would never occur. Nevertheless, Moshoeshoe II's close relationship with the MFP was heightened when Tsepo Mohaleroe, his legal adviser and intimate friend, displaced Seth Makotoko as leader of that party. Most likely, Moshoeshoe II and various MFP leaders had tired of Makotoko's haphazard and ineffectual leadership. While the King could not have expected the MFP to win the election, he may have hoped that the party would carry enough constituencies to hold the balance of power between the BNP and BCP. A man with Mr. Mohaleroe's legal expertise and lucid style would have been admirably suited to the bargaining process of coalition formation.

After ten years of struggle, the 1970 election found Moshoeshoe II playing a temporizing role, isolated from events, and holding far less real power than at the outset. Throughout his reign, the monarch had faced a series of constricted opportunities to restore the executive prerogatives of the Basotho Kingship. In responding, Moshoeshoe II had been trapped in short-term political expedients at the expense of broad, innovative strategies or daring attempts to break out of the mould of Basotho partisan politics. Nothing could have better symbolized the King's plight following Chief Jonathan's coup than the impromptu interview which he gave to a South African reporter through the chain mesh fence surrounding his palace. Moshoeshoe II is quoted as saying,

I have no knowledge of any state of emergency. I did not even know the election results. I am utterly perplexed, and have been told by the Prime Minister that I may speak to no one.[34]

PRINCE MOHATO'S INHERITANCE

In 1966 the Government newspaper, *Lesotho Times*, had warned that the eventual accession of Prince Mohato, Moshoeshoe II's eldest son, would depend on the development of good relations "between the Head (the King) and the Eyes, the Ears and the Mouth (the Prime Minister)".[35] On December 4, 1970, King Moshoeshoe II ended his eight-month "holiday" in The Hague and returned to Lesotho, but only after he had capitulated to Chief Jonathan's terms. Before being permitted to resume his reign, Moshoeshoe II was required to take an oath to conform to the provisions of the newly promulgated "Office of the King Order—1970". This document reaffirmed the King's right to be consulted, but gave the Prime Minister the "power to deem abdication" of the monarch or to act on the King's behalf should he "neglect or refuse to do any act in accordance with advice given to him".[36] Since consenting to these conditions, Moshoeshoe II has given every visible indication of having accepted a severely limited role. If these events are to be taken at face value, Prince Mohato must also be reconciled to rigidly circumscribed, symbolic functions.

Developments in Lesotho subsequent to Moshoeshoe II's "vacation" afforded him few alternatives if he hoped to preserve even the hollow shell of his Kingship. After a period of violence and desperate efforts to reach a negotiated settlement with the opposition, Chief Jonathan was able to consolidate his power and regain a modicum of international respectability. Two key factors facilitated the Prime Minister's recovery. The South African decision to maintain normal relations with Lesotho and to continue technical assistance and regular payment of shared customs and excise revenues was essential to the survival of the BNP regime. However, the long-delayed resumption of British diplomatic recognition and budgetary and economic aid on June 12, 1970, undoubtedly had the greatest immediate impact. As a result, the Prime Minister reaped the benefits of opposition concessions to disregard the abortive 1970 elections without his being compelled to give any ground such as permitting BCP or MFP representation of a government of national unity. Even the severe drought of summer 1970 seemed to work to Chief Jonathan's advantage by creating sympathy overseas and stimulating involvement of public and private foreign contributors in the famine relief effort. Thus, Prime Minister Jonathan felt confident enough to terminate negotiations with the opposition, to declare a five-year moratorium on partisan politics, and to offer Lesotho's services as a "bridge" for possible dialogue between South Africa and her critics.

Although these events may have led Moshoeshoe II to the conclusion that remaining in exile would be a futile gesture, it seems likely that neither the King nor the opposition politicians have given up their own aspirations. More likely they would subscribe to the sentiments of a Sesotho proverb quoted by Ntsu Mokhehle, namely, "When the ram withdraws, it is not retreating, but gathering power for the next attack".[37] Working on this assumption, a final assessment of the Basotho kingship's current assets and liabilities should prove informative.

On the positive side, the hereditary legitimacy of the current monarch is recognized by all groups in the society. To be sure, occasional comments are made about the "inferior" Batlokoa origins of Moshoeshoe II's mother and there is idle speculation on the vague pretensions of other branches of the royal family. But not even Leshoboro Seeiso, the King's half-brother born of an impeccable royal marriage, has a following that would genuinely support him against the incumbent monarch. Moshoeshoe II's lack of success in reversing the trend towards the emasculation of royal power belies his intelligence, charm, and seriousness of purpose. Relatively uncompromised by recent events, the thirty-five-year-old King is young enough to bide his time in the hope that the Basotho will ultimately turn to royal authority when trying to recreate viable political institutions from the constitutional wreckage left by Jonathan's coup.

Evidence of the fragility of Chief Jonathan's regime can be seen in the long absence of any constitution, in continued rule by ministerial decree, and in its dependence on the power of the small police force. In this uncertain situation, the monarchy might stand to gain from unpredictable events such as an assassination; the defection of segments of the police, chieftainship, or BNP; or an uncontrollable uprising of the opposition majority in Maseru. Indeed, Chief Jonathan has implicitly recognized the residual potence of royal legitimacy by his willingness to accept the risks of Moshoeshoe II's return to the Throne in preference to the greater uncertainties of installing a pliable king or proclaiming a republic. Of late he has emphasized the King's endorsement of the new five-year development plan to promote popular cooperation in fulfilling its objectives.

Still, Prime Minister Jonathan would appear to hold a significant advantage. Continued detention or surveillance of opposition leaders has made it incredibly difficult for them to organize a viable response. Meanwhile Chief Jonathan has had ample time to consolidate his control over the police and the administrative apparatus of the state. In addition, the Prime Minister has been the beneficiary of sharp increases in American aid to the three independent black enclaves in Southern Africa. Ntsu Mokhehle's growing despair has been demonstrated by his willingness to appear in conciliatory photographs with Chief Jonathan in return for less stringent detention and vague hints of some future political responsibilities. Moreover, the Prime Minister seems to have a further psychological and tactical edge. Much as Letsie I, Lerotholi, and Griffith declined to challenge British colonial rule, Moshoeshoe II and Mokhehle have hesitated to take the great risks of overthrowing Leabua Jonathan. Both the King and the BCP leader appear to have succumbed to gnawing fears that such actions would precipitate the even worse calamity of a permanent South African intervention on behalf of the BNP regime. In the interim, Chief Jonathan has begun to capitalize on opposition inertia by adopting a more stringent line toward South Africa which may reduce the range of the major, substantive conflicts about policy. Thus, any moves toward coalition government are likely to cast Chief Jonathan in the enviable role of a reasonable compromiser who has compelled his own party to forget past differences and work toward a national consensus.

Moshoeshoe II's opportunities to assume leadership have been circumscribed by complete isolation of the monarchy from administrative structures that might provide an organizational format. Since the remaining assets of the monarchy involve the person of the King, the death or renewed exile of the current ruler would be an especially cruel blow, subjecting the kingship to a long regency for Prince Mohato. Even the brief, eight-month interregnum of Queen 'Mamohato during her husband's "holiday" suggested that the permanent absence of an adult male ruler would assure the complete triumph of professional politicians over the monarchy. The Office of the King Order provides a menacing sanction against potential political indiscretions of the incumbent monarch, since any prior arrangements for succession or regency may be declared "null and void . . . in the event of the King abdicating or being deemed to have abdicated".[38] Should Moshoeshoe II defy his government again, Prince Mohato and his siblings might all forfeit their hereditary rights to the throne. Moshoeshoe II's hopes of creating a genuine executive role must be further dimmed by awareness that daring and successful royal action would probably work to the immediate advantage of the BCP. It is unlikely that a Mokhehle government would be willing to surrender the fruits of its long and bitter struggle for power to the kingship. For these reasons, Moshoeshoe II seems to have acknowledged the futility of further short-term confrontation with Chief Jonathan and to have concluded that royal influence can be enhanced, for the time being, by a high degree of cooperation.

Moshoeshoe II appears destined to preside over a symbolic constitutional monarchy. Such a fate is in keeping with the declining fortunes of royalty elsewhere in the world and with the typically poor prospects for the success of regimes which try to combine a ruling monarch and autonomous political parties.[39] Nevertheless, the Basotho political situation is so fluid that any outcome remains within the realm of possibility. The intangible assets of the Basotho kingship, especially its ability to evoke the emotion-laden imagery of Moshoeshoe I's political genius, may yet override the more mundane organizational talents and firepower of its enemies.

NOTES

1 This chapter is a substantially revised and shortened version of my paper *The Basotho Monarchy: A Spent Force or a Dynamic Political Factor?* which was presented at the Annual Meeting of the African Studies Association in Denver in November 1971 and was issued by the Ohio University Centre for International Studies as Paper No. 16 in its Africa Series in International Studies, 1972. I am grateful to the Foreign Area Fellowship Programme and to the Ohio University Center for International Studies for the research support that made this work possible.

2 The spelling and usage of Sesotho language terms and names throughout this chapter conform to current practice in the official English language publications of independent Lesotho. Quotations and other references retain the variant forms chosen by their authors. The following key may serve to clarify some meanings and pronunciations:

> Sotho (pronounced Suto) is one of the broad subdivisions of Southern Bantu languages. Mutually intelligible dialects are spoken by Tswana, Pedi and Southern Sotho peoples who also share a distinct cultural heritage.

> Sesotho (pronounced Sesuto) refers to the language and/or customs of the Southern Sotho.

> Mosotho (pronounced Mosuto) is the singular form denoting any individual who speaks Sesotho, but more usually a citizen of Lesotho.

> Basotho (pronounced Basuto) is the plural form referring to a group of Sesotho speakers, but unless otherwise indicated, to a group of citizens of Lesotho. Collectively, it refers to the Sesotho-speaking ethnic group, but, unless alternatively specified, will signify the nationals of Lesotho.

> Lesotho (pronounced Lesuto) refers to the country of the Basotho or for our purposes to the Basotho state originated by Moshoeshoe (with sundry changes in boundaries over time). Basutoland was the British colonial name which will be used where appropriate.

> Moshoeshoe is pronounced Moshwayshway. A genealogy of the royal house descended from Moshoeshoe I appears in Appendix I.

3 Electoral data appears in Appendix III.

4 The concepts selected are derived primarily from Samuel P. Huntington, *Political Order in Changing Societies*, esp. Chapter 3, "Political Change in Traditional Societies", (New Haven: Yale University Press, 1968), pp. 140–153; and Fred I. Greenstein, "The Impact of Personality on Politics: An Attempt to Clear Away Underbrush", *The American Political Science Review*, Vol. LXI, No. 3 (September 1967), pp. 629–641.

5 Major sources of historical, political, and social data on the origins of the Basotho monarchy are as follows: The Rev. T. Arbousset and F. Daumas, *Narrative of an Exploratory Tour to the North-East of the Colony of the Cape of Good Hope* (Cape Town: Solomon & Co., 1846; reprinted Cape Town: *Struik Africana Collecteana*, Vol. XXVII, 1968); Anthony Atmore, "The Passing of Sotho Independence 1865–1870" in Leonard M. Thompson, editor, *African Societies in Southern Africa* (New York and Washington: Praeger, 1969), pp. 282–301; Anthony Atmore, "Sotho Arms and Ammunition in the Nineteenth Century", *The Journal of African History*, Vol. XII, No. 4 (1971), pp. 535–544; The Rev. E. Casalis, *The Basutos* (London: Nisbet & Co., 1861; reprinted Cape Town: *Struik Africana Collecteana*, Vol. XVI, 1965); D. F. Ellenberger and J. C. MacGregor, *History of the Basuto: Ancient and Modern* (London: Caxton Publishing Co., 1912; reprinted New York: Negro Universities Press, 1969); Robert C. Germond, editor, *Chronicles of Basutoland* (Morija, Lesotho: Sesuto Book Depot, 1967); Sir Godfrey Lagden, *The Basutos* (London: Hutchinson & Co., 1909), 2 vols.; Martin Legassick, "The Sotho-Tswana Peoples before 1800" in Leonard M. Thompson, editor, *op. cit.*, pp. 86–125; William Lye, "The Distribution of the Sotho Peoples after the Difaqane" in Leonard M. Thompson, editor, *op. cit.*, pp. 191–206; Joseph M. Orpen, *Reminiscences of Life in South Africa* (Durban: P. Davis and Sons, 1908; reprinted Cape Town: *Struik Africana Collecteana*, Vol. X, 1964); P. B. Sanders, "Sekonyela and Moshweshwe: Failure and Success in the Aftermath of the Difaqane", *The Journal of African History*, Vol. X, No 3 (1969), pp. 439–455; Edwin Smith, *The Mabilles of Basutoland* (London: Hodder and Stoughton, 1939); George M. Theal, editor, *Basutoland Records*, 3 vols. (Cape Town: W. A. Richards, 1883; reprinted Cape Town: C. Struik, 1964); and Leonard M. Thompson, "Cooperation and Conflict: The High Veld", in Monica Wilson and Leonard M. Thompson, editors, *The Oxford History of South Africa*, Vol. I (New York and Oxford: Oxford University Press, 1969), pp. 391–346.

6 The Rev. E. Casalis, *op. cit.*, p. 155, 214.

7 Quoted in "Report on Constitutional Reform and Chieftainship Affairs", in *Basutoland Constitutional Handbook* (Maseru: Basutoland Government, 1960), p. 24.

8 Quoted in Edwin Smith, *op. cit.*, p. 314.

9 Questions of placing and succession are discussed in: *Basutoland Medicine Murder* (Jones Report) Cmd. 8209 (London: HMSO, 1951), pp. 35–39; Iam Hamnett, "Koena Chieftainship Seniority in Basutoland", *Africa*, Vol. XXXV, No. 3 (July 1965), pp. 241–251; and G. I. Jones, "Chiefly Succession in Basutoland", in Jack Goody, editor, *Succession to High Office*, Cambridge Papers in Social Anthropology, No. 4 (Cambridge: Cambridge University Press, 1966), pp. 57–81.

10 These terms are defined in David E. Apter, *The Politics of Modernization* (Chicago: University of Chicago Press, 1965), pp. 89–94.

11 The period of Cape rule, the Gun War and the resoration of Imperial sovereignty are discussed in: Lord William Hailey, *Native Administration in the British African Territories*, Part V, *The High Commission Territories: Basutoland, Bechuanaland Protectorate and Swaziland* (London: HMSO, 1953); Sir Godfrey Lagden, *op. cit.*; Edwin Smith, *op. cit.*; and G. Tylden, *The Rise of the Basuto* (Cape Town and Johannesburg: Juta & Co., Ltd., 1950).

12 E. Hugh Ashton, "Political Organization of the Southern Sotho," *Bantu Studies* (Johannesburg)), Vol. XII, No. 4 (December 1938), p. 290.

13 See the petition of Letsie II to King Edward VII reproduced in Sir Godfrey Lagden, *op. cit.*, pp. 620–623.

14 The question of incorporation is discussed in J. E. Spence, "British Policy toward the High Commission Territories", *The Journal of Modern African Studies*, Vol. 2, No. 2 (1964), pp. 235–244.

15 The development of the National Council is discussed in Lord William Hailey, *op. cit.*; Richard P. Stevens, *Lesotho, Botswana and Swaziland: The Former High Commission Territories in Southern Africa* (New York, Washington and London: Praeger Publishers, 1967); and "Report on Constitutional Reform and Chieftainship Affairs", *op. cit.*

16 The administrative reforms are discussed in: *Basutoland Medicine Murder*, *op. cit.*; Lord William Hailey, *op. cit.*; and Richard P. Stevens, *op. cit.*

17 The issues in the succession crisis are spelled out in "Basutoland High Court: Bereng Griffith V. 'Mantsebo Seeiso Griffith" (Lansdown Judgment) in Sir Harold Willan, editor, *The High Commission Territories Law Reports: 1926–1953* (Maseru: The High Court, 1955), pp. 50–84.

18 G. Tylden, *op. cit.*, p. 221.

19 The actual mother of Constantine Bereng Seeiso (now King Moshoeshoe II) is 'Mabereng Seeiso, the second wife of Seeiso. 'Mantsebo, the first wife, produced no male offspring.

20 *Basutoland Medicine Murder*, *op. cit.*, provides the most comprehensive analysis of *liretlo* available.

21 A chronology of Basotho political parties appears in Appendix II.

22 *Basutoland National Council: Legislative Council Debates, Second Meeting, Third Session* (Hansard), Vol. II, 20–26 March 1964, (mimeographed), pp. 1170–1171.

23 A thorough description of Moshoeshoe II's reign and of his conflicts with Chief Jonathan appears in J. H. Proctor, "Building a Constitutional Monarchy in Lesotho," *Civilizations* (Brussels), Vol. XIX, No. 1 (1969), pp. 64–85.

24 S. S. Matete, "Why Did I Resign Counsellorship?" *Mohlabani* (Maseru), Vol. 2, No. 2 (March 1956), p. 16.

25 A more complete analysis of Basotho political parties appears in Richard F. Weisfelder, "Lesotho", in Christian P. Potholm and Richard Dale, editors, *Southern Africa in Perspective: Essays in Regional Politics* (New York: The Free Press, 1972), pp. 134–139.

26 *Basutoland National Council: Legislative Council Debates, Second Meeting, Second Session*, (Hansard) Vol. 2, 26 January 1962 (mimeographed), pp. 1–2.

27 *Basutoland National Council: Legislative Council Debates, First Meeting, Third Session*, (Hansard) Vol. I, 20 August 1963 (mimeographed), pp. 15–21.

28 *Basutoland National Council: Report of the Basutoland Constitutional Commission, 1963* (Maseru: Basutoland Government, 1963), p. 39.
29 The distribution of electoral strength and National Assembly seats is shown in Appendix III.
30 "Speech Delivered by King Moshoeshoe II on the Occasion of Receiving from Her Royal Highness, Princess Marina, the Constitutional Instruments Establishing the Kingdom of Lesotho", *The Lesotho Times* (Maseru), Vol. IV, No. 91 (October 14, 1966), pp. 3, 10.
31 "New Basutoland Crisis: Moshoeshoe Hits Out at Constitution," *The Friend* (Bloemfontein), September 29, 1966, p. 1.
32 Analysis of these events and text of this document appear in Richard F. Weisfelder, "Power Struggle in Lesotho", *Africa Report*, Vol. 12, No. 1 (January 1967), pp. 5–7, 12.
33 Wilf Nussey, "Lesotho King Denies Story He Would Aid Coup: A Special Interview", *Cape Argus* (Cape Town), July 13, 1967.
34 David Barritt, "King Says He Was Not Consulted", *Sunday Times* (Johannesburg), February 1, 1970.
35 Caption to a photograph of the King, Prime Minister and Prince Mohato, *The Lesotho Times* (Maseru), Vol. IV, No. 62, March 18, 1966, p. 8.
36 "The Office of the King Order—1970", Order No. 51 of 1970, Supplement No 1 to the *Lesotho Government Gazette* of 20 November 1970 (Maseru: Government Printer, 1970), p. 547.
37 Quoted in "Mokhehle Interview: BCP Will Support Jonathan Coalition", *The Friend* (Bloemfontein), May 5, 1970.
38 "The Office of the King Order—1970", *op. cit.*, pp. 543–545.
39 This observation derives from Samuel P. Huntington, *op. cit.*, p. 184.

LESOTHO ROYAL LINEAGE AFTER MOSHOESHOE I

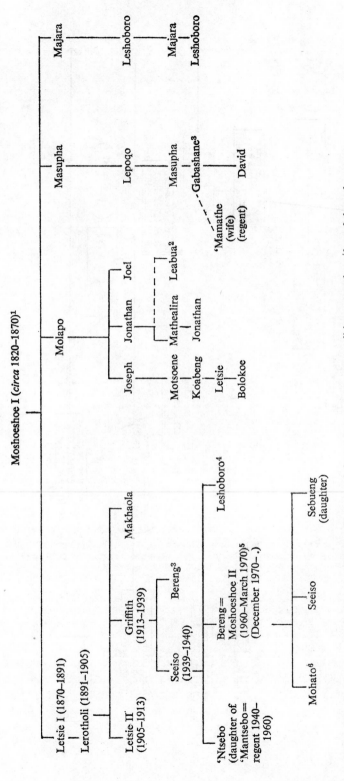

Moshoeshoe I (*circa* 1820–1870)[1]

1 Shows the major components discussed in this chapter and does not purport to cover all important branches of the polygynous royal family.
2 Prime Minister Leabua Jonathan, a son of a minor house of Jonathan.
3 Executed for medicine murder (1949).
4 Mentioned as an alternative to Moshoeshoe II.
5 Moshoeshoe II's only wife, 'Mamohato, served as regent from April to November of 1970.
6 Designated as heir to the throne.

Appendix II

CHRONOLOGY OF BASOTHO POLITICAL PARTY DEVELOPMENT

(Precursors of modern political parties)

Basutoland Progressive Association (BPA) 1907

Lekhotla la Bafo 1919 (Josiel Lefela)

Basutoland African Congress (BAC) 1952 (Ntsu Mokhehle)

(Renamed Basutoland Congress Party (BCP) 1958

Basho National Party (BNP) 1959 (Leabua Jonathan)

Basutoland Labor Party (BLP)* 1962 (E. E. Lethata)

Communist Party of Lesotho (CPL)* 1961 (J. Motloheloa)

Marematlou Party (MP) 1957 (S. S. Matete)

Marematlou Freedom Party (MFP) 1962 (S. S. Matete)

Basutoland Freedom Party (BFP) 1960 (B. M. Khaketla)

Lesotho Unity Party (LUP)* 1965 (L. Matlabe)

Marematlou Freedom Party (MFP) 1964 (Seth Makatoko)

Marematlou Party (MP)* 1964 (S. S. Matete)

Marematlou United Party (MUP)* 1968 ('Mamathe Masupha)

United Democratic Party (UDP)* 1968 (Charles Mofeli)

Lesotho Democratic Party (LDP)* 1967 (Charles Mofeli)

(Disintegrates) 1966

MFP 1969 New Leader (T. Mohaleroe)

MP* 1969 New Leader (S. Maphelleba)

Defections to BNP 1965-67

Alliance with BNP 1965-65

Royalist Independents 1970

BNP Independents 1970

1970: All parties disbanded by formal decree, but continue

*Parties with minimal popular base

Appendix III

ELECTORAL TRENDS IN LESOTHO GENERAL ELECTIONS

Party	Votes		Percentage		Seats	
	1965	1970	1965	1970	1965	1970
Basotho National Party (BNP)	108,169	129,434	41·6	42·2	31	23
Basutoland Congress Party (BCP)	102,974	152,907	39·6	49·9	25	36
Marematlou Freedom Party (MFP)	43,085	22,279	16·6	7·3	4	1
Marematlou Party (MP)	5,697	—	2·2	—	—	—
United Democratic Party (UDP)	—	345	—	·1	—	—
Independents	79	1,564	—	·5	—	—
TOTAL	260,004	306,529	100·0	100·0	60	60

Sources: 1965 polling station reports.

Nketu Oa Mara, Vol. 6, No. 9 (February 27, 1970), pp. 11–16.

W. J. A. Macartney, "Case Study: The Lesotho General Election of 1970", *Government and Opposition*, Vol. 8, No. 4 (Autumn 1973), p. 485.

PART IV

INCORPORATED KINGSHIPS: BUGANDA, ANKOLE AND IJEBU

6

BUGANDA

Crawford Young

It was not yet dawn—about 5.30 in the morning—when I was awakened suddenly by the sound of gunfire: quite near, I reckoned, certainly inside the wall that surrounds my palace and grounds. As I hurried into a shirt, some trousers and a pullover and sat on my bed to pull on some suede boots, I tried to work out more precisely what was happening and where the shots were being fired . . . I strapped on a webbing belt with a heavy automatic in the holster, grabbed a carbine, and dashed into the cool dark garden to look for the commander of the bodyguard.

The troops from the Uganda Army were attacking my palace on the orders of the Prime Minister, Dr. Obote . . . We had been suspecting such a move for weeks . . . Yet I was filled with a sense of outrage now that it was happening.[1]

Thus, seen through the eyes of Sir Edward Frederick William David Walugembe Mutebi Luwangula Mutesa II, Kabaka of Buganda, began the day of 14 May, 1966. Before the day was out, the Kabaka was in flight; the old palace of Mengo was in flames; the royal drum battery, the core symbol of the kingdom, was apparently destroyed. A fortnight later, the government announced plans to split the proud kingdom into four divisions under the central government administration. And on 30 June, 1966, President A. Milton Obote told Parliament:

There will be no discussions and no negotiations. Let no one think this government is restoring Sir Edward Mutesa as Kabaka. Sir Edward is no longer Kabaka of Buganda.[2]

So ended the Kingdom of Buganda, perhaps five centuries after the legendary Kintu had descended from the skies to found the throne, to which 35 Kabakas has succeeded. With the death of the exiled Kabaka in London in November 1969, the demise of the Kingdom appeared even more definitive.

Has the curtain of history now descended upon this extraordinary kingdom? Has the royal flame, which burned continuously at the entrance to the Lubiri (royal enclosure) during the reign of each Kabaka, been permanently extinguished? It had waxed incandescent during the nineteenth century, survived the Christian revolution which accompanied colonial penetration, and dominated the interlacustrine sky since the accession of the 29th Kabaka Suna about 1836. Its luminous rise drew to its court Zanzibari traders, European explorers, and Christian missionaries, all of whom contributed to its legend. A colonial territory was fashioned around the kingdom, and its traditional institutions were granted a special status consideration which were rare in the imperial era. It exploited the British connection to double its own size at the advent of the colonial period.[3] It provided the newborn Protectorate armies and an intrepid conquistador, Semei Kakungura, who subjugated Iteso, Bagisu, Sebei, Bagwere, Banyole, Basoga, and Padhola peoples in the Eastern Province, establishing the infrastructure of local administration—sufficiently thoroughly, in the Teso case, to eliminate the age-set basis of traditional structure before British presence began to make itself felt.[4] Baganda agents in most parts of the Protectorate fashioned the framework of "native administration". The exceptional qualities of the Kingdom of Buganda drew to its study a brilliant array of scholars, reaching a peak in the 1950s when it was subjected to a scrutiny unmatched in Africa; the mere recitation of a cast including Lucy Mair, Audrey Richards, D. Anthony Low, Lloyd Fallers, David Apter, R. Cranford Pratt, Martin Southwold, F. B. Welbourn, Christopher Wrigley, Peter Gutkind, and John A. Rowe is an eloquent commentary on its rayonnement.[5] Can one swift act of decapitation eliminate so prestigious a monarchy? Assuredly not, if one is to believe the deposed (and now deceased) Kabaka, who closes his book with the forecast: ". . . I believe utterly that the Baganda will show their devotion, though it demands great courage and perseverance. In the end I shall return to the land of my fathers and to my people."[6] Equally firm appears the conviction of the Obote government that there can be no turning back, that the monarchy in Buganda had proved itself incompatible with the nation-state of Uganda. Our purpose here is to evaluate the role of kingship in Buganda and Uganda politics. Although our focus is the post-independence period, such a venerable institution as Kiganda monarchy cannot be separated from its history. Continuity crowds change for the observer's attention; we must examine the past, to discover some of its rythms recurrent in the radically new context of the independent state of Uganda shorn of the special status won on pre-colonial battlefields, and enshrined in the Protectorate.

PRE-COLONIAL MONARCHY: RISE OF DESPOTISM

The genesis of the kingdom need not long detain us. Its foundation, generally attributed to Kintu,[7] was related to the diffusion of kingship in the interlacustrine area generally. The kingdom developed in particularly close symbiosis with its neighbour to the west, and constant rival, Bunyoro-Kitara. Until the eighteenth century, Bunyoro-Kitara greatly overshadowed Buganda, and indeed conquered it on occasion. The third Kabaka, Kimera, was almost certainly a Munyoro prince. In common with other lacustrine kingdoms, Buganda experienced an influx of Hima cattle herders; however, their numbers were small, although some still survive, and kingship never became associated with a conquering group distinctive in origin. The highly favourable rainfall and soil conditions in the arc of territory extending from the north to the west shores of Lake Victoria provided an ample and assured livelihood.[8]

The latter part of the eighteenth century, and greater part of the nineteenth saw the conjuncture of a phase of decline and disorder in Bunyoro-Kitara, and enhanced capacities on the part of Buganda, culminating in the successful reigns of Kamanya (1816–1836), Suna II (1836-56), and Mutesa I (1856–1884). During these decades the despotic power of the Kabaka was considerably enhanced, and important structural changes occurred in the Kingdom which enlarged the capacity of strong Kabakas to fulfill the absolutist potential of the office. It is the nineteenth-century version of the Kabakaship which serves as the baseline for more recent developments; Baganda and others who describe the traditional office of King extrapolate from a very particular historical model, when the Kabaka had succeeded in achieving a degree of untrammelled power which was itself an historical innovation.

In its pristine form Baganda society would appear to have been composed of exogamous, patrilineal clans, probably territorial at one point. Overlaid on the clan structure was the monarchy, which established a position as "Sabataka", or head of all the Baganda clans. The reigning Kabaka linked himself in marriage with many clans; through an ingenious adjustment in the descent system, which was not general in the interlacustrine kingdoms, the monarchy as an institution succeeded in linking itself to the clans, and giving them a high stake in its welfare. Although descent was normally patrilineal, royal princes (children of a Kabaka), better known as princes of the drum, reckoned their clan affiliation through the mother. Most sons except the oldest were eligible to succeed to the throne, and accordingly most clans could always hope that the next Kabaka would be one of their sons, guaranteeing a period of exceptional access to royal favour. No royal clan thus emerged, although some clans are held to be ineligible to produce a claimant to the throne. Of the 36 clans listed by Roscoe, 12 had at least one Kabaka, and 18 were said to be excluded from the succession.[9]

Control by the Kabaka over the clan structure was inhibited by the hereditary succession pattern for heads of clans and major lineages. Nomination of clan chiefs was made by the clan itself, from among the relatively narrow range of possible successors legitimated by the hereditary principle. The chief-designate was then presented for confirmation by the Kabaka. In the rare event of a royal veto, the clan put forward another nominee. Clans and major lineages also possessed ancestral estates, where their burial grounds were situated, and temples were erected. These lands were also hereditary, unlike the rest of the terrain, and theoretically beyond the power of the Kabaka to reallocate—although evidence suggests that nineteenth century Kabakas began to infringe upon clan and lineage estates.[10]

Clan and major lineage remain an important aspect of the individual's social identity. Mutual obligation remains operative; a Muganda will both seek and offer special assistance in securing a social niche, be it in a rural settlement or in the urban economy. In family matters, securing the welfare of children or aged dependents, commemorating death and honouring the forebears, clan affiliation is of central importance. The dispersion of

o

clan members, however, already advanced during the pre-colonial period, was vastly accelerated by the huge movements of people occurring in the coincident period of the Christian revolution and establishment of colonial rule, 1888–1900.

In the eighteenth and especially nineteenth century, new forms of political hierarchy appeared, which greatly enlarged the powers of the monarchy. A grid of territorial chiefs (Bakungu) was superimposed on the older clan structure. Unlike the clan chiefs, Bakungu were for the most part named at the pleasure of the Kabaka, carried no automatic presumption of hereditary succession, and were transferable. Buganda in the nineteenth century had ten great territorial divisions (saza), whose chiefs ranked in order of precedence. Each saza chief had a deputy, to act in his stead during the long periods in which his attendance at the royal court was required. The saza in turn was divided into lesser subdivisions (gombolola), with a ranked hierarchy of chiefs, named by the Kabaka on the basis of nominations by the saza chiefs. As agents of the Kabaka, the Bakungu enjoyed the same absolute powers over the commoners dwelling in the lands under their control which the Kabaka himself asserted at the centre.[11] Beneath this was the village, or cluster of homesteads, whose chief was also nominally invested (and sometimes actually) designated by the Kabaka.

The Kabaka progressively enlarged both the jurisdiction of the Bakungu, by extending their sway over lands once considered to be Bataka, and by eliminating the hereditary principle in selection of Bakungu; by the nineteenth century, two or three were still presumptively hereditary, or linked to a given clan head.[12] Bakungu were responsible for maintaining the excellent roads which linked each saza seat with the royal capital, levying taxes, resolving conflicts, and raising and leading armies for war expeditions. Appointment, tenure, and promotion of Bakungu was based upon achievement, in the sense of demonstrated capacity to perform the tasks required for the health and prosperity of the despotic kingdom.

Adding further complexity to the structure of the Kingdom were two other authority hierachies which grew up as part of the nineteenth century despotism, the Batongole, and the military leaders. The Batongole were specially appointed officers of the royal estates, scattered throughout the kingdom. Their jurisdiction over a tract of land included the people dwelling upon it; they were responsible directly to the Kabaka. Like the Bakungu, the Batongole were appointed entirely at royal pleasure, and as a reward for services rendered to the Kabaka. They offered the almost infinitely elastic source of offices to dispense to the faithful, as well as the advantage of introducing a competing source of rural authority to balance both the Bataka and Bakungu.

Finally, Mutesa I created for the first time a permanent standing army, with regiments under the command of a Mujasi, or General. Unlike the older military specialization of Gabunga (Admiral), the post of Mujasi was not linked to a clan, and provided another separate source of power. This was of particular importance in the nineteenth century, as warfare was a critical generator of resources to lubricate the monarchy. Buganda's military power was during most of this period greater than that of its neighbours, and accordingly plundering expeditions were likely to be successful. Sixteen major campaigns are recorded under Suna II (1836–1856), and sixty-six under Mutesa I (1856–1884).[13] The pelf acquired in this manner was not so much accumulated by Kabaka and chiefs, as converted into prestige and obligation by distribution in triumphant feasts and celebrations. When an expedition was decided upon, the Kabaka designated one or more saza chiefs to raise an army among his subjects and lead it; most frequently, those at the marches of the kingdom, Kyagwe on the east, Buddu at the southwest, were thus charged. Risks were high, as the chief himself was at the head of his troops; however, rewards were equally attractive, as the successful head of a military expedition not only pleased the Kabaka through delivery of a portion of the loot, but also could directly remunerate his followers through distribution of a share himself. Creation of permanent royal regiments gave the Kabaka an alternative to reliance on the Bakungu.

The Kabakaship had thus become the linch-pin of the complex Kiganda system. Below him were an intricate mosaic of overlapping authority systems, all of which had their apex at the throne. The distinction between the hierarchy systems was not as neat on the ground as their separate listing might suggest; Batongole and some Bakungu might simultaneously hold clan of lineage office.[14] Several of the royal household offices, and two or three of the saza chieftaincies were associated with given clans. The commoner might reside in a village belonging to Mutaka, a Mukungu, or Mutongole; he could and often did shift to a different location if life became intolerable under a given chief. Thus emerged a system which was intensely competitive, individualized the reward allocation system, and offered substantial status mobility. Personal advancement depended in part on maintaining a constant stream of vacancies at the top; the Kabaka and ambitious young men shared an interest in having a constantly replenished pool of offices open. A state of perpetual intrigue existed; alliances of chiefs formed and dissolved. Those in office faced the continual threat of *kuloopa* or malicious gossip, attributing conspiracy, alien birth, or other misdemeanour. The Kabaka's pleasure could be abruptly withdrawn; overnight, a Bakungu chief in the highest esteem could find himself seized, stripped of office and the lands which went with them, and even facing the executioner. As the able Ganda historian, M. S. M. Kiwanuka, has observed chiefs met in council "neither to legislate nor to advise, but to minister to the pride of the King who was the only source of legitimate authority".

The royal capital was the vortex of power and of its pursuit. The Kibuga (capital) was initially itinerant, but about 1885 became fixed on Mengo Hill. The royal enclosure itself contained some 500 dwellings, whereas the population of the capital drew various estimates from early visitors ranging from 3,000 to 77,000.[15] The two top-ranking Bakungu chiefs, who did not have territorial offices, had their enclosures in the vicinity of the palace, the Katikiro (chief minister) and Kimbugwe (guardian of the royal umbilical cord). For much of the time, the saza chiefs would be in attendance at the court. Proximity to the Kabaka placed one near the fount of royal favour; conversely, prolonged absence gave dangerous opportunities to potential rivals to organize intrigues and spread defamatory gossip. The court was also the focal point of the proto-educational system, and access point for inter-generational mobility. Some 400–500 young boys attended the court as pages. There they performed diverse menial and sometimes important tasks, observed the great men of the realm at close hand, were privy to the affairs of state, learned the legends and achievements of the kingdom, and, in most cases, acquired a taste for high office and a knowledge of the pathways to ambition fulfilled. It was primarily from the pool of young talent represented by the pages that the Kabaka recruited new officeholders. Social promotion therefore depended largely on placement at court as a boy. Chiefs had an obvious advantage in achieving this, but many pages were sons, relatives or even clients of quite low-ranking chiefs.

Maintenance of this complex, king-centred polity necessarily required men of extraordinary ability on the throne. The potentialities of the office as it developed for a highly centralized despotism were considerable; there was, however, no guarantee that they would be realized in a given reign. Indeed, the Kabaka himself was by no means secure against conspiracy directed against his person—although not, of course, against the Kabakaship. The very highest order of chiefly intrigue was that aimed at securing of favour by placing a new Kabaka on the throne. It was at the same time the most dangerous, as it required securing a legitimate successor, involving an adequate company of conspirators to execute the coup. To secure such a scheme from betrayal by a collaborator, seeking a safer shortcut to royal favour, was extremely hazardous, and the costs of failure most likely to be fatal. The Kabaka therefore had to exploit the multiplicity of structures, forestall the coalescence of dangerous cabals, and frequently employ drastic sanctions against incumbent chiefs to safeguard his position. On accession, a strong Katikiro, ruling in the shadow of the Kabaka's authority, could keep the machinery functioning; this was clearly the case of Katikiro Mukasa in the declining years of Mutesa I. But only dynamic leadership, by the Kabaka or in his name, could preserve the Kiganda system from serious disorder. Rowe ably summarizes the challenge of the institution to its incumbent:

> Ganda politics were fluid rather than static, opportunistic rather than tradition-directed. Each Kabaka faced anew the problem of preserving himself in his power. His success would depend on his skill in maintaining an individually competitive atmosphere and constant mobility among office holders, and on utilizing to the full the natural allegiance of the people.[16]

However difficult, successful rebellion was by no means unknown. Of the thirty cases of succession between Kintu and the interference of outside forces, no fewer than five were rebel princes.[17]

The full flowering of despotism in the nineteenth century may be attributed to several peculiarly favourable historic circumstances. Until the flagging fortunes of Bunyoro-Kitara were revived by the accession of

Kabarega beginning in 1870, and external penetration from the coast and down the Nile valley made itself seriously felt in the last quarter of the century, Buganda was thoroughly secure. The kingdom could pursue with relative impunity the role of predator state, providing the monarchy with a constant flow of new resources for distribution. Moreover, several long reigns occurred in succession, capped by men of exceptional talent, Suna II and Mutesa I. The inability of Mwanga to maintain his position, and the virtual eclipse of the Kabaka as the central focus of political power from 1888 until after World War I amply demonstrates the precarious position of the King himself.

There were virtually no limits upon the powers of the Kabaka, as they had developed by the nineteenth century. The various praise-names of the Kabaka exalted his strength, invincibility, and omnipotence. An anthology of proverbs invoked his majesty, his terrifying power, his right to kill any of his subjects.[18] The most important part of a coronation ritual was a ceremony on a historic site at Budo Hill, where the "Kabaka eats Buganda" (literally takes physical possession of), ritually symbolizing the total identification of King and Kingdom; henceforward, the Kabaka is the embodiment of Buganda. As one distinguished Maganda elder statesman, Serwano Kilubya, has indicated, it would be a gross breach of etiquette to refer to the Kabaka eating or sleeping; rather would the Kabaka simply "rest":

> ... To convey the idea that the Kabaka is always guarding his country and, hence, cannot fall asleep like the other people who have no responsibility; he merely takes a rest, meanwhile thinking out what he is going to do next." From the above it will be seen that the Kabaka was not looked upon as an ordinary human being. He was regarded as a kind of superman without the weakness of common folk. Theoretically, he requires neither food nor sleep, he was above such things.[19]

The Kabaka was the fount of custom; tradition was subject to royal repeal. Sir Edward Mutesa II states the traditional monarchical claim, which appears to have been borne out in practice:

> All authority flowed from the Kabaka. Just as he was the personification of the Baganda, so he and his actions were beyond judgement or question. A tradition that would be binding on all others ceased to be a tradition if he said so. The old might mutter and shake their heads at a discreet distance, but it simply was so. It is misleading even to say that if a Kabaka did something, it became right, because that implies that people considered and decided that such an action was acceptable. It was more automatic than that.[20]

The appointive power was a central lever in the Kabaka's authority. Only the Bataka chiefs lay outside his orbit. The King was thus the final arbiter of career prospects for the ambitious. Effective control over allocation of estates, limited to some extent by clan and lineage lands, but enhanced by continuous territorial expansion, was another pillar of authority. He was the final adjudicator of all cases, although the Katikiro frequently exercised this prerogative in his behalf. He had the power to establish and levy taxes. Collection was carried out by the Bakungu, but no tax could be exacted except under the authority of the Kabaka; Ham Mukasa lists nineteen different kinds of royal taxes.[21] He required the chiefs to maintain the road system. He raised armies; the Kabaka had the capacity to mobilize an enormous body of men. Stanley claims to have seen 150,000 men in an 1875 campaign against the Bavuma Islands.[22]

SYMBOLS AND SUCCESSION

The symbol of the kingdom is the battery of royal drums, known as Mujaguzo. Of these the most highly venerated is Kawulugumo, a drum which dates from the 15th Kabaka, Mutebi. The two other principal drums are Timba, which dates from the reign of the third Kabaka, Kimera, and Namanonyi, made by Juko, 16th Kabaka.[23] The battery in total consists of over 200 drums. To capture the drums was to capture the kingdom; in a literal sense, Mujaguzo incarnated the authority of the Kabaka. In mounting his throne, the new Kabaka beats Kawuluguma, the drum which rules all drums. Upon the death of a Kabaka, members of the Pangolin clan have responsibility for immediately securing Mujaguzo, and placing it under tight guard.[24] Kulubya, in summarizing customs of Buganda, gives special attention to the drums, which he describes as "very important." "Until this day," he continued, "this group of drums is held in high respect, so much so that it is a well-known fact that whenever they are heard it is a sure sign that the King is there is in person." Whenever a Kabaka dies, tradition held that the skins of two of the royal drums burst. Kulubya remarks wryly, "How this happens I am afraid I do not know; it may perhaps be suspected that a human hand plays a part in this." But, he added, after the death of Mutesa I, despite a guard posted by Katikiro Mukasa, the drums still burst.[25] The overwhelming importance of the royal drums as a symbol of king, kingdom and people was given remarkable demonstration when Mujaguzo was apparently destroyed by the Uganda Army in May 1966. Baganda of all ranks, from intellectual to commoner, including those who supported in most respects the central government against Mutesa, found the reports of the loss of the drums as a numbing personal trauma.

Other symbols of kingship include the flame lit by each new Kabaka, and which is kept alight throughout his reign. A royal stool, Namulondo, which dates from the ninth Kabaka Mulondo, serves once during each reign; after his designation, the new Kabaka mounts on Namulondo and stands, to allow all to see that he is Kabaka. A royal symbol of more contemporary vintage was the custom-made Rolls Royce belonging to Mutesa II. Buganda was careful to maintain its sense of special status during the colonial period by insuring that the royal vehicle (and stipend) were slightly larger than those of the British Governor.[26]

As with all despotic systems, a critical weak point was the moment of succession. The potential for conflict over the throne was aggravated by the very large number of eligible successors who were frequently available. Succession could pass to any prince of the drum, or son, or son's son, of a Kabaka. In practice, this meant that any Kabaka who succeeded in maintaining his throne for at least a few years was likely to accumulate a substantial number of sons; it was desirable to symbolize personal bonds with many clans through marriage, and clans would be desirous of assuring for themselves the possibility of having a Kabaka in the future by offering one of their daughters to the incumbent king. The brothers of a Kabaka were equally eligible and indeed their qualification for the throne was a mortal danger for the order of the kingdom; any brother of a Kabaka could be the instrument for a sudden cabal of chiefs. The choice was made immediately upon the Kabaka's death, by the Katikiro, the Kimbugwe, and Kasuju (guardian of the princes of the drum), and then presented to the council of chiefs (Lukiko) for ratification. The deceased Kabaka could have made his wishes known in advance, but since he was not present to superintend the proceedings, his desires could not bind the three electors. The choice had to be made instantly upon the expiry of the Kabaka. The stakes were enormous. The incumbent Katikiro had his own position to preserve. Purges of the chiefly ranks were likely to ensue, as a new Kabaka consolidated his power by installing men personally obligated to him. The new Queen Mother (Namasole) would be in a position to ensure special favours for her clan. The Katikiro had to keep news of the Kabaka's demise secret, as anarchy would swiftly intervene were even a brief interregnum to occur. When Suma II died in 1856, there were sixty-one eligible sons; all male issues of the Kabaka except the oldest were legitimate heirs. The Katikiro not only had to engineer the choice, but to assure that overwhelming numbers of reliable armed men were on hand when the Kabaka-designate was presented to the council of chiefs for approval and investiture.[27]

After investiture, the new Kabaka had to secure himself against rebellion, and consolidate his power. The early years of power were full of hazards; it took time to establish the plentitude of royal power. A young man needed to establish his authority over the Katikiro, who initially was likely to be in a far stronger position. The danger that any living legitimate successor automatically represented for an incumbent had generated elaborate safeguards. Princes of the drum were sent under close supervision to different corners of the kingdom. They were not permitted to reside at court, or to occupy any chieftaincy role which might serve as a catapult to early seizure of power. New Kabakas achieved theoretically absolute power, therefore, lacking the intimate familiarity with the network of intrigue which hundreds of pages had acquired, confronting an array of chiefs fearful of their own positions, masters of rumour-mongering, skilled in conspiracy.

There was thus a clear rhythm in the exercise of Kabakaship. The early years were ones of cautious consolidation of power, of uncertainty. Beginning with the reign of the 27th Kabaka, Semakokiro, after a period of instability and rebellion (the 12 Kabakas between 1700 and 1825 all had to fight for their throne), the practice developed of executing brothers of the Kabaka to forestall possible conspiracy centred about them.[28] After weathering the initial threats, the Kabaka then had to establish a more permanent security by balancing the different chiefly factions which formed. It was at this stage that the Kabaka could realize the full potential of his office. Old age was another perilous time; perspectives of imminent change were also likely to activate conspiracy. This pattern could clearly be seen in the reign of Mutesa I; in his first years, he was a shy and pliable king, dominated by the old Katikiro and Queen Mother. Within a decade, he had rid himself of both influences, and was at the zenith of power. The last five years of his life, he was hampered by a debilitating illness, and Katikiro Mukasa came to dominate the kingdom. A strikingly similar pattern may be discerned in the careers of the two Kabakas designated under British overrule. Daudi Chwa (1897–1939) was placed upon the throne as a one-year old infant. In the 1920s, after he had attained his majority, he began to challenge the great Protestant Katikiro Sir Apolo Kagwa. For nearly a decade, Daudi Chwa played a relatively active role, then during his last few years of life withdrew into sullen isolation. Sir Edward Mutesa II had a similar career pattern. He became Kabaka at the age of fifteen, then spent years finishing school, becoming a sportsman, enjoying the Mediterranean sun. He began to assert himself as Kabaka only about 1952. After his return from exile in 1955, Mutesa II and his henchmen, the "King's men", became a dominant political force.

The advent of British overrule introduced two important innovations in defining rules of succession. The epochal 1900 definition of Buganda-British relationships, which came to ensure a special status for the kingdom within the Protectorate, defined somewhat different rules of succession, extending eligibility to a wider range of collateral heirs. Article 6 of the agreement stipulated in part: "On the death of a Kabaka, his successor shall be elected by a majority of votes in the Lukiko, or native council. The range of selection, however, must be limited to the Royal Family of Uganda, that is to say, to the descendants of King Mutesa."[29] The surviving sons of Mutesa were executed by the unfortunate Kabaka Kalema in 1889. Mwanga, according to his grandson Sir Edward Mutesa II, had "uncertain and unsatisfactory" relations with women, and had no children until 1895, two years before his deposition. His first son, Daudi Chwa, was named Kabaka by the British and thus an important customary taboo, barring the eldest son from succession, disappeared.

The other critical change was the accession of a Christian Kabaka. This introduced strong pressures from the Anglican Church to restrict succession rights to sons born of the Christian marriage. Thus Daudi Chwa had more than a dozen sons but only Sir Edward Mutesa II from the church marriage.[30] Some would have preferred the choice to fall to another son, judged more promising, but the Native Anglican Church vigorously opposed. Sir Edward Mutesa II has two teenage sons, but both by the sister of his wife, whom he candidly avows to be his true love, in his autobiography.[31] Only one prince has been born of his Christian marriage. The church vigorously resisted his efforts to secure a divorce in the middle '50s; in the unlikely event that succession were again to become an issue, unravelling the diverse exclusions established by custom and Christianity would be a complicated problem.

One final dimension of the pre-colonial Kabakaship which merits examination, and serves as a useful link with the impact of the colonial and post-colonial periods, is the relationship of kingship and religion. Despite some distinguished representations to the contrary, it would seem misleading to classify the Kabaka with divine kingship.[32] The Kabaka was an omnipotent human being, but did not claim divinity. Traditional religion, *lubaale*, was utterly distinct from the Kabaka, and indeed one of the few potential sources of social influence and political power which eluded the control of the Kabaka. Although shrouded in the mists of legend, and containing obvious figurative elements, the myth of the origin of the dynasty does not assert a link with divinity. The first king Kintu, although he purportedly descended from the skies, is not described or worshipped as a god. The tombs of deceased Kabakas are revered shrines; the corporeal relics of former kings, the jawbones (before Mutesa I eliminated the practice), and umbilical cords are accorded high veneration, but appear distinct from saintly bones. They represent the projection into the past of the earthly kingdom rather than mortal vehicles for the divine spirit. The person of the living king was held in awe, and behaviour in his presence symbolized the great deference for the king. As Mutesa puts it, "Everyone knelt to speak to the Kabaka, and it was quite usual to lie full length before him in abasement. This is still the case."[33]

But a rigorous code of *lèse-majesté* is not equivalent to divinity. The Kabaka was not the intermediary with the spiritual world, and had no priestly functions. He made no rain, nor did he perform any other supernatural functions. The traditional religion, a pantheon of gods incarnating various natural and supernatural forces, had its own assortment of shrine attendants, temple guardians, and priests who were an island of autonomy. The *lubaale* cults tended to be identified with the clan structure; many shrines were in the particular custody of Bataka. They were therefore allied with the hierarchy over which the Kabaka had the least control, and constituted a political resource by Bataka against the encroaching authority of the Bakungu and Batongole.[34] As Suna and Mutesa I succeeded in extending the scope of centralized despotism, they came into conflict with the *lubaale* priests. Mutesa I in particular repeatedly expressed his contempt for the traditional cult to many visitors. His interest in the universal religions proposed to him, first Islam and later Christianity, was no doubt partly motivated by the hope that these might offer resources in the struggle against *lubaale*, if properly attached to the monarchy; to this must doubtless be added the more conventional assumption that the Christian missionaries and Zanzibari traders might be a source of guns or foreign alliance against the vague menace of alien intrusion from various quadrants.[35]

Many of the rites and ceremonies related to kingship, and the Kabaka on occasion had to propitiate the *lubaale* gods, of whom the most important was Mukasa, god of the lake, whose shrine was on the Ssese islands, tributary to but not fully controlled by the Kabaka. Traditional religion was thus a diffuse world of incorporeal spirits, not a systematic body of ideas. As Rowe suggests, the attitude toward religion had been rather casual on the whole, except at moments of crisis and calamity. Even then, efforts to secure supernatural intercession were to be supplementary to human efforts; the whole is aptly embodied in the Kigandda proverb, "God help me, but one must keep on running!"[36]

IDEOLOGY AND CONFLICT: THE CHRISTIAN REVOLUTION

Mutesa I began to attract Zanzibari traders and miscellaneous coastal technicians to his court in the 1860s, and listened with growing interest to their interpretation of the Holy Koran. In 1869, the Kabaka gave orders for Ramadan to be observed; the Islamic calendar and some dietary practices were adopted. About 1875, the Kabaka ordered the countryside to follow; mosques were hastily thrown up throughout Buganda.

The following year, a portentous conflict occurred. Zanzibari traders, and subsequently Christian missionaries, were confined by the King to the capital. Yet paradoxically this gave them direct access to the most crucial group on the country, the court pages. The centralization of the political recruitment process ensured that the overwhelming majority of the Kingdom's top personnel passed through the page corps. Able, ambitious and curious, the pages had ample time to sit at the feet of the foreigners at court. During the years of Mutesa's flirtation with Islam, a number of the pages became genuine converts, and accepted the circumcision that the Kabaka refused to contemplate. In 1876, the more devout pages began to criticize the role of the Kabaka in Islam, his unsuitability to lead prayers, the ritual impurity of the Kabaka's butcher. The Kabaka suddenly realized that a devastating new idea was abroad: that there was a higher law than the King himself, that the authority of the Kabaka could be questioned by his very pages. Stern measures were taken; about seventy Muslim pages were executed, and the mosques suddenly erected the preceding year were as swiftly demolished.[37]

But the following year, 1877, the first Christian missionaries appeared on the scene, from the Church Missionary Society. In 1879, they were joined by a Roman Catholic mission, dispatched by the French White Fathers. Both groups quickly established a coterie of "readers" among the royal pages, and Mutesa again displayed great interest. In 1879, he offered to join the Protestant church, and accept Catholic baptism in turn, but no reconciliation of views was possible on the monogamy issue. Despite the persecution of 1876, Islam also had a following among the pages, and, to a growing extent, among young chiefs. But the injection of three currents of religious belief and identity into Kiganda politics introduced a radically new factor: ideology. Groups began to crystallize around the religions, and had a stability, a basis for persistence through repeated crises, and a moral imperative transcending both the immediate pursuit of power, and the authority of the Kabaka. The task of the Kabaka was thus made infinitely more complex; the skills and instincts developed over generations of maintenance of supremacy through brokerage and manipulation of fluid coalitions of individuals, with the ultimate authority of the Kabaka beyond question, were suddenly no longer wholly relevant. Add to this the fact that

each of the religious groupings was backed by able foreign advisers—
Father Lourdel of the Catholics, Alexander Mackay of the Protestants,
an array of Zanzibari traders for the Muslims—who themselves became
skilled operators in Kiganda politics. It is superfluous to add that each
enjoyed plentiful access to external power resources, any one of which
could have overcome the Kingdom, and one can measure the full
dimensions of the Kabaka's dilemma.

Mutesa I survived the challenge of contending religious factions, but
Mwanga, who succeeded in 1884, paid the price. He faced the impossible
task of consolidating his power against the older chiefs, and at the same
time coping with the religious factions. Most of the new chiefs he named
were recent graduates from the page ranks, and Muslim or Christian
converts. Yet in 1885 he took his first dramatic step against the converts, executing three pages, and the following year about fifty Christian
readers were burned at the stake. Sir Edward Mutesa II describes his
plight:

> He was eighteen when he became supreme ruler of the country that had been
> held together—just—by the strength and subtlety of a remarkable man. The
> different religious groups had created factions, if not quite political parties.
> To continue to play them off against each other needed authority and courage.
> Neither Lourdel nor Mackay were easy men to manipulate, and they saw a
> chance to dominate this powerful youth. He knew that his selection from
> amongst his brothers as Kabaka had been opposed by his aunt, a formidable
> woman whom I was taken to visit as a child . . . He did not attend the Court
> while his father lived, but would stay with important chiefs out in the country.
> As a result, he was not experienced in the ceremonies and formality of the
> Court, nor did he have personal friends to turn to for guidance . . . Is it sur-
> prising that he wished to expel all the complicating foreigners, to return to the
> certainties of the old life?[38]

The resources of the despotic nineteenth-century Kabakaship, and of
its incumbent, simply could not face the new constellation of forces that
were confronted. Even after the Christian martyrdom, Mwanga named as
commanders of the royal regiments none other than Apolo Kagwa, the
ablest of the new Protestant generation, and Honorat Nyonyintono, a
dynamic Catholic leader (who lost his life in battle in 1890).[39] The end came
for the despotic model of the Kabakaship in 1888, when Mwanga did try
to mount a fantastic plot to maroon all the Muslims and Christians on a
deserted island in the middle of Lake Victoria. This temporarily united the
three religious factions against him; he fled across the lake himself, and
the Kabakaship went into more than three decades of eclipse.

Unlike the 1966 revolution, the 1888 revolutionaries could not con-
ceive of abolishing the monarchical institution. They were, however,
viewing the office in a radically new way. Muslim, Catholic and Protestant
sought to secure advantages and security for their factions. Monarchy
was the instrument of religion, and not, as Mutesa I had once hoped, the
contrary. The very choice of a pretender illustrates the newly instrumental
attitude the new political elite had towards *kingship*. They forced Kiwewa,
Mutesa's oldest son, to take the throne—whereas the oldest prince of the

drum was the one who was absolutely prohibited from the line of succession. In an older concept of monarchy, tradition could be altered by the Kabaka, but radical innovation in one of the most sensitive rules surrounding *kingship* would have been inconceivable.

The tensions between the three religious factions, and strains imposed by the conflicting ambitions and distrust among their foreign patrons and allies, quickly ruptured the brief triple entente. The Muslims won a temporary victory, as the vastly superior external strength potentially available to the Catholic and Protestant factions had not yet made itself felt. Muslims tried to make the monarchy an unambiguous instrument of Islam by requiring the Kabaka, Kiwewa, to submit to circumcision. This he adamantly refused to do, and made a pathetic effort to rally the traditional forces of the Kingdom to expel the Muslims. Before the year of the three Kabakas was over Kiwewa in his turn was placed under arrest and another son of Mutesa, Kalema, was perched precariously on the eroding throne by the Muslim faction.[40]

Mwanga made a brief return in 1890, backed by Christian armies, but in circumstances where the despotic powers of Kabakaship could not be restored. Captain F. D. Lugard, representing the Imperial British East Africa Company, arrived in Kampala the same year, and from that point forward decisive force was never in the hands of the monarchy. The first treaty between the Kingdom and the Company was signed at the end of 1890, and resident agents of the company began to serve as arbiters among the religious factions. In 1894, the Foreign Office officially confirmed a further treaty signed the previous year with Mwanga and the Bakungu chiefs, and Uganda became a Protectorate. For a time, British residents sought to maintain a balance between the Catholic and Protestant factions, and to offer some consolation to the Muslims. With the Palace at Mengo within range of Lugard's Maxim gun on Kampala hill, the new relation of forces was aptly symbolized. A battle between the Catholic (Bafransa) and Protestant (Baingelesi) in 1892 had been won by the latter, but through the 1890s the curious expedient of maintaining two Katikiros, a Protestant (Sir Apolo Kagwa) and a Catholic (Stanlislas Mugwanya) was preserved. Young Buganda was not long in recognizing the new situation. Although Kagwa records that there were only 2,052 confirmed Christians in 1895,[41] Christianity now made dramatic advances. Beginning in 1894, missionaries and Baganda catechists fanned out through the countryside; now backed by the authority of the chiefs, with the great counties divided up between Protestants and Catholics (with three small counties, Gomba, Basuju, and Butumbala. left to the Muslims), Christianity swiftly diffused. Social mobility now unequivocally lay through conversion, and Buganda responded with enthusiasm.[42]

The *coup de grâce* for the old monarchy came in 1897, when Mwanga fled into rebellion. He was captured in 1899, and exiled to the Seychelles, where he died in 1903. The Protestant party was now in full command. An infant son had been born to Mwanga on 8 August 1896, but, significantly, in the enclosure of the Protestant Katikiro Kagwa. Sir Apolo was made his guardian, and after the flight of Mwanga, the infant son Daudi Chwa became Kabaka in 1897. The new structure of Buganda was sealed and fixed in the 1900 treaty negotiated between Sir Harry Johnston and the Bakungu chiefs, with the Protestant faction clearly dominant. The implications of the 1900 treaty for kingship derive from the exceptional nature of the negotiating parties. Buganda was not simply a conquered state, to become an appendage of the Empire. Rather it became the keystone of the Uganda Protectorate, through an alliance between the British and a new revolutionary elite which had gained power within the Kingdom. The chiefs with whom Johnston negotiated were not traditionalists but a remarkable generation of new men, many already literate. They did not, of course, bargain from a position of full equality, but the situation was far less unequal than in most other early colonial relationships. The treaties of 1890 and 1893–4 were made with the Kabaka and chiefs, whereas before 1888 any negotiation would have been ratified by the Kabaka alone. In 1900, the negotiation was exclusively conducted by the chiefs. This was reflected in the extraordinary features of Buganda's Magna Carta. The political hegemony of the revolutionary generation of chiefs was given economic content, by the distribution of some 8,000 square miles of the best land in Buganda to some 1,000 chiefly claimants, partly in official lands attached to public office, and part in freehold property. (Ultimately, when the distribution had been made, there proved to be over 3,900 recipients.) The agreement contained a far more detailed description of the division of authority between Kingdom and Protectorate than colonial powers normally indulged in. At a later date, when a thorough European administration, hardly foreseen in 1900, had been established, the 1900 agreement seriously circumscribed its intervention in Kiganda affairs.

The position of the Bakungu chiefs was further reinforced by the simplification of the parallel traditional hierarchies which occurred. The bataka chiefs were simply not recognized, they had little representation in the negotiations, and lost heavily in the land settlement voted upon by the Bakungu chiefs. A single, territorially based hierarchy was recognized, salaries set and reasonable security of tenure in office afforded. The military offices were abolished, and the Batongole were absorbed as the bottom rung in the territorial (Bakungu) hierarchy.

MONARCHY IN ECLIPSE: THE BAKUNGU ASCENDENCY

Despite the wide range of autonomy which the Protectorate did allow to Buganda, the King and Kingdom were now locked irrevocably within a wider system. The pertinence of this fact was not immediately clear; for the first two decades, Buganda was the transcendant core of the Protectorate. The 1900 settlement had among other things permitted the Kingdom to double its territory, and ten new counties were added to the ten historic ones. Baganda political agents and catechists fanned out throughout the Protectorate; initially, the larger unit of which Buganda was a part simply offered wider horizons and new opportunities for the revolutionary generation of young Baganda. Later, when the empire-building era was over, Buganda continued to regard itself as occupying a special place in the Protectorate, a more intimate and state-to-state relationship with the British Empire than the other districts. Until the final years of colonial rule, the real threat was not Uganda, but submersion of Buganda in an East African Federation, likely to be dominated by Kenya's obstreperous settlers. The Omuwnika (Treasurer) of Buganda, Serwano Kulubya, travelled to London to argue a strongly stated brief against integration before the Joint Select Committee on Closer Union in 1931. In 1953, a chance banquet statement by the Secretary of Colonies suggested that an East African Federation might again be under serious consideration produced a violent reaction, precipitating the crisis leading to the deportation of the Kabaka.

Figure 1 STRUCTURE OF AUTHORITY[43]

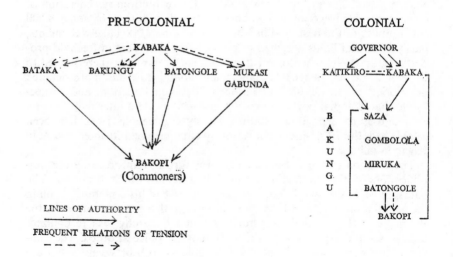

PRE-COLONIAL

COLONIAL

LINES OF AUTHORITY

FREQUENT RELATIONS OF TENSION

But of more immediate import was that the Protectorate introduced vitally important new actors in Kiganda politics, the British Governor, and his Resident (or Commissioner, as he was variously titled) in Buganda. Until the first World War, once the 1900 settlement had been signed, there was very little British participation in Buganda internal affairs. The colonial administration was very thin on the ground, and the budget deficits which persisted until 1916, plus the need to occupy and bring under administration the outlying areas, prohibited extensive deployment of expatriate personnel in Buganda. Further, under the strong leadership of Sir Apolo, the Kingdom was able to perform well all the tasks placed upon it. The revolutionary generation was well satisfied with the 1900 agreement, and became even more so when the introduction of cotton as a cash crop in 1906–1908 gave the land holdings an economic rent. By 1902, taxation was established. That year, the chiefs were given the imposing task of moving thousands of their subjects two miles away from the Lake Victoria shore, as an anti-sleeping sickness measure. Finally, imposition of cotton cultivation, and, in 1908, enforcement of stringent agricultural regulations to standardize the quality of the crop were all carried through without provoking serious disturbances. With very little British intervention, Buganda was thus able to carry out the early requirements of colonial order: administrative penetration, law and order, rudimentary health measures, regular taxation, and development of cash revenues for the peasantry to pay them.

Buganda politics were also kept singularly simple in the pre-war years by the absence of the Kabaka in the political equation. Daudi Chwa did not attain his majority until 1914; during his childhood years, he remained under the watchful guardianship of Sir Apolo Kagwa, and the Anglican missionaries. There was little turnover in the Saza and Gombolola chieftaincies, as the revolutionary generation, which had attained power early, lived out the satisfying careers opened by triumph in the 1890s, and the elimination of the earlier sources of competition.

The interwar years saw the political process return to more familiar patterns. The confluence of several factors agitated the political waters, and generated eddies of intrigue which recreated a more familiar environment of conflict. The British administration rapidly expanded, and began to undertake a wide range of new functions, implying more thorough intervention in Kingdom affairs, and more selectivity in designation of major chiefs and tended to become separated from office, as many estates allocated to chiefs in 1900 were inherited by sons who did not succeed to office. A comprehensive philosophy of colonial rule had taken form which, whatever its ambiguities, provided an important sense of purpose and direction to the Protectorate's relationships with Buganda. The Kingdom was divided into four districts, with British District Commissioners posted to offer direct supervision of local administration, seconded by a growing array of technical and specialized field staff. A revealing petition was submitted in the mid-1920s protesting this trend:

The Kabaka occupies a position at present which is tantamount to that of an ordinary Paramount Chief of one of the second rate tribes of Africa. He no longer has any power to control over his own chiefs and all and sundry officers of the Protectorate Government appear to have the right to have direct access to the Kabaka which right was exclusively reserved to the Governor alone . . . Any order issued to the Chiefs by the Kabaka or his Government has to be countersigned and approved by the P(rovincial) C(ommissioner) before it can be transmitted to the Chief concerned, with the result that the Chiefs are beginning to lose their sense of loyalty to their Kabaka . . . This is the effect of the practice brought about solely by the Administrative officers of the Protectorate Government which is entirely unjustified and clearly in conflict not only with time honoured traditions and principles of native administration in Buganda but also in the terms and intentions of the Uganda Agreement 1900.[44]

KING AND COMMONER: THE ALLIANCE FORMED

The crucial event marking the shift in relationships between Katikiro, Kabaka, and Protectorate was the elimination of Sir Apolo Kagwa in 1926. Sir Apolo did not take kindly to either the growing interventionism of the Protectorate or the less forceful ambitions of Duadi Chwa. Sir Edward Mutesa II records that "Sir Apolo was too accustomed to power to welcome my father's coming of age, and would have liked to ignore him as much as possible. An old and sick man, he was more or less forced to retire in 1926 by the Governor, who was aided by my father with the maximum discretion."[45] The newly appointed Provincial Commissioner, the trenchant J. R. Postlethwaite, was completely impatient with Sir Apolo, and precipitated the struggle, backed by Governor Sir William Gowers.[46] But Sir Apolo was a formidable man; on one occasion, in the midst of a discussion with the Governor and Kabaka, he displayed his mettle in an incident described by a later Kabaka:

> . . . Sir Apolo, a large powerful man, though no longer young, sprang to his feet and roared that he would fight Gowers there and then. Gowers was fifty himself, and did not appear to relish the contest. As Sir Apolo was stripping off his jacket, his son Mwebe, who was present as an interpreter, provided a timely distraction by fainting from emotion.[47]

A highly significant new social force appeared on the Buganda political scene in the 1920s as the Bakopi (Commoners) began to grow restive. Traditional obligation of labour and tribute owing to chiefs began to take on novel dimensions as the cash economy penetrated. Social obligation underwent a subtle metamorphosis into economic exploitation, as the beneficiaries of the 1900 settlement took on the appearances of a rentier class. The first stirrings of rural populism were fused with the grievances of the Bataka, and became expressed through the traditional idiom. At this juncture, the focal point for grievance was the Bakungu ruling oligarchy, and not the Kabaka himself. The surfacing of Bakopi disconent coincided with a phase in colonial thinking when paternal solicitude for the welfare of the commoner was transcendant, coincident with an interventionist predisposition. The Protectorate government forced the Buganda Lukiko to adopt in 1927 a Busulu and Envujo law, which sharply restricted the rents which could be collected from tenants, and limited the tribute which could be levied in labour or kind. Thus, the initial alliance of British and Bakungu was reversed; the Protectorate went through a phase of backing King and Commoner against the chiefs.

Daudi Chwa, after a few years of attempting to assert himself within the constructed framework of interwar Protectorate policy, became in his last years sullen and withdrawn. He did make a final bid for a confirmation of predominant power of the Kabaka against the three Ministers and chiefs in the mid-1930s. His proposals would have provided a definite five-year term for ministers, and twenty of the sixty nominated members of the Lukiko to be unofficials (and hence King's men) rather than chiefs as was then the practice. These failed to gain support, and the Kabaka responded with the only weapon remaining to him: non-cooperation. On one occasion he even threatened abdication. Generally, he ceased to be receptive to Protectorate advice.[48]

Daudi Chwa died in 1939, and the succession passed to his only son by the Christian marriage recognized by the Church, Sir Edward Mutesa II. Sir Edward, crowned at the age of fifteen, had been carefully tutored by Anglican missionaries and European teachers. As his father before him, he played very little role in his first years as Kabaka; the Katikiro, treasurer, and Chief Justice again were named as Regents during his minority. Sir Edward himself is the best witness to diffidence with which he began his royal duties: "I left political matters almost entirely in the hands of the three Regents. Sir Philip Mitchell, who was Governor from 1935–1940, used to come to see me occasionally and gave me chocolates, but I was not required to make decisions, only to accept and understand those that others had made."[49]

For more than a decade, Sir Edward made little effort to fill the office he had inherited. He hunted, attended Cambridge for two years, 1946–1948, became an officer in the Grenadier Guards, frequented English country estates and Mediterranean beaches.

POPULIST REVOLT

In this period when the office of Kabaka was virtually vacant, the political environment was undergoing radical transformation. Traditional patterns of intrigue and conspiracy among cliques of chiefs reasserted themselves. No longer were the Katikiro and his ministers able to dominate the scene in the fashion of Sir Apolo Kagwa. Populist impulses were quickening in the countryside, and were expressed both in traditional and a new nationalist idiom. The British tutelage no longer enjoyed the overwhelming prestige and unquestioned acceptance it had once possessed. The overrulers, in response, were moving beyond the dogma of indirect rule and pre-occupation with the future of "native States", to an initial and tentative concern with ultimate decolonization.

The first crisis in the reign of the new Kabaka was in the most classic mold of Kiganda conflict. An old reign had ended, a new one was not yet established. Katikiro Martin Luther Nsibirwa, who had held the office since 1927, and was the political heir of Sir Apolo Kagwa, exercised diminishing authority. The catalyzing dispute was of a traditional cast. The Queen Mother (Namasole) desired to remarry a commoner in 1941. Under Christian ethics, this was entirely acceptable, and the Protectorate endorsed her decision. However, there could be no more flagrant contravention of traditional norms. The young Kabaka gave his approval, but the issue became a spear of intrigue by a coterie of dissident chiefs. They were able to tap the growing currents of Bakopi disconent as a new political resource; few of the Katikiro's supporters dared speak out in open support of the Namasole's marriage. What is striking about this dispute is the pattern established, which has been a constant theme in contemporary Kiganda politics: rural effervescence, which in other contexts had been

P

channelled into radical protest, crystallized around the symbols of traditional politics. The Namasole was an important part of the matrix of the King-centred Buganda traditional institutions. Despite the endorsement of the incumbent King for the violation of traditional norms, popular discontents were articulated against the King but on behalf of kingship.

Other portentous developments reflected the changing British perspectives as to their colonial aims. The expectation of indefinite colonial tutelage, still dominant in the 1930s, gradually shifted to an acceptance by the postwar years that the terminal colonial period had begun. This broad trend overlay a much more complex process on the ground in Buganda, with the shift to decolonization proceeding in jagged fits and starts, and greatly affected by the particular personalities and predispositions of individual governors. Sir Charles Dundas, Governor from 1940–1944, had a marked impact in the pattern of ultimate decolonization, and a very particular set of ideas. He was strongly committed to transposing the doctrine of indirect rule to the new requirements of the terminal colonial period. His vision of a future Uganda was as a federation of "native states", a perspective rejected by all future Governors, but peculiarly coincident with the aims of many Baganda. Sir Charles produced a radical set of reforms in 1944, over the opposition of most of the Protectorate administration, which in effect dismantled many of the controls which had been built up over the '20s and '30s in Buganda. The District Commissioners were to be withdrawn, and only a Resident, based in Kampala, would exercise supervisory powers over the Kabaka's government. The chiefs would cease to be under the direct supervision of Protectorate personnel. These sweeping reforms were not wholly implemented in 1944, as their author was transferred shortly afterwards. They enjoyed little support from the lower reaches of the Protectorate staff, and neither the Kabaka nor the Katikiro then in office was able to take advantage of this opportunity to reassert control over the Kingdom. A decade later, when a similar opportunity was offered, the Kabaka's response was very different.

The years between the end of World War II and the crisis over the Kabaka's deportation have a peculiarly rudderless quality in Buganda. The new governor, Sir John Hall, reversed the direction of the Dundas reforms, and easily dominated the Kabaka; as Mutesa himself described the relationship, the Governor was very "straightforward". The Kabaka frequently visited Entebbe, played tennis with the Governor, and received his instructions. Sir John "would sit behind his desk, pour forth his views, and when he had finished it was clear that you were dismissed".[50] Sir Edward was far too compliant an instrument of the colonial will to serve as a focus for the burgeoning discontent. Animosity to the colonizer was growing rapidly, and serious disorders occurred in 1945 and 1949.[51] Samwiri Wamala had replaced Nsibirwa as Katikiro in 1941, and a bitter factional dispute aligned him against Serwano Kulubya, Omuwanika (Treasurer) since 1928. After the 1945 disorders, the Protectorate reinstated Nsibirwa as Katikiro, but he was almost immediately assassinated on the steps of the Anglican Cathedral at Namirembe Hill in Mengo. He was then succeeded by M. E. Kawalya-Kagwa, son of Sir Apolo, and the Protectorate led a purge of chiefs. But by now the position of chiefs loyal to the Protectorate was extremely difficult. The Kabaka was unable to give them effective backing, and the administrative embrace of the colonial staff was a painful encumbrance.

In this situation, commoner discontent was becoming explosive. In addition to a generalized hostility to British domination, an array of specific grievances troubled the countryside. Control of the rural economy by European and Asian buyers and processors of the cash crops, cotton and coffee, was increasingly resented. The government in the initial postwar years adopted a policy of holding down cotton and coffee prices to African producers, on the assumption that buoyant world market conditions were only temporary, and price stabilization funds had to be built up to protect against an anticipated return to more depressed price levels. European and Asian planters, however, were exempted from rigorous buying regulations on coffee, and received the full market prices. Asian buyers and "middlemen" were widely believed to cheat the growers, through manipulation of the scales and other sharp practices.

Groups which served as channels for awakening grievances were of several types. An elective principle was accepted in the Lukiko in 1945 and an assortment of traders and farmers joined the appointed chiefs. This group became obstructive; the Resident in Buganda was soon to accuse them in an Annual Report of showing "a lamentable lack of responsibility". "These people," the Resident maintained, "represented by a fraction of the electorate, such was the lack of interest in the elections shown by the ordinary Mugunda, normally used their newly-found power to criticize and attack constituted authority and to persuade the common people that it was they, and not the chiefs, to whom they should turn for help and guidance."[52]

The Bataka again became prominent, organized as a party, maintaining the continuity of vehicle clothed in traditional garb for the venting of contemporary discontents. A new set of structures, overlapping in leadership and membership with the Bataka Party, appeared at this time, aimed at political organization of rural Buganda. The Uganda Federation of African Farmers (under various labels) began organizing in 1947; out of it, in turn, was born the first nationalist party, the Uganda National Congress, in 1952.[53]

At this juncture, there seemed every reason to expect that the populist energies visible in the Buganda countryside would ultimately flow into the same channels which has already been established by nationalist movements in West Africa. The Kabaka appeared to be a frivolous and irrelevant young man; the institution of Kingship seemed unlikely to play a central role in the approaching final phase of the colonial epoch—the confrontation between colonizer and a new nationalist elite over the terms and timetable of independence. The outcome, in the event, was to prove radically different. Part of the explanation lay in the timing and cataclysmic nature of the conflict between Buganda and Britain, expressed through the monarchical institution, in 1953–1955, to which we now turn. Another set of factors derive, however, from certain particularities of Uganda as a polity, which set it apart from most African political systems; to these points we will return after considering the 1953–1955 crisis.

The (late) Sir Andrew Cohen took up the post of Governor in January 1952. In the Colonial Office, he had been an architect of post-war political reform in West Africa. He arrived on the scene, determined to impart a new momentum to political development in Uganda. However, he faced a series of dilemmas. He was determined to develop Uganda as a unitary state, yet confronted the fact that politization was mainly confined to Buganda, and was largely concerned with the relationship of the Kingdom to the Protectorate. To provide popular participation, it was proposed to move to a firm elected majority in the Lukiko, with Ministers responsible to it. At the same time, the Governor would need to have a mechanism through which to assure ultimate control, and enforce Buganda participation in the central institutions which were to take shape, departing from the Legislative Council. The Kabaka was to be the ultimate weapon of the Protectorate, yet his own position in the unitary state was far from clear, and his continued close association with the Protectorate as its instrument was a heavy liability to him. Pratt gives astute summation to the Kabaka's position:

> The Kabaka, in other words, was being pressed to support policies whose unpopularity might increasingly isolate him from his people and which, if successful, would seriously undermine his position.[54]

The advent of Sir Andrew as Governor roughly coincided with a metamorphosis of the Kabaka himself. He had reached full maturity and began to appreciate the difficulty of his position, and the need to take his distance from both Protectorate and the still missionary-dominated Church of Uganda. The separation was made easier by the departure of Sir John Hall as Governor; Mutesa's autobiography makes clear the paternal nature of this relationship. Also his closest religious mentor, Bishop Stuart, left Uganda at the end of 1952, and his successor, Bishop Brown, never established as close a relationship. Simultaneous with his conflict with Sir Andrew, the Kabaka reached the point of near rupture with the Church of Uganda over his desire to divorce his wife Damali, in order to regularize his relationship with her sister, Sarah Kisosonkole.

The crisis was triggered by a speech by Colonial Secretary Oliver Lyttleton on 30 June, 1953, mentioning the possibility of East African federation. This statement on the heels of the formation of the abortive Central African Federation, had an explosive impact on Buganda. Sir Andrew had in fact been closely associated with the moves toward amalgamation in the Rhodesias and Nyasaland, and made no secret of his conviction that what he believed to be the economic benefits of the scheme would have ultimately silenced the African objections, especially in what is now Malawi. Thus, the fear that the British might try to exert all their influence in favour of such an undertaking was by no means empty, even if exaggerated.

The Kabaka at this juncture for the first time exerted active leadership and independence for the throne. He rejected as inadequate the reassurances proffered by Entebbe and London that no alterations would be made without taking local public opinion fully into account. In addition, he entered new demands that the affairs of Buganda be transferred from the Colonial to the Foreign Office, and that a timetable be set for the independence of Buganda.[55] Total impasse was reached on whether the Kabaka would nominate three Buganda members for the Legislative Council (Legco). As part of his program of political development, Sir Andrew wished to enlarge the African representation on Legco. Buganda remained suspicious of the body, as it had been since the establishment of Legco in 1920. Accepting participation in the Legislative Council, it was argued, implied acceptance of its legitimacy, whereas the degree of representation allowed would inevitably make Buganda influence marginal. Membership might imply a commitment to accept decisions without a real possibility of influencing them. Further, the multi-racial complexion of the Legislative Council implied evolution toward a multi-racial state, which Buganda emphatically rejected. Although in March 1953 the Kabaka had agreed to name the three members, with the toleration but not the consent of the Lukiko, in October, at the request of the Lukiko, he retracted his offer. The Kabaka further complicated the Governor's dilemma by enlisting the support of the monarchs of the three other kingdoms of Bunyoro, Toro, and Ankole in demanding a revision of their status with the British government. The Kabaka had by now succeeded in unifying his kingdom behind him, and casting himself as militant spokesman for their own aspirations; symptomatic of this development was the gesture of the previously anti-Kabaka party, UNC, in advancing as its own the Kabaka's program for a timetable for Buganda independence, and shift of responsibility to the Foreign Office. Sir Andrew found himself with few remaining options; the only African opinion then being articulated was solidly behind the Kabaka. Yet accepting the Kabaka's terms would have meant the end of his program of political development for Uganda as a unitary state.

Sir Andrew, however, did not improve his position by his next move. He appears to have miscalculated the possibility of undermining Sir Edward's position by the expedient of exile—as indeed had the French in their almost simultaneous move to remove the troublesome Sultan Mohammed V—who, like Mutesa, was rescued by martyrdom from the stigmas of excessive pliability to colonial wishes in the early years of his reign. The Governor, before acting, took counsel with academic experts and others as to the Kabaka's popularity, and received testimony that the prestige of King and Kingship was in decline. On 27 November, Sir Edward Mutesa was suddenly arrested, and placed on an R.A.F. plane for Britain. Efforts were made to persuade his older half-brother, George Mawanda (who had been passed over in 1939, although he had been educated in England and was considered by some more promising at the time) to accepting the throne. Mutesa affirms that he was offered the guarantee of a substantial private income if he would agree to abdicate.[56] But these initiatives stood no chance of success.

The reaction was instantaneous and overwhelming. Buganda was entirely solidified behind the throne. The many currents of post-war politics flowed together. Bataka, Bakopi, nationalist politician, and Mengo functionary formed a solid phalanx. Many had grave reservations about Mutesa—but monarchy as an institution, and above all as a symbol of Kiganda identity, was now under attack. Political awareness in the Buganda countryside had been steadily increasing; it now found its moment of total participation, but around the central core of identity. Those who might have been disposed to sympathize with the deportation, or share Sir Andrew's views on a unified, democratic Uganda as the appropriate political goal could not possibly raise their voice against the flood of resentment. The UNC itself had dispatched a delegation of protest to London within a month of the deportation. Politics was, at this crucial juncture, still essentially a Buganda phenomenon; it was not yet possible to view African political response to colonial rule in a larger frame. Political activity was beginning in other areas, but was not yet oriented to Kampala or the national scene.

The results of the crisis were a rearrangement of social forces in Buganda of critical importance in the years immediately ahead, when the final shape of the independent state was to be hammered out. It soon became clear that the British confronted a total impasse. The rest of Uganda was insufficiently politicized to serve as a counterweight to Buganda. The position of the loyalist faction of chiefs who still manned many of the countries and gombololas was completely undermined. The very process of democratization to which the government was now committed implied enfranchisement of the most vociferously pro-Kabaka sentiments. The hopelessness of Sir Andrew's position was epitomized in the paradoxical fact that the Buganda countryside was most actively angry at the very moment when as a result of sharp policy shifts by the Governor, prosperity had never been so high (nor has it been since). A rapid expansion of schools and welfare facilities had been undertaken. The first steps had been initiated in permitting African participation in buying and processing the crops. Most important, the price stabilization policy was abandoned, and cotton and coffee prices both surged to levels never before—or since—attained. Within little more than half a decade, cotton prices tripled, and coffee prices (increasingly the major Buganda crop) went up six-fold.[57] Rusting automobile hulks in rural Buganda today are a monument to the material prosperity of this period—while its political legacy was a resurrection of the monarchy to a level of power which it had not held since the death of Mutesa I in 1884.

The Protectorate government at this stage lacked the authority and prestige to impose a decision on its own, without allies. Its case was weakened by a shrewdly hatched legal challenge to the decision, pleaded by two brilliant imported Queen's Councel, Kenneth Diplock and Dingle Foot. Although the deportation was sustained, it was held by the Court to have been improperly justified. This was celebrated as a major triumph by all

Buganda. A veritable cult of Mutesa developed, exemplified by the following "Mutesa Psalm" published in a vernacular newspaper:

We thank you, oh Mutesa, everyone utters your name for your wonderful acts. The Country praises the honour of Mutesa. Uganda will follow his example. Mutesa is our shepherd. He has reared us in the pastures of new Uganda and filled our minds with encouragement.
He has guided us on the right path for the virtue of his name.
When we pass through the valley and the shadow of death we will not fear for he is with us.
His words and his education please us.
He has prepared for us a new Uganda before the face of our enemies.
Our self rule is near at hand.
His example will always be followed.
We shall dwell in Mutesa's new Uganda for all our lives.
May glory everlasting be to Mutesa II and his subjects.[58]

What is unusual about this catechism is not the style or content, but the object of the message; many such poems are found in the ephemera of African politics in the 1950s, but their adoration has been lavished upon charismatic nationalist heroes, not monarchs.

There was no recourse but acceptance of negotiation for the return of Mutesa. A commission under Sir Keith Hancock, with four Lukiko nominees, was established to negotiate with the Governor the terms of a constitutional settlement in Buganda (and a possible return of Mutesa). After long and careful discussions, the Governor announced the results to the Lukiko but the disorder was so great that he was unable to complete his speech. The Lukiko then rejected the Hancock proposals almost unanimously, and appointed a new commission to propose alternatives; the balance on this second group lay with more traditional and royalist elements. The British succeeded in coming to terms with the second commission, although at the cost of some additional concessions. In sum, Buganda agreed to cease impeding the institutional development at the centre; the British in turn conceded virtual internal autonomy to Buganda. The Protectorate abandoned its powers to influence appointments of chiefs to an all-Baganda Appointments Board; such supervision as was to continue would take place entirely through the Kabaka's Government at the top. An extremely important concession made to the second commission was that the Kabaka himself would name the Chairman of the Appointments Board.

The high water mark of the monarchy in modern politics was the triumphant return of the Kabaka on 17 October 1955. Amid scenes of indescribable enthusiasm, all Buganda turned out to receive its king, descending, like Kintu, from the skies to resume possession of the Kingdom. We may defer to Mutesa for a description of his shining hour, the twenty-mile journey from the airport at Entebbe to Kampala with crowds estimated as high as 1,000,000 thronging the arrival route:

We set off on the most remarkable journey of my life. The twenty-two miles to Kampala took over two hours. The whole of the route was lined with banana trees about five feet high and covered with decorative arches. People on both sides reached a point of hysteria as we arrived, throwing themselves about, lying on the ground, screaming, waving their arms, while the car inched its way forward, followed by a lengthy cavalcade. My Rolls Royce held up to the strain, but many did not: one began to smoke and had to pull off the road, while the clutches of many lesser makes collapsed. Finally the crowd grew so thick I had to get out and walk the last thirty yards.[59]

The alliance between Kabaka and Bakopi now operated to conduct a relentless purge of the county and sub-county chiefs. From the rural folk came a wave of populist retribution directed at "collaborator" chiefs, felt to have been lukewarm toward the Kabaka in his absence. Characteristic of the mood of the times was a possibly apocryphal story making the rounds that a chief who has sworn to cut off a leg if the Kabaka ever returned was confronted with a deputation of peasants who proposed to enforce the conditions of the wager with fate.[60] Mobs attacked houses and fields of those accused of disloyalty. The Kabaka, now the unchallenged spear of the nation, quickly moved to exploit the end of British supervisory power over rural administration. Seven of the twenty county chiefs were sacked by the new Buganda Appointments Board, on which the Kabaka placed as chairman his royal uncle, Prince Badru Kakunguru.[61] The mere number understates the magnitude of the purge; these counties contained well over two thirds of the population, and included the crucial areas of Kyagwe, Buddu, and Kyadondo. The chiefs, the cornerstone of the Protectorate system, were now effectively boxed between the Kabaka and the people.

This link between populism and monarchy is central to an appreciation of terminal colonial and post-independence politics. Sir Andrew was not alone in entirely failing to forsee this eventuality. Audrey I. Richards, former Director of the East African Institute of Social Research, and a leader of the team of out-standing historians and social scientists who made as painstaking a survey of Buganda as any traditional African Kingdom has received, admitted in 1964:

> We confess that even after making this intensive study of the kingship in Buganda we did not anticipate the immediate and dramatic success of the traditional royalist Kabaka Yekka or "Kabaka only" party which became dominant in 1961.[62]

KINGSHIP AT FLOOD TIDE

The vagaries of historical sequence conspired to produce an environment peculiarly favourable to the resurrection of monarchy. The Kabaka was now clearly in the ascendant phase of his career. The years of minority, education overseas, and frivolous early adulthood were behind; the King was now a shrewd, subtle politician well equipped to exploit the potential of Kingship. Political mobilization occurred several strategic years earlier in Buganda than in the rest of the country: in response to it the colonial power conceded virtual autonomy to the monarchy, and surrendered its capacity to exert real influence on domestic affairs in Buganda. In these circumstances, even more than in the era of indirect rule, the very

ideology of terminal colonialism provided a framework for the consolidation of royal power, and its legitimation in the most impeccably modern
terms. Democracy and representative government in the Buganda of the
dying days of the Protectorate, simply operated to provide the Kabaka a
parliament of King's men duly anointed by the electoral process.

Buganda enjoyed an interlude permitting the consolidation of the
rejuvenated monarchy before the rest of the country effectively entered the
arena. Until this time, the political process in other areas had been almost
exclusively district focussed; although political notables had emerged,
many of whom later earned top positions in the national arena, it was not
until the late 1950s that the remainder of the country began to make its
numbers felt. Buganda, despite its economic and social hegemony and
historic prominence, contained only 25 per cent of the population of
Uganda, of whom 40 per cent were immigrant farm labourers and tenants
from western and northern Uganda, Rwanda and Burundi. Thus the final
phase of the transition to independence necessarily produced a radical
alteration in the political balance, as the representative national system
based upon universal suffrage was established.

In 1958, the greater part of the Legislative Council (although Buganda
did not participate) was directly elected. Two national political movements,
outside the framework of royalist politics in Buganda, took form. The
Democratic Party, organized at the stimulus of and utilizing the
communication channels of the Catholic Church was created in 1956.
The Catholics organized politically as a group which regarded itself as
systematically disfavoured by a Protestant Establishment, both British and
African. In 1960 a kaleidoscope of ephemeral factions coalesced into the
Uganda People's Congress (UPC), which was at bottom an alliance of
non-Ganda political notables determined to terminate Buganda domination of modern politics.[63] In 1955, Buganda stood alone, and in the shadow
of its pre-eminence in Protectorate life was cast to the farthest corners of
the territory. By 1960, Buganda again stood alone—but now in total
isolation, its demands for federal protection for its autonomy spurned by
the rest. Buganda, bitter in her hour of loneliness, refused to cooperate in
the creation of national institutions. The Lukiko expressed the bitterness
of the kingdom in an overwhelming vote for a vociferously-worded resolution at the end of 1960, declaring Buganda independence as of 1 January,
1961. No steps were taken to give effect to this momentous resolve, and
both the Kabaka and the Governor departed for overseas destinations
at the moment it was to occur.

Terminal colonial negotiations were founded on the work of two
commissions, The Wild Commission in 1959, and the Munster Relationships Commission in 1961,[64] completed by episodic negotiations. The Wild
Commission took a predominantly unitary line, while the Munster Report
shifted in the direction of the conceding of a federal structure. Despite the
strong protests of Buganda, the first full national elections based on
universal suffrage took place in 1961. The Kabaka opted for an electoral
boycott in 1961; this tactic had the paradoxical effect of both demon-
strating the overwhelming capacity of the monarchy and the King's men

to enforce its directives, and yet placing adversaries in power. The boycott was followed by 97 per cent in Buganda; however the remaining 3 per cent went to the DP, which on the basis of this infinitesimal poll swept the 19 Buganda seats, which added to 23 won elsewhere, gave the DP a 43–35 majority over the UPC.

The DP was led by a Muganda, Benedicto Kiwanuka, who took over as first Prime Minister in 1961–1962. The dominant Buganda reaction was well expressed by the Kabaka:

> After the election Kiwanuka was puffed up with pride and success. He must have understood as clearly as everyone else that almost half his support was fictitious, the result of the boycott, and that his position was therefore insecure to say the least . . . Now he became intolerable. He made personal attacks on me, and said that I had arranged the boycott. This was not in fact true as the people had understood without instructions from me, but I would not have been ashamed had I done so. Feeling against the DP in Buganda remained intense, and it was our vision of life under such a government as the worst of all possible futures that led us astray.[65]

Perhaps the greatest apostasy of Kiwanuka was the acceptance of a position which gave him precedence over the Kabaka.

Kiwanuka's back provided the bridge between the UPC and the Buganda monarchy. Buganda, as the preceding statement by Mutesa suggests, now realized that the options were few. Independence was bound to come, and there was simply no way to effect withdrawal, against the combined opposition of the British and the rest of the country. The arithmetic of the religious cleavages which governed voting elsewhere in Uganda was such that the UPC could not gain a majority without support in Buganda, and the latter simply could not be obtained except through an alliance with the throne; populism was pre-empted by the Kabaka. The UPC and Buganda found common cause in their animosity toward the DP. The British, preoccupied at this juncture with securing a power transfer formula promising some prospect for post-independence stability, insisted on arrangements which both guaranteed a united, if not unitary Uganda, and the willing participation of Buganda. Only one possible outcome maximized the rewards for the main actors: a UPC-Kabaka alliance. The UPC made important concessions to achieve this. It was agreed that Buganda would retain the prerogative of opting for designation of its parliamentary delegation by the Lukiko, and substantial autonomy in a semi-federal Uganda. The UPC agreed to desist from campaigning in Buganda. In return the UPC would be senior partner in the national government, and the Lukiko was to be directly elected for the first time. In the face of a firm alliance between populism and monarchy, this concession strengthened rather than weakened the Kabaka.

KINGSHIP IN INDEPENDENT UGANDA

This, then, provided the basis for Uganda independence on 9 October 1962. The independence elections produced a firm majority for the UPC-Buganda coalition. The UPC won 37 seats elsewhere in Uganda, to 24 for the DP. In Buganda a new movement arose to give modern political form to the royalist populism which swept the kingdom; its essence was well epitomized in its name, Kabaka Yekka (Kabaka alone). Welbourn records that men presenting themselves to the chiefs to register as voters were asked "oyagala Kabaka?" (do you love the Kabaka?).[66] Yes, came the overwhelming response at the ballot box. KY presented itself to the Buganda voters with a chair as symbol, which Mutesa coyly suggests that "people chose to connect with the throne".[67] Protestants, Muslims and Catholics, Bataka and Bakungu, Bakopi and elite, Baganda and immigrant tenants, all registered their fealty through election 69 of 72 Lukiko members from the KY slate. This in turn ensured that the parliamentary elected by the Lukiko were a solid KY brigade of twenty-one.

The independent state of Uganda thus reposed upon an extraordinary political formula, in which Kiganda Kingship was a key element. The sheer force of numbers, in a parliamentary system, placed the centre of gravity outside Buganda for the first time. However, the numerical weight of the north, east and west was diluted by the tremendous role played by religious cleavage in determining voting alignment elsewhere. The Catholic base of the DP won for its 24 seats, while the UPC garnered 37. In Buganda nationalism, linked to the Kabakaship, transcended the religious divisions, and thus compelled the political leaders from other regions to deal with Buganda as a bloc. The weight of Buganda in national politics was enhanced by its strategic location at the centre of the country, enveloping the capital of Kampala. The early entry of Baganda into modern roles meant that their representation was strong in the upper ranks of the central bureaucracy, the educational establishment, and the professions.[68] Illustrative of the social pre-eminence of Baganda is the fact that 160 of 212 superscale positions in the Uganda public service in 1965 were held by Baganda. Finally, the semi-federal constitution negotiated in 1962 gave the central government very little effective control over Buganda.

The crux of the capabilities displayed by the Kabakaship in the initial post-independence phase of politics lay in its ability to mobilize the twin resources of populism and Buganda nationalism. These two themes deserve exploration, as their confluence lies at the heart of the apparent paradox of reinforcement of kingship by modern politics, and also of the dilemmas faced by the post-1966 Obote government in ruling Uganda as a unitary state.

POPULISM

Populism is an essentially modern phenomenon in Buganda politics.[69] The very nature of the pre-colonial politics offered neither structural opportunity nor a supporting *weltanschaung* for peasant participation. Low argues that, especially in the nineteenth century, the steady expansion of the Kingdom, and success of plundering expeditions generated sufficient resources to keep the Bakopi largely satisfied. Bakopi had some social options, in particular migration. For chiefs of all hierarchies, people were more important than territory, and a sustained loss of clients diminished their social resources; this fact was a constraint upon their behaviour, but did not make the Bakopi as a group an operative factor on politics at the kingdom level. When Mwanga tried to raise a people's rebellion against the Bakungu-led religious factions in 1897, he failed utterly.

By the 1920s, however, rural unrest came to be a feature of the social landscape. The authority of the Protestant Bakungu oligarchy which triumphed in the Christian revolution and the establishment of the Protectorate was eroding, and the diffusion of a cash economy, linked to the radical alteration in land tenure patterns ratified by the 1900 agreement, created a new sense of economic exaction. Populist ferment grew during the 1940s, with serious disorders in 1945 and 1949.

The Bataka movement was resurgent. Populist syncretic religious movements, such as the Balokole ("the saved ones") gained a large following.[70] Ignatius Musazi stimulated an enormous outburst of enthusiasm for his Uganda Federation of African Farmers, even though it lacked the organizational capabilities to carry out the ambitious tasks of buying and processing cotton and coffee which it set for itself.

The 1953 deportation of the Kabaka provided the catalytic, extra-ordinary, realigning event which redirected populist energies into royalist channels. Kingship entered a new phase; its role of supreme spokesman for Buganda discontent enabled it to become the rallying symbol. It would be entirely wrong to see this new link between King and people as being a simple manipulative relationship directed from the top; it was a two-way channel, with the Kabaka compelled to lead by following populist pressures. Symptomatic of the new relationship was the purge of chiefs which followed the Kabaka's return in 1955. The wave of attacks upon both the persons and property of chiefs accused of disloyalty was not ordered by the Palace; it is most unlikely that the Kabaka could have stopped them, even had he engaged the full prestige of the throne behind an appeal for calm. It is equally true that the weight of populist pressure was instrumental to the Kabaka in implementing the 1955 purge, and the acute sense that chiefs thereafter felt of potential populist pressure was a constraint inducing full loyalty to the throne.

Another highly revealing episode illustrating the relationship of the Kabaka and the populists was a trade boycott organized in Buganda in 1959. The organizational framework for the boycott was supplied by a suddenly formed party, the Uganda National Movement (UNM), organized by a broad front of Baganda politicians as a riposte to the formation of an anti-Ganda coalition among non-Baganda members of the Legislative Council, the Uganda People's Union (UPU). The UNM swiftly became, in Low's words, "the most powerful political party which either Buganda or Uganda had ever seen".[71] The UNM seized upon the issue of British support for special representation in the Legislative Council for non-Africans. In protest, a boycott of non-African trade, which quickly escalated into widespread assaults upon people and property, as populist enforcement measures were taken against backsliders. The boycott was disavowed by non-Baganda, and disliked by many Baganda elite; yet it commanded overwhelming popular support, both from farmers, and from the web of small traders, taxi drivers and others who emerged to provide much of the *de facto* leadership of the movement. Mutesa's description of this movement is interesting and revealing:

> This enlisted strong emotional support as the Indians had a powerful stranglehold on trade, and long after the leaders had been transported to the wilds of the north and the movement itself forbidden, the boycott flourished . . . The boycott, ably led by a demagogue, Augustin Kamya, lasted many months, and though it affected politics, its vitality was not political. Europeans were left alone and it did not affect my own buying, but Indian shops and foreign goods could not be patronized by the most distinguished and loyal Africans with impunity. Beer was the most noticeably banned commodity. A man was shot in a bar for no other reason than that he was holding a pint . . . Empty beer cans outside the house betrayed many . . . If a man bought some foreign product in one part of Kampala and then went on his way to buy the bananas on which we live at an African market, he would find himself preceeded by a stranger walking with a slightly peculiar gait, with the toes turned out, and goods would become unobtainable or prices soar as he arrived. The Lukiko and I were in a difficult position, not wishing to attack the boycott publicly . . . Under some pressure, I made a speech with a discouraging reference, but it was not thought strong enough by the Governor . . . Fines and threats were used, which placed the organization on the wrong side of the law, and so beyond my official approval. Also it made an unfortunately easy cover for those who had old scores to settle. On the other hand, it was an impressive display of our strength.[72]

Kabaka Yekka itself, when it took form as a royalist movement in 1961, was another reflection of the strongly populist flavour of Buganda politics. Over half the KY candidates in 1962 were farmers or traders; it was in no sense an oligarchical movement.[73] In the post-independence period, the monarchist KY paradoxically was Uganda's closest analogue to the mass single party model which appeared to be the dominant political force in Africa at the moment of African independence.[74] Symbolic of the fusion of populism and monarchism was the key role of boycott organizer Kamya as a principle founder of KY, and Eric Swebug, organizer of the short-lived militant populist movement Bawajjere (Common Man), who became Organizing Secretary of KY in 1963.[75]

The resurgence of traditional religion, *lubaale*, was another manisfestation of populism. The Christian revolutionary generation believed they had suppressed the old gods, and indeed there was relatively little evidence of traditional religion during much of the colonial period. However, with the deportation of the Kabaka, there was a sudden resurrection of *lubaale* worship. Shrines reappeared in many banana gardens and the argument was heard that only the old gods could restore the Kabaka to his throne. During the 1962 Lukiko electoral campaign, the following prayer was widely offered:

> O Muwanga, who ordered this land, we kneel and pray Thee so to order it again as Thou didst order it in ages past. Guard our Kabaka and the Throne, together with the ancient traditions of our tribe, that they may again become as they were in the beginning. For ever and ever. Amen.

O blessed Muwanga, have mercy upon us.
O blessed Mukasa of the lake, have mercy upon us.
O all ye blessed ones of old, who disappeared, have mercy upon us, We
    beseech you.
O all ye blessed ones of old, who fled because you feared the atrocities of the
    European, Arise and join with us that we may restore our land and establish
    it as it was of old.
For ever and ever. Amen.[76]

The Kabaka, the Lukiko, and Baganda became a traditional trinity.
Mutesa after his return gradually came to terms with *lubaale* cult leaders,
and by the time of independence traditional prayers were again being
heard within the royal enclosure. Welbourn argues persuasively that the
Kabaka wound up achieving what had eluded his pre-colonial
predecessors: the full absorption of *lubaale* into the matrix of supports
for the monarchy.[77] The Kabaka was now head of not only the clans and
the Bakungu hierarchy, but also of the *lubaale* pantheon.

NATIONALISM AND KINGSHIP

Buganda nationalism was the other pillar of neo-monarchism. The
nature of identity in the pre-colonial past can only be a matter of
speculation. The evidence available from the scrutiny of accounts by early
travellers to the Kingdom suggests that Ganda identity was already well
established. One may speculate that a number of aspects of the Kingdom's
social structure may have generated a fairly pronounced sense of Ganda-
hood. The clans, although they were probably the most important foci of
identity, were well dispersed territorially throughout the Kingdom. The
nature of Kingship and the structure of the court rendered the monarchy
itself the vortex of Ganda identity. All roads led to the royal court; social
mobility for young men passed through the palace page corps. A sense of
national enmity toward Bunyoro-Kitara permeates the historical
chronicles of Buganda. Frequent mobilization of armies to march for the
Kabaka against neighbouring groups also no doubt contributed to a sense
of membership in a community.

Incipient Buganda nationalism received major support from the
reactions of the first generation of explorers and adventurers who reached
Lake Victoria. Most early visitors came away with (and published in
Europe) highly favourable impressions of the Baganda. Henry Stanley,
whose voluminous chronicles wove a rich embroidery of ethnic stereotypes
for central Africa, gave a verdict characteristic for its time:

(The Baganda were) . . . an extraordinary people, as different from the bar-
barous pirates of Uvuma, and the wild, mop-headed men of Eastern Usukuma,
as the British in India are from their Afridi fellow-subjects, or the white
Americans of Arkansas from the semi-civilized Choctaws . . . Mutesa impressed
me as being an intelligent and distinguished prince, who, if aided in time by
virtuous philanthropists, will do more for Central Africa than fifty years of
Gospel teaching unaided by such authority, can do.[78]

The fundamentally favourable stereotype which Buganda enjoyed, at least compared with its neighbours, was of considerable import in the development of Buganda nationalism. Mutesa himself expresses a view which may be accepted as general:

> Perhaps another reason for the calm of the Baganda is that, unlike many Africans, they have not lost their identity. The changes in the country have not been so fundamental as elsewhere in Africa.
> Our way of life has been altered—improved—in external things by the advent of the British, while the basic beliefs and ways of life have remained. ... Of course, other changes in over seventy years have been enormous. But the sense of identity is precisely what has remained. We are invariably accused by our detractors of being tribalists in a sense of the word that it is a wicked, retrogressive thing to be. I have never been able to pin down precisely the difference between a tribe and a nation and see why one is thought so despicable and the other is so admired. Which ever we are, the Baganda have a common language, tradition, history and cast of mind. While we stood alone, we were accepted as the most civilized and powerful of the kingdoms. Does this justify our being totally dominated by our neighbours, unnaturally yoked to us as they were by Britain? It was through the qualities of Baganda that Europeans were attracted to the country, hurrying through Kenya and Tanzania to reach the "pearl of Africa", as Stanley called Buganda.[79]

The Baganda did not undergo the experience of realizing that they were despised as a group by Europeans. From the outset, the natural inclination to assume one's superiority to neighbouring groups received consistent support from European observers, from whose verdict, in early colonial days, there was no appeal.

Baganda self-confidence was sanctified by the 1900 agreement, viewed by Baganda of recognizing that special, distinctive status was appropriate for a more advanced people. Equally natural was the special role made available to Baganda as chiefs and administrative cadres in other parts of the Protectorate, to establish a framework of "native administration" based upon the Kiganda model. Nothing could be more natural than the Katikiro's attendance at the coronation of King Edward VII, and the deference he and Ham Mukasa were accorded in London in 1902.[80]

From the 1920s on, Buganda nationalism began to take on new flavour, as populism extended the bounds of the conscious political community, and as the question of Buganda's relationships with the rest of Uganda and East Africa began to be perceived as a potential threat. Fears came more sharply into focus beginning with the tenure of Sir Andrew Cohen as Governor, with the beginning of vigorous moves toward self-government. The threat was two fold: the looming menace of a settler dominated East African Federation on the one hand, and a unitary Uganda state in which Buganda would be relegated to secondary status on the other.

Until 1958, the congeries of political movements arising in Uganda were all dominated by Buganda. The crystallization of what appeared to be an anti-Buganda parliamentary group in the Legislative Council by 1959 dramatized the new dangers to Buganda. The new Baganda political elite as well as those around the throne began to realize the strength of anti-Baganda sentiments in other parts of the Protectorate. This strengthened the potent link between populism and royalism; the reaction to this threat was to face the nation as a unified entity. Buganda could only protect its interests by remaining as one; an atmosphere emerged when the popular pressures on all Baganda to rally round their identity were overwhelming. As with the populist impulses, ethnic identity found as its focus and symbol the monarchy itself. Young intellectuals such as Abu Mayanja, not a scion of the Mengo establishment, rallied to the Kabaka's government, and became the first Muslim Minister. Buganda was by no means united or homogeneous in political outlook; amongst the Baganda intellectuals and prominent central civil servants and professionals were many strongly committed to a united Uganda. But the linkage of the throne to the dynamic new forces of populism and Buganda nationalism made the appeal of KY irresistible to all.[81]

TOWARD CONFRONTATION

The UPC-KY alliance seemed initially to offer reasonable satisfaction to both members. The short-lived era of good feeling was capped by the UPC's cooperation (after a bitter internal struggle) in electing the Kabaka as Chief of State for Uganda in 1963. Serious consideration was given by Buganda leaders to joining the UPC en masse. A facinating document in 1963, signed by KY members of parliament, meeting under the Chairmanship of Amos Sempa, one of the most belligerent of Buganda nationalists, urged that Buganda could best promote its own interests, and preserve the throne, by more wholeheartedly integrating itself into Uganda as a whole. The option of secession so seriously urged in 1960, was now utterly unrealistic; the central government had the power and will to keep Buganda in by force, if necessary.[82]

However an important reservoir of mistrust remained. The merger proposal of 1963 was never implemented. The nature of the political balance was silently altered by a growing pattern of carpet-crossing; by August 1964, the UPC had an absolute majority, and was able to govern alone without KY. At that time, ten of the twenty-four KY members, led by the Baganda portfolio holders in the Obote government, joined the UPC benches. In January 1964, the short-lived mutiny of the Uganda Army was first met by British troops, then by swift Africanization which tended to enhance Obote's control over the security forces. Obote moved swiftly in September 1964 to eliminate a chronic dispute between Bunyoro and Buganda over territories awarded by Britain to Buganda by the 1900 agreement. Two counties had substantial Banyoro majorities, and the mere organization of a referendum could produce no other outcome than a Bunyoro victory—and parenthetically warm gratitude from a strategic district.[83] A wave of popular indignation swept Buganda; Michael Kintu, Katikiro since 1955, was thrown out of office for his failure to adequately secure the interests of the Kingdom.

There ensued a year of growing tension, with the Palace apparently torn between several alternative courses of action. It was whispered that the Kabaka himself was considering joining the UPC, although there is no hint of this in his autobiography. Indeed, Mutesa expresses some resentment at the KY carpet-crossers, although there were many rumours at the time that the Baganda ministers had retained their portfolios with the Kabaka's blessing.[84] An atmosphere of conspiracy began to saturate the country. Mistrust toward the central government in Buganda, kindled by the lost counties issue, was also intensified by a fall in coffee prices, and a widespread conviction that somehow the Obote government was responsible. Whatever the divisions among Baganda intellectuals, there could be little doubt at this juncture that the countryside looked upon their government as the Kabaka's government, and the Obote regime as an alien entity. Obote, who travelled frequently to the countryside, never felt able to make an official tour through Buganda, although he had married a distinguished Ganda lady after independence; the wedding which might have been interpreted, in part, as a gesture of unity, gave rise to considerable grumbling in Buganda.

The possibility of an alliance with the DP was also entertained in Mengo, but by 1964 the DP had been badly eroded at the top by parliamentary defections. In 1965, there began to take shape a loose "Bantu" front, which by joining to the Buganda bloc much of the rest of southern Uganda, plus the remaining DP delegates, might have been able to bring about the downfall of the Obote government by parliamentary means. This network began to coalesce around the Secretary-General of the UPC, Grace Ibingira, in the latter part of 1965. There can be little doubt that this move enjoyed the patronage of the Kabaka, although he vigorously denies paternity in his autobiography. Contacts were also discreetly made with other highly placed individuals, including the security forces. Brigadier General Sabama O. Opoloto, who had close family ties in Buganda through marriage to a daughter of former Katikiro Paulo Kavumu was a regular visitor at the Palace.

The issue was decisively joined on 4 February, when a motion was passed calling for a commission of inquiry into allegations that Obote and two of his closest associates had personally benefited from $350,000 worth of gold and ivory placed in the hands of Uganda authorities by Zairian rebels, presumably for the purchase of military supplies. To general astonishment, with Obote absent touring the north, one UPC member after another rose to support the call for an inquiry, including six ministers. For a brief moment, the Obote government seemed on the verge of disaster; however, after methodically completing his tour through the north, Obote returned to establish the Commission of Inquiry. Then at a cabinet meeting on 22 February, 1966, police suddenly appeared to size five ministers of the Ibingira "Bantu" group, including one Muganda, Dr. E. B. S. Lumu. Two days later, he suspended the constitution, assumed all powers and abolished the Kabaka's office of President. By 3 March, Obote felt sufficiently secure to make his first public charges against the Kabaka, accused of soliciting foreign (British) intervention. On 15 April, Obote suddenly convened Parliament to announce a new constitution, which was then endorsed by members before they had read it, creating a presidential system with himself as chief executive.

Q

The final phase of the confrontation between Uganda and Buganda came five weeks later. The Kabaka and Lukiko had made clear their rejection of the suspension of the constitution, and the new one proclaimed in its place. The Lukiko slowly escalated its rhetoric, and finally on 20 May, with the clear support of the Kabaka, passed a belligerent motion calling for the Obote government to remove offices from Buganda soil by 30 May on the grounds that it was illegal and unconstitutional. The Obote government seized the opportunity to label this resolution as an act of rebellion, and to move decisively against Buganda itself. Thus occurred the battle of Mengo Hill on 23 May, which saw the flight of the Kabaka, the apparent destruction of the royal drums, and subsequently the obliteration of both the Kabakaship and Buganda as an entity.[85]

CONCLUSIONS: KINGSHIP AND POST-INDEPENDENCE POLITICS IN UGANDA

We may now return to the questions which opened our discussion, and raise some more general issues of the role of monarchy in contemporary African politics. In the specifically Ugandan context, can the Kingdom of Buganda be abolished? What are the consequences for Baganda, Buganda, and Uganda of the exile and subsequent death of the Kabaka in November 1969? Have we arrived at the moment of empirical validation of Apter's well-known hypothesis that "modernizing autocracy (the Kiganda system) can adapt and adjust institutions without great difficulty until the point is reached where the principle of the kingship itself is challenged. At that point either modernization and change are halted, or the entire system shifts to a different principle of authority, conforming to either a consociational or mobilizational type?"[86] More broadly, does the apparent outcome of the confrontation between monarchy and the state confirm a trend toward disappearance of the venerable institution of kingship in modern Africa? Are kings relics of a pre-colonial past, artificially preserved during the imperial age, whose paraphernalia will be consigned to the exhibition halls of national museums?

In Africa, as elsewhere, the institution of monarchy was critical to the historical process of state formation. Centralization, and the establishment of a territorial basis for the state, were associated with the extension of royal power. Superimposed upon this nascent state system was the territorial grid of the colonial partition. We would suggest that the most important single factor affecting the post-independence prospects of monarchy is the relationship between it and the contemporary independent state, heir to the colonial unit. Enclosed within the confines of a state whose central institutions it could not control, the monarchy is clearly imperilled. Kingship in Morocco, Ethiopia, and Swaziland may well survive for a considerable period; the norms of interstate relations prevail in governing interaction with neighbours. But locked within a larger state, the monarchy finds itself arrayed against a central government which the mores of the world state system provide warrant for unlimited and uninhibited intervention, extending to the liquidation which took place in 1966.

The unusual relationship between the Protectorate and the Kingdom had failed to establish, during the colonial period, the unambiguous primacy of the central institutions. Buganda was able to see itself as enjoying a special treaty relationship with the British crown. It clearly took precedence over what were looked upon as the wild places which lay beyond the borders of the Kingdom. Many historic kingdoms were reduced to the humble status of mere chiefdoms during the colonial era; not so Buganda, whose sense of its monarchical proportions and importance remained more than intact. The self-image of the kingdom, and its achievement of virtually complete internal autonomy well before Ugandan national leaders achieved control at the centre, made an early clash with the central state very likely. We would suggest that monarchy so domesticated as to have wholly adjusted to a status of local government agency may survive after independence. Kingship whose aspirations approach such sovereignty is a threat to the central state.

Although the argument is hypothetical and thus speculative, we would argue that the monarchy in Buganda would not have been internally overthrown. Had its arena been differently defined, it could have survived the transition to political independence. Unitary nationalists from other parts of Uganda, and from within the kingdom, had expected and hoped that the ideology of mass nationalism which the UPC tried to convey to Buganda would unite the common man with the central leadership against the perquisites and privileges of the Kabaka and the "Mengo clique". The early years of independence had brought about the dissolution of these hopes; the Kiganda monarchy was, in their eyes, an irreducible obstacle to the fulfilment of their vision of a united Uganda. Thus, in one important sense the Apter dilemma has not yet been posed in Buganda; the principle of kingship did not come under effective challenge from within the system, but was destroyed from without.

Both Obote and Mutesa appeared to act upon the assumption of incompatibility between Buganda kingship and a central state not under its domination. The fears frequently expressed in Mengo about the nature and consequences of independence were, from the standpoint of the interests of the monarchy, justified. Only separation, as threatened in 1960 and 1966, or domination of Uganda's central institutions could guarantee the survival of kingship. The uneasy federal compromise which provided the formula for independence was never satisfactory to either protagonist. The elevation of the Kabaka to the Chief-of-State position gave the shadow but not the substance of power. The enhanced dignity was insufficient protection to the monarchy when it was unaccompanied by effective control of any of the real levers of central power, the bureaucracy, or the security forces. The gamble of a conspiracy which would have brought to power a coalition friendly to the Kabaka in 1965–1966, had it succeeded, could well have given Kiganda monarchy a sufficiently strong position at the centre to defer the day of reckoning for a prolonged period. But even this would have fallen short of establishing the kind of domination of the monarchy over the central state which would have permanently guaranteed the Kabakaship against intervention from without the historic kingdom.

However, it is well to recall that the outcome in 1966 could have been different; the Ibingira plot came close to succeeding, and history would appear to provide different lessons for the future had this been the case.

As a second hypothesis, we may suggest that post-independence prospects for monarchy depend upon the way in which kingship both as institution and symbol relates itself to dominant social forces during the successive historic stages of colonial encounter, imperial subjugation, and nationalist response. A prime reason for the vitality of kingship in independent Uganda, and the felt necessity to eliminate it, was the linkage of monarchy, as institution and as symbol, to key forces of change in the society. Here we are clearly speaking of the office and not the incumbent; one of the more striking aspects of kingship in Buganda in the last century is the resiliency of the institution in the face of inefficiency of recent incumbents, and even long periods of virtual vacancy. Mwanga's reign was expended in the forlorn pursuit of a viable role; collaboration and resistance were both tried, without success. The pathetic, short-lived reigns of Kiwewa and Kalema led to a swift and tragic end for both. During the long minority of Daudi Chwa, there was, in effect, no reigning Kabaka; again in his final years, in the 1930s, he withdrew into a sullen inactivity. Mutesa II was another boy king, and did not really assert himself until shortly before his deportation in 1953.

But even while Mwanga the king was moving toward the final desparate phase of revolt, the institution of monarchy had been firmly captured by the Christian revolutionary elite, who were the dynamic force within the kingdom during the first three decades of colonial rule. The symbols of monarchy were a vehicle for the forceful leadership of Sir Apolo Kagwa. Beginning in the 1920s, new forces began to make themselves felt; the *bakopi* (commoners) began to weigh in the political scales, and rural populism, expressed through the neo-traditional idiom of the *bataka* claims, became visible. More recently, particularly after World War II, the growing sense of animosity to the colonial power, and the Asian commercial intermediaries of the colonial system, coalesced into an active sense of nationalism. In Buganda, except for a section of the professional, civil servant and intellectual elite, nationalism after 1953 became crystallized around the kingdom, and focused upon the symbols of the monarchy. During the 1945 and 1949 disturbances, the king and kingship appeared under attack. But the deportation crisis realigned the twin forces of populism and nationalism behind the symbols of kingship. And Mutesa II now entered a phase of his career when he was able to use the institution of the Kabakaship to bind himself to these forces. The 1959 Asian boycott, the swift organization of KY and its 1962 electoral sweep in Buganda, the heavy and spontaneous rural participation in the 1966 disorders on behalf of King and Kingdom, all give testimony to the potency of this support.

However, the situation was radically transformed by the Obote revolution of 1966. As an institution, the monarchy has been suppressed. The possibility of a restoration has been made much more remote by the death of the exiled Kabaka. The monarchy has now been placed before its most unstable contingency, succession. Although there is no lack of princes of the drum, who conceivably might succeed, the means to choose and consecrate a new Kabaka are beyond their reach. But the elimination of monarchy as a symbol will be far less simple. A whole new set of legends about the Kabaka has developed since May 1966. The inevitable mystery which surrounds his solitary death in a humble East London flat does nothing to dispel these myths. The idea of the monarchy, a fraternal and reassuring memory, will continue to haunt the four administrative districts into which the former kingdom has been partitioned. The passage of time without restoration will make increasingly likely the permanence of the demise of the institution of monarchy; aligning the symbols of politics to this new reality will be a long process.

The present challenge to the national leadership is, in effect, to invert the Apter hypothesis. Although kingship in Buganda is dead, its principle has not yet been effectively challenged. Until it has been, no alternative basis for legitimation of central power in the Buganda countryside is likely to be effective. Despite some organizational efforts, the ruling UPC appears quite unlikely to provide this alternative at the present time. The bureaucratic apparatus of the state has supplanted the Kabaka's government, but appears able only to generate passive acquiescence, and little support. The opportunity for sharing in a national system offering broader perspectives than Buganda itself has definite attractions for the elite, whose professional and administrative careers have been undisturbed. A significant segment of the elite had come to regard kingship as an anachronism and an obstacle to change. However at the moment this portion of the elite seems unable to carry rural society with it.

The centrality of Buganda makes the challenge all the more severe. The decapitated kingdom is the nexus of social and economic communication. The rapidly growing metropolis of Kampala dominates the urbanization process. The careful efforts of the Uganda government to diffuse development opportunities throughout the country cannot in the immediate future compensate for the commanding lead which Buganda assumed in the colonial period. The cumulative nature of economic transformation, extent of its infrastructure, and unalterable ecological advantages of soil and rainfall conspire to maintain Buganda at the forefront of development. Strategies of encapsulation available to national elites in Zambia in dealing with the Kingdom of Barotseland are simply not feasible. The nation of Uganda cannot be secure as long as its wealthiest region, geographical core, and cradle of its elite, is not bound to its central institutions by meaningful affective ties. The king has perished, but the symbol of monarchy continues to interpose a formidable competing principle of legitimacy.

Where they do not territorially coincide, nation and kingdom appear incompatible in the era of independence. The Buganda case suggests that either nation triumphs through dismantlement of kingdom, or kingdom mates nation through conquest of its central institutions, or through secession to render territory and kingdom congruent.

NOTES

1 Sir Edward Mutesa, Kabaka of Uganda, *The Desecration of My Kingdom* (London: Constable, 1967), p. 9.
2 *Uganda Argus*, 11 June, 1968, 1 July, 1968.
3 A. D. Roberts, "The Sub-Imperialism of the Baganda", *Journal of African History*, III, 3 (1962), 435–450; A. H. Cox, "The Growth and Expansion of Buganda", *Uganda Journal*, XIV, 2 (September, 1950), pp. 153–159.
4 H. B. Thomas, "Cape Imperii—The Story of Semei Kakunguru", *Uganda Journal* VI, 3 (January, 1939), pp. 125–136.
5 To mention only major works produced by this array, we may cite Lucy Mair, *An African People in the Twentieth Century* (London: Routledge, 1934); A. I. Richards (ed.), *Economic Development and Tribal Change* (Cambridge: W. Hefner and Son, 1954), and *East African Chiefs* (London: Faber & Faber, 1959); D. Anthony Low and R. Crawford Pratt, *Buganda and British Overrule* (London: Oxford University Press, 1960); Low, *Religion and Society in Buganda 1875–1900* East African Studies No. 8 (Kampala: East African Institute of Social Research); Lloyd A. Fallers (ed.), *The King's Men* (London: Oxford University Press, 1964); David Apter, *The Political Kingdom in Uganda* (Princeton: Princeton University Press, 1961); Martin Southwold, *Bureaucracy and Chiefship in Buganda*, East African Studies No. 14 (Kampala: East African Institute of Social Research, 1961); F. B. Welbourn, *East African Rebels* (London: S. C. M. Press, 1961); and *Religion and Politics in Uganda* (Nairobi: East African Publishing House, 1966); C. C. Wrigley, *Crops and Wealth in Uganda*, East African Studies No. 12 (Kampala: East African Institute of Social Research, 1959), and "The Christian Revolution in Buganda", *Comparative Studies in Society and History*, II, 1 (1959), 33–48; Peter Gutkind, *The Royal Capital of Kibuga* (The Hague: Mouton & Co., 1963); John A. Rowe, *Revolution in Buganda 1856–1900—Part One* (unpublished dissertation, University of Wisconsin, 1966). For full bibliographies on Buganda, see especially Fallers and Rowe.
6 Mutesa, *op. cit.*, 194.
7 Although there are some traditional accounts which deny the genesis role to Kintu, and claim an older line extends further back; Charles E. S. Kabuga, in "The Genealogy of Kabaka Kintu and the Early Basekabaka of Buganda", *Uganda Journal*, XXVII, 2 (September, 1963), pp. 205–216, claims Kintu was the eighth Kabaka.
8 For the early history of Buganda, John Roscoe remains a standard source, *The Baganda* (London: Macmillan, 1911). Roscoe relied heavily on the great Protestant Katikiro, Sir Apolo Kagwa, as a source; Sir Apolo himself has been a crucial contributor, with *Basekbaka be Buganda* (Kampala: 1901); *Ekitabo kye Mpisa za Buganda* (Kampala: 1905), and *Ekitabo kye Bika bya Buganda* (Kampala: 1908).
9 Roscoe, *op. cit.*, pp. 138–140. There is some ambiguity about the total number of clans. Occasionally both consolidation and scission of clans have occurred. Also, a continuing expansion of Baganda during the two centuries before 1900 meant a constant accommodation of new population.
10 Audrey I. Richards, *The Changing Structure of a Ganda Village* (Nairobi: East African Publishing House, 1966), p. 17.
11 Southwold, *op. cit.* provides an excellent account of the consolidation of the Bakungu hierarchy. Elsewhere, he raises the interesting question whether Kiganda tradition as filtered through students of the Kingdom may not have exaggerated the omnipotence of its despotism; see Southwold, "Kingship in Buganda", *Mawazo*, I. 2 (December, 1967), pp. 17–23.
12 Lloyd A. Fallers, "Despotism, Status Culture and Social Mobility in an African Kingdom", *Comparative Studies in Society and History*, II (1959–1960), p. 18.
13 Fallers, *The King's Men*, p. 83.
14 This is made clear by the fascinating studies by various scholars associated with the former East African Institute of Social Research, which mapped sample parishes in exhaustive fashion to unravel the nature of the overlap. See especially Richards, *Ganda Village*, and Fallers, *The King's Men*, pp. 64–116 and *passim*.

15 M. S. M. Kiwanuka, *Mutesa of Liganda* (Nairobi: East African Literature Bureau, 1967), p. 4.
16 Rowe, *op. cit.*, This analysis of the 19th century Kabakaship is greatly endebted to Rowe's graceful and persuasive portrait of the Kingdom. See also D. A. Low, "The Advent of Populism in Buganda", *Comparative Studies in Society and History*, VI (1963–64), pp. 424–444.
17 Martin Southwold, "Succession to the Throne in Buganda", in Jack Goody (ed.), *Succession to High Office* (Cambridge: University Press, 1966), p. 90.
18 Ham Mukasa provides a number of striking examples in "The Rule of the Kings of Buganda", *Uganda Journal*, X, 2 (September 1946), pp. 136–143.
19 Owekitibwa S. W. Kulabya, "Some Aspects of Buganda Customs", *Uganda Journal*, IX, 2 (May 1942), p. 53.
20 Mutesa, *op. cit.*, p. 31.
21 Mukasa, *loc. cit.*, p. 137.
22 Henry M. Stanley, *Through the Dark Continent*, Vol. I (New York: Harper & Brothers, 1878), p. 53.
23 Allen J. Lush, "Kiganda Drums", *Uganda Journal*, III, 1 (July 1935), pp. 7–25.
24 F. Lukyn Williams, "The Kabake of Buganda: Death of his Highness Dandi Chwa, K.G.M.G., K.B.E. and Accession of Edward Mutesa II", *Uganda Journal*, VII, 4 (April 1940), pp. 176–187. For another exhaustive account of the ritual of ascension to the throne, see R. A. Snoxall, "The Coronation Ritual and Customs of Buganda", *Uganda Journal*, IV, 4 (May 1937), pp. 277–288.
25. Kulubya, *loc. cit.*, pp. 50–51. It is worth remembering that this contribution was his Presidential address to the Uganda Society in 1941; needless to say, he was the first African to achieve such recognition and for that matter, the last for many years.
26 Fallers, *The King's Men*, p. 287.
27 Rowe, *op. cit.*, pp. 3–5, in Goody, *op. cit.*, pp. 82–126. See also the detailed account of succession rules by Southwold. For much of the Kingdom's life, succession by brothers of the deceased Kabaka was more likely than transmission of the throne to a son.
28 *Ibid.*, p. 22.
29 The text of the Treaty may be found in Low and Pratt, *op. cit.*, pp. 350–366.
30 Mutesa, *op. cit.*, p. 76.
31 *Ibid.*, p. 98.
32 For the contrary argument, see H. P. Gale, "Mutesa I.—Was He a God?" *Uganda Journal*, XX, 1 (March 1956), pp. 72–87. A whole dissertation erroneously citing Buganda as the prototype of Frazerian divine kingship was contributed by Tor Jistang, *The King of Ganda* (Stockholm: Museum of Sweden, New Series Publication No. 8, 1944). Jan Vansina argues the sacralization of kingship although not its divinity in "A Comparison of African Kingdoms", *Africa*, XXXII, 4 (October 1962), pp. 324–335.
33 Mutesa, *op. cit.*, pp. 32–33.
34 F. D. Welbourn, "Some Aspects of Kiganda Religion", *Uganda Journal*, XXVI, 2 (September, 1960).
35 C. C. Wrigley, "The Christian Revolution in Buganda", *Comparative Studies in Society and History*, II (1959–1960), pp. 33–48.
36 Rowe, *op. cit.*, p. 60.
37 *Ibid.*, pp. 85–91.
38 Mutesa, *op. cit.*, pp. 42–43.
39 Rowe argues persuasively that the Christian purge was only half-heartedly carried out; "The Purge of Christians at Mwanga's Court", *Journal of African History*, V, 1 (1964), pp. 55–71.
40 For details on this revolutionary year, see Sir John Milner Gray, "The Year of the Three Kings of Buganda, Mwanga-Kiwewa-Kaleme, 1888–1889", *Uganda Journal*, XIV, 1 (March 1950), pp. 15–52.
41 A. M. K. Mayanja (translator), "Chronology of Buganda, 1800–1907, from Kagwa's Ebeke", *Uganda Journal*, XVI, 2 (September 1952), p. 154.

42 For details on the swift advance of Christianity, see Low, *Religion and Society*; John V. Taylor, *The Growth of the Church in Buganda* (London: SCM Press, 1958).
43 The writer is indebted to D. A. Low for the left side of the above figure; the right-hand side is adapted from it.
44 Quoted in Raymond Buell, *The Native Problem in Africa* (New York: 1928; reprinted Frank Cass, London, 1965), 576–577. The best analysis of this period is provided by Pratt, in Low and Pratt, *op. cit.* See also Apter, *op. cit.*
45 Mutesa, *op. cit.*, p. 74.
46 J. R. Postlethwaite records his version of the melodrama in his memoirs, *I Look Back* (London: Boardman and Co., 1947).
47 Mutesa, *op. cit.*, p. 74.
48 Low and Pratt, *op. cit.*, p. 247.
49 Mutesa, *op. cit.*, p. 84.
50 *Ibid.*, pp. 109–110.
51 Both were the object of investigations by Commissions of Inquiry. See *Report of the Commission of Inquiry into the Disturbances Which Occurred in Uganda During January, 1945.* (Entebbe: Government Printer, 1945), and *Report of the Commission of Inquiry Into the Disturbances in Uganda During April, 1949* (Entebbe: Government Printer, 1950).
52 *Ibid.*
53 On the colourful history of Ignatius Musezi and the Uganda Federation of African Farmers, see George Shepherd, *They Wait in Darkness* (New York: John Day, 1955).
54 Low and Pratt, *op. cit.*, p. 323.
55 Mutesa in his autobiography (119) confirms the interpretation by Pratt (325) that he did indeed mean Buganda independence in referring to "our country" in his document; in his words, "By 'we' I always mean the Baganda, as any of my people would."
56 Mutesa, *op. cit.*, p. 125.
57 Uganda Protectorate, Department of Agriculture, *Annual Report*, 1955.
58 From *Uganda Eyogera*, reprinted in translated form in Low and Pratt, *op. cit.*, pp. 340–341. The detailed analysis of the 1953–1955 crisis presented in Low and Pratt is the most useful summary of these events. See also Apter, *op. cit.*, pp. 263–300.
59 Mutesa, *op. cit.*, p. 144.
60 D. A. Low in *The Times*, 15 October, 1955, Mutesa recounts this episode in his autobiography, *op. cit.*, p. 147.
61 Prince Badru, titular head of the Uganda Muslim community, was the son of Prince Mbogo, leader of the Muslim faction in the 1890s, and grandson of Kabake Suna II. For a valuable account of Islam in Buganda, and its complex schisms, see T. W. Gee, "A Century of Muhammadan Influence in Buganda, 1852–1951", *Uganda Journal*, XXII, 2 (September 1958), pp. 139–150.
62 Fallers, *The King's Men*, p. 358.
63 For excellent treatments of terminal colonial politics, see D. A. Low, *Political Parties in Uganda, 1949–1962* (London: Athlone Press, 1962); F. B. Welbourn, *Religion and Politics in Uganda, 1952–1962* (Nairobi: East African Publishing House, 1965).
64 Uganda Protectorate, *Report of Constitutional Committee* (Wild Report); (Entebbe: Government Printer, 1959), *Uganda Relationships Commission* (Munster Report), (Entebbe: Government Printer, 1961).
65 Mutesa, *op. cit.*, pp. 159–160.
66 Welbourn, *op. cit.*, p. 48. On the formation of Kabaka Yekka, see also Cherry Gertzel, "How Kabaka Yekka Came to Be", *African Report*, IX, 9 (October 1964), pp. 9–13.
67 Mutesa, *op. cit.*, pp. 159–160.
68 For figures illustrating the strategic social position of Baganda, see J. E. Goldthorpe, *An African Elite* (Nairobi: Oxford University Press, 1965); see the calculations on the Civil Service by David Gogin, *Africanization of the Ugandan Public Service*, unpublished doctoral dissertation, University of Wisconsin, 1967, pp. 139–143.

69 D. A. Low has argued this case with particular force in various of his writings; for a succinct statement, see "The Advent of Populism in Buganda", *Comparative Studies in Society and History*, VI (1963–64), pp. 424–444. John Saul has entered an interesting caveat to this utilization of the term "populism", in his chapter in Ghita Inoescu & Ernest Gellner (eds.), *Populism: Its Meanings and National Characteristics* (London: Weidenfeld and Nicolson, 1969). It is urged that the term implies an explicit worship of the people, and a reaction of small rural folk to the penetration of the capitalist economy. We retain the term, although would note that it did not imply an ideology of exaltation of the people; remarkably, the symbol of monarchy served as a surrogate for the "people". The economic aspect was present, as evidenced by the massive participation in the boycott of Asian traders in 1959.

70 See especially F. B. Welbourn, *East African Rebels* (London: SCM Press, 1961).

71 Low, *Political Parties in Uganda*, p. 32.

72 Mutesa, *op. cit.*, pp. 154–155.

73 Low, "The Advent of Populism in Buganda", p. 442.

74 This evaluation rests upon the writer's observation of party organization in Uganda in 1965–66.

75 J. M. Lee, "Buganda's Position in Federal Uganda", *Journal of Commonwealth Political Studies*, III (1965), p. 173.

76 Welbourn, *Religion and Politics* in Uganda, p. 44.

77 L. C. Fallers takes Low to task for neglecting the nationalist element in rural Buganda political response, in his comments on "The Advent of Populism in Buganda", *op. cit.*, pp. 445–448. Welbourn also lays particular stress on this element in *Religion and Politics in Uganda*.

78 Stanley, *op. cit.*, I, pp. 187–193.

79 Mutesa, *op. cit.*, pp. 78–79.

80 See the interesting record of this oddysey by Ham Mukesa, *Uganda's Katikiro in England* (London: Hutchinson and Co., 1904).

81 This summary statement necessarily compresses the complexity of the situation into a simple assessment. Welbourn, *Religion and Politics in Uganda*, offers an excellent analysis of the intricacies of Baganda nationalism not fully treated here. See also the valuable paper by M. S. M. Kiwanuka, "Nationality and Nationalism in Africa: The Uganda Case", typescript, 1969.

82 "Fresh Political Approach in Buganda. Basis of the M.P.'s Recommendation for K.Y.–U.P.C. Merger." (Kampala: Uganda Bookshop, for Dr. S. J. L. Zake and others, n.d. (1963).

83 For useful background on the immediate post-independence period, see Cherry Gertzel, "Report from Kampala," *African Report*, IX, 9 (October, 1964), pp. 3–8.

84 Mutesa, *op. cit.*, p. 176.

86 Apter, *op. cit.*, p. 21.

7

ANKOLE

Martin R. Doornbos

Though largely overshadowed in public attention by the more dramatic overthrow of the Buganda monarchy, the kingdom of Ankole deserves more by the way of an epitaph than a mere footnote in the obituary of its better-known neighbour. Incorporated into the Uganda framework by an accident of colonial history, the Ankole kingship experienced many of the familiar strains and stresses that followed in the wake of European colonization. What was traditionally the linch-pin of the social system in this process became confronted with the demands of an entirely different organizational framework, that of a colonial administrative state. Although the effect of these changes has been to make the monarchy increasingly obsolete as an institution, ultimately its abolition, on September 8, 1967, did not so much result from its lack of popular support as from a challenge to the integrity of the wider Uganda polity, a challenge, moreover, which originated from outside the Ankole sub-system.

Nor is this the only factor that lends special interest to Ankole. That the abolition of the Ankole monarchy should have elicited few strong reactions from the local populace is no less intriguing considering the upheaval provoked under similar circumstances in Buganda. Part of the explanation lies in the different processes of adjustment and interaction that have taken place over the years *within* Ankole and Buganda as well as *between* each of them and the Uganda-wide political system. In Buganda the fate of the monarchy was decided in a head-on confrontation between the Government of Uganda and the Kabaka's government, which until then had commanded substantial powers. And since, unlike what happened in Ankole in 1967, many Baganda interpreted the overthrow as a threat to themselves as a people, their sense of cultural loss was far more deeply felt—and noticeable—than in Ankole.

To better understand the relative ease with which the removal of the Ankole monarchy was effected we will need to examine the structural transformations which over the years have affected the role of kingship in Ankole society. Rather than a one-to-one substitution of modern for traditional authority structures, the social, political and geographical contexts of the kingdom were transformed at the same time that the kingship itself was being restructured. At the turn of the century, when colonial rule was introduced, the formal boundaries of the kingdom underwent considerable expansion; these territorial gains were offset, however, by the political limitations arising from its incorporation into

236

Uganda. From that point on, the very existence of the monarchy came to depend on policy considerations of an entirely different nature from what might have been the case had the kingdom been treated as a distinct political entity.

Moreover, various characteristics of the social structure of Ankole had a significant bearing on the changing role of kingship, in particular the ethnic division between Bairu and Bahima and the loss of influence suffered by the traditional ruling clan, the Bahinda. In the wake of colonization new patterns of relationships emerged among groups, and these in turn gave rise to new perceptions of the role of kingship in the system. In brief, a rather complex set of factors must be taken into account if one is to appreciate the roots of this transformation. Before coming to grips with the central question raised in this chapter—to what extent has the redefinition of kingship affected the capacity of the institution to operate as a meaningful element in the political system?—a necessary first step is to sketch the key characteristics of the traditional political system; another is to identify the processes of incorporation and resulting structural transformations which eventually led to the redundancy of the institution of kingship.

THE TRADITIONAL CONTEXT OF ANKOLE KINGSHIP

A major feature of the socio-cultural setting in which the Ankole kingship was embedded was the pronounced cleavage between Bahima and Bairu. To this day each ethnic group has retained its distinctive cultural attributes and much of its distinct way of life. Bahima life has traditionally centred around their famed long-horn cattle, which for them was not only a means of subsistence but a symbol of wealth, power and prestige; the Bairu, on the other hand, have generally been cultivators and at first did not own any cattle. The Bahima, who presently constitute about five per cent of the population, traditionally stood as a political elite, whereas the Bairu were much less involved in the politics of the kingdom.

The Bahima are said to have migrated into the Ankole area some four or five centuries ago, at which time they proceeded to set up the centralized state structures which have been handed down through time.[1] Nonetheless, the inauguration rites of the King or *Omugabe* of Ankole included some rather un-pastoral ceremonies, such as the planting of millet seed, which might indicate the existence of kingship in an era before the Bahima assumed political control.[2] It seems possible, therefore, that the Bahima-dominated state structure has been projected back into history to establish a claim on its origin. On a mythological plane the royal clan of Ankole, the Bahinda, supposedly had an origin which was distinct from that of both Bahima and Bairu;[3] but the Bahinda led essentially the same type of life as the Bahima and have generally identified themselves with Bahima interests. The Bahima are normally considered to be a Bahima clan, though a somewhat special one. Ankole could thus be called a Bahima state,[4] notwithstanding the references to the myth of origin which Bahima often made. The function of this myth was basically a legitimizing one, as it purported to establish a statutory equality between Bahima and Bairu, and thus to conceal the social distance between them.

Ankole was not only a state of the Bahima, but primarily for the Bahima. Although some Bairu were directly subservient to Bahima elements, and most had fewer rights and privileges than Bahima, there can be little doubt that a good proportion of the Bairu must have lived a fairly autonomous existence: even more certain is that the political life of the kingdom revolved around matters that were almost the exclusive concern of Bahima, such as warfare, cattle raising, the adjudication of disputes and the like.[5] Some Bairu were required to provide produce and services to the Omugabe and other senior Bahima, and at times such requisitions may have been rather arbitrary, but there is little indication of a pervasive and continuous exercise of Bahima political control over all of them. While in a general sense Bairu were a subject category, their lack of participation in the political process may in part be explained by the nature of the Bahima state, which was especially geared to the requirements of pastoralism. The social structure of Ankole, therefore, comprised two distinct types, or levels of political relationships: between Bahima and Bairu, relationships tended to be intermittent and hierarchical, based on a "premise of inequality";[6] within the Bahima stratum, however, relationships were more frequent and basically egalitarian.[7]

The King (Omugabe) was the pivot around which the system revolved. To most Bairu, he was the ultimate embodiment of legitimate power and, in principle, the supreme arbiter of conflicts among men.[8] In fact, however, the office was quite far removed from day-to-day Bairu affairs. While the Omugabe clearly stood as the central figure in the traditional polity and his position no doubt inspired considerable awe to most Bairu, the ties that linked them to the Omugabe were not especially conducive to strong affective identification with the political system. For the Bahima, on the other hand, the Omugabe stood at the epicentre of their political relationships. They certainly enjoyed a much more intimate relationship with the Omugabe. Not only was his way of life much the same as theirs, but he was also regarded as the protector of their interests. The traditional system of Ankole thus differed in a fundamental way from, for instance, traditional Buganda with its more homogeneous population. Contrary to what its mythology would imply, traditional Ankole was not a system in which Bairu and Bahima were basically united in a mystical identification with its kingship.

On closer inspection the kingship in Ankole reveals some paradoxical features. While in theory the Omugabe was all-powerful, in practice his powers were far more circumscribed. In theory, he was the supreme decision-maker, but in practice he could not afford to disregard the demands of the political elite, especially the Bakungu or territorial chiefs. Again, in theory the Omugabe could rely on coercion to impose his will, yet compliance with his policies depended largely on inducements.

These apparent contradictions can best be understood in the light of the patron-client relationships operative in the traditional society. Based on solidarity ties between political actors commanding unequal resources (power, land, cattle, etc.), patron-client relations provided the crucial connecting links between the Bakungu chiefs and their personal followings (whether Bahima or Bairu), and indeed between the king on the one hand, and Bakungu chiefs and non-chiefly Bahima and Bairu on the other. The Bakungu, in charge of territorial divisions, were largely drawn from the Bahinda ruling clan; to a lesser extent from the Bahima sub-stratum; and in exceptional cases from amongst the Bairu. While in effect helping to legitimate the authority of the Bakungu, the personal links between them and their clients were further reinforced by expectations of mutual benefits. In return for the protection accorded by the Bakungu to their clients, the latter would send tribute, whether in the form of cattle or agricultural produce, to the Bakungu, who might then utilize this flow of resources for further solidifying their bases of support. In most instances, those Bakungu who stood as "clients" in relation to the Omugabe did not need resources in kind. The transaction, typical of the patrimonial pattern, involved the conferment of "status" in return for administrative services and personal loyalty. Only insofar as it involved non-chiefly Bahima or Bairu did the clientage relationship between the Omugabe and his followers involve the exchange of resources in kind.

Patronage was especially important as a political resource for Bahinda aspiring to succeed to, or displace, an Omugabe. The choice of an Omugabe being largely determined by superior strength, it was essential for potential pretenders to command as strong a body of supporters as their resources permitted. Patronage was the major avenue to build this support. Once installed, an Omugabe again needed to mobilize support to stay in office. He had to master sufficient strength to ward off external threats and counter-act internal fissures. But if patronage helped to maintain the Omugabe in office, it did not define the role of that office. As a network of relationships the patron-client ties constituted one sub-system, but did not encompass the totality of the political or social system. Though itself heavily dependent upon the support of clientage networks, the institution of kingship also served to uphold the integration of the system through reference to the values of high authority with which it was identified. To facilitate the discharge of this function, the incumbent needed to maintain lines of support in a rather more concrete sense, and functioned basically as a *primus inter pares*. The sum of these factors, therefore, was that structurally the system was characterized by dispersed powers and collective decision-making, while normatively it featured strong hierarchical values about authority. Moreover, the structural and normative aspects were critically interconnected, since hierarchical values made sense primarily in relation to the participatory style of decision-making. They provided a source of cohesion against potentially disruptive political forces. In this context, the role of kingship was unmistakably meaningful.

THE EXPANSION IN SCALE OF ANKOLE'S ORIGINAL BOUNDARIES

After the redrawing of the kingdom's boundaries, early in this century, the Ankole monarchy came to compromise an area which was several

times the size of the nineteenth-century kingdom of Nkore.[9] This spectacular expansion was in part the result of conquests and territorial
accretions antedating the arrival of the British, and in part the consequence
of the further territorial enlargements affected under the auspices of British
colonial policy in the name of administration efficiency.

Spheres of influence had always been fluctuating in the interlacustrine
area, but during the latter half of the nineteenth century Nkore ascended
to a considerably enhanced role in the region. This "imperialism" of Nkore
was directly related to the decline of its northern neighbour Bunyoro and
it reached its peak during the rule of Ntare V, shortly before the arrival
of the British. Several smaller neighbouring kingdoms, Igara, Buhweju and
Buzimba, were made to recognize Nkore's paramountcy and pay tribute
to its ruler. And when, at the turn of the century, the British assumed
control over the entire region, they subdued and incorporated additional
areas, including Bunyaruguru as well as a large section of Mpororo
kingdom. Thus, in addition to the original Nkore kingdom which lay in the
present Isingiro, Kashari and Nyabushozi counties, Ankole's expansion was
largely the result of the annexations to the west of Rwampara and Shema
counties (at the cost of Mpororo) and of Igara, Bunyaruguru, Buhweju
and Mitooma to the north (the latter at the expense of Bunyoro).[10]

Formal expression was given to these annexations in the Ankole
Agreement of 1901, although Kajara was not added until 1914. Nominally,
all these areas were placed under the rulership of the Omugabe of Ankole,
which should be remembered when considering the role of the kingship
in the present century. Evidently, from that moment on the Ankole
dynasty had few traditional roots, if any, in more than half of its domain.
This does not necessarily mean that kingship *per se* was an alien element
in incorporated areas. Most of the areas comprising Ankole exhibited
significant similarities in terms of language, social organization and ways
of life, including the presence of an ethnically distinct ruling stratum, the
Bahima. Although the proportions of Bahima and Bairu varied from one
area to the next, and in Nkore proper showed a somewhat larger Bahima
population than in the other areas, the recurrence of an analogous ethnic
division in these various regions (added to the general cultural unity of
the area) appears to have strongly facilitated the enlargement of scale of
Ankole. In historic times the fluctuating balance of power had often
caused a change of rulership, as was indeed expressed in the Bairu proverb
"it does not matter who takes over, they are all kings". Nonetheless, for
a kingship which was to be put to the test of generating new meaning and
functions, the lack of direct historical roots in a large section of its domain
would doubtless make this task more difficult. In terms of its territorial
jurisdiction, therefore, the Ankole monarchy found its traditional bases
of legitimacy significantly reduced at the beginning of this century.

ANKOLE AS A SUBSYSTEM

Simultaneous to the British-sponsored expansion of Ankole, the kingdom was itself brought into the wider orbit of Uganda. From then on the

perpetuation of the kingship as an institution rested no longer on its intrinsic strength, but on considerations of political expediency extraneous to Ankole. These considerations were of two kinds, the first being the familiar strategem of employing traditional structures of authority for the purpose of consolidating colonial control. (The implications of this policy for Ankole will be discussed below in the context of the new administrative framework in which the Omugabe and chiefs found themselves inserted.) A second ground for preserving the kingship gradually eclipsed the former in importance, however, and retained its relevance even in the post-independence period: of special significance in this connection were the problems arising from the over-all political situation in Uganda, and centering primarily around the Buganda issue.

As noted earlier, in contrast with Ankole, the kingdom of Buganda formed a powerful political subsystem, whose integration within the rest of Uganda posed serious problems first to colonial officials and subsequently to nationally-oriented African politicians. For a long time, both felt that Buganda could not be dethroned from its dominant position without seriously compromising the viability of Uganda as a whole.[11] Until recently the solution adopted to contend with the Buganda issue was to try to balance its influence by enhancing that of the smaller kingdoms, and even of the districts of Uganda, which hence were turned into minor replicas of Buganda. Insofar as possible, the traditional and quasi-traditional rulers of these divisions were placed on an equal constitutional footing with the Kabaka of Buganda, and this effort contributed in no small part to the exaltation of offices such as that of the Omugabe of Ankole.

As also noted earlier, the immediate motive for abolishing monarchical structures throughout Uganda stemmed from the application of a similar policy in regard to Buganda. When, in 1966, the Buganda crisis came to a head, the Uganda Government decided to seize upon this opportunity to dismantle once and for all the Kabaka's stronghold. Following an open clash with the armed forces of Uganda, the Buganda monarchy was destroyed and its Kabaka fled the country. With the Buganda kingship eliminated, the smaller kingdoms instantly lost their raison d'être from the standpoint of the central Uganda government; moreover, their abolition was positively valued because it "soothed the pill", as it were, for Buganda.

From the perspective of Uganda-wide politics, this sequence of events provides a dramatic illustration of the part played by "national" political considerations—and more specifically by the necessity of creating an internal balance of power situation—in both retaining and, ultimately abolishing the Ankole monarchy: whether or not the Ankole kingship enjoyed legitimacy within its own society was of secondary importance.

The loss of legitimacy suffered by the Ankole monarchy, as evidenced at the time of its abolition, cannot be exclusively attributed to the exigencies of Uganda-wide politics. The institution might conceivably have retained, or developed, functions which would have tied it more closely to Ankole society, and this in spite of the fact that its prolongation ultimately depended on extraneous factors. The possibility of successful adaptation, albeit in a different situational context, has been demonstrated in the case of a few European monarchies and there seems to be no particular reason why this pattern could not have repeated itself in Africa.[12] Thus, if Ankole's incorporation into Uganda, as well as its prior territorial expansion, entailed severe limitations upon the exercise of monarchical authority, for a fuller understanding of the consequences of these moves something must be said of the interplay of social and political forces set in motion by the impact of colonial rule.

CONTENTION FOR PRE-EMINENCE IN THE NEW FRAMEWORK:
THE BAHINDA-BASHAMBO CONFLICT

Once the colonial framework was established, the stage was set for a violent competition between the representatives of traditionally influential ruling clans, the Bahinda and the Bashambo, each seeking access to positions of wealth and privilege. The result was that, early in the century, the role of the monarchy was put to a severe test by the elimination of a large part of its traditional entourage, the Bahinda clan, as a political force.

The introduction of new political resources under British rule, and the fact that they came to circulate in an expanded political market, led to the culmination of a longstanding rivalry between the Bahinda and the Bashambo, from which the latter emerged triumphant. The Bahinda, it will be recalled, formed the royal clan of Ankole, whose members had exclusive title to the Omugabeship and to various senior chieftainships. The Bashambo were the royal clan of the neighbouring kingdom of Mpororo, of which parts were incorporated into Ankole at the time of British intervention.[13] Both were Bahima clans and stood in a similar relationship to the Bairu population in their respective areas. In the nineteenth century, the Bashambo had been gaining ground as rulers in various other areas which subsequently came under the suzerainty of Ankole, and the Bashambo thus had to be counted as a force of no small significance in the expanded Ankole kingdom. But not only did the Bahinda-Bashambo strife become increasingly salient due to the incorporation of neighbouring territories into Ankole; it was also directly stimulated by the imposition of colonial overrule. While the British were offered thus a golden opportunity to exploit inter-clan rivalries to consolidate their power in Ankole, it was the Bashambo who in fact took advantage of the British presence to further their own political interests. As it turned out, however, their interests appeared to coincide largely with those of the British, so that the end result might not have been very different had the British tried to take deliberate advantage of the situation.

It is not too surprising, therefore, if the Bahinda-Bashambo conflict took a decisive turn precisely during the years which immediately followed the introduction of British overrule. Since shortly before the signing of the Ankole Agreement in 1901, the Enganzi, then "principal chief" in Ankole, was a Mushambo, Nuwa Mbaguta.[14] Mbaguta was to remain on the scene almost as long as the then ruling Omugabe, Kahaya, namely until the late 1930s; although they initially enjoyed reasonably cordial relationships with each other, these relationships soon deteriorated into mutual rivalry and hostility. In the eyes of the British, Mbaguta was cooperative, interested in innovations, and eager to follow their instructions. With the backing of his British "overlords" he asserted himself as a shrewd and powerful potentate. From the point of view of Protectorate officials, Mbaguta emerged as the ideal kind of "native authority". Through him many administrative measures were introduced and implemented in Ankole, earning him laudatory comments in the records of British officers. As he proved himself an effective and reliable instrument, the scope of his influence was gradually enlarged by the administration. Almost unnoticed, the office of Enganzi gained a prestige and significance equal to the stature of the incumbent, thus conferring upon Mbaguta a degree of influence and respect unknown among his predecessors. In fact, only one pre-1900 Enganzi seems to be vaguely remembered in Ankole, as against several generations of Abagabe.[15] And so, Mbaguta, the "brightest star near the moon", as was the original meaning of the word "Enganzi", came to eclipse even the Omugabe himself in actual influence.

Being an outsider to the traditional establishment of Ankole, Mbaguta was seen by the British as a more neutral and manipulable agent of transformation than might otherwise have been the case. Being the leader of the Bashambo clan, Mbaguta did his best to exploit all possible opportunities to curtail Bahinda influence and further Bashambo interests. As a key contact man of the British, several such chances soon offered themselves. The establishment of a colonial administration, which necessitated a considerable amount of accommodation on the part of the senior chiefs, in large number Bahinda, gave Mbaguta the power as well as the opportunity to displace the most recalcitrant among the Bahinda chiefs. Since the traditional chiefs were incorporated in an administrative command system which not only imposed specific duties but also implied considerable restrictions to their exercise of authority, many were the Bahinda chiefs who felt that the objectives of bureaucratic control involved more restraints than they could endure. And their awareness of the part played by Mbaguta in diminishing their traditional prerogatives contributed in no small way to further reduce their threshold of tolerance.

Early in the century this culminated in a series of incidents. Government officers were engaged in strong actions against Igumera, the leader of the discontented Bahinda, and his followers. For some years after the death of Ntare V, in 1895, Igumera had been the strongest chief and virtual ruler of Ankole.[16] Upon the establishment of British control he was relegated to the position of a county chief and in many other ways found his influence severely curtailed. When these restrictions caused him to rebel, the British exiled him to Buganda, a measure for which Mbaguta deserves special credit. Many other chiefs were also dismissed during these early years. With only three exceptions the senior chiefs of all ten counties were replaced in the years between 1901 and 1908. The effect of these

R

measures was thus to leave Mbaguta's power virtually unchallenged among the Ankole elite. Many Bahinda preferred to take refuge in Buganda and elsewhere, rather than face further humiliation, and after the murder of a British officer, St. Galt, in 1905, the exodus took on major proportions. (The background of this murder has largely remained a mystery, although many people in Ankole believe that it originated directly from the Bahinda-Bashambo conflict.')[17]

Although Ankole historiography has been surprisingly inexplicit or inconclusive about this period, the fact is, however, that most of the Bahinda aristocracy fled from Ankole out of fear for punitive sanctions by Mbaguta and the British. So widespread and lasting was the exodus that by the early 1930s, a special recruitment effort was necessary in Buganda to find an eligible Muhinda candidate to succeed the incumbent Omugabe. Meanwhile a number of positions left vacant were taken over by Bashambo and other Bahima, and a good many chieftainships were filled by Baganda elements especially recruited for that purpose by Mbaguta. Divorced from his Bahinda kinsmen, the reigning Omugabe, Kahaya, thus came to stand rather isolated and, whenever possible, Mbaguta did not fail to further circumvent his basis of authority.

With the elimination of the Bahinda stratum disappeared a major element of the traditional political structure of Ankole. Severance of his links with the Bahinda aristocracy was a source of uneasiness and frustration for the Omugabe, as it deprived him both of the power structure and the traditional frame of reference that once defined his position in the system. Once the traditional ties of patronage had been ruptured, the Omugabe had no choice but to turn elsewhere to solidify his political resource base.

KING AND CHIEFS IN THE COLONIAL FRAMEWORK

The Bahinda-Bashambo strife not only mirrored but indeed accelerated the process of institutional change inaugurated under the aegis of British rule. As a consequence kingship itself was restructured. The colonial bureaucracy heavily impinged upon the authoritative and symbolic roles of Ankole kingship, eroding its traditional functions and causing it to lose its essential meaning.

Even when exercised with utmost benevolence, colonial rule was basically authoritarian. It established a bureaucratic state in which all actions originated from orders sent by high-ranking officials to their subordinates, and in which elaborate reporting at all levels placed further controls upon the execution of policies. It had the qualities of briskness and efficiency characteristic of sportsmanship and military style.[18] Its values were rational, and geared towards the maintenance of law and order. Its lines of command comprised colonial officers as well as African chiefs, and while the distinction between these ranks was strenuously maintained, both sectors applied similar criteria of hierarchy and administrative competence. The dispersal of power that once characterized traditional Ankole thus gave way to a distinctively hierarchical structure;

for the metaphysical authority norms operative in the traditional society were in time substituted with a set of instrumental and pragmatic values. To be sure, a semblance of continuity was maintained through the person of the Omugabe, and occasional lip-service was paid to the traditional values attached to his office. On the whole, however, the effect of these cumulative transformations was to turn the Omugabe into an instrument of bureaucratic rule, with traditional values and symbols increasingly relegated to the sphere of local folklore. Belated attempts to adorn the institution of kingship with a new overlay of ceremonialism, and to draw new distinctions between the ideal and actual powers of kingship, failed to reverse the trend. What finally emerged was little short of a caricature of the traditional institution of kingship, which in turn led to a further erosion of the affective sentiments it once inspired.

As a way of facilitating their adaptation to the system, the British promised the Omugabe and other senior chiefs the right to nominate their successors.[19] In addition they were to enjoy such privileges as the right to a share of the revenue collected, land grants, and various other fringe benefits. According to the Agreement of 1901, "Chief" Kahaya was "recognized by His Majesty's Government as the Kabaka or supreme chief" of Ankole, and it was further stipulated that "so long as the aforesaid Kabaka and chiefs abide by the conditions of this Agreement they shall continue to be recognized by His Majesty's Government as the responsible chiefs of the Ankole district". However, the document added a stick to the carrot, for it was made explicit that, should they fail to abide by these stipulations, removal from office might follow. Moreover, "should the Kabaka of Ankole—Kahaya or his successors—be responsible for the infringement of any part of the terms of this agreement, it shall be open to His Majesty's Government to annul the said Agreement, and to substitute for it any other methods of administering the Ankole district which may seem suitable". Clearly, the terms of the Agreement were characteristically British, as was the new order it inaugurated.

At first the Omugabe was not unwilling to comply with British directives. In a sense, of course, he had no choice; yet British backing provided a new, and perhaps an even more secure, basis for the enjoyment of his formal prerogatives. A semblance of traditional authority was maintained which tended to conceal the loss of effective power suffered by the incumbent. To the average villager or herdsman, at any rate, the implications of colonial rule were not immediately visible. There followed a period of incubation, during which the old order continued to shape popular allegiances, making it possible for the Omugabe to draw upon residual traditional loyalties. The colonial administration was naturally interested in making use of this goodwill to solidify its control over the country; moreover, in Ankole as elsewhere, it was felt that removal of a traditional ruler might cause consternation and resistance, reactions, which to the minds of British officials were definitely to be avoided.

The incorporation of monarchical authority into the new system entailed some profound ambiguities. Even among those European administrators who had more than a passing interest in the exotic, the value of traditional authorities was assessed mainly in terms of their ability to command obedience. The assumption was that "all you could in fact do was to explain what you wanted to some 'Native Authority'; and as he— or she—was generally only too anxious to please, the result was usually that it was done".[20] The legitimacy of traditional authority had to be maintained if it was to remain serviceable. Yet to treat a king or chief in those early days with all the pomp and protocol characteristic of a later period might have stimulated a renewed consciousness of their role and a taste for more and more authority. This could easily have conflicted with the conduct of an efficient colonial administration. Thus a fragile balance (if not open tension) developed between the requirements of continued legitimacy and the exigencies of external control.

Ambiguities were especially noticeable in regard to the Omugabe's position vis-à-vis the administrative chiefs. For some time these relationships were not laid down in very explicit terms. Moreover, the official line in regard to these matters tended to change over time. For many years the policy was evidently to have it both ways, that is, to keep full control over the chiefs with the district administration, while adhering to the idea that all authority was exercised in the name and under the supervision of the Omugabe. Chiefs of counties and lower divisions were appointed by and held responsible to the district administration.[21] District officials inspected their books, kept records of their administrative performance, and reported on their diligence in implementing by-laws. Yet the Omugabe was officially regarded as the chiefs' superior, and this in more than a purely nominal sense. From the British viewpoint, his capacity to exercise influence over the subordinate chiefs had a practical usefulness. For this, however, he had to be given the opportunity to display his authority. Hence, the Omugabe was also asked to tour and inspect and report; at this point, however, new problems arose which in time caused considerable strain between the incumbent and British officials. For one thing, the standards of good administration entertained by the Omugabe were not necessarily the same as those of British officials, and disagreements would almost inevitably arise between them. Chiefs would either find themselves confronted with conflicting demands, or else the Omugabe would follow the official line and communicate directives which he secretly disapproved of.

Moreover, the relationship between the Omugabe and the chiefs was evidently different from the relation that obtained in pre-colonial days. Although the Omugabe had to perform in an administrative command system, in the minds of British administrators his traditional legitimacy was expected to assist him in the assumption of this new role. Yet, precisely because this legitimacy was associated with an earlier and rather different authority relationship, this new role did not instantly click, but instead created puzzles and embarrassment on all sides. Moreover, as the scope of his authority had been left exceedingly vague, the chances of a successful adaption were all the more problematic.

Finally, to function effectively within the district organization a certain amount of administrative proficiency was required of the incumbent. The whole system was designed to work on the basis of paperwork and bureaucratic codes; and failure to master these bureaucratic skills could easily spell administrative and political failure. Largely untrained for his new role, the Omugabe naturally felt inadequate in discharging the multiplicity of administrative tasks devolved upon him. Rather more surprising is that the problems created by this situation were not readily appreciated by British officials. Not until 1938, when the Omugabe himself finally asked for copies of reports to be sent to him, did a District Commissioner begin to wonder "has the Omugabe facilities for starting a filing system of his own?"[22]

These ambiguities and contradictions led to increasingly strained relations between the Omugabe and British officials. Lack of interest in and resentment of the British administration came more and more to characterize the Omugabe's attitude, and a vicious circle ensued in which growing impatience and irritation on the part of colonial officers and increasing apathy and surliness on the part of the Omugabe were some of the more salient elements.

Long after the early days of self-confident colonialism had passed, British officers developed a more balanced understanding of the structural innovations they had enacted. As Mitchell reflected in 1939:

> Few of us realized . . . that the instrument which we were using could not retain its effectiveness if we deprived it—as we generally did—of most of its powers and responsibilities, to say nothing of its revenues. I have often wondered since those early days that the Chiefs thought it worthwhile even to try to carry out our wishes, when we had taken from them the power to punish and often looked upon the tribute and service from their people, without which they could not exist, as being corrupt extortion.[23]

This contradiction is fully borne out by the record. The frequency with which the institution of kingship was used to induce compliance with administrative policies was inversely related to its actual usefulness for that purpose; accordingly, its employment tended to produce ever more marginal results. For some time it was felt that if only the Omugabe himself could be interested in the innovations proposed by the district administration, there would be no problem in getting the rest of the population to follow suit. However, the result turned out to be very different, because the role designed for the Omugabe was as foreign to the Banyankore as it was to the man himself. As redefined by the British administration, the role of the Omugabe departed in some major ways from pre-colonial conceptions. This was not only because the Omugabe became a subordinate of Protectorate officials. The idea of a bureaucratic line of command itself was alien to the indigenous political culture of Ankole. The traditional meaning of kingship was to symbolize the political integration of a pluralistic polity through hierarchical authority values. This aspect was lost once kingship became converted into an instrument for gaining acceptance of immediate, concrete ends. This policy assumed the existence of sources of actual power which the Omugabe had never had. It further assumed that the prestige of his office would automatically survive the structural transformation of colonial rule. Both assumptions turned out to be fallacious.

When the Omugabe was asked to convey the wishes of the British administration to his people, they saw him perform in a capacity which made little sense either in the old or in the new framework. Even the relatively rare visits he made to various areas were felt as a burden and a nuisance by the people concerned, as shown in the repeated complaints over the requirement to provide food for him and for his retinue. Increasingly, therefore, the Omugabe was met by a lack of understanding and interest on the part of his own people which only enhanced his own disinterest in, and discomfort with, his role and ultimately led him to retreat into apathy.

These remarks are not intended to support the view, held by some anthropologists, that successful innovation requires that it be harnessed to existing cultural patterns.[24] New situations, after all, may generate new orientations and values. Institutional transformation and change of orientations are bound to occur wherever there is any justaposition of new and old elements. To assume that one can manipulate at will an institution such as kingship and at the same time expect popular orientations and allegiances toward it to remain unaffected, would be profoundly misleading. The attempt to use the traditional role of kingship in Ankole was based on this erroneous assumption; although far-reaching structural changes were introduced, all along the official assumption was that the orientations which supported the old monarchical order would remain unaffected. In fact, the structural transformations introduced in Ankole could only lead to the growing obsolescence of the monarchy.

ETHNIC CONFLICT

A final element bearing on the destiny of the Ankole kingship has to do with the Bairu-Bahima division. As we have seen, in the pre-colonial era, Bairu and Bahima had different orientations to the monarchy. In order to preserve its legitimacy the monarchy needed to "equalize" the symbolic identification of its ethnic "constituents" and give Bairu and Bahima a sense of shared involvement in the affairs of the kingdom. This requirement, however, ran counter to the established "premise of inequality". Ankole's ethnic stratification, as it turned out, imposed an additional limitation on rejuvenation of kingship.

As the monarchy was being restyled, Bairu and Bahima simultaneously developed divergent attitudes toward the office, which, in a sense, led to a replication of earlier divergencies. Although the Bahima maintained a close identification with the monarchy, the source of this identification changed considerably. The Bairu, on the other hand, had never been very closely related to the monarchy, and when the institution lapsed into obsolescence, their reaction was one of growing indifference. There was also another strand of opinion among Bairu, however. As the monarchy was identified with Bahima overrule, its legitimacy was questioned at the same time that Bahima supremacy was challenged by Bairu. So far from promoting the unification of ethnic segments through their joint identification with kingship, the Obugabe became a symbol of increasing tension between Bairu and Bahima.

The rise of ethnic hostility was the concomitant of a restratification process begun during colonial rule. In traditional times, the distinctive ethnic hierarchy does not appear to have been seriously questioned in Ankole. In view of the lack of perspective on alternative arrangements, it seems understandable that the Bairu generally submitted to the inferior social position they were given. Following the Ankole Agreement, the principle of ethnic inequality was variously reaffirmed and even strengthened. For instance, the Bairu were obliged to perform labour duties, pay tax and provide food supplies for extractive agents who were largely Bahima chiefs, and who themselves enjoyed a substantial share of this revenue. Again, in the recruitment of senior chiefs preference was given to Bahima and other non-Bairu such as Baganda, until about the middle of the century. Moreover, the subordinate position of the Bairu was consistently re-emphasized and acted out by the Bahima elites, reaffirming their feeling that they were a despised group.

But the colonial rule also prompted social developments that increasingly caused the Bairu to question not only specific discriminatory practices but the whole rationale behind the "premise of inequality". The effect of modern education was to instill egalitarian orientations and aspirations among an increasing number of Bairu, a growing sense of dissatisfaction over their traditional status as "second-class citizens". Bairu also developed an awareness of greater self-sufficiency from their mastery of modern skills, as well as from the new sources of income made available to them through the cultivation and sale of cash crops. The result of all this was the emergence in the 1940s and 1950s of a Bairu-led and Bairu-inspired protest movement which formalized and intensified the claims of Bairu elements to a fuller participation in Ankole affairs. Owing to this pressure, increased Bairu participation in the political life of Ankole was in fact forthcoming. But this was a slow process, and the relations between Ankole's ethnic groups were consequently marked by prolonged hostility.[25]

If the monarchy became a focal point of conflict, this was not so much the result of its own doing as a reflection of intensified ethnic antagonisms. These occurred at a time when the influence of the Omugabe was at its lowest ebb, and when the new functions vested in the Omugabe seemed strangely reminiscent of the Emperor's new clothes. In contrast with the situation in adjacent Rwanda, the monarchy in Ankole was too weak to become a significant factor in the ethnic strife; yet ethnic rivalry was bound to occur at some point, and if for no other reason than to strengthen their respective claims, the contestants could scarcely resist the temptation of politicizing the issue of monarchical legitimacy.

To the Bairu, kingship was a constant reminder of Bahima claims to hegemony. Whatever pronouncements the Omugabe made to the effect that all Banyankore were equally his subjects,[26] these were inevitably received with a sense of strong disbelief by educated Bairu elements. As Bairu protest became increasingly vociferous during Gasyonga's reign, the latter's attitude became the target of growing criticisms on their part. Even though they knew that the kingship no longer had any direct influence in politics, any semblance of involvement of the Omugabe with Bahima tactics was invariably denounced by the Bairu as "proof" of ethnic favouritism.

To the Bahima, the monarchy also became a symbol in a new political sense. Traditionally, the kingship symbolized, and in a way ensured, their political unity. Although the practical utility of the institution was now very much in doubt, the Omugabe's continued presence in the office during a time of ethnic status transformation nonetheless strengthened Bahima feelings of identity and security. As they sensed the threats posed to their political supremacy most Bahima sought to reverse the trend as best they could given the political resources available to them. Since the 1940s, tension focused particularly on the number of senior chieftainships occupied by Bahima, as the displacement of Bahima chiefs inevitably meant a loss of resources, power and status for the group as a whole. While the ethnic distribution of these posts changed slowly, in the long run the numerically weaker Bahima were bound to suffer a decline of their privileged political status. Though forced to relinquish their position of pre-eminence, the Bahima derived a sense of unity and continued recognition from the conviction that the kingship was still "theirs." That this conviction was largely illusory is beside the point. Precisely because they were victims of this illusion, they failed to realize the full extent of their eclipse as a political elite, a fact which also helps to explain their relative quiescence during the transition. Retention of the monarchy through the period of ethnic restratification has thus probably smoothed the reversal of ethnic status in Ankole.

Somewhat anti climatically, the contrasting attitudes of Bairu and Bahima almost never led to explicit demands for either the abolishment or the retention of the Ankole monarchy. Several factors mitigated ethnic tension and hence diminished the degree to which the monarchy became an issue in the dispute. One such factor was related to Ankole's status as a sub-system of Uganda, as discussed earlier. The essential point to note in this connection is that the national arena offered alternative avenues for upward social mobility for both Bairu and Bahima to those available in Ankole proper. Many of the best qualified Banyankore found employment in other parts of Uganda; while slowing down local competition for positions, this also helped to attenuate ethnic tension. For this reason intergroup conflict in Ankole never assumed the global proportions that it did in the ethnically stratified but closed system of Rwanda.[27] Nor did the survival of kingship become an all-pervasive issue, as in Rwanda.

Another explanation for the staying power of the Ankole monarchy lies in the emergence of sub-cleavages among the Bairu. European proselytization in Ankole has tended to divide the population into roughly equal proportions of Catholics and Protestants. Converted Bahima are almost exclusively Protestants, while Catholic Bairu are in slightly larger numbers than Protestant Bairu. In time, different patterns of socialization and different economic opportunities have tended to make the Protestant Bairu more antagonistic to the traditional Bahima establishment than were the Catholic Bairu.[28] In the late 1950s, the Catholic Bairu aligned themselves with the Bahima against the Protestant Bairu in the Ankole branch of the Democratic Party, although many Catholic Bairu insist on pointing out that this was done less out of a predilection for traditional authority than for reasons of political expediency. The Catholic-Bahima alignment involved an implicit understanding, however, that the position of the monarchy would remain unquestioned. Meanwhile, the Protestant Bairu found their way into the Uganda People's Congress and in the early 1960s faced a need to attract votes from either Catholic Bairu or Bahima to stand a chance of winning elections. As a result, while the UPC membership would have been the most likely group openly to challenge the kingship, electoral considerations caused them to refrain from doing so. Ironically, the two political parties were indeed so concerned not to be identified publicly with anti-monarchical opinion that at times each of them purported to represent the interests of the most loyal defenders of the Omugabe. Little of this stemmed from genuine sympathy for the kingship; but it did help to prolong the relatively undisturbed existence of the monarchy.

Ethnic tension was at its height in Ankole in the middle and late 1950s. However, this was also the time when important advances towards ethnic equality were made, stimulated by political as well as educational and economic conditions.[29] By the time of independence, in 1962, remnants of inequality were certainly still present in Ankole, but the principle of Bahima supremacy was no longer operative, and in most spheres of life Bairu could be found who stood on an equal footing with Bahima. The friction between Bairu and Bahima slowly subsided, and Bairu protest declined correspondingly. A core of Bairu militants continued to press for full equality, however, who did not envisage the possibility of full political emancipation short of a formal abolition of kingship. Its elimination, as it turned out, came at a time when equality had by and large been achieved. This was not unlike what happened to another symbol of "ethnic" domination in Uganda, namely the statue of King George V in Kampala, from which the identifying plaque was not removed until several years after the country attained independence.

THE NEO-TRADITIONALIZATION OF ANKOLE KINGSHIP

The kingship thus increasingly came to be a lonely station. So far from being the axis from which radiated an innovating tradition, in its terminal years the monarchy did little more than reflect the orientations of its environment. And the shine it produced was just as faint as the popular identifications which it inspired.

A lonely monarch, the Omugabe's loneliness was made even more apparent by the pedestal on which he was placed during the last phase of his reign. Whereas in earlier colonial times his status had been deliberatedly downgraded in the interest of administrative efficiency, throughout the fifties and the early sixties the tendency was just the opposite. Only in these later years was formal recognition given to some of the Omugabe's traditional titles. In 1951 the Provincial Commissioner gave his approval to the use of the title of "Rubambansi the Omugabe", "on all formal occasions as a matter of courtesy".[30] Similarly, when discussing the proposals for local government reform outlined in the 1953 Wallis Report, members of the *Eishengyero* (Ankole Council) suggested that the Omugabe be treated as the political Head of the Kingdom "as he had always been".[31] It was further decided in that same year that from now on all by-laws would be ratified by the Omugabe before being published in the Gazette. Moreover, as if to reaffirm his newly-gained pre-eminence, the Omugabe was allowed to officiate over the annual opening ceremonies of the *Eishengyero*, and to award Certificates of Honour to those Ankole Government employees deemed worthy of such distinction.[32]

Up until the mid-fifties the *Eishengyero* remained largely a Bahima establishment. After 1955, however, following franchise extensions, its composition underwent a major change; from then on until about 1961, the position of the Bahima elite suffered a sharp decline. This transformation was reflected in the *Eishengyero*'s increasingly cavalier treatment of certain proposals aiming at buttressing the symbolic aspects of the Omugabeship, such as the defeat of the motion introduced in 1957 seeking the confirmation of all appointed chiefs by the Omugabe.[33] Nonetheless, the loss of effective powers incurred by the Omugabe was paralleled by further attempts to enhance the formal appurtenances of his office.

The inflation of the Omugabeship reached its peak shortly after Uganda attained independence. The stature and dignity of the office of Omugabe gained unprecedented recognition—a phenomenon which is best understood in the light of two fundamental realities of post-independence Uganda politics. One was the adoption of a special kind of federal structure for the new state; another had to do with the somewhat capricious course of party competition in the years immediately following independence.

"Federalism" explicitly put Ankole on the political map of Uganda as a Kingdom. As noted earlier, there was a variety of reasons for adopting a pluralistic constitutional framework for Uganda, the most decisive being the position of Buganda. This framework was federal in respect to Buganda, and semi-federal or quasi-federal in respect to Ankole, Toro, Bunyoro, and the "Territory" of Busoga. Until this pattern was laid down, the term "Kingdom" had been used in an informal sense in respect to Ankole and the other semi-traditional units, the common official reference being "District". Shortly before independence, however, the "Kingdom of Ankole" and the other Western kingdoms gained constitutional recognition *qua* Kingdoms. Ankole's monarchical status was formalized in a new Ankole Agreement, concluded on 30 August, 1962, and was reaffirmed in the 1962 Independence Constitution of Uganda as well as in subsequent legislation. The wording used for defining the position of the Omugabe was the same in the Ankole Agreement and the Uganda Constitution:

1 (1) The Omugabe (King), who is the Ruler of Ankole, shall enjoy all the titles, dignities, and preeminence that attach to the office of Omugabe under the law and custom of Ankole.
(2) The Omugabe, the Omwigarire (Queen) and members of the Royal Family, that is to say, descendents of Omugabe Rwebishengye (Abanyiginya n' Abanyiginyakazi), shall enjoy their customary titles and precedence.[34]

The signing of the 1962 Ankole Agreement was hailed as the "biggest ceremony in Ankole history",[35] and for several dignitaries it was indeed an opportune moment to look back into the past. The Bishop of Mbarara outlined three stages in the development of Ankole—"the period when the Kings of Ankole were supreme, their period under British protection, and the time after the agreement had been signed by the Governor and the Omugabe".[36] The Enganzi, for his part, pointed to the changes which had occurred since 1901 and asked "those present to join with him in asking the Governor to convey to the Queen (of England) and her Government the deep gratitude of the people of Ankole" for the work they had done.[37] The Omugabe, the Enganzi, and the Governor all expressed satisfaction with the constitutional arrangements which had just been agreed upon.[38]

While the new Ankole Agreement substantially enhanced the formal status of the Omugabe, this trend was further accentuated by the local implications of party rivalries at the national level. It is well to remember in this connection that at the time of independence, in 1962, the central government of Uganda was under the control of a coalition between the Uganda People's Congress (UPC) and Kabaka Yekka (KY), while the Ankole government was under the control of the Democratic Party (DP). By 1963, however, the UPC had evicted the DP from its leading position in Ankole, and before 1964 drew to a close a growing tension emerged between the UPC and KY, in time causing the collapse of their alliance at the centre. Exclusive control over the central government passed into the hands of the UPC leadership; meanwhile the tension between the UPC and KY reached unprecedented proportions.

In 1962, Kabaka Yekka began to solicit the support of Baganda and non-Baganda elements residing in Ankole. In response to what was officially regarded in Ankole as an unwarranted intrusion into the political life of the Kingdom, the DP government of Ankole initiated measures to counteract the KY tactics. Thus when groups of individuals in Ankole began to wear badges bearing the words "Kabaka Yekka", the Ankole government reacted by prohibiting the display of such badges on the ground that it amounted to "praising a King in another Kingdom", and this was contrary to customary law as it "belittled the honour and authority of the Omugabe".[39] One Muhamudu Kasumba was arrested and convicted for not heeding the Ankole government's instructions, and a case grew out of the incident in which the action of the Ankole government was finally upheld as valid by the Uganda High Court.[40] The matter became rather more complicated because some members of the Uganda cabinet did not, at that time, share the view that wearing a KY badge constituted an affront to the Omugabe. At a political rally in Mbarara in July 1962 some central government ministers went so far as to publicly denounce the order which sought to prevent the wearing of KY badges. The Minister of Justice, himself a Munyankore and UPC member, "shouted praises of Kabaka Yekka and told a big gathering that any one was free to wear a Kabaka Yekka badge in Ankole".[41] These controversies led to a growing estrangement between the Ankole and Uganda governments, and similarly between the Minister of Justice and the High Court. The issue took a new turn when those who sought to spread KY influence in Ankole adopted an alternative strategy. With characteristic shrewdness, they substituted another label for the previous one and soon new badges were circulating bearing the inscription "Omugabe Wenka" ('The Omugabe Only'). The display of these badges was immediately prohibited, however, and "Omugabe Wenka" turned out to be an exceedingly short-lived affair. It seems a fair presumption that even without the government's prohibition its impact would have remained minimal. Neither the persons wearing these badges nor the slogan itself carried much of an appeal in Ankole. The comments of the Omugabe further contributed to defuse the issue:

> I am above politics and the use of my name by any one political party as a slogan would only divide my people and endanger their happiness and the progress of my Kingdom . . . I do not discriminate against any of my people and I regard all of them in Ankole, irrespective of their political or religious beliefs, as my beloved subjects and for that reason I do not permit a section of my people to use my name for political ends.

In regard to Kabaka Yekka, the Omugabe's view was:

> My Enganzi and the Eishengyero have publicly condemned Kabaka Yekka activities in Ankole and I strongly endorse their condemnations as I would not personally permit any other ruler to exercise his rule in my own Kingdom.[42]

The KY threat against the Omugabe's Kingdom was repeated a few years later, but now in an entirely different political context. Ironically, the renewed Kabaka Yekka infiltration caused the UPC government then in office in Ankole to use much the same argument as its DP predecessor had done. On 14 September, 1965, the Enganzi stated "I have today been informed that a movement called 'Kabaka Yekka' has started infiltrating into this Kingdom to try and hinder the progress of this Kingdom". He further pointed out that "saying Yekka here in Ankole and wearing Kabaka Yekka shirts in Ankole means that the Kabaka is the only King . . . even in this Kingdom of Ankole", and warned that "I, as the guardian of the constitution under the Ankole schedule, and the Omugabe's Government as a whole, cannot approve of this".[43] To the Omugabe, the Enganzi gave his reassurance that "this Government and your loyal subjects shall never allow any external movement seeking to lower your dignity. The exodus of KY to this Kingdom is truly calculated at lowering your dignity and seeks to cause division among your loyal subjects. Banyankore are well-known to be peace-loving and tolerant, but they might be forced to reach a point beyond which they will tolerate no more if KY tries to force its way through to this Kingdom."[44]

That point was never reached, however, partly because of the restrictions placed upon KY activities, and partly because far more critical developments were in the offing. From the end of 1965 until mid-1966, Uganda experienced the first acute crisis of its history as an independent state, and through the spring of 1966 everyone's attention was focused on the impending trial of strength between the Kingdom of Buganda and the central government of Uganda. The outcome of the crisis was to bring about a major change in the national balance of power and in time produced a fundamental overhaul of the entire governmental structure. The preparation of the new constitutional arrangements took considerable time, however, and while new proposals were being formulated many pre-existing arrangements and institutions were temporarily left untouched. Among these were the kingships of Ankole, Toro, and Bunyoro. In 1966, an interim constitution was introduced which for all intents and purposes abolished federalism, but nonetheless reconfirmed the legitimacy of these three remaining monarchies. As the Enganzi said to the Omugabe, in his opening address of the Eishengyero, "nothing in this constitution had prejudiced your position as the Omugabe of Ankole Kingdom, as you will soon hear . . . Part one paragraph one to ten of the Ankole New Schedule, which honours you Nyakusinga, has not been altered either by letter or punctuation."[45] The provisional 1966 Constitution was in effect for a little over a year, that is, until the constitutional arrangements for a unitary republic in Uganda were ready. The Ankole kingship lasted until just that time.

The Ankole monarchy, then, lost its traditional functions and met formidable obstacles while trying to develop new ones. One might argue that the Ankole kingship was in a state of political decay throughout the colonial period, and hence that the only type of development experienced was "regressive" development. If the sole criteria for assessing political development are the fortunes of a particular institution (in this case the kingship), this view cannot be logically disputed. As we have seen, the Ankole kingship did not "develop" into a strong, adaptable political institution in the present century. It lacked the conditions for developing new goals, it did not exhibit a significant increase in functional complexity; its institutional development was consequently thwarted.[46] However, one wonders whether there is any point in employing these criteria.[47] The functions of the Ankole monarchy were eroded when a new and more inclusive organizational framework was imposed upon it; there was no compelling reason for the kingship to survive as a strong institution in that framework. Since there happened to be a monarchy in Ankole, its retention could be justified on the ground that a premature decapitation might generate popular reactions which could hamper the development of an effective administration. In point of fact, its continuation during the building of the new political and administrative structures probably helped obviate a major legitimacy crisis. Its own problems and ambiguities were no less severe when serving that purpose, however; indeed these problems were rendered all the more acute by the process of self-liquidation to which the kingship found itself subjected. The main significance of the Ankole monarchy is that it helped redefine the cognitive map of many members of Ankole society at a time when major transitions were under way. As these transformations were reaching completion, the monarchical "shell" could finally be thrown away. The decline of the monarchy was thus both a result and an accelerator of institutional change on a broad, nation-wide scale. In this sense the role of the Ankole kingship, even as a decaying institution, can conceivably be correlated with political development. As such it merely illustrates a universal phenomenon, namely, that growth processes throw up redundancy.

NOTES

1   This has been a standard explanation for the origin of a number of interlacustrine states, including Ankole, ever since Speke's account of his exploration. See J. H. Speke, *Journal of the discovery of the source of the Nile*, 1963, 246. Yet, there is no *a priori* reason why the establishment of centralized state structures should have coincided with the arrival of Bahima elements. The origins of the Bahima have long been the source of considerable speculation among anthropologists, historians and others. Whereas it is usually assumed that Bairu were indigenous to the area, an astounding variety of geographical origins has been attributed to the Bahima, most often Ethiopia, but also ancient Egypt as well as ancient Israel. See J. F. Cunningham, *Uganda and its People* (London, 1905) x-xi; Sir Harry Johnston, *The Uganda Protectorate*, Vol. I (London, 1904). p. 210; Robert P. Ashe, *Two Kings of Uganda* (London, 1889; 2nd ed., with a new introduction by John Rowe, Frank Cass, London, 1970), 337–338. Illustrative of a prevalent body of opinion on the origins of the Bahima is Sir Albert R. Cook's observation that "everyone has remarked their extraordinary likeness to the old Egyptian mummies"; similarly Alfred R. Tucker describes the typical Muhima as "a man the very image, you would say, of Ramses II". Sir Albert R. Cook, *Uganda Memories (1897–1940)*, (Kampala, 1945; reprinted Frank Cass, London, 1973), p. 118; Alfred R. Tucker, *Eighteen Years in Uganda and East Africa*, (London, 1911), p. 272. Recently, the debate has shifted to biochemical arguments, but still without much conclusive evidence one way or the other. See Merrick Posnansky, "Kingship, Archaeology and Historical Myth", *Uganda Journal*, 30, 1, 1966, pp. 6–7, and G. C. Cook, "Tribal Incidence of Lactase Deficiency in Uganda", *The Lancet*, April 2, 1966, pp. 725–730.

2   F. Lukyn Williams, "The Inauguration of the Omugabe of Ankole to Office", *Uganda Journal*, IV, 4, 1937, p. 309.

3   The legitimising myth of Ankole kingship was that Ruhanga, the Creator, has put his three sons, Kakama, Kahima, and Kairu, to a competitive test on the basis of which he entrusted each of them with a different task. The test involved watching over a full milkpot during one whole night. Kakama successfully passed the test and was consequently charged with the rule of the country. Kahima, who had given some milk to Kakama, was made to look after the cattle, while Kairu, who had spilled all his milk was ordered to till the soil. See H. F. Morris, *A History of Ankole* (Kampala, 1962), p. 6. This legend will be recognised as a local adaption of a mythical heritage found throughout the inter-lacustrine area, but even in Ankole there are further variations on this theme. A distinctly Bairu version is related in P. J. Gorju, *Entre le Victoria, l'Albert et l'Edouard* (Rennes, 1920), pp. 279–281.

4   The term "Bahima State" was introduced by K. Oberg. See K. Oberg, "The Kingdom of Ankole in Uganda", in M. Fortes and E. E. Evans-Pritchard (eds.), *African Political Systems* (London, 1940), p. 128.

5   Oberg, *op. cit.*, 129–130; W. L. S. Mackintosh, *Some Notes on the Abahima and the Cattle Industry of Ankole* (Mbarara, 1938), p. 20; Audrey I. Richards (ed.), *East African Chiefs* (New York, 1959), p. 152.

6   The phrase is borrowed from Jacques J. Maquet, *The Premise of Inequality* (London,

O.U.P., 1961). However, while in Ankole, as in Rwanda, there was a "premise of inequality", this does not imply that hierarchical relationships were structured identically in the two cases.

7 Cf. Oberg, "The Kingdom of Ankole", *op. cit.*, pp. 128–136; see also Jacques Maquet, "Institutionalisation feodale des relations de dependence dans quatre cultures interlacustres", paper presented at the *Colloque du Groupe de Recherches en Anthropologie et Sociologie Politiques* (Paris, 1968).

8 Oberg, "The Kingdom of Ankole", p. 131; Richards, *East African Chiefs, op. cit.*, p. 153.

9 The name Ankole is a mixed Luganda-English corruption of Nkore. For a more detailed account of the expansion of the kingdom, see H. F. Morris, "The Making of Ankole", *Uganda Journal*, 21, 1957, pp. 1–15 and H. F. Morris, *A History o Ankole* (Kampala, 1962).

10 A full list of Ankole's annexations is given in Richards, *East African Chiefs, op. cit.*, pp. 156–157.

11 See David E. Apter, *The Political Kingdom in Uganda: A Study in Bureaucratic Nationalism* (Princeton, 1961).

12 While it is legitimate to consider the tenacity of institutions in this way, it is quite a different proposition to raise the adaptive capacity to the level of a norm. This is, however, the tenor of the argument in Samuel P. Huntington, "Political Development and Political Decay", *World Politics*, XVII, 3, 1965, pp. 386–430. Carried to its logical conclusion, the argument implies that all political structures ever established should ideally have maintained themselves.

13 See H. F. Morris, "The Kingdom of Mpororo", *Uganda Journal*, 19, 1955, pp. 204–207, and Morris, *A History of Ankole*, pp. 17–22.

14 F. Lukyn Williams, "Nuwa Mbaguta, Nganzi of Ankole", *Uganda Journal*, 10, 1946, pp. 196–208.

15 The Enganzi was Muhigi. It should be noted, however, that the memory of past Abagabe appears to have been fluctuating. Roscoe writes that when he first visited Ankole ". . . it was impossible to obtain from the people any information as to the names of their previous rulers". However, on his second visit he found that "contact with other tribes, especially with the Baganda and the Bakitara, aroused a desire to have a genealogy of the royal family, and a list of kings was prepared for the purpose". See Roscoe, *The Banyankole* (Cambridge, 1923), p. 34. (Abagabe is the plural of Omugabe.)

16 H. F. Morris, *A History of Ankole, op. cit.*, p. 35.

17 A good introduction to the puzzle is H. F. Morris, "The Murder of H. St. Galt", *Uganda Journal*, 24, 1960, pp. 1–15. Despite lengthy and meticulous inquiries, the background to this incident has long remained a mystery. The most plausible hypothesis is that the murder was the result of a Bahinda plot to thwart Mbaguta's popularity with the British. The alleged murderer was a Mushambo who was himself killed immediately following the St. Galt murder. Whether this was in fact an attempt to implicate Mbaguta by provoking an incident for which the onus would come to lay on the Bashambo remains unproved. Its result, at any rate, has been to strengthen Mbaguta's position.

18 This is aptly illustrated by the following excerpt from *Notes for Officers appointed to Uganda*, published by the Crown Agents for the Colonies (London, 1934): "In Entebbe, Kampala and Jinja and the larger centres the population and facilities permit of most English games being pursued. Golf, cricket, tennis, soccer and occasionally rugger are played, and in the majority of out-stations there are tennis courts and rough golf courses. If, however, in bush stations these facilities are entirely lacking, regular exercise should always be taken, such as a brisk walk or a stroll with a shot gun" (p. 19).

19 See *Ankole Agreement*, 1901, para. 3.

20 Uganda Protectorate, *Native Administration* (Entebbe, 1939), p. 4.

21 With a single exception, i.e. Buhweju county, the provision in the Ankole Agreement that the principal chiefs were entitled to nominate their successors soon fell into oblivion.

22 A note in the margin of the minutes of the meeting of saza chiefs held on 19 May, 1938. This note as well as the documentation referred to below, is available in the archives of the District Commisisoner's Office, Mbararra. The access granted to this material by the Ministry of Regional Administration and the kind assistance of the District Commissioner, Ankole, and his staff, are gratefully acknowledged.

23 Uganda Protectorate, *Native Administration*, p. 4.

24 E.g. "a change in any one part of the culture will be accompanied by changes in other parts, and . . . only by relating any planned detail of change to the central values of the culture is it possible to provide for the repercussions which will occur in other aspects of life". Margaret Mead (ed.), *Cultural Patterns and Technical Change* (Paris, 1953), p. 10.

25 The development of ethnic conflict in Ankole is traced in greater detail in Martin R. Doornbos, "Kumanyana and Rwenzururu: Two Responses to Ethnic Inequality", in Robert I. Rotberg and Ali A. Mazrui (eds.), *Protest and Power in Black Africa* (New York, 1970), pp. 1088–1136.

26 For instance, after a visit to Rwanda, the Omugabe stressed the unity he expected of the Banyankore in the following terms: "In Ruanda, there are three types of people, namely Bahutu, Batutsi and the Batwa. They work together in co-operation and . . . their motto is 'Omuguha gw'enyabushatu' (a rope with three strands) representing these classes of people in Ruanda. You will agree with me that no country should expect progress if there is lack of cooperation and disunity. Division and hatred engineered by subversive elements in a country exhibit a gloomy picture and their ends are fatal. I should like you to be 'Omuguha gw'enyabushatu' That is when we shall achieve Ankole's will as a nation." From the "Speech by Rubambansi the Omugabe at the Opening Ceremony of the Eishengyero of Ankole", 17 January, 1956.

27 Some further differences are suggested in Martin R. Doornbos, "Protest Movements in Western Uganda: Some Parallels and Contrasts", in *Kroniek van Afrika*, 1970, p. 3.

28 See Doornbos, "Kumanyana and Rwenzururu", *loc. cit.*

29 *Ibid.*

30 Letter from Provincial Commissioner, Western Province, to District Commissioner, Ankole, 23 July, 1951.

31 Minute 3 of the Eishengyero, May, 1953.

32 Minute 70 of the Eishenbyero, 1954.

33 Minute 25 of the Eishengyero, 1957. The idea was copied from Buganda, where the presentation of chiefs to the Kabaka was known as *Okweyanza*.

34 See Schedule 2 of the *Constitution of Uganda*, 1962.

35 *Agetereine*, 14 September, 1962.

36 *Uganda Argus*, 31 August, 1962.

37 *Ibid.*

38 The Agreement had been worked out in consultation with the Governor by a Constitutional Committee consisting of Ankole representatives. There had only been two points of difference which needed to be referred to the Colonial Secretary for settlement. One of these was whether or not the Ankole Ministers were to enjoy individual or collective responsibility, the other concerned the number of guns to be fired for the Omugabe on ceremonial occasions. On the first issue, the final decision was that they were individually responsible, which meant they were essentially department heads. On the number of guns "the Committee demanded fifteen while the Governor was only prepared to grant nine". (Uganda Argus, 8 March, 1962.) In the end, he got nine.

39 News release, Enganzi of Ankole, undated (August, 1962).

40 Criminal Revision, No. 30 of 1962 of the Kashari County Court of Ankole.

41 Open letter from Enganzi to Governor of Uganda, 10 August, 1962.

42 *Uganda Argus*, 9 February, 1962.

43 "Official Statement by the Enganzi; Warning to KY Infiltration in Ankole", 14 September, 1965, mimeo.

44 "Speech by Owekitinisa the Enganzi on the 20th Coronation Anniversary of

Rubambansi the Omugabe of Ankole, Sir Charles Godfrey Gasyonga II", 27 September, 1965, mimeo.

45   "Speech by Ow'Ekitinisa the Enganzi on the Opening of the First Eishengyero of Ankole", 21 April, 1966, mimeo.

46   Huntington, "Political Development and Political Decay", *loc. cit.*

47   Cf. Martin R. Doornbos, "Political Development: The Search for Criteria", *Development and Change*, I, 1, 1969, pp. 93–115.

8

IJEBU

Peter C. Lloyd

Some of the kingdoms of pre-colonial Africa have developed into modern states without any substantial changes in their long established boundaries; such as Rwanda, Burundi, Lesotho, Swaziland to cite examples discussed in this volume. Other states however are of such an extant that they embrace a number of kingdoms of one or more culture complexes. In these the rulers, in as much as they have retained their power and prestige, have operated within the sphere of local government. And it is, thus, their evolving roles in this sphere which have substantially determined their importance and influence at the national level. The Yoruba kingdoms and their rulers of Western Nigeria fall into this category.

The political structure of the Yoruba kingdoms was far from being static before the colonial period; we may usefully see the political process in terms of a competition for power in each kingdom between the oba and the various grades of subordinate chiefs. Events in the nineteenth century seemed, generally, to favour the chiefs at the expense of their obas. The British colonial government, however, in seeking to base its local administration upon the indigenous office holders and in instituting the formal native authority system, both imposed new demands upon the obas and provided opportunities for them to exploit new sources of support. In short the obas became more autocratic than before. This brought them into conflict with their chiefs, who challenged this shift in the balance of power, and later with the growing number of educated young men who saw themselves as the heirs of colonial power. The rather sudden withdrawal of British support as Nigeria moved towards consti-tutional independence left the obas in a most vulnerable position still trying to maintain a status which, in the previous two or three decades, was slowly becoming institutionalized. The events in the reign of one such oba form the subject of the present chapter.

I. COLONIAL RULE AND ITS AFTERMATH

The Yoruba, now numbering ten million people, have, from time immemorial constituted a large number of independent kingdoms of varied size.[1] In their origin and myths the respective rulers trace ultimate descent from Oduduwa, the supposed progenitor of the Yoruba people at Ile Ife. Some of the older among existing dynasties perhaps originated in the fourteenth century or earlier. A fairly common pattern of royal

260

paraphernalia, installation ceremonies and the like is still found throughout Yoruba country. The Western Region of Nigeria, established in 1951
as a unit within the Federation, ultimately exercising internal self-government, included most but not all of the Yoruba kingdoms.[2]

The British colonial government, which established its rule over most of
Yoruba country by an Order in Council in 1901, administered the area
under a system of native administration conventionally known as "indirect
rule".[3] The new territorial units followed very closely the boundaries of the
kingdoms and of the ethnic divisions within the Yoruba people—into
Oyo, Egba, Ijebu, Ijesha, Ekiti, etc. The obas or kings, together with their
subordinate chiefs were gazetted as "Native Authorities" and were the
instruments of British rule. Whilst maintaining the status of the obas the
British did in fact substantially reverse their roles, for the oba became
dependent upon the colonial government whereas he had previously been
dependent upon his chiefs. But, in as much as the impact of British rule
was, at the local level, slight most obas managed to fulfill adequately the
expectations both of the British administrative officers and of their chiefs.
Crises were apt to occur however when, in the 1930s and '40s, educated
obas developed, with British encouragement, far more autocratic roles
vis-à-vis their chiefs, who reacted by attempting to exile and depose them.
For many years colonial administrators saw their Native Authorities as
the basic units in the future independent Federation; but these schemes
vanished in the 1940s with the realization that many Native Authorities
were not viable units for the management of the social services increasingly
expected and that local government elected councils and not native administration by traditional rulers was the pattern of the future.[4]

A head-on clash between the nationalist politicians and the traditional
rulers, contesting power at the Federal or Regional levels, never materialized. But in the Western Region the Action group leaders championed
the cause of the elected local government councillors in curbing the autocracy of the obas. Their attitude towards the obas was however ambiguous.
The upsurge of cultural nationalism, for instance in the wearing of Yoruba
rather than western dress and the taking of chieftancy titles by educated
politicians and such leaders, also included a deep respect for the traditional
institution of kingship. (The Yoruba have for long regarded kingship as a
mark of superiority over neighbouring peoples whose traditional political
systems were of a more rudimentary nature.) In a practical vein, the new
political leaders sought the support of obas in winning the votes of their
electorates. The educated obas, sharing a similar scholastic and occupa-
tional background with the politicians, wooed by them, and conscious
of the fact that they now held the ultimate powers of appointment and
deposition tended to favour and support the Action Group. But party
politics divided the Yoruba towns and kingdoms as British rule had never
done; local factions took party labels to enhance their demands and rival
communities supported different parties. The obas could no longer play
the role traditionally expected—that of being "father of the people" and
impartial in their dealings with all. During the thirteen years of rule by
Action Group and its successor, the Nigerian National Democratic Party

(led by Chief Akintola) the obas failed to develop a satisfactory new role, and slowly declined in power and prestige. Thus when military rule drove the politicians from office at both national and local levels the obas were not able to stage a dramatic come-back. The government of their towns rested instead with the Nigerian administrative officers and the local government staff. The obas and chiefs were but one among many groups whom the administrative officer might consult. Nevertheless, many obas continued to bear the brunt of popular complaints against taxation and stagnant standards of living in the middle 1960s.[5]

I have elsewhere developed most of the themes introduced in the foregoing paragraphs. In this article I shall illustrate them with reference to the events and issues of two years, 1952–4, in the reign of the Awujale, oba of Ijebu. The story of the reign of the Awujale is rather more dramatic and violent than that of most obas, but in so being it does emphasize the major conflicts which arose during the late colonial and post colonial period.

The Ijebu kingdom is one of the largest and its ruler, the Awujale, was regarded by the British as a First Class Chief—a rank held by the Oni of Ife, the Alafin of Oyo, and the Alake of Abeokuta. Due to the proximity of Lagos, Ijebu migrants and commuters form a large part of its population. Through these two factors local Ijebu issues have received an unusual prominence in the national press. The traditional political system of the Ijebu kingdom, differs, as will be elaborated below, from that of most Yoruba kingdoms in that some of the highest titled offices are open to all citizens, (and not restricted to men of a specific descent group); hence very wealthy men—who so often seem to come from humble homes—can aspire to that political power which matches their economic status. The struggle between the Awujale and his wealthiest citizen, Timothy Adeola Odutola, which is related below has much in common with that in Benin between the Oba and Gaius Obaseki, his Iyase.[6] The Ijebu people are, furthermore, the wealthiest and most advanced in education among the Yoruba. The heartland of their kingdom is situated on an escarpment the soils of which are not suitable for cocoa; the area is very densely settled. The Ijebu rely therefore on crafts and trading and in the present century have migrated throughout Nigeria in pursuit of these occupations. Ijebu Ode town is remarkable for the number of imposing houses, but most of these belong to men still absent. The popular stereotype of the Ijebu is of a pushing entrepreneurial type; in as much as there is any scientific foundation to this belief (and psychological tests to differentiate personality types within Yoruba country have not, to my knowledge, been carried out) it may derive from the lack of land which forces men into crafts and trades or from the cognatic descent system which gives the Ijebu much greater scope in manipulating different relationships to gain given goals.[7]

Before outlining the background to the Ijebu conflicts I must briefly summarize a mode of analysis which I have already developed in published papers. Firstly I have distinguished between traditional African kingdoms on the basis of the distribution of political power, viz. the manner in which the councils of chiefs which advise the kings were selected. Competition for power would take a different form in each of the three ideal types—

two "open" types in which chieftaincies were either hereditary within descent groups or available to all men, one "closed" type where the king selected his chiefs from kin, affines or followers.[8] Subsequently I developed the analysis of conflict between king and chiefs in Yoruba kingdoms contrasting the two roles of the oba—on the one hand a consecrated monarch installed by a complex set of rituals, on the other hand an arbiter between chiefs and descent groups, each of which is individually competing for power.[9] With his consecrated power the oba may become autocratic; but the chiefs have the right to depose him. To portray a static balance between oba and chiefs is but an heuristic device, for both compete for the control of new resources—in the pre-colonial period, incomes from trade, booty from war, land seized from conquered neighbours. In the twentieth century novel resources existed in the exploitation of new forms of wealth and in the manipulation of the colonial administrative system. In particular the educated oba accepted with alacrity the opportunities provided by the British conception of a more active role in local government.

In asserting his power he offended his chiefs who tried to depose him; they failed, of course, and in their failure, together with their inability, through their poor salaries, to maintain their prestige associated with chieftaincy, lost the support of their people. The educated oba appealed directly to his people and became a benevolent and popular autocrat. His success in establishing this new role was, however, short-lived as the same forces which had facilitated his own aggrandizement were also contributing to the general increase in wealth and education and the rise of nationalist political parties. Once they were given the opportunity of playing an active part in local government, through elected councils, the educated and wealthy young men of the town challenged the autocracy of the oba, claiming to assume not only the statutory duties of local government but also, on occasion, the traditional duties of kingship. In this contest the oba was in the weaker position and has invariably lost. The loss of authority was paralleled by a reduction in income as the prerequisites attached to many duties were no longer received; the oba's wealth, relative to that of rich businessmen in his town, declined and his attempts to exploit new sources of income raised, as often as not, fresh complaints against his rule. The costs of maintaining the oba as a ceremonial figure-head seemed comparatively high and incompatible with the ever-growing demands for improved social services. Increasingly it is becoming acknowledged, not least by the more astute obas themselves, that the long-term future of Yoruba kingship is bleak.

II. THE KINGDOM OF IJEBU

(a) Structure

The legends of Ijebu describe how the present kingdom was founded by Obanta who came, it is alleged, from Ile-Ife (though a Benin origin seems more likely); he met crowned rulers in the area but these acknowledged his superiority and he established his own capital at Ijebu Ode. This was probably in the fourteenth century, the reigning Awujale at the time of the narrative below being the 51st in succession.[10]

Ijebu Ode is, today, a small town by Yoruba standards having a population of only 69,000. But the settlement pattern of the Ijebu kingdom differs from that of the northern Yoruba. Ijebu Ode is surrounded by a large number of small villages but these are autonomous units, each with its own chiefs and individually subordinate to the Awujale. Ijebu Ode has very little farmland within its own limits. Thus, whereas the vast majority of the inhabitants of the northern Yoruba town are farmers, the population of Ijebu Ode is engaged in urban occupations—19 per cent of the adult men are craftsmen, 28 per cent are traders, 5 per cent are professionals and 23 per cent are in a residual category including labourers, unemployed and retired; only 20 per cent are farmers (1952 Census). This has had an undoubted impact on the political life of the town.

The explanation of this difference is to be found in Ijebu social structure. The basic social unit here is the cognatic descent group, not the agnatic group found in the northern kingdoms. Thus a man is member of groups descended from as many ancestors as he can remember. Active participation in these groups is of course restricted by such factors as time and distance, and a man's primary allegiance will always be to the group in whose village or compound he lives. But a man can always exploit his relationship with other groups in order to gain certain advantages—better or more land, a title held by the group, the patronage of an influential member. Thus farmers will move from Ijebu Ode to the villages, traders and craftsmen in the reverse direction.

Ijebu Ode town is divided into three major sections and twenty-five wards. Each ward—a street, in fact—contains the compounds of one or more descent groups, the apical ancestor of the group being described as an immigrant to Ijebu Ode, usually in the early years of its history. Each group has its own shrine and a hereditary priest; these priests are in charge of cults concerning the whole town. The secular head of the ward is the *oloritun*—usually its oldest male inhabitant presuming that he has lived most of his life in the ward.

In the past every Ijebu belonged to an age-set; these were constituted at three-yearly periods among the adolescent youths. The age-sets formed a basis for the organization of public work and seem, too, to have one means of representation in the ward council.

The traditional political structure of Ijebu is highly complex; it has, furthermore, decayed to an extent unparalleled among Yoruba kingdoms. It is possible, today, to list the major offices but difficult to assess their roles and duties a century, for instance, ago. Contemporary explanations of the traditional role are likely to be expressed in terms of that sought by the aspiring incumbent.

The *ogboni* association, known in Ijebu as *osugbo*, was highly important. All free-born men were expected to join and one could rise through a series of grades to one of the six *iwarefa* titles of the highest rank; the Oliwo was the senior *iwarefa* and he was assisted by his messenger the Apena. The *osugbo* was the highest judicial tribunal of the kingdom. All other titled chiefs (and even the Awujale himself, though a representative) were members, though ineligible for titled office.[11]

Three chiefs, the Agbo, the Lapoekun and the Kakanfo were respectively in charge of the age-sets—collectively described as *ipampa*—in the three sections of Ijebu Ode.

Citizens of the Ijebu villages participated in the age-set and the *osugbo* but membership of the palace associations was *de facto* confined to residents of the capital. The most senior palace servants were the *odi* who were responsible for a number of rites, for the funeral of the Awujale and for presenting eligible candidates for the throne to the senior chiefs. The *ifore* association was open to free-born Ijebu; a man could join by indicating his wishes to the *odi*, paying the necessary fees and being installed by the Awujale; it was headed by the Olotuifore. The Ogbeni-Oja was selected alternately from among the *odi* and *ifore* members; this was a very high-ranking title in the political structure of the kingdom.

The most senior title holder in Ijebu Ode is the Olisa. This title is hereditary in one descent group. Its holder is said to rank as ruler of the town, in contrast with the Awujale who rules the entire kingdom. Junior to him is the Egbo whose title is similarly hereditary.

The Olisa and the Egbo, the Ogbeni Oja, the senior *ifore* chiefs, and the *opampa* chiefs traditionally constituted the *ilamuren*, the highest political association in the kingdom, the decisions of which were conveyed to the Awujale and issued as his commands. The multiplicity of the titles and the difficulty of ascribing modern roles to the various associations has led to all but the most senior titles becoming vacant in the present century. The senior title-holders were given salaried offices in Native Authorities and in the Native Courts; but the cost of taking a title (given the degree of affluence expected of a chief in Ijebu Ode) has deterred men from taking up those titles to which no salary is attached.

(b) Recent history[12]

The kingdom of Ijebu maintained its integrity, being relatively little affected by the massive displacement of people and subsequent wars caused by the collapse of Oyo. It was, during this century, in a most strategic position controlling one of the major routes from Lagos to Ibadan and the Yoruba interior. Ijebu could thus not only exact a profit from trade along this route but also, to some extent, control the flow of arms to Ibadan, at many periods her powerful enemy. The Ijebu maintained their monopoly by refusing to allow non-Ijebu traders to enter the kingdom (though Ijebu were active in Lagos and Ibadan). They gave a cool, and often hostile, reception to missionaries and consular officials. Thus the introduction of western education into Ijebu was delayed, although many of its citizens were senior officials in Lagos.

Exclusiveness, however, did not mean isolation. It is difficult to reconstruct the internal crises of the kingdom in the late nineteenth century, but they certainly existed. Awujale Fidipote fled from his capital to exile in Epe in 1885 and from this date the palace at Itoro seems to have fallen into ruins; subsequent Awujales reigned in their own houses. The traditional Ijebu political system does not seem to have provided an effective army and the Ijebu forces in the latter decades of the nineteenth century were led by Baloguns—men who were almost free-lance warriors, rising to pre-eminence through their ability and recruiting on the basis of their prestige and ability to supply their followers with guns and powder. If they acted independently of the Awujale and his chiefs the latter could exercise little restraint. At the turn of the century Balogun Kuku was clearly the most wealthy and powerful man in the capital.

Ijebu's exclusiveness resulted in a British military expedition against the kingdom in 1892; after a brief skirmish south of the capital a small force of soldiers entered the capital destroying the *osugbo* meeting house and remaining as a garrison for several years. The Ijebu however did not sulk in defeat. The speed with which they accepted Christianity embarrassed the missionaries; nevertheless Islam seems to have gained a strong foothold in the town at an earlier period so that of the present-day population of Ijebu Ode over two thirds are Muslim, one third are Christian (in the surrounding rural area however the proportion of Muslims and Christians is nearly identical). The Ijebu eagerly accepted education, too: the Grammar School was opened in 1913 for instance, and in 1954 on the eve of the introduction of free primary education, a higher proportion of Ijebu children were in school than in any other Yoruba area. Today the Ijebu occupy a relatively high proportion of senior posts in the public services and in teaching and are dominant in many spheres of commerce— all of which rouses the jealousy of other Yoruba ethnic groups.

In the first decade of this century the British administrative officers in Ijebu Ode seem to have been deeply involved in local administration, the consequence of the garrison being stationed in the centre of the town with the administrative officer's house next to it. At an early date a council was formed including non-chiefs; but later, a council of chiefs alone was constituted. The chiefs were given specific portfolios—of transport, forests and the like. Many of the British officers seem to have been highly autocratic, concerning themselves intimately with the administration of justice (punishing the Awujale if he heard cases privately in the palace) and with the cleanliness of the market. With the institution of the native authority system throughout Yoruba country in 1917 the methods of administration in Ijebu followed more closely the pattern evolving in other kingdoms.

In this period of rapid administrative change, the reigns of successive Awujales have not been without crises. In 1903 the Awujale and several of his chiefs fled to Ejinrin but they were reinstated by the administrative officer. The next Awujale was appointed in 1904 without any apparent dispute and he reigned until his death in 1915. It was then the turn of Tunwase ruling house to present candidates for the throne but its only eligible member, Adenuga, was still very young. An elderly man from another ruling house was recognized by the resident administrative officer but not by his superiors. He was deposed by his *odi* and a man of Tunwase house, though not possessing all the elements of eligibility was recognized by the local administrative officer. However in 1917 the first of these two rival rulers was reinstalled and he reigned until his death in 1925.

Adenuga then ascended the throne without apparent trouble. But within three years he was exiled. He was a young and educated man who, from all later accounts, was popular in the town both with his chiefs and with the mass of the people. A young letter-writer nicknamed Frugality apparently refused to undertake his share of communal labour and the Awujale and chiefs had him arrested on a charge of counterfeiting coins and gave him an excessively heavy sentence. This raised the suspicions of the administrative officers who, on investigation, held that the charge was framed against Frugality and exiled Adenuga to Ilorin.

The situation posed by Adenuga's exile led to claims by Tunwase house that they should provide a substitute ruler; counterclaims were, of course, made that the house had had its turn and it was now the turn of the next house in line. The possible candidates who were born to reigning Awujales were ineligible on other grounds and the chiefs agreed to waive the rule, selecting an elderly man, Ogunnaike. He was, of course, not able to carry out the full installation ceremonies since Adenuga was still living. The chiefs perhaps hoped that an elderly ruler would not encounter the same problems as the young Adenuga; but equally he was not likely to fulfil the British expectations of the role.

Ogunnaike reigned for less than four years and was succeeded in 1933 by Daniel Adesanya, the principal actor in the narrative which follows, one significant feature of which is the manner in which the allegedly traditional norms and values, so often flouted in practice, are yet still powerful weapons to use against one's adversaries.

III. THE REDEFINITION OF THE ROLE OF THE AWUJALE

Daniel Adesanya was in his mid-forties when he ascended the throne. He had been a tailor by occupation. He was also a church-warden of St. Saviour's, the leading Anglican Church in Ijebu Ode. Thus, though he had not completed his primary education, Adesanya occupied a prestigious position in the more westernized community in Ijebu. He is said to have been a relative and close friend of Dr. N. Olusoga, at that time Ijebu's member of the Legislative Council. As a tailor he is believed to have had a number of contracts for the government such as sewing uniforms for native authority employees. His eligibility for the throne was, however, marginal.

Gbelegbuwa house, to which Adesanya belonged through his mother, was considered "defunct"; that is, the children born on the throne of its last ruler (who reigned at the end of the eighteenth century) had long since died without acceding to the throne. But the lack of eligible candidates from the extant houses and the recent precedents in installing as Awujale a man not born on the throne led the members of Gbelegbuwa house to claim the right to present candidates for the throne. Adesanya was active in this petitioning and the claims of the house were recognized by Awujale Ogunnaike and his chiefs.

Thus when Ogunnaike died members of Gbelegbuwa house were anxious to establish their claims lest, in being overlooked, they became forgotten again. But the house was at first far from unanimous in the selection of candidates. Adesanya's membership through his mother was a severe handicap (at the time he was known as Daniel Otubusin—he assumed his mother's family name only upon selection for the throne). The other royal houses were reluctant to see a new competitor in the rotation but seem to have had no strong candidates themselves. There was very strong support for the reinstatement of Adenuga, especially from the Muslims in the town and the Ijebu in Lagos. The chiefs, *odi* and elders responsible in their various capacities for selecting the Awujale found it very difficult to come to a clear decision and were not unwilling to accept the choice of the British Administrative Officers to get them out of the impasse. The latter however insisted that "native law and custom" should be followed except where a departure was expressly desired by the chiefs. They were, too, reluctant to bring back Adenuga for in their eyes a criminal offence was an irremovable barrier to public office. The District Officer, in charge of the everyday administration of the town, minutes that the townspeople were strongly in favour of Adenuga and that Adesanya was both unpopular and of weak moral fibre. The Resident, in charge of the whole Province, ignored these comments in making his own reports to his superiors and strongly advocated the claims of Adesanya. Thus in August 1933 government recognition was given to Adesanya, eight months after the death of Ogunnaike.

A year later, as he was celebrating the first anniversary of his installation, one Yesufu Idumota shot the Awujale, causing him the loss of his right arm. Idumota protested that he had acted solely on his own initiative, arguing that he felt that Adesanya had no right to the throne, that the Resident had ignored petitions in favour of Adenuga and that Dr. Olusoga was also instrumental in supporting Adesanya and denigrating Adenuga. However the Olisa and the Egbo, together with the Native Authority Treasurer were, with others, tried in the Supreme Court for conspiracy to murder and by this court were found guilty. On appeal, it was held that the evidence of one woman witness was contradictory and they were acquitted. The two chiefs had both been installed in the reign of Ogunnaike; the Olisa had been a sanitary inspector and the Egbo was semi-literate. In the course of the trial allegations were made that the Awujale was trying to stop bribery in the courts, that he usually communicated directly with the Resident without informing the chiefs of the content or outcome of his discussions, and that the Awujale attempted to secure the support of his chiefs by paying their debts. The evidence was however very confused as the chiefs (both those charged and those who were witnesses) were not united—they had for instance supported different candidates for chieftaincies; they were competing for salaried posts in the Native Authority (some such appointments altering the traditional ranking of titles) and they were aggrieved by unfulfilled promises of reward for political support.

At the installation of the Awujale, the Governor of Nigeria, Sir Donald

Cameron, spoke at length of the role which he conceived for the oba in native administration; the same themes were later incorporated into a major policy document *The Principles of Native Administration and their Application*, published in July 1934.

He explained that under customary law the Awujale could not enforce his orders in any Nigerian court; but as "Native Authority of Ijebu Ode" he became a part of the colonial administrative structure. However, a policy of governing through chiefs failed if the chiefs were not educated in the new role; the Resident and District Officers would henceforth work closely with the oba though all orders would be issued through the latter. He concluded

> You, Awujale, must trust me when I say again, that I am doing all this to strengthen your position, so that the policy of ruling a people through their chief may continue and endure, gathering strength through the years to come. According as the Chief's administration gains strength in this manner, according as he is more able to stand by himself in administering his people in accord with civilized standards so will the measure of control by the Resident be withdrawn as it has been withdrawn in other parts of the British dependencies.[13]

Daniel Adesanya did, in fact, soon learn his new role. He converted the former District Office into a modern imposing palace (being reluctant, it was alleged, to live in any of the traditional buildings for fear that the supernatural powers residing in regalia would cause the death of an unconsecrated oba). The upper floor contained his private apartments, the ground floor his offices and audience chambers. Most of the Native Authority offices were sited either within the palace walls, or just outside its gates. The impression was thus given that the Awujale had close control over all activities. He would spend most of the morning in his office dealing with files sent from his own Native Authority departments and from the District Officer and Resident. He would greet his chiefs each morning but not spend long with them unless attending a formal meeting. Petitioners were encouraged to visit the Awujale in his office and he was expected to countersign a variety of permits and licences. Complaints against Native Authority officials were brought before the oba for settlement.

Since the Awujale was gazetted as the "Sole Native Authority" for Ijebu, all councils were purely advisory to him. In the early 1920s a small council, composed predominantly of traders and with a secondary school teacher as secretary, was set up in Ijebu Ode to advise the Awujale. At the divisional level the Awujale had been advised by the Judicial Council, comprising the four most senior subordinate rulers. In 1937 a Central Advisory Council for the Division was established with fifty-four chiefs and nine commoner councillors, the latter nominated by the Awujale. This council was reorganized in 1946 to contain sixty-three chiefs and seventy-one councillors. A later reform in 1951 changed the proportion to thirty-five chiefs and one hundred councillors. Ijebu Ode had too, its own District council for the town and surrounding villages. This consisted in 1945 of the Olisa as Chairman, twenty-one councillors, and representatives, totalling forty-four, of the chiefly associations, the *osugbo*, the age-sets, the *odi*, the royal houses, women and Hausa immigrants. This council was reformed in 1951 to include thirty-nine councillors and only twelve chiefs. The councillors were elected by acclamation in their wards; they were mostly traders and professionals and their standards of literacy were high—two of them lawyers.

With the rising levels of literacy and wealth among the Ijebu the autocracy of the Awujale as "Sole Native Authority" came under severe attack. He relinquished the designation only in 1949 and was in fact the last major Yoruba to do so. In a statement to the Divisional Advisory Council he claimed that he had never exercised his power in an autocratic manner. The Resident added that any change in the designation of the Native Authority did not alter the traditional prerogatives of the Awujale in respect of chieftaincies and land.

The Awujale's denials of autocracy were usually fully supported by the Residents in their reports to their superiors; but hostility among the Ijebu people ran high and one of the foremost campaigners for the relinquishing of Sole N. A. status was Mr. T. A. Odutola. In the mid-1940s action had been taken in the Supreme Court to have the Awujale's appointment nullified but this was lost.

One symbolic result of the recognition of the councils of chiefs and elected commoners as Native Authorities was the gradual transfer of offices from the palace environs to Itoro where they would enjoy greater freedom from interference by the Awujale.

Although the Awujale enjoyed, until 1949, and thereafter in diminishing degree, great power in his kingdom, he exercised it substantially in the traditional manner. He appeared little in public and then always with great dignity. At public council meetings he spoke rarely and then to summarize a decision rather than to make a substantive contribution. He won support not through public debate but through negotiations conducted by his palace servants and loyal chiefs. This is the mode traditionally expected of the oba; but in the modern context when the oba is the chief executive of his kingdom it quickly gives rise to allegations of intrigue, unfulfilled promises, blackmail, double-dealing and the like. A very skilful man could perhaps manipulate others in such a way as to avoid substantial criticism of himself. Daniel Adesanya seems to have been, at times, rather inept in his dealings with people.

The fact that a literate tailor, an office holder in the premier church of the town, could be selected as the Awujale was itself symptomatic of the social and economic change in Ijebu. The area was probably the wealthiest and most literate part of Yoruba country outside Lagos. Its wealth came not from peasant crops, for cocoa is grown only on the margins of the kingdom, but from the profits of trade and crafts pursued elsewhere in Nigeria. The Ijebu were among the most travelled of Nigerian peoples. In the early 1950s a higher proportion of Ijebu children were attending primary school than in any other administrative division of the country. Ijebu traders and clerks collectively, had a wide experience of conditions throughout Nigeria; individually they were active, and especially in Lagos, in the nascent nationalist political parties. These men retained their loyalties to the towns of their birth; they displayed this through the imposing two-storey residences which they built. Nor did they feel that the parish-pump politics of the home town were too trivial for their attention. It is thus not unnatural that the other important actor in our narrative in the early 1950s, Mr. T. A. Odutola, was a man who had attained the highest possible status in commerce and in colonial government.

Odutola's father had been a trader of very moderate wealth and came from a family of no great distinction. But the son attended the Ijebu Ode Grammar School reaching the highest class—then Class IV—in the mid-1920s. He first became a Native Court Clerk but then turned to cocoa-buying and lorry-owning, following his elder brother who was already becoming prosperous. Mr. T. A. Odutola was highly successful—as were many other Ijebu, most of whom were much less educated. He, however, turned to the establishment of modern enterprises, exploiting timber concessions in the Ijebu forests and setting up a tyre-retreading factory in Ibadan. In both enterprises he employed European managers. He became, in the post-war years, the richest Ijebu man and among the wealthiest among all Yoruba. His status in Ijebu was symbolized by his car number plate—J 2, the Awujale having J 1. He built a very large house of unusual design in the newly developing area on the edge of Ijebu Ode. He was active in town affairs and established his own secondary school which cost him a considerable annual sum to maintain. Equally, he was respected by the colonial administration and was appointed to the Legislative Council as representative of Ijebu and awarded the Order of the British Empire. In 1951 he stood for election to the Western Region house of Assembly as an NCNC candidate, this party seeming more popular in Ijebu Ode. He topped the poll but changed his allegiance to the Action Group when it was apparent that this party had not only won a majority of seats in the Region but also most Ijebu seats, due to the proliferation of NCNC candidates which caused all but Odutola to be unsuccessful.

Most Yoruba feel that a man cannot be a national leader unless he is also a leader in his home community; a man of education and wealth who chooses to ignore his home town will earn the disapproval of most. Odutola quite clearly sought political power in Ijebu Ode commensurate with his wealth and status in national affairs. His earlier lack of popularity is illustrated by a pre-prepared resolution carried at a public meeting at Itoro on February 5, 1951 under the auspices of the *oloritun* and the local branch of the Nigerian National Democratic Party. The charges raised, whatever their foundation, do illustrate the type of criticism made against men such as Odutola. He was said to have been lax in attending local council meetings and to have used his membership of them and of the Legislative Council to further his own ends. (Many councillors make their elective office their main occupation; chiefs are expected so to do; a successful entrepreneur will obviously have many other claims on his time.) He was alleged not to have championed the cause of the poor—he was instrumental in passing an N. A. rule that sawyers should deposit £50 before being issued with permits to fell trees, thus in effect reserving the timber trade to the richer men. (In fact, indiscriminate felling of trees was destroying the Ijebu forests.) He was said to have sought the title of Ogbeni Oja through non-traditional means; to have led a local agitation which divided the town into opposing camps, and then to have changed sides. (This charge probably referred to his championing the agitation for the Awujale to relinquish his Sole Native Authority status, and Odutola's subsequent support of the Awujale when, it is said, he was seeking timber concessions from him.) Odutola had allegedly failed to provide overseas scholarships to deserving Ijebu youths, and had not helped any of his own employees to success; he had acquired land from dishonest individuals rather than from the proper descent group heads and representatives, thereby causing litigation, and had supported the vendors financially. (A great number of land sales result in court actions.) The Yoruba are essentially an egalitarian people, and a meteoric rise from poverty to great wealth is often attributed to the use of supernatural means; it is further supposed that the costs of such practices include the barrenness of wives or the death of wives and children. Such calamities are therefore often attributed to the rapacity of the successful man. Such stories circulated about Odutola.

These allegations show the type of criticism that a wealthy man has to endure and which must be countered if he is to establish such a personal following as to merit, according to traditional values, the reward of high political office. In the event, Odutola was able to exploit the antagonism felt towards the Awujale in Ijebu Ode to the extent that he was regarded as the leader of the opposition to the oba. At the same time there were some popular causes which he could not fully support, since to do so would have caused severe conflict with his role as a leading member of the Action Group.

Four issues were paramount in Ijebu Ode in the early 1950s. The first was the salary of the Awujale. The power to depose an oba rested with the Colonial government (and was rarely exercised); but the salaries of obas and chiefs were decided by each Native Authority, and as educated councillors exercised greater control over the annual budget (instead of leaving it for the District Officer to prepare), they were inspired to use salary cuts as a form of punishment. But the fear existed that a cut once made could not later be restored, and that in reducing the salary of the Awujale they were jeopardizing the status of a future ruler who would, hopefully, be more popular. An attack on the kingship *per se* would have had almost no popular support. A second issue was the appointment to the vacant title of Olisa, the rival factions each supporting their own candidates. Thirdly, there was the reluctance of the *oloritun* to collect taxes on the grounds that their percentage of them was too small. Fourthly, there were several situations in which the integrity and honour of the Ijebu kingdom were questioned.

One looks almost in vain for well-defined pressure groups operating within Ijebu. This is partly because few individuals have specific personal interests in the issues listed above. The chiefs of Ijebu Ode were generally opposed to the Awujale during the period under review. In fact, only one appeared to be consistently loyal. He was literate and the head of a descent group owning a large area of valuable land on the edge of the town and presumably needed the support of the Awujale in his sales and leases of this land. He was hoping, too, that his title would be recognized as giving him overlordship of a number of Ijebu villages so that he might justifiably claim the presidency of the local native court. The remaining chiefs expressed the grievances usually cited by chiefs against their oba. Their salaries were low and the oba did nothing to raise them, preferring to tell the District Officer that increases were not justified. The oba received petitioners directly, thus depriving the chiefs of their perquisite, and he intrigued against and between his chiefs.

The *oloritun* or ward heads do not seem to have had any traditional collective organization. But in the late 1940s and early 1950s they were led by a semi-literate mallam, Ali, whose general political attitude was to be strongly pro-British and anti-affluent Nigerian politicians. He favoured the NCNC; he was violently critical of the Awujale. On a number of occasions he led the *oloritun*—elderly and usually illiterate men—in public demonstrations of protest. Their implicit grievances were that elected councillors were tending to supercede them as ward leaders—pressure was always being put on the councillors to give full reports to ward assemblies.

Political parties were not strongly organized in Ijebu Ode. The influence of Lagos was strong and many men retained allegiance to the National Nigerian Democratic Party formerly led by the late Herbert Macaulay; they were lukewarm in support of the NCNC alleging Ibo domination. At one time the local leader of the NNDP was a letter writer who explicitly used the party label in expressing local grievances. In 1951 he was lured by the Action Group into becoming their local paid organizer. Though prominent politicians of both major parties frequently visited Ijebu Ode, little formal organization was created and party allegiance was usually demonstrated by membership of one of the town's factions, the leader being identified with a party.

The study of Ijebu factions is, however, rendered extremely difficult by their ephemeral nature. One's impressions are that the relationships between the leader and his hierarchies of followers are predominantly ones representing immediate self-interest rather than more abiding relationships of close kinship or permanent interests. Thus although there were in Ijebu Ode two Muslims for every Christian, religious divisions seemed weak; the Awujale was a Christian—but his main opponents were both Christian and Muslim. As a consequence the membership of factions appeared to be highly fluid. An exacerbating factor seemed to be the practice of some leaders to lead their followers to the brink and then suddenly desert to the other side, thus claiming the full reward for loyalty from the erstwhile opponent and leaving their followers, bereft of a leader, to suffer the maximum punishments.

IV. IJEBU: 1952–4

Let us start our narrative of Ijebu events in the latter months of 1950. A year had passed since the Awujale had relinquished his status as Sole

Native Authority. In 1950 he was made a Commander of the Order of St. Michael and St. George, perhaps as a compensation for his loss of power. When he visited Ijebu Ode and addressed the Council, the Chief Commissioner of the Western Provinces, in congratulating the Awujale, observed that the honour was well deserved. The council minutes of January 17 report that the Chief Commissioner "was of the opinion that the final settlement and removal of political misunderstanding between the two great sections [i.e. the pro- and anti-Awujale factions] of the Ijebus was long overdue and he appealed to both sides to come together in the spirit of 'give and take' ".

There was, however, still a strong current of ill-feeling against the Awujale. The Divisional Council minutes for 25 October, 1950 record:

> The Awujale disclosed how he had been hearing rumour about bringing back his salary to £1,700 from £2,400. Nobody brought such things to his notice. He was however in sympathy with the suffering of poorly paid chiefs and to alleviate their suffering he was prepared to surrender voluntarily £700 out of his salary for that purpose. It should not be taken as a precedent that Awujales must bring down their salaries.

The Council resolved on 4 April, 1951 "that where a Town or Group council desires to maintain the *status quo ante* in respect of chief's salaries, the Council is prepared to accept the maintenance of the salaries in force, subject to a corresponding reduction in the social services for the area, but future successors to the stool shall conform rigidly to the formula prescribing one-eighth of tax revenue as salary for chiefs." This had been moved by two Action Group members of the House of Assembly but most speakers in the council had urged that no salaries should actually be reduced. The cut in the Awujale's salary was, in fact, short-lived; for in August 1951 the Council voted him £800 a year as "entertainment and ceremonial expenses".

The native authority system had increased the autocracy of the Yoruba obas, giving a most active role in administration to men like the Awujlae, educated ruler of a large kingdom. This role was increasingly resented by the educated traders, clerks and teachers who now constituted the elected element on the councils. They felt that duties performed by the Awujale should devolve upon them. As a general principle this would not generate much enthusiasm among the mass of the people who would certainly prefer the autocracy of the oba, constrained by the traditional values of kingship, to the petty despotism of minor bureaucrats. Nor were any individual incidents of sufficient importance or magnitude to arouse popular resentment.

In controlling the native authority estimates the educated councillors had one weapon with which to attack the Awujale—the control of his salary. But, as has been mentioned, in reducing the salary of the present Awujale they feared to create a precedent which would affect subsequent more popular rulers.

Thus it proved in practice extremely difficult to divorce the two roles of the Awujale—that of traditional oba and native authority—and to separate the individual from these roles. However, a new issue was to

arise—the appointment of a new Olisa—which was not only important
enough to arouse mass enthusiasm but also allied the literate councillors
with the masses. For the Awujale could be shown to be using his status as
native authority to flout traditional norms. For Odutola, this issue
presented an opportunity to assume the mantle of popular leadership.

In February 1951 Sonubi, the Olisa, resigned after holding office for
only four years. His stated reason was that the worship of "sticks and
stones" was repugnant to him as a Muslim; he said that he had hoped to
persuade his own *odi* to modify the customary rituals, but he had failed.
This sounded feeble to most Ijebu; why had the Olisa taken four years to
discover it? Some said that he had promised at his installation to carry out
all the necessary sacrifices. A petition from his own descent group asked
that he should reassume the title on the condition that the *odi* would
perform the sacrifices if the Olisa would pay for them. Sonubi had, it seems,
at times offended his own descent group by omitting certain rituals and by
wearing trousers instead of the wrapper obligatory for Ijebu chiefs. The
general consensus of opinion was that the Olisa could not afford to maintain himself. The salary of the former Olisa had been £350 but on Sonubi's
succession this was reduced to £200, and only later increased to £300. A
petition claimed that the Olisa incurred expenses at Christian, Muslim and
Yoruba ceremonies; costs of palm wine, rams, kola nuts, yams, etc. for
the various festivals amounted to £128 a year. His *odi* cost him £50 a year
and the official entertainment of visitors £30. His family cost him £250 and
he spent £100 a year to maintain a chiefly style of life—clothes, car, etc.
It was alleged that Sonubi had sold land vested in his title in order to avoid
debt.

The various branches of the descent group began to fight over the
right to present candidates. Members of Sonubi's own segment argued
that since he had not completed the installation ceremonies they should
be allowed to present a substitute; they feared that their segment might
be declared "defunct" and ineligible to present candidates on future
occasions. The other segments pressed their own claims. The choice of the
new Olisa was seen to rest, in the early part of this dispute, with the *odi*
of the Olisa and the Olawaberu, a priestly office holder. (In 1946 the
Egbo and Odutola had been the leading members of a commission of
inquiry which ruled in this manner.) The chosen candidate would then be
ratified and installed by the Awujale.

On October 19, 1951 the Divisional Native Authority council debated
the right of the Awujale to settle chieftaincy disputes. It was subsequently
resolved that "all chieftancy issues are matters within the surveillance of
the Awujale under Native Law and Custom and he is the only person
qualified to settle them".

At a meeting at Itoro in December 1950 before the Awujale and chiefs,
it was decided that the Jasan segment of the Olisa descent group should
provide candidates. Ten were originally proposed but most of these were
soon eliminated and the contest lay between Olusoga and Akinsanya.
Olusoga seems to have been the choice of the descent group and its head,
of the *odi*, of the *oloritun* and, initially, of the Awujale. Akinsanya became

T

the choice of Odutola and his faction. It is alleged that the candidate originally favoured by this faction was rejected by the Awujale; some say he was too outspoken and that the Awujale sought a more pliable chief.

The *odi* installed Olusoga in office in mid-1952 with the apparent connivance of the Awujale. The other chiefs of the Ijebu Ode immediately protested, saying that the new Olisa should be "a capable, efficient, intelligent and literate person". Akinsanya was the choice of the descent group and should therefore be recognized (thus contraverting the resolution of the Divisional Council cited above). In September Odutola moved a motion in the Ijebu Ode District Council to amend customary law.

The resolution proposed that candidates for the title of Olisa should be sponsored by unspecified members of the eligible family, but selected by the senior titled chiefs (by majority vote if necessary); the candidate so selected would be immediately approved by the Awujale without further discussion. The Native Authority Council would finally give its own approval.

Such a resolution was legitimate inasmuch as Native Authorities were empowered to propose amendments to customary law for ratification by the administrative officers. It went further than the intention of this rule, however, in giving the elected councillors a decisive voice in a chieftaincy dispute. The resolution was held by the Resident to be *ultra vires*. He is believed to have supported the candidature of Olusoga, and rumours in October that he was about to formally recognize him brought a renewed outburst of protests. In July the Awujale had said that he would reopen the issue, and in August that he supported Akinsanya, although most people seem to have felt that he continued in private to press the claims of Olusoga. It was felt that if the Awujale were to support unambiguously the candidature of Akinsanya, the administrative officers would accept this and give formal recognition. That they hesitated to do so was therefore evidence of the Awujale's perfidy. The Awujale was attacked in a public meeting at Itoro and the Ijebu Ode District Council called for a full enquiry into his administration. But this vehemence was not fully supported in the Divisional Council and the Administrative Officers took no positive action. Odutola therefore raised the issue in the District Council in the following February. He accused the Awujale of making money from chieftaincy issues and referred to a vote of no confidence in the Awujale, passed by the town council but apparently ignored by the colonial administration.

After some further discussion, a resolution was unanimously passed expressing concern at the attitude of the Regional Government and stating that "the Ijebu-Ode chiefs and people be advised . . . that they are entitled to taking up the matter with Daniel Adesanya Gbelegbuwa II the Awujale of Ijebu land in the way and manner in which like matters were being handled in Ijebu-Ode before the British advent".

In order to intensify the pressure against the Awujale a fresh attack on his salary was launched, the grounds on this occasion being different from hitherto. When Remo was excised from Ijebu Division in 1937 a sum of £400 was paid by the former as a contribution to the Awujale's salary in recognition of his continuing traditional sovereignty: when Remo ceased payment, the Ijebu Divisional Council carried the sum but at a meeting on November 14, 1952 Odutola moved its discontinuence. He failed to carry the Council with him—perhaps because of the Awujale's presence throughout the discussion and the vote by a show of hands. It seems that most of the proponents of the motion, though not all, were councillors from Ijebu Ode, and that the Awujale's support lay in the subordinate towns and villages (Ijebu Ode was represented on the Council by two chiefs and fifteen elected councillors). On the following day the Divisional Council urged a reconciliation between the Awujale and his opponents in Ijebu Ode rather than debate the Town Council's resolution to cease payment of its own share of the Awujale's salary.

Whilst tension was rising in Ijebu Ode over the delay in installing a new Olisa, other issues arose which attracted considerable popular interest. One of these was taken as another opportunity to attack the Awujale. A lengthy law suit between Ijebu and Ondo over their respective boundaries was concluded in Ijebu's favour with the award of two hundred guineas costs. As was usual in such land cases action was taken by the obas of each kingdom. The costs of the action were not met by Native Authority funds but were paid by the obas from their personal estate, specifically supplemented by public subscriptions. When the announcement of Ijebu's victory was made it was asked if the Awujale would pocket the two hundred guineas himself or refund it proportionally to subscribers. In the past obas had made no distinction between their private and public expenditure (the distinction was not in fact so recognized) and kept no formal accounts. As this issue indicates, obas were now expected to attract income in the traditional manner, by gifts and the like, whilst accounting for it in a modern manner.

When the results of the 1952 Census were published, citizens of Ijebu Ode were horrified to find that their town was smaller than Ijebu Igbo, one of the subordinate towns in the kingdom. A letter of protest to the District Officer elicited the response that he was satisfied that the census had been properly conducted. In the District Council Meeting on January 29, a number of chiefs and councillors protested that certain houses in their own wards had not been enumerated. Odutola said that he was not in town at the time so did not know whether his house was counted, but that he was sure that the count would not have been accurate. He moved that, if the Government was not prepared to undertake a re-count, the Council should print its own forms and carry out the task itself. It was finally agreed that renewed pressure should be put upon the government for a re-count. (This was not conducted.)

Finally, in early 1953 a levy, known rather unfortunately as the Capitation Tax, was introduced by the Western Region Government. This was a flat rate of 10 shillings imposed on all male taxpayers, intended to meet the costs of the increased social services provided by the government. The new tax was explained to the Town Council on February 3 by Odutola and there was little debate; it was argued that other towns in the Region had accepted the tax and Ijebu Ode should follow them. The Regional Premier,

Obafemi Awolowo addressed the Divisional Council at its meeting on February 21, and here too chiefs and councillors accepted the tax, both because they recognized its necessity and because most of them were Action Group supporters. The unpopularity of the tax developed later in the year with, as will be described below, the *olorituns* of Ijebu Ode refusing to collect tax and rioting among the people of Ago Iwoye, a large subordinate town in the kingdom. However, neither faction in the contest between the Awujale and Odutola sought to exploit this issue for its own ends.

The position of the Awujale was further weakened by the retirement of the Resident, Mr. W. Fowler, a man of the "old school" who felt strongly that the oba should be protected at all costs. His successor saw his task as the building of strong local government institutions and was loath to get involved in local intrigues as these were increasingly becoming national political issues.

In the early months of 1953 the Awujale was in an extremely weak position. The intensity of feeling over the appointment of the Olisa was such that the popular leaders were advocating the deposition of the Awujale in the traditional manner. Strictly construed, this constituted an invitation to take his own life, but rumours of assassination circulated wildly. The Awujale was portrayed by his opponents as using his powers, derived from his native authority status, to flout traditional law in refusing to accept a candidate properly selected by his family and the chiefs. Similarly, in his actions concerning the moneys due from Remo Division and the financing of the legal dispute with Ondo, the Awujale was portrayed as failing in his traditional role. To cap these issues, popular discontent was running at a high level with the introduction of the new taxes. Finally, the decreasing involvement of British administrative officers in local disputes and the immediate departure of the Resident, one of the "old guard", deprived the Awujale of one of his main supports.

Passions ran so high in the town that violence seemed not unlikely. Were this to have occurred the outcome would almost certainly have been a victory for the Odutola faction and defeat for the Awujale. Such a situation would furthermore have endangered the status of all obas, most of whom were, at this time, contesting power with the elected local government councils. Thus on March 13, a "peace mission" of Yoruba obas visited Ijebu Ode; its members were the Alafin of Oyo, the Oni of Ife, the Alake of Abeokuta, the Oba of Lagos and the Odemo of Ishara; all, with the exception of the Alafin, were well-educated men; all with the exception of the Oba of Lagos were prominent members of the Western Region House of Chiefs. The obas first met with the Ijebu chiefs in the Government Rest House and then went to the palace where they persuaded the Awujale to avert the threatening crisis by recognizing Akinsanya as the Olisa elect. The obas then took Akinsanya, together with his supporters, to the palace to pay homage to the Awujale. During the day's proceedings Odutola played a most prominent part in acting as host to the visiting obas. The British administrative officials took no part in the affair.

On the day of the "peace mission" excitement ran high in Ijebu Ode. A small detachment of Nigeria Police marched through the town with riot equipment as a warning against violence. Women in the market place chanted songs in abuse of the Awujale; one ran, "Ijebu is leaving you behind, Father who is fond of bribery" (*Ijebu de hin lehin re o, Baba onije kuje o*). Rumours were rife; it was said that Olusoga had spent £1,000 in his effort to win the title and that Odutola had spent £6,000, much of it at the time of the "peace mission" when he was ostentatiously generous in seeking support. It was alleged, too, that money had been guaranteed to defend any taxi driver who might cause the death of the Awujale in a motor accident should he leave the palace. But the day passed without major incident.

The appointment of Akinsanya as the Olisa was announced at the Divisional Council meeting in March and he carried out his traditional ceremonies of installation in the following month with a strong police presence in the town as a consequence of the rumours of an assassination attempt.

Many leading Ijebu citizens argued, at this juncture, that the campaign against the Awujale should cease. But others insisted that the issues raised earlier should also be prosecuted to a conclusion.

In the District Council Odutola successfully moved the withholding of the Awujale's £800 entertainment allowance. But when it was proposed that the Division Council should abrogate the "Remo" £400 the Awujale mobilized the support of chiefs and councillors from the subordinate towns and villages; they were absent from successive meetings and the Divisional Council was dissolved.

In the following months the Ijebu Ode chiefs continued to boycott the palace and the Awujale was not overtly active in public affairs. When he realized that the chiefs planned to boycott the Agemo festival—one of the major annual ceremonies held at Itoro—the Awujale invited all the expatriates to attend. This gave the occasion a certain grandeur in the eyes of the masses; but the expatriates were not in a position to give the Awujale any effective support—they attended largely out of a sense of duty and were visibly annoyed when the traditional rituals were delayed and they were kept from their own ritual of the Saturday curry lunch. Later in the year the Awujale celebrated the twentieth anniversary of his installation by giving a small cocktail party for the resident British officials; in other circumstances the oba would have used such an occasion for lavish public entertainment.

In his position of weakness the Awujale was unable to exploit some issues which might have brought him popularity. In 1953 the Action Group was advocating the incorporation of Lagos into the Western Region; the NCNC argued that it should be a Federal capital territory. A corollary of the latter arrangement might have been the transfer of Ikorodu and Epe, Ijebu towns in Colony Province, to Ijebu Province. NCNC supporters in Ijebu Ode urged the Awujale to campaign for the restoration of the integrity of Ijebu land. But he refused to take a position publicly, saying that he owed his allegiance to the Action Group.

Though he seems to have tacitly supported the Action Group on this issue and refused to seek popular support, Odutola was not always a completely loyal member of the party. The Action Group decreed that

Coronation Day 1953 should be a "day of mourning" in protest against the slowness of constitutional changes leading to independence. But most Yoruba towns organized lavish ceremonies to mark the occasion and Odutola was one of the leading actors in those held in Ijebu Ode.

In November a new issue arose which, once again, showed the Awujale to be incapable of maintaining the traditional status of his office. A Provisional Divisional Council was constituted, to replace that which had become defunct through its failure to reach a quorum; this council was thought by many to have been selected by the Awujale himself. By virtue of his status as the traditional ruler of the Ijebu kingdom the Awujale had always presided over meetings of any Divisional Council. But at the first meeting of this Provisional Council, Odutola moved that a chairman be selected by secret ballot—a method of voting not usually practised at such meetings.

The Awujale stood as a candidate against the Orimolusi of Ijebu Igbo and the Dagburewe of Idowa—both subordinate crowned obas. The Orimolusi won easily and the defeat of the Awujale was interpreted in Ijebu Ode as a slight to the capital. The Orimolusi acted with great tact and efficiency; he shared his office with other subordinate obas and ostensibly fought for the provision of electricity in Ijebu Ode. He was held, throughout Ijebu, as a popular oba who maintained the traditional dignity of the kingship.

The attacks on the Awujale continued. There were persistent rumours in Ijebu Ode at this time that the Awujale was being pressed by his opponents to sign a document in which he promised to limit the exercise of his powers. (Such a document was signed under pressure by the Alafin in 1954.)[14] The demands being made of the Awujale included the following: that he should not give out crowns without the consent of the Divisional Council; that he should not appoint new chiefs without the concurrence of existing chiefs; that he should not sign land leases or gun licenses, that he should maintain a strict account of all moneys received, that he should not interfere with court judgements and that he should not communicate with the Resident or the District Officer without the consent of the Council. Early in 1954 he fell ill and went to Lagos suddenly for treatment. The Divisional Council members claimed that it was contrary to custom for an oba to leave his town (at least without due notice); they resolved that his salary should be suspended completely. This time the Regional Government stepped in and ordered its restoration; for it was reluctant to see local government councils exercising such a controlling power over the obas and the Awujale had proved himself a loyal Action Grouper.

In March 1954 it was rumoured that Odutola was about to be installed as Ogbeni Oja. The significance and duties of the office had virtually been forgotten in Ijebu Ode during the fifty years that it has been vacant. But the supporters of Odutola were ready to reconstruct the role. It was said that the Olisa had, in the past, remained largely confined to his official residence, in the manner of an oba, and that the Ogbeni Oja had been the effective leader of the *ilamuren* furthermore upon the death of the Awujale the Ogbeni Oja acted as Regent. Against Odutola it was said that he sought a chieftaincy title to enable him to sit in the House of Chiefs whereupon he would seek to dominate this august body. This title would have almost certainly given its holder membership of the highest local government councils and customary courts and its bestowal upon Odutola was resented by other wealthy men whose titles gave them prestige but not this effective power. However, with due ceremony Odutola assumed the title.

At this point we must break off our narrative of events in Ijebu Ode. The contests for power of course continued. In 1959 the Awujale died; he was succeeded in the following year by Sikiru Adetona. He came from the ruling house whose turn it was to occupy the throne; but the four eligible candidates, being born to a reigning ruler, were elderly illiterate men. Adetona was a son of one of these. He had completed his secondary education in Ijebu Ode and was in England studying accountancy when called to assume office.

Odutola continued to take an active part in local politics. A new Divisional Council was elected in 1955 under the provisions of the 1952 Local Government Law. The elections were fought on party lines and the Action Group was a majority of seats. The Action Group councillors came to the inaugural meeting with a printed list of members to be elected to various offices and committees together with the proposers and seconders of motions. Odutola was duly elected chairman; he was furthermore described as the leader of the party and it was arranged that all "parliamentary members" should meet in his house on the day before each Council meeting to arrange business. The meetings of the Council were conducted with an exaggerated parliamentary formality.

But Odutola's pre-eminence was later to be challenged by the Olisa and the new Awujale. In their first months in office both these men acted with caution and acknowledged the support given to them in contesting their title. Once in office, however, they began to assert themselves and to strive to protect their own status from loss of power, wealth or prestige.

V. CONCLUSION

In few Yoruba towns has the bitterness and violence of the conflicts in Ijebu Ode been matched. In this narrative I have centred the description upon the manoeuvres in the Native Authority Councils. However, throughout the period, the Ijebu themselves saw the contest as being fought not only by these constitutional means but equally by medicines and the supernatural. To detail many of the rumours which circulated would probably be libellous to those concerned; to deny completely their veracity would be distorting. Most Ijebu substantially believed these rumours of intrigue, corruption, and plots of murder and based their own actions upon them—and that is what is most important.

The Ijebu story has nevertheless much in common with events in other Yoruba towns. The major conflicts of interest, for instance, are the same, lying between the oba and his chiefs, the oba and the wealthy and literate men of his town. Similar too, are the conflicts between the capital and its subordinate towns and villages; new councils gave the latter a share of seats proportionate to their populations, thus terminating the dominance of the chiefs and leading citizens of the capital; the gap in the provision of social services was narrowed too, so that citizens of the capital argued that they were being left behind.

The situations in which these conflicts were resolved were provided by the transformation of the Native Authority System, in which chiefs had predominated, into a local government structure with elected councillors outnumbering the chiefs by three to one. A major issue here lay in deciding which of an oba's duties should pass to the new statutory bodies and which he should continue to exercise as traditional ruler.

Those seeking to wrest power from the obas frequently tried to redefine the traditional role in modern terms. Thus it was argued, with a little justification, that the oba had always been a constitutional monarch; they then ascribed to the present incumbent the role of a contemporary British monarch. Some elements were new, however—for instance, the argument that the Awujale should keep a record of all money received. When it came to attacking the oba, the criticisms tended to be formulated according to traditional values. The oba should entertain munificently all distinguished visitors to his town (the supply of tribute being ample for this); the Awujale failed inasmuch as he had to call for specific contributions from his chiefs even though his own salary was so much greater. The oba is responsible for the prosperity of his town; the Awujale failed inasmuch as electricity did not come to the town. The oba should ensure peace in his town and settle disputes; the Awujale failed inasmuch as the Nigeria Police were brought into the town to maintain order.

During the period considered here the Awujale appeared to play a largely passive role, attempting to maintain his salary and power but not creating any new role. In part this was due to his personality. But other obas, much more astute and better educated, fared no better in finding a new role though they did avoid crises such as those beset the Awujale. The opponents of the Awujale, for their part, were no more specific in outlining the role which they thought proper for their oba. They attacked him on specific issues, in a large measure to further their own goals, which were but indirectly related to the status of the oba. A persistent theme was the desire to punish and hurt Adesanya without seriously affecting the status of kingship. (And those who were less concerned to maintain the kingship would certainly not have made a public issue of it.) The kingship emphasized the ethnic identity of the Ijebu (as for other Yoruba groups), and the importance of its capital vis-à-vis similar towns. Though the chiefs opposed their oba it is difficult to see their offices being maintained in the absence of kingship.

The slow demise of Yoruba kingship is thus not due to any broadly-conceived policy by one or more interest groups capable of ensuring its acceptance: rather, it is the unintended outcome in the resolution of a series of conflicts of interest and incompatibility of roles; the alleged traditional status of the oba is still stressed.

NOTES

1   See P. C. Lloyd, *Yoruba Land Law* (London: Oxford University Press, 1962); and P. C. Lloyd, "The Yoruba", in J. L. Gibbs (ed.), *Peoples of Africa* (New York: Holt Rinehart and Winston, 1965).

2   Political developments in Nigeria are described in James S. Coleman, *Nigeria: Background to Nationalism* (Berkeley and Los Angeles: University of California Press, 1958); and Richard K. Sklar, *Nigerian Political Parties* (Princeton; Princeton University Press, 1963).

3   See E. Baillaud, *La Politique indigène de l'Angleterre en Afrique occidentale* (1912); and M. Perham, *Native Administration in Nigeria* (1937).

4   Sir Bernard Bourdillon, "The Future of Native Authorities", *Africa*, XV, 1945, pp. 123–128.

5   P. C. Lloyd, "The Development of Political Parties in Western Nigeria", *American Political Science Review*, XLIX, 1955, pp. 693–707; and P. C. Lloyd, "Traditional Rulers", in J. S. Coleman and C. Rosberg (eds.), *Political Parties and National Integration in Tropical Africa* (Berkeley and Los Angeles: California University Press, 1964).

6   R. E. Bradbury, "Continuities and Discontinuities in Pre-Colonial and Colonial Benin Politics 1897–1951", in I. M. Lewis (ed.), *History and Social Anthropology* (London: Tavistock Publications, 1968).

7   P. C. Lloyd, "Agnatic and Cognatic descent among the Yoruba", *Man (n.s.)*, Vol. No. 4, 1966, pp. 484–500.

8   P. C. Lloyd, "The Political Structure of African Kingdoms: an Exploratory model", in M. Banton (ed.), *Political Systems and the Distribution of Power* (London: Tavistock Publications, 1965).

9   P. C. Lloyd, "Conflict Theory and Yoruba Kingdoms", in I. M. Lewis (ed.), *History and Social Anthropology* (London: Tavistock Publications, 1968); P. C. Lloyd, *The Political Development of Yoruba Kingdoms in the Nineteenth Century* (London: Royal Anthropological Institute, 1970).

10   P. C. Lloyd, *Yoruba Land Law*, Ch. 6.

11   In the neighbouring small Egba kingdoms the *ogboni* had been the principal political associations; at its meetings the decisions of government were taken. This was not so in the Ijebu capital where decision making rested with the oba and the *i'amuren* chiefs. But the *osugbo* could perhaps be seen as representing popular opinion against the palace; cf. P. Morton-Williams, "The Yoruba Ogboni cult in Oyo", *Africa* XXX, 1960, pp, 362–374.

12   For Yoruba history in the nineteenth century see J. F. Ajayi, *Christian Missions in Nigeria 1841–1891* (London: Longmans, 1965); and E. A. Ayandele, *The Missionary Impact on Modern Nigeria 1842–1914* (London: Longmans, 1966). For Ijebu in the twentieth century see E. A. Ayandele, "The Changing Position of the Awujales of Ijebuland under Colonial Rule", in M. Crowder and O. Ikime (eds.), *West African Chiefs: Their Changing Status under Colonial Rule and Independence* (Ile Ife, Nigeria: University of Ife Press, 1970).

13   *Nigeria Gazette*, Vol. 68, No. 20, 1933.

14   Published in the *Nigerian Tribune*, 10 December 1954; see also "A Crown Falls", *West Africa*, 2000, 25 June, 1955.

CONCLUSION

MONARCHICAL RESPONSES TO SOCIAL CHANGE:
A Spectrum of Strategies

Our aim in this volume has been to assess the conditions which in recent times have affected the viability of African kingships, and, given these conditions, to evaluate the part played by individual monarchs in regulating the processes of change initiated under the aegis of colonial rule. In this concluding chapter the emphasis is on the second of these dimensions. Drawing upon the empirical evidence presented in the preceding essays an attempt is made to identify the nature and range of strategies employed by African rulers to ensure their own political survival in the midst of a rapidly changing social and political environment.

When one emphasizes the element of choice involved in these strategies one does not mean to imply that African rulers were everywhere and at all times faced with a fixed range of alternatives. If, as J. H. Plumb contends, "stability becomes actual through the actions and decisions of men, as does revolution",[1] there are limits to how far such actions and decisions can actually influence the course of events. In the case of the polities discussed in this book, these limits were in part set by the capacity of monarchical institutions to meet the changing needs of society and in part by the structure of society itself. To return to the typology outlined in the Introduction, one might say that the more "monopolistic" the institutional framework of monarchical rule, and the more "open" the social structure, the greater the area of choice available to the incumbent.[2]

But one needs to take into account more than just institutional or societal variables. The success or failure of monarchical strategies has often been conditioned by chance occurrences over which political actors had relatively little control. Whether attributable to a caprice of fortune, the vicissitudes of life, or the vagaries of political succession, these occurrences have had a direct bearing on the destiny of some monarchies.[3] Similar uncertainties have arisen from the imponderables of colonial rule—from the variable dispositions of colonial civil servants, the unpredictability of their responses to monarchical demands, or the unintended consequences of specific administrative decisions. Difficult though it may be to generalize about the effect of these contingencies on the destinies of African monarchs, that they did entail significant advantages or liabilities is undeniable. Scarcely more predictable were the effects of the constitutional moves which accompanied the termination of colonial rule. Their impact on the range of options available to African monarchs emerges with striking clarity from the recent histories of Buganda and Ankole: the according to Buganda by the British Protectorate of a semi-federal status which was denied to Ankole certainly contributed to encourage the former's separatist leanings, and did much to discourage the latter's propensities in this direction.

For all these reasons the term "strategy" may suggest a wider range of alternatives, as well as more rationality in the selection of these alternatives, than seems justified in the context of this discussion. Nonetheless, in attacking problems of political emancipation and survival, of political modernization and institutionalization, most African monarchs have been faced with a strategic choice among several possible courses of action: a choice among prospective allies on which came to depend the identity of their future enemies, a choice between the short-run advantages of political expediency and the longer-run costs of political inefficiency, and between the requirements of political survival and the exigencies of political modernization.

For purposes of analysis a distinction must be drawn at the outset between the conditions of terminal colonialism and the exigencies of the post-independence period. During the first of these phases the strategies available to African monarchs were conditioned by the nature of their relationship with the emergent forces of nationalism: with the attainment of independence, the critical issue was no longer how best to exploit the resources of nationalism but rather how to maintain themselves in power—or simply in office—in the face of increasing demands for social, economic and political modernization. Their chances of success in achieving the second of these objectives often depended on the choices they made to attain the first. The broader the range of interests associated with the throne in the period of terminal colonialism, the more diversified the strategies of survival available in the period following independence.

STRATEGIES OF EMANCIPATION

Neither the involvement of African kingships in nationalist politics, nor the choices forced upon them through such involvement, can be properly assessed unless one tries to clarify the relationship of the throne to its supporters, actual or presumptive. Where the power of the throne had already suffered a major erosion (as in Ankole), or where the sheer exiguousness of its territorial jurisdiction ruled out the possibility of a lasting coalescence between nationalist and monarchical loyalties (as in Ijebu Ode), relatively little effort was made by the incumbent to draw political advantage from the circumstances of the ending of colonialism. Instead of nationalism serving as a major prop of an efficient monarchy, the relationship was rather the opposite: the symbols of the monarchy as well as the image it evoked in the minds of the masses were consciously manipulated by nationalist politicians to further their immediate political objectives.

No matter how threadbare the power of the throne, the mere presence of a monarchical order has often been instrumental in the creation of a supporting environment for the claims of reformist or nationalist politicians. Thus, while casting occasional aspersions on the obaship, Awolowo was far too conscious of its symbolic significance in the eyes of the Yoruba masses to advocate its suppression. Similarly, however distasteful the idea of ruling monarchy might have been to Rwagasore, and for all his "populist" inclinations, the outward veneration he showed towards the symbols of kingship goes far in explaining his short-lived apotheosis as the chief spokesman of Burundi nationalism. Or consider the case of Lesotho: in a vein reminiscent of Coillard's views on "kingly socialism",[4] the leaders of the Pan-Africanist oriented Congress Party apparently saw in Moshoeshoe's rule the prefiguration of certain major tenets of African Socialism. In the official imagery of the BCP leadership, writes Weisfelder, Moshoeshoe emerged as "a dynamic, innovative leader whose forging of a voluntary union of African people to thwart alien rule might serve as a prototype for contemporary black liberation struggles against foreign domination and white racism". Although the theme of monarchical legitimacy has evidently lent itself to many variations,[5] in each of these instances the embedded meanings of kingship were deliberately seized upon by the nationalist elites to enhance their own political stature.

Elsewhere, however, and most notably in Buganda, Rwanda and Swaziland, nodules of power had persisted around the throne which, in the hands of an energetic ruler, could play a determining role in shaping the orientation of nationalist sentiment and activity. In their attempt to subordinate the forces of nationalism to the throne the choice faced by African monarchs was essentially twofold: They could prosecute a policy of "divide and rule" aiming at the creation of competing factions within the nationalist movement, and thus cast themselves in the role of "honest brokers"; or they could openly identify themselves with the goals of secular nationalism, and in so doing assert the supremacy of the Crown as a symbol of nationalist legitimacy. In one case the capacity of the monarchy to aggregate power was conditioned by its ability to maintain or encourage intergroup rivalries and elite segmentation, and in the other by its ability to mobilize the solid loyalties of all nationalist elements behind the throne.

The first of these strategies is nowhere better illustrated than in Morocco. Only by consciously encouraging the emergence of rival organizations to the Istiqlal could Mohammed V, and later on Hassan II, cast himself in the role of the "charismatic trimmer". Only then could Mohammed V claim "the function of honest broker among the groups he had encouraged (Mouvement Populaire) or disparaged (Istiqlal) without being identified with or indebted to any of them".[6] As the case of Burundi also demonstrates, the political fragmentation achieved by the monarchy may be the precondition of its own political survival. In contrast with this policy of *divide et impera*, the history of Buganda prior to independence is reducible to a rapid consolidation of nationalist forces in defence of the throne, with the latter emerging as a prime symbol of cultural unity and organizational solidarity. "The language of kingship", in A. I. Richards' words, "with its rich emotive values, was the basis for the call for unity by the *Kabaka Yekka* leaders. The queen ant (*Namunswa*) protects the termite

hill against attack. In these circumstances adherence to any political party
except the *Kabaka Yekka* came to seem an act of treason, not only because
it might stand for a different policy but because it divided the country at a
time of danger."[7] The link between populism and monarchism, crystallized
by the deportation of the Kabaka, was not "a simple manipulative relationship directed from the top"; as Young goes on to note, "it was a two-
way channel, with the Kabaka compelled to lead by following populist
pressures".

Different strategies called for different tactics. To discharge successfully
their arbitral functions, African monarchs had to meet certain minimum
requirements, namely to check effectively the tendencies to hegemony of
any single political group; to ensure the survival of as many political
contenders as seemed compatible with the maintenance of monarchical
arbitration; and to avoid too close an identification with any of the several
aspiring factions, so as to enable the Crown to hedge its bet, and thus
facilitate its disengagement from the embrace of any of its supporters when
the circumstances required.

Where monarchical strategies aimed at pre-empting the force of secular
nationalism, the tactical requirements were essentially two-fold: to
promote an emotional commitment to the symbols of the monarchy, and
to draw maximum advantage from the resources of nationalism in order
to legitimize the perpetuation or aggrandizement of monarchical power.
In Buganda, as Young's discussion makes clear, these conditions were
ideally met by the nature of the Kabakaship. Just as in the traditional
society "all roads led to the royal court", the ideology of the final struggle
against colonialism "provided a framework for the consolidation of royal
power and its legitimation in the most impeccably modern terms: democracy and representative government in the Buganda of the dying days of
the Protectorate simply operated to provide the Kabaka with a
parliament of King's men duly anointed by the electoral process". As a
further prop to the Crown, the latent resources of populism were quickly
seized upon by the throne and channelled into its political arsenal, to be
used, if need be, as a counterweight to the more progressively-oriented
Ganda nationalists.

In contrast with Buganda, where the political setting was admirably
suited to the revitalization of the Kabakaship and thus minimized the
importance of tactical considerations, in Swaziland the operational skills
of the Nggwenyama (King) played a far more decisive role in reactivating
the powers of the throne. As in Buganda, the symbolic meanings attached
to the kingship were certainly instrumental in giving the *Imbokodvo* an
aura of legitimacy unmatched by its competitors. But as Potholm's
analysis shows, this alone may not have sufficed to tip the scales on the
side of the monarchy. Equally important was the electoral strategy devised
by the *Imbokodvo* leadership, in close cooperation with the throne, aiming
on the one hand at maximizing its electoral support through the "placement" of safe candidates (for the most part related to the royal family)
in key constituencies, and, on the other hand, at drawing maximum
advantage from its temporary alliance with the European-dominated

United Swaziland Association (USA). Much of the credit for the spectacular renaissance of the Swazi monarchy in the years preceding independence goes to the Ngwenyama himself. Seldom anywhere has the fate of a monarchy been so overwhelmingly dependent upon the tactical skills of the monarch himself.

In the absence of an appropriate setting monarchical symbols are of relatively little help to build an emotional consensus behind the throne. Such a consensus is unlikely to occur unless the stimulus of nationalism operates in a sufficiently homogeneous cultural environment. In a political climate saturated with ethnic tension, the chances are that the monarchy will become the first casualty of ethnic conflict: besides being denied the opportunity to exploit fully the ideological resources of nationalism, there is also the possibility that the symbolic resources of the monarchy will be exploited by its opponents to accelerate its demise (as happened in Rwanda).

Just as nationalism in many instances created the predisposing circumstances that helped foster sentiments of devotion to the throne, the advent of independence greatly lessened the "stock" of ideological and symbolic resources available to African monarchs. As the stimulus of nationalism declined, so did the charismatic qualities attributed to the monarch. The circumstances of post-independence politics increasingly forced African monarchs in the position of "transactional leaders", seeking to devise a new kind of legitimacy for themselves: Faith in the monarch's ability to deliver the goods, rather than faith in his capacity to achieve deliverance, became the essential ingredient of monarchical legitimacy.

STRATEGIES OF SURVIVAL

In most cases the ideological consensus built around the throne in the heyday of the nationalist crusade proved extremely short-lived. Because of the heightening of expectations that followed in the wake of independence, a growing imbalance has developed between the supply of, and demand for, political resources. As political inflation gathered momentum, monarchical symbols proved increasingly inadequate to maintain existing political exchange standards. In these conditions African monarchs could either seek to salvage what little symbolic prestige they still claimed by relinquishing the substance of power, or they could insist on retaining or accumulating power—but at the risk of being overthrown by the very forces they sought to contain.[8]

In the spectrum of strategies resorted to by traditional African rulers to preserve or enlarge their bases of power at least four deserve mention; though employed with varying degrees of success by different rulers they nonetheless illustrate the nature of processes involved in the search for personal power.

(a) *Building up the Royal Image.* In their attempt to strengthen the legitimacy of their office African rulers have everywhere sought to generate feelings of devotion to their person. They tried to convey a vision of themselves as both "sacred and good", so as to focus upon their person the symbolic reference world of the "exemplary centre".[9] Typical of the attitudes fostered through this kind of imagery is the Ethiopian view that "the big men around the court are no good; only the Emperor is for us".[10] In this type of environment the language of kingship takes on compelling connotations. Political opposition to the Crown can easily be identified with disloyalty to the monarch, and dealt with on grounds of heresy.

The role played by monarchical symbols in shaping popular perceptions of the royal image emerges with striking clarity from the various case studies contained in this book. The impression one gets is that monarchical symbols served, in Lasswell's words, "as 'key signs', providing a unifying experience, (and) fostering sentiments that transcend the limitations of culture, class, organization and personality".[11] What many of these studies also demonstrate is that the process is by no means automatic. Monarchical symbols alone do not suffice to project this kind of transcendent image; the latter has to be affirmed and fashioned by the incumbent himself.

A variety of manipulative techniques entered into the art of making the royal image. One of these concerns the redefinition of traditional leadership styles through the appropriation of unallocated symbolic resources—a phenomenon perhaps best illustrated by Young's discussion of the manner in which elements of the traditional Ganda religion (lubaale) were inserted into the symbolic matrix of the Kabakaship, in 1962. The Kabaka, according to Young, "wound up achieving what had eluded his precolonial predecessors: the full absorption of the lubaale into the matrix of supports for the monarchy". Although the result was evidently different in the case of Rwanda, a somewhat similar process of symbolic redefinition can be detected in the eleventh hour attempt made by Mutara Rudahigwa to emphasize the "myths of unity and equality" of the Rwanda monarchy, and at the same time minimize the diffusion of the "myths of inequality". Alternatively, the traditional reference world that once gave symbolic expression to monarchical legitimacy may also be used to legitimize new political practices. Or else a new set of legitimizing symbols may be added to the traditional panoply of African kingships.

As symbol manipulators, African monarchs tried to draw maximum advantage from the expressive resources of their respective cultures. But their success at manipulating symbols has tended to depend to a considerable extent on their ability to control and coordinate both traditional and modern channels of communication. Haile Selassie of Ethiopia has been notoriously successful in enlisting the support of modern networks of communication to turn the spotlight on the religious and secular aspects of his leadership and to make maximum use of the opportunities offered through traditional channels. According to Clapham, "the channels of communication leading to the Palace are not restricted, fixed, institutional, but on the contrary multiple, fluid and personalized. This gives Haile Selassie scope for the manipulation and manoeuvre at which he excels, maximizing the information and range of choices open to him". Clapham's terse characterization of the game of politics in Ethiopia applies equally well to Burundi until 1965: "If all goes well the Emperor claims the credit; if not, others take the blame."

Where modern media of communication tended to evade the control of the palace, the synchronizing of traditional and modern networks of communication was made all the more problematic—a situation nowhere better illustrated than in Rwanda. Not only was the image of the Mwami conveyed through the Hutu-controlled press evidently at variance with his own conception of the Mwamiship; but the contradictory messages emanating from the ranks of the Tutsi stratum (reflecting in large part a cleavage between the Western-educated and traditional elites) added yet another element of confusion in the content of political communications attributed to the monarchy. The inability of the throne to control effectively traditional channels of communication turned out to be as much of a handicap for the Rwanda monarchy as its inability to gag the propaganda apparatus of its opponents.

The building-up of an effective image also requires the maintenance of popular beliefs about the capacity of the incumbent to perform well. Achievement criteria based on performance and success were by no means inevitably absent from the matrix of supports of traditional kingships. With the emasculation of traditional symbols, however, performance and success assume an increasingly high order of priority as a source of legitimation. No matter how much reassurance the rural masses may find in the traditional idiom of kingship, the urban intelligentsia are more likely to be drawn to the throne by clientelistic rewards than by purely symbolic ones.

(b) *The Uses of Political Clientelism.* Defined as an exchange relationship between actors commanding different resources (rather than as a special case of dyadic ties involving a lopsided friendship), political clientelism has been part and parcel of the political arsenal of African kingships since time immemorial.[12] Where the relationship tends to take on a novel quality is in the kind of resources through which African rulers have in recent times sought to enlarge or consolidate their following. Rather than through the mere extension of protective guarantees to their clients, African kings have increasingly sought to use their monopoly of modern bureaucratic and economic resources to solidify the loyalties of their supporters and adulterate the animosities of their opponents. Public office in these conditions becomes a major source of patronage. Furthermore, patronage "may go towards personal acquisitions (real estate, import licenses, commercial licenses, non-competitive contract bidding), or may trickle down the arteries of patron-clientele alliances".[13]

In this setting patronage is not merely intended to disarm the opposition through material and psychic rewards, but also to foster enough competition within the ranks of the bureaucracy to justify the intervention of the Crown. It is at this level that the resurgence of traditional techniques of manipulation manifests itself most clearly. Traditionally, as Bradbury reminds us, "the oba's capacity to exercize personal power depended on his ability to maintain a balance of power between competing groups and individuals within the political elite, and his success in keeping open multiple channels of communication with other sectors of the population".[14] These techniques are still very much part of the political game in Swaziland,

U

Morocco and Ethiopia. By resorting to "pre-emptive" and "strategic" appointments, as one observer had recently noted, Hassan has been able both to "deaden the criticisms of the opposition from which the appointee came" and at the same time increase the leverage of the Crown.[15] In Ethiopia, in Clapham's words, "the Emperor . . . stands at the centre of a web of competing intelligence networks, each of which is concerned to maximize the information flow which it controls. Conflict situations are thus deliberately fostered as a centralizing instrument—a technique which requires very delicate handling".

These techniques alone are no guarantee that political clientelism will serve its intended purpose. The evidence from Ethiopia points to the crucial role played by attitudinal predispositions in ensuring the success of clientelistic strategies: the client-patron nexus is very strongly anchored in the cultural matrix of the monarchy, thus providing a basis of legitimacy for processes of exchange between the throne and its clients; but attitudes alone may not suffice to ensure the perpetuation of a clientelistic monarchy. Of at least equal importance is the volume of resources available to the throne to meet the expectations of its potential clients. Yet a third variable concerns the nature of the recipients: Where clientelism merely tends to perpetuate the privileged position of an entrenched oligarchy, as seems to be the case in both Swaziland and Ethiopia, the rewards accorded by the royal patron to his wards may serve as the chief motive for his overthrow.

There is yet a final point to be stressed: the workings of clientelism may in some instances produce a reversal of patron-client relationships. Resources may gravitate into the hands of his clients to such an extent as to make the royal patron a captive of his subordinates. Burundi is a case in point: no matter how hard Mwambutsa may have tried to regain the initiative, once he had decided to place a number of influential Bezi elements in key positions the balance of power was drastically tilted in favour of the *ganwa* oligarchy. From 1963 onwards the real power behind the throne were the descendents of princely families. The irony of this situation is that the very loss of autonomy incurred by the throne temporarily contributed to its staying power. Just as in medieval Europe the barons, by directing their attacks against the king's "wicked advisers" rather than against the king himself avoided "a direct clash with the theoretical basis of the monarchy",[16] a convincing case can be made for the view that the attacks made upon Bezi notables by Hutu and Tutsi politicians for a while served to deflect criticisms away from the king's person to his courtiers, thus giving the monarchy an extra lease on life.

In a sense political clientelism may be said to reflect the generalized failure of parties, parliaments and elections to take root in the cultural soil of African monarchies. In the absence of "institutionalized guarantees for an individual's security, status and wealth", as James Scott has recently observed, personal reciprocities need relatively little prodding to take the place of "impersonal contractual arrangements".[17] Nonetheless, this extreme weakness of institutionalized, legally-based, means of political exchange may also reflect the very nature of the strategies employed by traditional African rulers to pull the rug from under the feet of their opponents. Save for Buganda and Swaziland, where parliamentary institutions and clientelistic strategies have tended to be mutually supportive, in most other cases African rulers have deliberately sought to curtail or deny political participation via electoral and parliamentary processes.

(c) *Restricting Political Participation.* Depending on the juncture at which it occurred, political participation has served both to reinforce and weaken the power of African monarchs. The introduction of the suffrage, on the eve of independence, significantly heightened the potency of monarchical symbols. With the disappearance or weakening of chiefly authority, and the entry into the political arena of a new breed of politicians, many of them operating on the basis of an entirely new set of political rules, the Crown emerged as the only familiar symbol to which the peasant masses could relate in any meaningful sense. Nor was the significance of this fact lost on the nationalist elites. Their repeated efforts to use monarchical symbols to fortify the appeal of their own political claims further intensified popular perceptions of the Crown as a key "condensation symbol".[18]

With the advent of independence, however, the continued activation of popular energies through electoral processes entailed major liabilities for monarchical institutions, and, where independence had long been a *fait accompli*, as in Ethiopia, processes of modernization carried similar threats. Electoral competition, like modernization, can so intensify intergroup conflict as to endanger the very legitimacy of monarchical institutions. The alternatives at this point are either for the monarch to cast himself in the role of a figurehead, or to retain power by limiting the expansion of popular participation, but at the risk of unleashing a major constitutional crisis.

Most African monarchs have opted for the second of these alternatives: by June 1965 Hassan had dissolved Parliament and gathered all power into his hands; in July of the same year Mwambutsa had made clear his intention to "reign and rule", thus reducing the newly-elected National Assembly to a rubber stamp; in Ethiopia, as Clapham points out, the Senate still serves as a "place of retirement or disgrace for noblemen", while the Chamber of Deputies "serves mostly as a forum for local grievances and does not articulate national problems in any coherent way". Only in Swaziland and in Buganda was a genuine effort made to reconcile monarchical and parliamentary forms of legitimacy. Although it is still too early to tell how long, in Swaziland the compromise may last, since Swaziland lacks the traditional conciliar infrastructure of Buganda as well as the cohesive impetus which Buganda derived from it encapsulated status, the experiment may well prove equally short-lived, though for evidently different reasons.

Enough evidence can be gathered from the recent evolution of Ethiopia in support of the proposition that the chances of survival of African monarchs are inversely proportional to the scope of political participation.[19] The case of Burundi, however, makes only too plain the nature of the risks involved in the reduction of popular participation once the latter has already been extended to the masses. The activation of ethnic loyalties which usually follow in the wake of increasing demands for participation may cause a vertical split to emerge between two mutually antagonistic "stability groups". The resulting threats to the regime may call its very existence into question.[20]

Whether or not a regime can afford to dispense with elections and parliaments while at the same time retaining a modicum of legitimacy depends in part upon its ability to provide alternative structures for participation, or opportunities for involvement, ineffectual though these may be for registering individual choices. Political involvement, after all, may express itself in different forms and through different channels. At one end of the spectrum are the periodic ceremonies and festivities which form part of the political folklore of every monarchy. Whether organized in the name of tradition or as an alternative to it, the aim is not simply to give the incumbent confirmation of his right to rule, as by a plebiscite, but also to communicate to the masses a vicarious sense of participation in the political life of the kingdom. A somewhat similar result can be achieved through consultative assemblies at the local level (as in Swaziland), through an innocuous electoral ritual (as in Ethiopia), or through the "orchestration" of political party activity from the commanding heights of the palace (as in Burundi until 1965). But as the rate of social and economic modernization increases the point is eventually reached where the continued denial of effective political participation can only be enforced through coercion or threats of coercion. Ultimately the survival of the monarch depends on his ability to command the loyalty of the armed forces and the police.

Rarely, however, can the throne rely on the undivided loyalty of the military. What may appear on surface as a trial of strength between the palace and the army may actually conceal a far more serious confrontation between different segments of the armed forces. In Ethiopia the abortive coup of December 1960 was in part traceable to a latent opposition between certain key figures in the Imperial Body Guard and the senior army officers; a crucial factor behind the series of coups and counter-coups that led to the overthrow of the Burundi monarchy was the opposition between Hutu and Tutsi officers within the police and the army; and the military coup that disposed of the Libyan monarchy was essentially a coup of the captains against the colonels, or, as one observer put it, of the "young and thin against the old and the portly".[21] Whether primarily institutional, ethnic or generational, these cleavages must be assessed in the light of the informal configurations of power that prevail within the king's "inner circle"; many of these informal linkages, however, are determined largely by the nature of the social forces at work in society. There are no simple formulas through which the loyalty of the army to the monarch can be ensured. Neither the blocking of promotions of junior officers (as happened in Morocco between 1956 and 1959), nor the monarch's readiness to meet the officer's demands for higher pay (as shown by Haile Selassie in 1961, 1964 and 1974), nor the shuffling of military personnel or the encadrement of police and army officers by foreign advisers (as was the case in Burundi until 1965, and as is still the case in Swaziland), are sufficient guarantees. Symbolic ties and material rewards may be instrumental for a while in muting criticism, but as new generations of officers move up the promotion ladder the demands for participation voiced by the intellectuals are likely to find an increasingly receptive echo among the junior officers. While the decline of monarchical legitimacy prompts the monarch to rely more and more on the coercive power of the army, this very situation may sow the seeds of his own undoing.

One possible way out of this dilemma, as Huntington suggests, is for the monarch to curb popular demands for participation by simultaneously limiting or reversing the process of modernization. But once modernization has "caught on", the chances of arresting it are extremely slim.[22] Meanwhile, "the slowdown in reform itself, while it may reduce the appearance in the future of more groups hostile to the regime also will intensify the hostility of those which already exist".[23] Where clientelistic strategies are no longer effective to neutralize the opposition of the educated elites the monarch may in last resort turn to the international arena for replenishing his stock of political resources.

(d) *Capitalizing upon External Resources.* There is nothing particularly intriguing about a strategy aiming at transforming the resources of the international environment into capabilities relevant to the pursuit of domestic policies. Where the strategy takes on a somewhat incongruous colouration is in the hiatus observable between the "radical" image projected by some African monarchs on the international plane and the conservative objectives which this image is intended to serve in the domestic arena. As the case of Ethiopia demonstrably indicates, striking a militant posture on the international plane can help restore a measure of legitimacy to a monarch bent upon a conservative course in the domestic realm. The radical stance adopted by King Mohammed V during the early phase of the Congo imbroglio enabled him to project an image of "progressivism" ideally suited to steal the thunder from his domestic opponents. By seizing the initiative in convening the Casablanca Conference, in January 1961, and then publicly stating his support for Lumumba, Mohammed V effectively silenced his left-wing critics. Similarly, by placing himself at the vanguard of the movement for African unity and subsequently securing the location of the OAU headquarters in Addis Ababa, Haile Selassie acquired a new "aura of legitimacy" in the eyes of many who, under different circumstances, might have disavowed his leadership. As one observer put it, "it enabled the Emperor effectively to undercut the opposition of those modernizing elements who had criticized his aloofness from the mainstream of continental politics"; furthermore, "the new emphasis on African unity also served to broaden the horizons of loyalty of Ethiopians who were asked to think of themselves as Africans and Ethiopians, not as Shoans, Tigreans, or Amharas".[24] However unimpressive his record as a modernizing monarch, there can be no gain saying Haile Selassie's talent for converting his international status (both as a mediator in inter-African disputes and a pretigious advocate of African unity) into a source of domestic legitimacy.

Another way in which to stave off political bankruptcy is for the monarch to appeal to foreign governments to improve his resources. The borrowing of economic, informational or coercive resources from abroad can thus be used to make up for the domestic shortage of such resources, and, if properly invested, significantly prolong the life-span of the monarchy. Although the examples of Swaziland and Ethiopia suggest a reasonably close relationship between the capacity for survival of African monarchies and the extent of their dependency on foreign governments, this strategy is not without certain major liabilities. Where external links of dependency take on the quality of a satellite relationship considerable discredit may be cast upon the monarch's claim to embody the nationalist ethos of his people. In this case the question arises as to whether the resources available from external sources are at all sufficient to make up for the loss of legitimacy incurred by the throne by the very nature of this relationship. Moreover, whether real or imagined, the identification of the throne with a particular government may prompt similar moves on the part of its domestic opponents. As the cases of Lesotho and Burundi demonstrate, once domestic conflicts are converted into an extension of international rivalries, severe limitations are placed on the monarch's ability to act as an impartial arbiter. Rather than easing the task of managing conflict for the Crown, the carry over of international rivalries into the domestic arena merely serves to accentuate the dichotomous nature of internal conflict (as in Burundi), or else causes the palace to be increasingly drawn into the vortex of East-West rivalries (as in Lesotho). In either case the ability of the monarch to steer a neutral course is seriously compromised.

The greater the monarch's inclination to rely on the economic and military support of any given foreign government, the lesser the chances that he can successfully capitalize upon the "status" resources that might otherwise accrue from his diplomatic role-playing. Similarly, the fewer the chances that he can successfully contain popular demands for participation. Insofar as foreign influences may contribute to activate previously inert elements, support from external sources runs directly counter to the monarch's effort to engage in a strategy of limited political participation.

The strategies we have discussed are not necessarily consistent with each other. Conversely, the success of any given strategy may in turn depend on the ruler's ability to meet other strategic or tactical requirements. That any given set of strategies is likely to include elements of interdependence which may facilitate or inhibit the attainment of long-range objectives becomes even clearer in the light of the developmental options faced by African monarchs.

STRATEGIES OF DEVELOPMENT

However wide the area of disaccord among political scientists as to how political development should be conceptualized, that it involves in essence a problem of choice among priorities is a point on which there seems to be substantial agreement. Priorities may refer to what resources should come first—"whether agriculture should precede industry or vice versa; when services should be expanded; whether to expand technical or liberal education, etc."[25]; or they may refer to the means by which resources can be generated, or to the criteria according to which they ought to be allocated. Or the alternatives may involve a choice between the short-run exigencies of institutional stability and the long-run goals of "growth", defined by Eisenstadt as "the ability to absorb varieties and changing types of political demands and organizations".[26]

A major difficulty is that the element of choice involved in the setting of developmental priorities may suffer serious restrictions as a result of prior strategic commitments. The dilemma, in Huntington's phrase, is one of "success v. survival". Success in promoting modernization, according to Huntington, requires the centralization of power in the monarchy, yet "this centralization makes difficult or impossible the expansion of power and the assimilation into it of new groups produced by modernization". Since the assimilation of new groups "can only come at the price of the monarchy", the monarch finds himself impaled on the horns of a "fundamental dilemma"—whether to survive as a mere symbol by giving in to the demands of new groups in society, in which case he must presumably give up all hopes of initiating reforms, or to concentrate power into his own hands and face the risk of being overthrown.[27]

Where Huntington's thesis is likely to engender skepticism is in the assumption that centralization goes hand-in-hand with the promotion of social, economic and cultural reforms. Neither in Ethiopia nor in Rwanda has centralization been especially conducive to innovation in the social and economic realms. At least as much evidence can be gathered from this volume in support of the contrary argument, namely that centralization rather than dispersion of power is what enabled African monarchs to survive politically, and, further, that the costs of centralization have often placed insuperable obstacles on the path of socioeconomic reforms. To put it somewhat differently, assuming with Huntington that the key to development lies in the building of strong and durable institutions, may not the amount of resources invested in the process of institutionalization be counter-productive from the standpoint of a policy of innovating outputs?

(a) "Positional" v. "Innovative" Strategies. In the light of the evidence supplied in this volume several areas of incompatibility emerge between the strategies of survival employed by African monarchs and their ability to deal with problems of growth and development. For one thing, if much of the success met by the rulers of Swaziland and Ethiopia in maintaining themselves on their thrones can be traced to what Zartman calls "position politics",[28] so can many of the liabilities they face in promoting social and economic reforms. As part of the tactics of clientelism, position politics requires the perpetual probing of power constellations. The monarch's position as supreme arbiter thus depends on the continuous control of his clienteles. It requires tactical alliances and disengagements, sub-rosa manoeuvres to cultivate potential aspirants and discredit eventual opponents. Crisis-management in these conditions inevitably takes place at the expense of long-range planning.

It is not only the "style" of position politics that sets limitations on developmental strategies but the drain of economic and financial resources which often accompanies the rewarding of prebends to the faithful. Prebends and patronage have always been a necessary adjunct of inherited power. In eighteenth-century England, as J. H. Plumb reminds us, "it was patronage that cemented the political system, held it together and made it an almost impregnable citadel, impervious to defeat, indifferent to social change".[29] Even though the result may not be conducive to the same adamantine stability, patronage serves as a major source of political cohesion in Morocco and Ethiopia. And it also played a significant part in extending the life-span of the Burundi monarchy. The reverse side of the coin is that the costs of patronage may far exceed the amount of expendable resources available to the regime. Furthermore, where ethnic conflict can no longer be tempered through prebends, and where the prospects of instability are high, the more insatiable become the demands of the king's clients. A vicious circle is thus set in motion whereby the absence of social and economic reform heightens the prospects of instability while at the same time absorbing more and more of the resources necessary for the implementation of such reforms.

Yet another consequence of clientelistic strategies is that they may narrow the span of the recipients to the point where processes of exchange take place in a closed circuit, eliminating from the political system those very elements whose skills are most needed for implementing reform. Evidence of this phenomenon can be gathered from Burundi, Ethiopia and Swaziland. Alternatively, the constraints of clientelistic relationships may neutralize initiative and lead to inertia. Conformity rather than innovation is what keeps the system going. Whatever talent happens to be incorporated into the patron-client relationship is thus emptied of all usefulness for the purposes of development.

(b) *Expressive v. Entrepreneurial Strategies.* Expressive strategies,[30] focused on symbol manipulation, do not necessarily exclude entrepreuneurial or problem-solving strategies. That each type of strategy may indeed be mutually supportive is made abundantly clear by the political style of Prince Rwagasore, in Burundi, a style which involves a considerable amount of political dramaturgy as well as a keen appreciation of the need for pragmatic initiative. Expressive and entrepreneurial ingredients are also implicit in Apter's characterization of "modernizing autocracies". Symbolic ideology, according to Apter, is what enables the monarch to traditionalize and sanctify innovation. This is what prevents fragmentation and allows "new groups to form which, often fulfilling new needs in society, remain essentially supportive rather than destructive forces".[31]

Modernizing autocracies have not always been equally successful in promoting modernization, however, and the reason may lie in part in the varying mixtures of expressive and entrepreneurial styles which came to characterize the modus operandi of their respective monarchs. Where the emphasis is primarily on manipulation of symbols, or where such manipulation becomes a substitute for problem-solving or entrepreneurial skills, the chances of fomenting significant structural change are slight. Another liability involved in the use of expressive strategies is that their repetitiveness often generates their own irrelevance and thus leads to interia. As Nettl perceptively observed, "greater familiarity with the relevant show, in terms of more frequent performances, may mean less involvement and hence less relevance". Explaining why "the development component of developmental nationalism as a process does not lend itself readily to dramaturgical presentation", Nettl goes on to note that "just as the content of theatrical plays has tended, over the years, to reduce the possibility of structured audience participation in terms of clapping, shouting and singing, so the preoccupations with administration and economic development for the purpose of providing welfare offer little means for audience participation but demand a different form of involvement".[32] While political survival presumably requires the maintenance of a political cartharsis between the ruler and his audience, political development demands a more rationally, pragmatically-oriented commitment from both actors and audience.

Moreover, expressive strategies may prompt the use of tactics which positively hinder the fashioning of entrepreneurial roles. Whereas entrepreneurship suggests, in Apter's words, "a potential for imaginative choice" as well as an inclination to "explore alternatives and test feasibilities",[33] expressive strategies may on the contrary discourage the exercise of choice and reduce or eliminate alternatives through a lack of information. As our previous discussion of royal "image-making" tends to suggest, the patterning of responses associated with the image of venerability conveyed by the monarch is not particularly conducive to rational choice. And where the gathering and diffusion of information is systematically manipulated for the sake of image-making, the possibility of "exploring alternatives and testing feasibilities" becomes all the more uncertain. It is not simply a matter of monarchical image-making becoming its own justification; the tactics involved in this process also become the main justification for restricting or falsifying information.

In drawing attention to these contradictions our intention is not to deny the stabilizing effect of monarchical symbols in situations of rapid social change—a point cogently argued by Doornbos in his discussion of Ankole. Our sole purpose is to stress the limitations placed on developmental strategies when the perpetuation of symbolic legitimacy becomes an end in itself. Besides committing informational and other resources almost exclusively to maintaining the system, rather than to developmental goals, the result may also be an overemphasis on maintenance of a sub-system at the expense of national integration—a situation most clearly illustrated by the case of Buganda.

(c) *Secessionist v. Encapsulating Strategies.* Incorporation within a wider state inevitably confronts the monarch with the alternative of adjusting his perspectives to the exigencies of national unity (which means relinquishing at least part of his political resources to the central government), or, on the contrary, resisting incorporation by seceding from the central state. The options involved are directly affected by the situational context in which they arise, and the potential for economic development inherent in the incorporated unit. The higher the potential in resources of the incorporated kingdom, the greater the attractiveness of secessionist policies. Such, at any rate, is the conclusion which emerges from a comparative examination of Ankole and Ijebu Ode on the one hand, and Buganda on the other. Unlike Buganda, Ankole and Ijebu Ode had been reduced to the status of agencies of local government long before independence. Buganda by contrast had succeeded in wresting from the British Protectorate a "special relationship" which, moreover, continued unimpaired for some time after independence. Compared to Buganda's relatively rich economic potential, the resource base of Ijebu Ode and Ankole seemed scarcely serviceable for autonomous developmental purposes, neither one possessing the cumulative advantages of economic wealth, of a highly developed infrastructure, and the ecological assets of soil and rainfall, all of which, as Young points out, "conspired to maintain Buganda at the fore-front of development".

It is difficult to tell how far these parameters can be said actually to determine the course of monarchical strategies. Significant as they were in the case of Buganda, lack of economic viability was effective in mitigating the secessionist proclivities of the Litunga of Barotseland. Nor can one infer from the economic potential of the incorporated unit definitive conclusions about the effectiveness of its developmental policies in the social and economic realms. Without in any way denying the capacity for innovation of the Buganda kingship, one must also recognize that many of the decisions taken by the Kabaka's government, or by the Kabaka himself, were made on the basis of political expediency, with little attention paid to economic rationality. A case in point is the disastrous Ndaiga Settlement scheme, started in 1963. Not only did it fail to bring Buyaga county (one of the "Lost Counties") into the fold of Buganda, as the Kabaka had hoped; but the financial costs of political failure were equally high. An estimated £100,000 was spent on the Ndaiga scheme, an investment entirely lost to Buganda when the majority of the inhabitants in Buyaga voted to join Bunyoro in the 1964 referendum.[34] If Buganda's "royal" road to development was in part traced out in the economic map of the kingdom, the situation nonetheless left ample room for tactical choice. The irony in this case is that although the tactics employed by Buganda were intended to solidify its political pre-eminence as a separate entity, in the end the result was to subsidize the economic development of Bunyoro.

The greater the capacity of the monarch to tap and monopolize the developmental resources of the encapsulated kingdom, the slighter his chances of political survival after independence. The very success of his developmental strategies at the level of his kingdom, while making the prospect of seccesion all the more attractive for his subjects, also increases the chances of a head-on confrontation with the central government. Only where monarchical institutions have ceased to provide meaningful opportunities for social, economic and political advance will strategies of encapsulation hold any attraction for the educated elites, if not necessarily for the monarch himself. The obstacles placed in the way of social and economic modernization by the scelerosis of monarchical institutions may thus serve as a major inducement for the elites to throw their weight behind the central political institutions.[35]

To return to Huntington's query: "Must the monarch be the victim of his own achievements? Can he escape the dilemma of 'success *v.* survival'?" From the evidence available from the "incorporated kingdoms" discussed in this book, there seems to be no clear way out of the impasse. As Young tersely puts it, "either nation triumphs through dismantlement of kingdom, or kingdom mates nation through conquest of its central institutions, or through secession to render territory and kingdom congruent". Nowhere in Africa has an incorporated kingdom been able to assert its primacy over the institutions of the incorporating state, and where secession was attempted the outcome has been the obliteration of the monarchy as an institution. What few incorporated kingships are still in existence in Africa owe their survival to their sheer impotence, i.e. to their inability to perform the centralizing functions which Huntington regards as essential for promoting social, economic and cultural reform.

Where the formal boundaries of the kingdom coincide with those of the state, the answer is far more ambiguous. The problem lies in part in the definition one gives of "success". As noted earlier centralization alone is no guarantee of success if by that is meant the ability to promote reform. The least one can say is that the record of centralizing monarchies is a very mixed one, ranging from a near absence of innovating policies (as in Libya and, to a lesser extent, Ethiopia), to marginal innovations and piecemeal reforms (as in Morocco). Centralization of power around the throne may so overload the system as to impair its efficiency; or else centralizing policies may become their own justification, meanwhile threatening not only the success of the kingship as a modernizing institution but also its very survival.

To equate political development with institution-building thus leaves unanswered the question of the serviceability of political institutions for purposes of social and political innovation. Criteria of "adaptability, autonomy, coherence and complexity"[36] do provide important reference points for assessing the nature of the institutional parameters within which decisions are made. In and by themselves, however, these criteria have relatively little heuristic value for assessing what the chances of innovation are in any particular context. Ultimately, whether a political system is capable or not of innovation depends in most cases on the strategic choices made by the individual rulers in their attempt to cope with the changing circumstances of their environment. Although institutions like events, may influence the perceptions of costs and advantages involved in a particular course of action, institutional variables alone rarely suffice to explain developmental choices. Our comprehension of the decisions made by individual African rulers at certain critical junctures is at least as illuminating from the standpoint of pre-colonial history as the nature of the institutions through which they established their right and capacity to rule. Just as the growth and decline of archaic kingdoms can best be understood in terms of the political resources individual monarchs were able to generate and of the limits set by their opponents upon their choices, the survival and fall of contemporary African monarchies must be seen in a similar light.

It may be that in seeking to analyze the limits of political development in monarchical settings we have done little more than unwittingly open ourselves to Huntington's charge that "the concept of political development serves in effect as a signal of scholarly preferences rather than as a tool for analytical purposes", and hence that "the principal function which political development [has] in fact perform[ed] for political scientists [has been] neither to aggregate nor to distinguish, but rather to legitimate".[37] Nonetheless, since Huntington must himself be credited with the thesis that political development should be identified with political institutionalization, to point out the limitations of his argument is perhaps not entirely beyond the scope of a scholarly investigation of the concept of development. That the "principal function" which political development has in fact performed for African monarchs happens to be precisely the reverse of that which it has performed for political scientists is perhaps as much a reflection of the limitations involved in a strictly institutional approach to development as a commentary on the frailty of monarchical institutions in contemporary Africa.

NOTES

1   J. H. Plumb, *The Origins of Political Stability: England 1675–1725* (Boston, 1967), p. xvii. For a similar argument, in a different context, see Roger Letourneau, *The Almohad Movement in North Africa in the Twelfth and Thirteenth Centuries* (Princeton, 1969), p. 43.

2   See Introduction, p. 18 ff.

3   Clinical records of the physical disabilities suffered by African monarchs are unfortunately far too scarce or unreliable to follow up the interesting line of analysis suggested in Hugh L'Etang's work on *The Pathology of Leadership: A History of the Effects of Disease on 20th Century Leaders* (New York, 1970). Although the evidence is limited, there can be little doubt that the conduct and leadership of African monarchs has at times been directly affected by their physical conditions. According to Rowe, the attack of gonorrhea suffered by Mutesa of Buganda in 1862 "was serious enough to have been recorded in Ganda history, and must have temporarily checked both his active life and his growth in political power". (See John Rowe, *Revolution in Buganda: 1856–1900*, unpublished Ph.D. thesis, University of Wisconsin, 1967, p. 69.) One might also note in this connection that it was during his visit to Turkey, apparently motivated by reasons of health, that King Idriss of Libya lost his throne; similarly, Mwambutsa's frequent trips to Switzerland, where he apparently underwent medical treatment, almost inevitably coincided with a political crisis of one kind or another.

4   L. H. Gann and P. Duignan, *Colonialism in Africa* (Cambridge, 1969), Vol. I, p. 29.

5   Particularly intriguing in this connection is the use of monarchical symbolism made by the Konzo and Amba tribesmen of Western Uganda in their attempt to evade the domination of the Toro, immediately after Uganda's independence. The men who took the initiative in founding the Rwenzururu Kingdom used monarchical symbolism as a lever with which to assert "independence from and parity with the Toro Kingdom", and this in spite of the fact that monarchical symbols were fundamentally alien to the traditional political culture of both Konjo and Amba. See Martin R. Doornbos, "Kumanyana and Rwenzuru: Two Responses to Ethnic

Inequality", in R. Rotberg and A. Mazrui (eds.), *Protest and Power in Black Africa* (New York, 1970), pp. 1088–1136.

One might also note in passing the part played by the Kongolese kingship in the emergence of modern nationalist sentiment in Angola. According to Marcum, the failure of [Bakongo] monarchical nationalists to depose the puppet king, Dom Antonio III and replace him with a pretender more sympathetic to their aspirations is what "eventually led to the creation of the UPNA (later UPA) and to the Angolan uprising of March 1961". John Marcum, *The Angolan Revolution* (Cambridge, Mass,. 1969), Vol. I, p. 339.

6   John Waterbury, *The Commander of the Faithful* (New York, 1970), p. 146.
7   See Lloyd Fallers (ed.), *The King's Men* (London, 1964), p. 41.
8   The argument is further developed in Samuel Huntington, *Political Order in Changing Societies* (New Haven, 1968), p. 177 ff.
9   The expression is borrowed from Clifford Geertz, "Ideology as a Cultural System", in David Apter (ed.), *Ideology and Discontent* (New York, 1964), p. 66. Geertz associates the "theory of the exemplary center" with "the notion that the capital city (or more accurately the king's palace) was at once a microcosm of the supernatural order—an image of the universe on a smaller scale—and the material embodiment of the political order". *Ibid.*
10 Donald Levine, *Wax and Gold* (Chicago, 1965), p. 188.
11 Harold Lasswell, *Psychopathology and Politics* (New York, 1960), p. 184.
12 For further information, see R. Lemarchand, "Political Clientelism and Ethnicity: Competing Solidarities in Nation-Building", *The American Political Science Review*, LXVI, No. 1 (March 1972), pp. 68–90.
13 John Waterbury, *op. cit.*, p. 277.
14 R. E. Bradbury, "Continuities and Discontinuities in Pre-Colonial and Colonial Benin Politics", in I. M. Lewis (ed.), *History and Social Anthropology* (London, 1968), p. 2,00.
15 John Waterbury, *op. cit.*, pp. 271–2.
16 Joel T. Rosenthal, "The King's 'Wicked Advisers' and Medieval Baronial Rebellions", *Political Science Quarterly*, Vol. LXXXII, No. 4 (1967), p. 597.
17 James Scott, "Patron-Client Politics and Political Change", *American Political Science Review*, LXVI, No. 1 (March 1972), pp. 91–113.
18 Unlike "referential symbols", which are "economical ways of referring to the objective elements in objects or situations", "condensation symbols", according to Edelman, "evoke the emotions associated with the situation. They condense into one symbolic event, sign or act patriotic pride, anxieties, remembrances of past glories or humiliations, promises of future greatness; some of these or all of them". Murray Edelman, *The Symbolic Uses of Politics* (Urbana, 1964), p. 6.
19 A point repeatedly emphasized by Huntington in several articles and in particular in *Political Order and Changing Societies*, p. 177 ff.
20 See Donald Horowitz, "Three Dimensions of Ethnic Politics", *World Politics*, Vol. XXII, No. 2 (1971), p. 238 ff.
21 *The Economist*, December 6, 1969, p. 26.
22 Huntington, *Political Order and Changing Societies*, *op. cit.*, p. 188.
23 *Ibid., loc. cit.*
24 Robert L. Hess, *Ethiopia* (Ithaca and London, 1970), p, 237.
25 D. Apter and S. S. Mushi, "Social Science and Development: The Role of Political Science", a paper presented at the VIIIth World Congress of the International Political Science Association, Munich, Aug. 31–Sept. 5, 1970.
26 *Ibid.*
27 S. Huntington, *Political Order in Changing Societies*, *op. cit.*, p. 177.
28 W. Zartman, "Kingship in Morocco", unpublished MS.
29 J. H. Plumb, *The Origins of Political Stability—England 1675–1725*, *op. cit.*, p. 177.
30 The expression is borrowed from H. Feith, *The Decline of Constitutional Democracy in Indonesia* (Ithaca, 1962).
31 D. Apter, *The Political Kingdom in Uganda* (Princeton, 1967), p. 27.
32 J. P. Nettl, *Political Mobilization* (New York, 1967), p. 266.

33 D. Apter, *The Politics of Modernization* (Chicago, 1965), p. 71.
34 For further information see M. Hall, "Agricultural Planning in Buganda: 1963–1966", *East African Journal of Rural Development*, Vol. I, No. 1 (1968), 52–59.
35 The case of Barotseland is a prime example; see T. O. Ranger, "Nationality and Nationalism: The Case of Barotseland", *Journal of the Historical Society of Nigeria*, Vol. IV, No. 2 (1968), p. 245 ff.
36 *Ibid.*, pp. 12–24.
37 Huntington, "The Change to Change", *Comparative Politics*, Vol. III., No. 3 (1971), p. 304.

SELECTIVE BIBLIOGRAPHY

GENERAL WORKS ON AFRICAN KINGSHIPS

Bruyas, Jean. "La Royauté en Afrique Noire", *Annales Africaines* (1966), 157–228.
Crowder, Michael and Obaro, Ikime, *West African Chiefs* (Ile-Ife, Nigeria: 1970).
Davidson, Basil. *African Kingdoms* (Amsterdam: 1967).
Davidson, Basil. *The African Genius* (Boston: 1969).
Fage, J. D. *A History of West Africa* (Cambridge: 1969), esp. 18–46.
Gluckman, M. *Order and Rebellion in Tribal Society* (London: 1963).
Goody, Jack, ed., *Succession to High Office* (Cambridge: 1966).
Ibn, Khaldun. *The Muqaddimah*, trans. by F. Rosenthal (New York: 1958) 2 vols.
Kaberry, P. M. and Forde, Daryll. *West African Kingdoms in the Nineteenth Century* (Oxford: 1967).
Kaberry, P. "Primitive States", *British Journal of Sociology*, VIII (1957), 224–234.
Lewis, Herbert S. "The Origins of African Kingdoms", *Cahiers d'Etudes Africaines*, VI (1966), 402–407.
Lloyd, P. C. "Traditional Rulers", in James S. Coleman and Carl J. Rosberg, eds., *Political Parties and National Integration in Tropical Africa* (Berkeley and Los Angeles: 1967), 382–412.
Lloyd, P. C. "The Political Structure of African Kingdoms: An Exploratory Model", Michael Banton, ed., *Political Systems and the Distribution of Power* (London: 1965), 63–109.
Lloyd, P. C. "The Political Development of West African Kingdoms", *Journal of African History*, IX (1968), 319–329.
Mair, L. *Primitive Government* (Baltimore: 1962).
Maquet, Jaques. *Africanité Traditionnelle et Moderne* (Paris: 1967).
Mazrui, Ali A. "The Monarchical Tendency in African Political Culture", *British Journal of Sociology*, XVIII (1967), 231–250.
Mills-Odoi, D. G. *Divine Kingship and Its Occurrence in West Africa*, mimeo. (Legon: 1967).
Murdock, G. P. *Africa Its People and Their Culture History* (New York: 1959).
Posnansky, Merrick. "Kingship, Archaeology and Historical Myths", *Uganda Journal*, XXX (1966), 1–16.
Richards, Audrey I., ed., *East African Chiefs* (New York, 1959).
Richards, Audrey I. "African Kings and Their Royal Relatives", *Journal of the Royal Anthropological Institute*, 91 (1961), 832–412.
Trouwborst, Albert. "Sociologische Achtergronden van het Sacraal Koningschap in Afrika", *Africa*, XIX (1965), 360–364.
Vansina, Jan. "A Comparison of African Kingdoms", *Africa*, XXXII, (1962), 324–335.
Vansina, Jan. *Kingdoms of the Savanna* (Madison, Wis: 1966).
Vansina, J.; Mauny, R., and Thomas, L. V., eds., *The Historian in Tropical Africa* (London: 1964).

Williams, David. "The Changing Role of Chiefs in Africa", *Optima*, XVI (1966), 215–220.

I. THEOCRATIC KINGSHIPS

1. Ethiopia
Abir, M. *Ethiopia: The Era of the Princes* (London: 1968).
Budge, E. A. W. *A History of Ethiopia, Nubia, and Abyssinia* (London: 1928).
Caquot, A. "La royauté sacrale en Ethiopie", *Annales d'Ethiopie*, II 1957.
Clapham, C. S. *Haile-Selassie's Government* (London: 1969).
Clapham, C. S. "The Ethiopian Coup d'Etat of December 1960", *Journal of Modern African Studies*, VI (1968), 495–507.
Clapham, C. S. "Imperial Leadership in Ethiopia", *African Affairs*, 271 (1969), 110–120.
Del Boca, A. *The Ethiopian War 1935–1941* (Chicago: 1969).
Greenfield, R. Ethiopia: *A New Political History* (London: 1965).
Haberland, E. *Untersuchungen zum Athiopischen Konigtum* (Wiesbaden: 1965).
Hess, R. L. *Ethiopia: The Modernization of Autocracy* (Ithaca: 1970).
Huntingford, G. W. B. *The Galla of Ethiopia* (London: 1955).
Huntingford, G. W. B. *The Land Charters of Northern Ethiopia* (Addis Ababa: 1965).
Jesman, C. *The Ethiopian Paradox* (London: 1963).
Levine, D. N. *Wax & Gold* (Chicago: 1965).
Levine, D. N. "Ethiopia: Identity, Authority, and Realism", L. W. Pye and S. Verba, *Political Culture and Political Development* (Princeton: 1965).
Lipsky, G. A. *Ethiopia: Its Peoples Its Society Its Culture* (New Haven: 1962).
Luther, E. W. *Ethiopia Today* (Stanford: 1958).
Marcus, H. G. "The Last Years of the Reign of the Emperor Menilek", *Journal of Semitic Studies*, IX (1964).
Marein, N. *The Ethiopian Empire: Federation and Laws* (Rotterdam: 1955).
Mathew, D. *Ethiopia: The Study of a Polity, 1450–1935* (London: 1946).
Mosley, L. *Haile Selassie: The Conquering Lion* (London: 1964).
Pankhurst, R. K. P. *An Introduction to the Economic History of Ethiopia* (London: 1961).
Pankhurst, R. K. P. *State and Land in Ethiopian History* (Addis Ababa: 1967).
Pankhurst, R. K. P. *Economic History of Ethiopia* (Addis Ababa: 1968).
Perham, M. F. *The Government of Ethiopia* (London: 1948 and 1969).
Rubenson, S. "Some Aspects of the Survival of Ethiopian Independence in the Period of the Scramble for Africa", *Historians in Tropical Africa* (Salisbury, Rhodesia: 1962).
Rubenson, S. *King of Kings Tewodros of Ethiopia* (Addis Ababa: 1966).
Sandford, C. *Ethiopia under Haile Selassie* (London: 1946).
Schwab, P. *Ethiopia and Haile Selassie* (New York—forthcoming).
Trimingham, J. S. *Islam in Ethiopia* (London: 1952; reprinted Frank Cass, London, 1965).
Ullendorff, E. *The Ethiopians* (London: 1960).

II. STRATIFIED KINGSHIPS

2. Rwanda
Albert, Ethel. "Socio-Political Organization and Receptivity to Change: Some Differences between Rwanda and Burundi", *Southwestern Journal of Anthropology*, XVI (1966), 46–74.
Codere, Helen. "Power in Rwanda", *Anthropologica*, IV (1962), 45–85.
d'Arianoff, A. *Histoire des Bagesera* (Brussells: 1952).

d'Hertefelt, Marcel. "Les élections communales et le consensus politique au Rwanda", *Zaire*, XIV (1960), 403–38.

d'Hertefelt, Marcel. "Myth and Political Acculturation in Rwanda", in Allie Dubb, ed., *Myth in Modern Africa* (Lusaka: 1960), 114–135.

d'Hertefelt, Marcel and Coupez, Andre. *La Royaute Sacree de l'Ancien Rwanda* (Tervuren: 1964).

Heusch, Luc de. *Le Rwanda et la civilisation interlacustre* (Brussells: 1966).

Hubert, Jean. *La Toussaint Ruandaise et sa Répression* (Brussels: 1965).

Kagame, Alexis. *La Poésie Dynastique au Rwanda* (Brussels: 1951).

Kagame, Alexis. *Le Code des Institutions Politiques du Rwanda Précolonial* (Brussels: 1952).

Kagame, Alexis. *Les organisations Socio-familiales dans l'Ancien Rwanda* (Brussels: 1954).

Kandt, Richard. *Caput Nili* (Berlin: 1921).

Lacger, L. de. *Le Ruanda* (Kabgaye: 1961).

Louis, Wm. Roger. *Rwanda-Urundi: 1884–1919* (Oxford: 1963).

Lemarchand, René. "Power and Stratification in Rwanda: A Reconsideration", *Cahiers d'Etudes Africaines*, VI (1966), 592–610.

Lemarchand, René. "Political Instability in Africa: The Case of Rwanda and Burundi", *Civilisations*, XVI (1966), 307–337.

Lemarchand, René. "Revolutionary Phenomena in Stratified Societies: The Case of Rwanda and Zanzibar", *Civilisations*, XVIII (1968), 1–34.

Lemarchand, René. "La Relation de Clientèle Comme Moyen de Contestation: Le Cas du Rwanda", *Civilisations*, XIX (1969), 1–27.

Lemarchand, René. *Rwanda and Burundi* (London: 1970).

Maquet, Jacques. *The Premise of Inequality in Rwanda* (Oxford: 1961).

Maquet, Jacques. "La Participation de la Classe Paysanne au Mouvement d'indépendence du Rwanda", *Cahiers d'Etudes Africaines*, IV (1964), 552–568.

Maquet, Jacques and d'Hertefelt, M. *Elections en Société Féodale* (Brussels: 1959).

Nkundabagenzi, F. *Rwanda Politique*, 1958–60 (Brussels: 1961),

Pagès, R. *Un Royaume Hamite au Centre de l'Afrique* (Brussels: 1933).

Pauwels, Marcel. *Imana et le Culte des Mânes au Rwanda* (Brussels: 1958).

Van Overshelde, A. *Un audacieux pacifique: Monseigneur L. P. Classe* (Namur: 1948).

Vansina, Jan. *L'évolution du royaume Rwanda des origines a 1900* (Brussels: 1962).

Vidal, Claudine. "Le Rwanda des Anthropologues ou le fetichisme de la vache", *Cahiers d'Etudes Africaines*, IX (1969), 384–401.

Webster, John B. *The Political Development of Rwanda and Burundi* (Syracuse: 1966).

3. Burundi

Albert, Ethel. "Une étude de valeurs en Urundi", *Cahiers d'Etudes Africaines*, II (1960), 147–160.

Albert, Ethel. "La Femme en Urundi", in Denise Paulme, ed., *Femmes d' Afrique Noire* (The Hague: 1960), 173–206.

Albert, Ethel. " 'Rhetoric', 'Logic' and 'Poetics' in Burundi: Culture Patterning of Speech Behaviour", *American Anthropologist*, Special Issue (1964–65), 35–54.

Baeck, L. *Etude Socio-economique du centre coutumier d'Usumbura* (Brussels: 1957).

Cart, Henri-Philippe. "Conception des rapports Politiques au Burundi", *Etudes Congolaises*, IX (1966), 1–22.

Cart, Henri-Philippe and Rousson, Michel. "Prestige et Connaissance des Professions au Burundi", *Revue de l'Institut de Sociologie*, IV (1969), 635–57.

Chrétien, J. P. "Le Burundi" *Notes et Etudes Documentaires*, 3364 (1967).

Gorju, Msgr. J. *En Zigzags à travers l'Urundi* (Namur: 1926).

Gorju, Msgr. J. *Face au Royaume Hamite du Rwanda: Le Royaume Frère de l'Urundi* (Brussels: 1938).

Lechat, Michel. *Le Burundi Politique* (Bujumbura: n.d.).

Lemarchand, René. "Social Change and Political Modernization in Burundi", *The Journal of Modern African Studies*, IV (1966), 14–24.

Lemarchand, René. "The Passing of Mwamiship in Burundi", *Africa Report*, XII (1967), 14–24.

Paradis, J. "Le contrat d'Ubugaburu", *Bulletin des Jurisdictions Indigènes et du Droit Coutumier Congolais*, 3 (1947), 137–146.

Rodegem, F. M. *Structures Judiciaires Traditionelles au Burundi* (Bujumbura: n.d.).

Ryckmans, Pierre. "Organisation politique et sociale de l'Urundi", *Revue Générale Belge* (1921), 461–484.

Sebiva, Gatti. "Burundi: Détente entre le Parlement et le Gouvernement", *Etudes Congolaises*, 8 (1963), 42–44.

Simons, Eugene. "Coutumes et Institutions des Barundi", *Bulletin des Jurisdictions Indigènes et du Droit Coutumier Congolais*, 7 (1944) 137–283.

Trouwborst, Albert. "La mobilité de l'individu en fonction de l'organisation politique des Barundi", *Zaire* XVIII (1959), 780–800.

Trouwborst, Albert. "L'organisation polique et l'accord de clientèle au Burundi", *Anthropologica*, IV (1962), pp. 9–43.

Trouwborst, Albert. "Kinship and Geographical Mobility in Burundi", *International Journal of Comparative Sociology*, IV (1965), 166–182.

Trouwborst, Albert. "Le Burundi", in J. Vansina et al., eds., *Les Anciens Royaumes de la zone interlacustre meridionale: Rwanda, Burundi, Buha* (Tervuren: 1962).

Vansina, Jan. "Notes sur l'Histoire du Burundi", *Aequatoria*, XIV (1961), 1–10.

Vansina, Jan. "The Use of Process Models in African History", in Raymond Mauny, L. V. Thomas and J. Vansina, eds., *The Historian in Tropical Africa* (London: 1964), 375–390.

Vansina, Jan. *De La Tradition Orale: Essai de Méthode Historique* (Tervueren: 1961).

Ziegler, Jean. "L'intégration sociale et politique entre Batutsi et Bahutu dans la région extra-coutumière de Bujumbura", in Atteslander P. and Girod, R., eds., *Travaux Sociologiques*, I (Bern: 1966), 267–290.

III. ETHNIC KINGSHIPS
4. Swaziland

Best, Alan C. *The Swaziland Railway* (East Lansing: Michigan State University Press, 1966).

Davidson, Basil. "Country of King Sobhuza", *New Statesman*, 46, September 19, 1953, p. 308; October 3, 1953, pp. 367–8.

European Advisory Council, *Minutes of the Reconstituted European Advisory Council* (Mbabane: Mimeographed, 1949–1964).

Great Britain, Government of. *Cmnd No. 2052* (London: Her Majesty's Stationery Office, 1963).

Great Britain, Government of. *Cmnd No. 3119* (London: Her Majesty's Stationery Office, 1966).

Great Britain, Government of. *The Swaziland Order-in-Council, 1963* (London: Her Majesty's Stationery Office, 1963).

Great Britain, Government of. *Swaziland* (London: His Majesty's Stationery Office, 1946–1953).

Great Britain, Government of. *Swaziland* (London: Her Majesty's Stationery Office, 1954–1967).

Holleman, J. F. (ed.) *Experiment in Swaziland* (Capetown: Oxford University Press, 1964).

Kuper, Hilda. *An African Aristocracy: Rank Among the Swazis* (London: Oxford University Press, 1947).

Kuper, Hilda. *The Swazis: A South African Kingdom* (New York: Holt, Rinehart and Winston, 1963).

Kuper, Hilda. "The Swazis of Swaziland", J. L. Gibbs (ed.), *Peoples of Africa* (New York: Harcourt, Brace and World, 1965).

Kuper, Hilda. *The Uniform of Color* (Johannesburg: University of Witwatersrand Press, 1947).

Marwick, Brian. *Abantu Bakwa Ngwane* (Capetown: University of Capetown Press, 1939).

Marwick, Brian. *The Swazis* (Cambridge: Cambridge University Press, 1940).

Potholm, Christian. "Changing Political Configurations in Swaziland", *The Journal of Modern African Studies*, Vol. IV, No. 3 (1966).

Potholm, Christian. "Swaziland in Transition to Independence", *Africa Report*, Vol. XII, No. 6 (1967).

Potholm, Christian. "Swaziland", in C. P. Potholm & Richard Dale (eds.) *Southern Africa in Perspective: Essays in Regional Politics* (New York: The Free Press, 1972).

Potholm, Christian. *Swaziland: The Dynamics of Political Modernization* (Berkeley: University of California Press, 1972).

Stevens, R. P. "Swaziland Political Development", *The Journal of Modern African Studies*, Vol. I, No. 3 (1963).

Stevens, R. P. *Lesotho, Botswana and Swaziland* (New York: Frederick A. Praeger, 1968). *Times of Swaziland*, January 1, 1960–January 1, 1969.

Welch, Claude E. "Constitutional Confusion in Swaziland", *Africa Report*, Vol. VIII, No. 4 (April, 1963).

Zwane, Timothy. "The Struggle for Power in Swaziland", *Africa Today*, Vol. XI, No. 5 (May, 1964).

5. Lesotho

Arbousset, Rev. T. and Daumas, F. *Narrative of an Exploratory Tour to the North-East of the Colony of the Cape of Good Hope* (Cape Town: 1846).

Ashton, Hugh. *The Basuto* (London, New York, Toronto: 1967).

Atmore, Anthony. "The Passing of Sotho Independence 1865–70", *African Societies in Southern Africa*, Edited by Leonard Thompson. (New York, Washington: 1969).

Casalis, Rev. E. *The Basutos* (London: 1861).

Chakela, Koenyama S. *The Past and Present Lesotho* Cairo: The Organization for Afro-Asian Peoples Solidarity, n.d.

Duncan, Patrick. *Sotho Laws and Customs* (Cape Town: 1960).

Edwards, Isobel. *Basutoland Enquiry* (Southwick: 1956).

Ellenberger, D. F. and MacGregor, J. C. *History of the Basuto: Ancient and Modern* (London: 1912).

Germond, Robert C. *Chronicles of Basutoland* (Morija, Lesotho: 1967).

Hailey, Lord. *The High Commission Territories: Basutoland, the Bechuanaland*

x*

Protectorate and Swaziland. Part V of *Native Administration of the British African Territories* (London: HMSO, 1953).

Halpern, Jack. *South Africa's Hostages* (Baltimore: 1965).

Hamnett, Ian. "Koena Chieftainship Seniority in Basutoland". *Africa*, XXXV (1965).

Jones, G. I. "Chiefly Succession in Basutoland", in *Succession To High Office*, Jack Goody, ed. (Cambridge: 1966).

Lagden, Sir Godfrey. *The Basutos* (London: 1909).

Legassick, Martin. "The Sotho-Tswana Peoples before 1800", *African Societies in Southern Africa*, Edited by Leonard M. Thompson (New York and Washington: 1969).

Lye, William. "The Distribution of the Sotho Peoples after the Difaqane", *African Societies in Southern Africa*, Edited by Leonard M. Thompson (New York and Washington: 1969).

Macartney, W. J. A. "African Westminster? The Parliament of Lesotho", *Parliamentary Affairs*, XXIII (1970).

Orpen, Joseph M. *Reminiscences of Life in South Africa* (Durban: 1908).

Proctor, J. H. "Building a Constitutional Monarchy in Lesotho", *Civilizations*, XIX (1969) 64–85.

Sanders, P. B. "Sekonyela and Moshweshwe: Failure and Success in the Aftermath of the Difaqane", *Journal of African History*, X (1969), 449.

Sheddick, Vernon G. J. *Land Tenure in Basutoland*, Colonial Research Studies, No. 13 (London: Commonwealth Relations Office, 1954).

Sheddick, Vernon G. J. *The Southern Sotho. Southern Africa.* Part II of *Ethnographic Survey of Africa*, edited by Daryll Forde (London: 1953).

Smit, P., Leistner, G. M. E., Wyk, H. J. van, and Merwe, E. J. vander. *Lesotho* (a compendium of various African Institute publications about Lesotho) (Pretoria: 1969).

Smith, Edwin. *The Mabilles of Basutoland* (London: 1939).

Spence, J. E. "British Policy Towards the High Commission Territories", *The Journal of Modern African Studies*, II (1964), 235–244.

Spence, J. E. *Lesotho: The Politics of Dependence* (London: 1968).

Stevens, Richard P. *Lesotho, Botswana and Swaziland: The Former High Commission Territories in Southern Africa* (New York: 1967).

Thompson, Leonard M. "Cooperation and Conflict: The High Veld", *The Oxford History of South Africa*, I, Edited by Leonard Thompson and Monica Wilson (Oxford: 1969).

Tylden, G. *The Rise of the Basuto* (Cape Town and Johannesburg: 1950).

Wallman, Sandra. *Take Out Hunger: Two Case Studies of Rural Development in Basutoland* (New York: 1969).

Ward, Michael. "Economic Independence for Lesotho?" *The Journal of Modern African Studies*, V (1967), 355–368.

Weisfelder, Richard F. *Defining National Purpose in Lesotho.* Papers in International Studies, Africa Series No. 3. Ohio University Center for International Studies, Africa Program (Athens, Ohio: 1969).

Weisfelder, Richard F. "Lesotho: The Politics of Desperation", *Perspectives on Southern Africa.* Edited by Richard Dale and Christian Potholm (forthcoming).

Weisfelder, Richard F. "Power Struggle in Lesotho", *Africa Report*, XII (1967), 5–13.

IV. INCORPORATED KINGSHIPS
6. Buganda

Apter, David. *The Political Kingdom in Uganda* (Princeton: 1961).
Ashe, R. P. *Two Kings of Uganda* (London: 1890; 2nd. ed. with a new introduction by John Rowe, Frank Cass, London, 1970).
Ashe, R. P. *Chronicles of Uganda* (London: 1894; 2nd. ed. with a new introduction by John Rowe, Frank Cass, London, 1971).
Cox, A. H., "The Growth and Expansion of Buganda", *Uganda Journal*, XIV (1950), 153–159.
Fallers, Lloyd A. "Despotism, Status Culture and Social Mobility in an African Kingdom", *Comparative Studies in Society and History*, II (1959–1960), 11–32.
Fallers, Lloyd A. (ed.), *The King's Men* (London: 1964).
Fallers, M. C. *The Eastern Lacustrine Bantu*, International African Institute, Ethnographic Survey of Africa, East Central Africa, Part XI (London: 1960).
Gale, H. P. "Mutesa I—Was He a God?" *Uganda Journal*, XX (1956), 72–87.
Gee, T. W. "A Century of Muhammaden Influence in Buganda, 1852–1951", *Uganda Journal*, XXII (1958), 139–150.
Gertzel, Cherry. "How Kabaka Yekka Came to Be", *Africa Report*, IX (1964), 9–13.
Gertzel, Cherry. "Report From Kampala", *Africa Report*, IX (1964), 3–8.
Goody, Jack, ed., *Succession to High Office* (Cambridge: 1966).
Gorju, Pere J. *Entre Le Victoria, L'Albert, Et l'Edouard* (Rennes: 1920).
Gray, Sir John Milner. "The Year of the Three Kings of Buganda, Mwanga-Kiwewa-Kalema, 1888–1889", *Uganda Journal*, XIV (1950), 15–52.
Gugin, David. *Africanization of the Uganda Public Service.* Unpublished Dissertation, University of Wisconsin (1967).
Gutkind, Peter. *The Royal Capital of Kibuga* (The Hague: 1963).
H., J. W. *A. M. Mackay: Pioneer Missionary of the C.M.S. to Uganda. By His Sister* (London: 1890; reprinted by Frank Cass, London, 1970).
Hancock, T. R. "Patriotism and Neo-traditionalism in Buganda: The Kabaka Yekka ('the King Alone') Movement, 1961–1962", *Journal of African History*, XI (1970), 419–434.
Jistang, Tor. *The King of Ganda* (Stockholm: 1944).
Johnston, H. *The Uganda Protectorate* (London: 1902).
Kabuga, Charles E. S. "The Geneology of Kabaka Kintu and the Early Basekabaka of Buganda", *Uganda Journal*, XXVII (1963), 205–216.
Kagwa, Sir Apolo. *Basekabaka Be Buganda* (Kampala: 1901).
Kagwa, Sir Apolo. *Ekitabo Kye Bika Bya Buganda* (Kampala: 1908).
Kagwa, Sir Apolo. *Ekitabo Kye Mpisa Za Buganda* (Kampala: 1905).
Kiwanuka, M. S. M. *Muteesa of Uganda* (Nairobi: 1967).
Kulubya, Owekitibwa, S. W., "Some Aspects of Buganda Customs", *Uganda Journal*, IX (1942), 49–50.
Lee, J. M. "Buganda's Position in Federal Uganda", *Journal of Commonwealth Political Studies*, III (1965), 165–181.
Low, D. Anthony. "The Advent of Populism in Buganda", *Comparative Studies in Society and History*, VI (1963–1964), 424–444.
Low, D. Anthony and Pratt, R. Crawford. *Buganda and British Overrule* (London: 1960).
Low, D. Anthony. *Political Parties in Uganda, 1949–1962* (London: 1962).
Low, D. Anthony. *Religion and Society in Buganda 1875–1900*, East African Studies, No. 8, East African Institute of Social Research (Kampala: 1957).
Lush, Allen J. "Kiganda Drums", *Uganda Journal*, III (1935), 7–25.

Mair, Lucy. *An African People in The Twentieth Century* (London: 1934).

Mukasa, Ham. "The Rules of the Kings of Buganda", *Uganda Journal*, X (1946), 136–143.

Mukwaya, A. B. *Land Tenure in Buganda*, East African Studies, No. 1, East African Institute of Social Research (Kampala: 1953).

Mutesa, Sir Edward. *The Desecration of My Kingdom.* (London: 1967).

Postlethwaite, J. R. *I Look Back* (London: 1947).

Report of the Commission of Inquiry into The Disturbances in Uganda During April 1949 (Entebbe: 1950).

Report of the Commission of Inquiry into The Disturbances Which Occurred in Uganda During January 1945 (Entebbe: 1945).

Richards, A. I. *The Changing Structure of A Ganda Village* (Nairobi: 1966).

Richards, A. I., ed., *East African Chiefs* (London: 1959).

Richards, A. I., ed., *Economic Development and Tribal Change* (Cambridge: 1954).

Roberts, A. D. "The Sub-Imperialism of the Baganda", *Journal of African History*, III (1962), 435–450.

Roscoe, John. *The Baganda* (London: 1911; 2nd edition, Frank Cass, London, 1965).

Rowe, John A. "The Purge of Christians at Mwanga's Court", *Journal of African History*, V (1964), 55–71.

Rowe, John A. *Revolution in Buganda 1856–1900—Part One.* Unpublished Dissertation, University of Wisconsin (1966).

Shepherd, George. *They Wait in Darkness* (New York: 1955).

Snoxall, R. A. "The Coronation Ritual and Customs of Buganda", *Uganda Journal*, IV (1947), 277–288.

Southall, A. W. and Gutkind, R. C. W. *Townsmen in The Making.* East African Studies No. 9, East African Institute of Social Research (Kampala: 1956).

Southwold, Martin. *Bureaucracy and Chiefship in Buganda.* East African Studies, No. 14, East African Institute of Social Research (Kampala: 1961).

Southwold, Martin. "Kingship in Buganda", *Mawazo*, I (1967), 17–23.

Stanley, Henry M. *Through The Dark Continent* (New York: 1878).

Taylor, John V. *The Growth of the Church in Buganda* (London: 1958).

Thomas, H. B. "Capex Imperii: The Story of Semeikakunguru", *Uganda Journal*, VI (1939), 125–136.

Thomas, J. R. and Scott, R. *Uganda* (London: 1935).

Tucker, A. R. *Eighteen Years in Uganda and East Africa* (London: 1908).

Welbourn, F. B. *East African Rebels* (London: 1961).

Welbourn, F. B. *Religion and Politics in Uganda* (Nairobi: 1966).

Welbourn, F. B. "Some Aspects of Kiganda Religion", *Uganda Journal*, XXVI (1962), 171–182.

Williams, F. Lukyn. "The Kabaka of Buganda: Death of His Highness David Chwa, K.G.M.G., K.B.E., And Accession of Edward Mutesa II", *Uganda Journal*, VII (1940), 176–187.

Wrigley, C. C. "The Christian Revolution in Buganda", *Comparative Studies in Society and History*, II (1959), 33–48.

Wrigley, C. C. *Crops and Wealth in Uganda*, East African Studies No. 12, East African Institute of Social Research (Kampala: 1959).

Young, Crawford. "The Obote Revolution", *Africa Report*, XI (1966), 8–14.

7. Ankole

Doornbos, Martin R. "Protest Movements in Western Uganda: Some Parallels and Contrasts", *Kroniek van Afrika*, 3 (1970).

Doornbos, Martin R. "Kumanyana and Rwenzururu: Two Responses to Ethnic Inequality", in Robert I. Rotberg and Ali A. Mazrui, eds., *Protest and Power in Black Africa* (New York: 1970), 1088–1138.

Doornbos, Martin R. and Lofchie, Michael F. "Ranching and Scheming: A Case Study of the Ankole Ranching Scheme", in M. F. Lofchie, ed., *The State of the Nations* (Berkeley and Los Angeles: 1971—forthcoming).

Gorju, P. J. *Entre le Victoria, l'Albert et l'Edouard* (Rennes: 1920).

Ingham, K. "Some Aspects of the History of Western Uganda", *Uganda Journal*, XXI (1957), 131–149.

Katate, A. C. and Kamugungunu, L. *Abagabe b'Ankole, Ekitabo I and II* (Kampala: 1955).

Mackintosh, W. L. S. *Some Notes on the Abahima and the Cattle Industry of Ankole* (Entebbe: 1938).

Morris, H. F. A History of Ankole (Kampala: 1962).

Morris, H. F. *The Heroic Necitations of the Bahima of Ankole* (Oxford: 1964).

Morris, H. F. "The Making of Ankole", *Uganda Journal*, XXI (1957), 1–15.

Morris, H. F. "The Murder of H. St. G. Galt", *Uganda Journal*, XXIV (1960), 1–15.

Mungonya, Z. C. K. "The Bacwezi in Ankole", *Uganda Journal*, XXII, (1958), 18–21.

Mushanga, Musa T. *Folk Tales from Ankole* (Kampala: 1969).

Nganwa, Kesi K. *Abokozire eby' Okutangaza Omuri Ankole* (Nairobi: 1948).

Oberg, K. "The Kingdom in Uganda", in M. Fortes and E. E. Evans-Pritchard, eds., *African Political Systems* (London: 1940), 121–164.

Oberg, K. "A Comparison of Three Systems of Primitive Economic Organization", *American Anthropologist*, XLV (1943). 572–587.

Posnansky, M. "Kingship, Archaeology and Historical Myth", *Uganda Journal*, XXX (1966), 1–12.

Roscoe, John. *The Banyankole* (Cambridge: 1923).

Roscoe, John. "Bahima, a Cow Tribe of Enkole in the Uganda Protectorate", *Journal of the Royal Anthropological Society*, XXXVII (1907).

Stenning, D. J. "The Nyankole", in Audrey I. Richards, ed., *East African Chiefs* (London: 1959).

Stenning, D. J. "Salvation in Ankole", in M. Fortes and G. Dieterlen, eds., *African Systems of Thought* (Oxford: 1965), 258–275.

Taylor, Brian K. *The Western Lacustrine Bantu* (London: 1962).

Thiel, Paul van W. F. "The Music of the Kingdom of Ankole", *African Music Society Journal*, IV.

Williams, F. Lukyn. "The Inauguration of the Omugabe of Ankole to Office", *Uganda Journal*, IV (1937), 300–312.

Williams, F. Lukyn. "Nuwa Mbaguta, Nganzi of Ankole", *Uganda Journal*, X (1946), 124–135.

Williams, F. Lukyn. "Hima Cattle", *Uganda Journal*, IV (1938).

Wrigley, C. C. "Some Thoughts on the Bacwezi", *Uganda Journal*, XXII (1958), 11–18.

8. Ijebu

Lloyd, P. C. *Yoruba Land Law* (London: 1962).

Lloyd, P. C. "Installing the Awujale", *Ibadan*, 12 (1961), 7–10.

Lloyd, P. C. "Sungbo's Eredo", *Odu*, 7 (1959), 15–22.

Lloyd, P. C. "Osifekunde of Ijebu", in Philip D. Curtin, ed., *Africa Remembered: Narratives of West Africans from the Era of the Slave Trade* (Madison: 1967), 217–288.

Lloyd, P. C. "Agnatic and Cognatic Descent Among the Yoruba", *Man* (N.S.), I (1966), 484–500.

Johnson, S. *History of the Yorubas* (Lagos: 1921).

Ayandele, E. A. "The Changing Position of the Awujales of Ijebuland under Colonial Rule", in M. Crowder and O. Ikime, eds., *West African Chiefs* (Ife: 1970), 231–254).

INDEX

Abanyaraguru people, Burundi, 118
Abeokuta, Alake of, 262, 278
abiiru (Rwanda custodians of Esoteric Code), 70, 72, 84, 95
Action Group, Nigeria, 261, 271, 272, 273, 274, 279–80, 281
Addis Ababa, 38, 42, 43, 45, 47, 48, 55, 56, 58
Adenuga, Awujale of Ijebu, 266–7, 268
Adesanya, Daniel (Daniel Otubusin), Awujale of Ijebu, 267–70, 276, 281
Adetona, Sikiru, Awujale of Ijebu, 281
Adwa, Italians routed by Menilek at (1896), 38
Afa-Negus (Ethiopian Chief Justice), 51, 52
African Heads of State Conference (1963), 55
African socialism, 149, 164, 287
age, effect on royal leadership of, 19–20
Agemo festival, Ijebu, 279
age-sets: in Swaziland, 131, 138–9, 139; in Buganda, 194; in Ijebu, 264, 265, 269–70
agriculture: in Ethiopia, 36–7, 46; in Rwanda, 79, 82; in Swaziland, 135–6, 139; in Lesotho, 163–4; in Buganda, 208–9, 213, 216
Ahmad Gran, 37, 42
Akinsaya, *Olisa* of Ijebu, 275–6, 278–9, 281
Akiutola, Chief, 262
Aksum, 36, 40
Albert, Ethel, 97
Ali, Mallam (of Ijetsu), 273
Almeida (Jesuit), 51
Amhara, 36
Amin, Idi, President of Uganda, 124
ANC, South Africa, 177–8; Youth League, 174
anciens séminaristes, 80
Anglican Church (Protestants), 75; in Buganda, 202, 204–7, 209, 214, 219, 221, 222, 223, 230; in Ankole, 250–1; in Ijebu, 267
Anglo-American Corporation, 144
Anglo-Boer War (1899), 131, 132
Ankole, 1, 5, 9, 10, 13, 15–16, 17, 215, 236–59, 286, 299, 300; traditional context of kingship, 237–9; expansion in scale of original boundaries, 239–40; as a subsystem, 240–2; contention for pre-eminence in the new framework: the Bahinda-Bashambo conflict, 242–4; king and chiefs in the colonial framework, 244–8; ethnic conflict, 248–51; neo-traditionalization of kingship, 251–6
Ankole Agreement (1901), 240, 242, 245, 249; (1962), 252–3
Ankole Council (*Eishengyero*), 252
Apter, David, ix, 6, 165, 194, 229, 231, 298, 299
Aqabe Sa'at (Ethiopian system of appointments with Emperor), 56
Arkell, A. J., 6
army, armed forces; in Ethiopia, 11, 48, 54, 55, 59; in Rwanda, 70, 77, 78; Burundi, 112, 113, 116–17, 118, 119, 120, 121, 122; Swazi regiment system (*lifbutfho*), 137, 138–9; and Sobhuza II's paramilitary force, 156; in Ijebu, 266
asbestos mining, 139, 146
Ashanti, 1, 2, 6, 7, 133
Astridiens (*Cercle Scolaire d'Astrida*), 80, 82, 105, 107
Awolowo, Obafemi, Regional Premier, Nigeria, 278, 287
Awujale (Ijebu king), 16, 17, 22, 23, 262, 265, 266–7; redefinition of role of, 267–73; during years 1952–4, 273–82; salary of, 274, 276–7, 282; *see also* Ijebu

Badru Kakunguru, Prince of Buganda, 218
Bagehot, Walter, 177
Bagisu people, 194
Bagwere people, 194
Bahima clan, Ankole, 237–8, 239, 240, 242, 244, 248–51, 252
Bahinda clan, Ankole, 9, 15–16, 17, 237, 239, 242–4
Bairu clan, Ankole, 237, 238, 239, 240, 242, 248–51

316 INDEX

Bakaffa, Emperor of Ethiopia, 41
Bakopi (Buganda commoners), 210–14, 216, 218, 221–4, 230
Bakungu chiefs (Buganda), 15, 17, 196, 197, 199–200, 203, 206, 207–9, 210, 221, 222; (Ankole), 239
Baloguns (Ijebu warriors), 266
Balokole religious movement, Buganda, 222
Bantfu Baka Ngwane (the people of Ngwane), 130–1
Bantu, 10–11, 72, 130
"Bantu" front, Uganda, 227
Banyiginya clan, Rwanda, 23, 78
Banyole people, 194
Baranyanka (Batare chief), 105, 106, 107
Barotseland, 8, 24; Litunga of, 129, 133, 300
Bashambo clan, Ankole, 15–16, 17, 242–4
Basoga people, 194
Basotho monarchy, 8, 160–89; emergent kingship, 161–6; restructuring under colonial rule, 166–9; loss of initiative by, 169–74; restricted rule of Moshoeshoe II, 174–83; *see also* Lesotho
Basutoland, 132, 140, 154; *see also* Lesotho
Basutoland African Congress (BAC), 174
Basutoland Congress Party (BCP), 164, 175, 176, 177–8, 180, 189, 287
Basutoland Constitution (1959), 175–7
Basutoland Executive Council, 175, 176
Basutoland National Council, 22, 23, 170–1, 172, 173, 174, 175–6
Basutoland National Party (BNP), 160, 175, 177, 178, 179–80, 181, 182, 189
Basutoland Progressive Association, 170
Bataka clan, Buganda, 17, 72, 196, 199, 210, 213, 221, 222, 230
Bataka Party, Buganda, 213, 216
Batare clan, Burundi, 17, 22, 107; struggle for power between Bezi and, 22–3, 24, 99–111 *passim*, 121
Batongole (royal officers, Buganda), 196, 197, 203
Bawajjere movement, Buganda, 223
Beattie, J. H. M., 6
Bechuanaland Protectorate, 132, 140, 146, 154; *see also* Botswana
Bega clan, Rwanda, 23
Belgium, Belgians, 3, 16; indirect mandate in Rwanda, 15, 67, 71, 74–80, 87–8; and Groupe de Travail's visit to Rwanda (1959), 83–4; in Burundi, 103–7, 108, 111, 121
Bemba people, 133
Benin, *Oba* of, 262
Bereng Griffith of Lesotho, 171, 172

Bereng Seeiso see Moshoeshoe II, King, 175–6
Bezi clan, Burundi, 17, 107, 108–10; struggle for power between Batare and, 22–3, 24, 99–111 *passim*, 121
Bhunu, King of Swaziland, 131
Biafra, 55
Big Bend sugar plantation, Swaziland, 146
Bihumagani, Léopold ("Biha"), 106, 107, 108, 116, 117
Bilegeya, Prince, 178
Bimazubute, Gilles, 116
Bimpenda, Germain, 106
Binder, 5
Biroli, Joseph, 107
Bitwadad (Ethiopian official), 51
Bled es-Siba, Morocco, 17
Boers, Boer republics: war with Britain (1899), 131, 132; settlers in Swaziland, 141; expansionist aims in Lesotho, 163, 166–7; *see also* South Africa
Bordihn, Jerry, 151
Botswana, ix, x, 140
Boyd Orr, Lord, 1
Bradbury, R. E., 291
Bramson, Leon, 7
Britain, British colonial rule, 14, 16; in Ijebu, 17, 22, 266, 268, 273, 274, 276–7, 278, 279, 280; Ethiopia buys Canberra bombers from, 55; in Swaziland, 130, 131, 132–3, 140–55; expansion in South Africa, 131; and Boer War, 131, 132; High Commission Territories in Southern Africa of, 132, 154–5; disengagement from Southern Africa, 140; in Basutoland, 160, 166–74, 176, 177, 178, 181, 182; in Cape Colony, 163, 167; in Buganda, 193–4, 202, 206–20; in Ankole, 236–7, 239, 242, 244–55 *passim*; in Yoruba kingdoms, W. Nigeria, 260–3
British Colonial Development and Welfare Corporation, 139
British East Africa Company, 206
British High Commission Territories in Southern Africa, 132
British South Africa Company, 8
Brown, Bishop (Uganda), 214
Bruce, 41
Buganda, 1, 2, 3, 11, 15, 16, 17, 19, 25, 35, 72, 109, 129, 193–235, 286, 293; deportation of Kabaka (1953–5), 3, 214–18; monopolistic resource allocation in, 9, 10, 11, 12; overthrow of monarchy (1966), 16, 20, 228; pre-colonial monarchy: rise of despotism, 194–200; symbols and succession, 200–4; ideology and conflict: the Christian revolution, 204–7; 1900 Treaty with Sir Harry